SINGULAR REBELLION

SINGULAR REBELLION

Saiichi Maruya

Translated by Dennis Keene

KODANSHA INTERNATIONAL
Tokyo, New York and San Francisco

Publication of this translation was assisted by a grant from the Japan Foundation.

Originally published in 1972 by Kodansha Ltd. under the title *Tatta hitori no hanran*. In-house editor: Stephen Shaw.

Distributed in the United States by Kodansha International/ USA Ltd., through Harper & Row, Publishers, Inc., 10 East 53rd Street, New York, New York 10022. Published by Kodansha International Ltd., 12-21, Otowa 2-chome, Bunkyo-ku, Tokyo 112 and Kodansha International/USA Ltd., with offices at 10 East 53rd Street, New York, New York 10022 and the Hearst Building, 5 Third Street, Suite No. 400, San Francisco, California 94103. Copyright © 1986 by Kodansha International Ltd. All rights reserved. Printed in Japan.

LCC 85-45785
ISBN 0-87011-763-7
ISBN 4-7700-1263-2 (in Japan)

First edition, 1986

1

There's a lot to be said for having a girl fall in love with you because she's mad about your good looks, or—if your looks aren't up to much—your friendly, cheerful personality. There's even more to be said for having her succumb to a protracted campaign of pure attrition. But for her to take a liking to you on account of your great-grandfather is surely eccentric; and yet I can't help feeling it wasn't until we got on to the subject of that grand old man that Yukari started showing any interest in me. Right up to the moment when my ancestor of three generations past, Jukichi Mabuchi, became the topic of our talk, I'd been playing a shrewd (as I saw it) second fiddle to Oguri, this being the first time I'd met Yukari and friend, but from that point onward we seemed to get on fine. I know it's never all that easy to interpret and judge things of this kind, but in support of my view I can offer the fact that, once we'd parted from Oguri and Mayo late that night, the first thing Yukari chose to talk about in the taxi was my great-grandfather.

Yukari edged closer to me in the dim light of the back seat, either because she was drunk or pretending to be, and I must say the light touch of her warm, soft limbs was nice, very nice indeed. It also just happened that one of her enormous earrings was dangling right in front of my mouth, occasionally brushing my lips. The stimulation this provided brought back a vivid memory of the weird, pink, plastic objects she was wearing, and that in turn brought to mind the ears themselves, so I felt it necessary to whisper something appropriate into the nearest one.

"I really enjoyed this evening. . ."

I admit that it was a remark of striking banality, and Yukari's reply was no great improvement.

"Me, too. . ."

While this sparkling conversation was in progress, my right hand happened to brush against Yukari's left hand and, after a moment's hesitation, I plucked up enough courage to give the small hand a definite squeeze. She immediately entrusted it to my care, and though the gesture was perfectly ordinary, even predictable, nothing can be more confidently guaranteed to arouse deep feeling in the breast of a middle-aged man than the slim fingers and slightly sweaty palm of a girl.

"That was really fascinating, the story about your great-grandfather," Yukari went on to say, in a whisper it's true, yet still apparently unable to find a subject more pertinent to the situation of having her hand fondled in the dark by a man. No doubt it was a strange, even ludicrous remark, as I became aware later on when I thought about it; but at the time I was too excited to notice.

"Oh, I'm glad to hear that," I said, taking a more studied delight in the feel of her slender hand, and gazing at her face, pale and vague in the half-light; then, almost groaning in ecstasy, she added:

"Especially that part about the gold watches... Oh, that was wonderful!"

She spoke as if implying some powerful admiration for me personally, although I soon sensed it was my narrative art alone that was being praised. I also started to feel that this young woman might be much more innocent and inexperienced than she looked, since she seemed remarkably ignorant of what should be talked about in situations of this kind.

The story about the gold watches was one I'd heard during a summer vacation at home when I was a university student during the war. I heard it from the lips of our local historian, a long-retired teacher from the town's technical college. I was walking along by the river when he stopped me, generously treated me to a small water ice, and then let me into the secret of this "hidden episode" in my great-grandfather's life, an incident that showed his true greatness of soul. According to him, Jukichi Mabuchi had acquired a popular dancing girl of the region as his mistress, but this amazing beauty had come down with tuberculosis. There was nothing she liked better than a gold watch, despite the fact that she was unable to tell the time, because she enjoyed the sound it made when her patron clicked open the lid. So, whenever he had a moment to spare, he'd sit by her sickbed flipping open his gold watch, which he did with such frequency that the spring would eventually break. He would then acquire another one from Tokyo or Osaka and continue snapping and clicking away. Within a year or two his

2

mistress died, and by then some dozen gold watches with broken lids had accumulated by the side of her pillow.

The old local historian had insisted, with tears in his eyes, that this had all happened in the 1880s when the cost of any Swiss watch (particularly a Zenith, as these must have been) was astronomical. He applauded not only the extravagant generosity of buying a dozen of them, but also the gentleness, the compassion, it showed toward the sick. What a tale was this to move the heart, how typical of our pioneer for commerce in this area, he exclaimed, with an expression that suggested he could barely endure the emotion his own words had raised. My own inner response at the time had been to question the wisdom of this acquisition of twelve watches. Surely it would have made better sense, when one watch had broken down, to trade it in for a new one; but though I remained skeptical on this point, it seemed slightly vulgar to voice any actual objection, so I didn't. After all, Jukichi Mabuchi had been a real force in the political and business worlds of the north in the late years of the nineteenth century, and it didn't seem right for a close relation like me to criticize him. This natural restraint, however, only seemed to inflate the importance of the doubt, and so I was less than moved by this moral tale. In fact I'd only brought up the subject to get a laugh, but Oguri alone obliged me, while the two girls, Yukari and Mayo, both sighed in simultaneous and passionate chorus, their faces flushed by dreams of the romantic past.

As this was the very opposite of the reaction I'd looked for I felt a certain confusion, wondering if it was an indication of the passion all women have for presents, or perhaps of the remarkable humorlessness of girls employed as fashion models. This was the first time I had ever gone out drinking with two of them; in fact I'd never even spoken to one before.

It was Oguri I had to thank for landing me in their company, starting off with dinner and then a tour of the night spots. He'd been in the same class as me at high school, a large, easygoing person who was good at football. We hadn't got on badly, but we'd never been particular friends either. All I can remember of our acquaintance at university was that he'd come to see me on two or three occasions, mainly to borrow money, and we'd played a few games of chess. He had been in the sociology department, then taught at a school before entering publishing, but the publisher had gone broke and Oguri had been reduced to earning a living through the lower forms of journalism. This meant doing draft translations of detective stories, which would then be improved by a more skilled hand, although it seems he did finally graduate to doing it all himself; or writing the scandal pages in screen and stage magazines, and scripts for disc jockeys. He'd done this for quite a long time, and then a few years ago he'd been taken onto the editorial staff of a publicity magazine put out by a beer-making company; and since his immediate superior died shortly afterward in a plane crash, he found himself promoted to the rank of editor-in-chief. This gave him section head status in the company, and finally he was able to settle down in comfort—or so I heard from a mutual acquaintance, a newspaper reporter we'd both known at school. Consequently, when I joined my present company, he was one of the people I sent a formal card to, announcing the fact. Most people ignore such things, but he telephoned me almost imediately suggesting we get together sometime and have a drink. I promised to do so but, as usually happens, nothing came of it and we didn't meet.

On the day in question I'd gone to his beer company on business. There was a rumor they were about to place a large order for refrigerated display cases and I went there to put out a few feelers. In fact this wasn't really my job as head of the planning department, but once I'd told our operations division about this, they asked me if I'd go and look things over for them. Quite unlike the situation in government service, there is no rigid role demarcation in business enterprises (which is a polite way of saying people are always trying to pass the buck somewhere else), and I was well aware of this even though I'd been pretty surprised by it at first; so I simply reconciled myself to the fact that I'd bought it again and went. I admit it had crossed my mind that I was visiting the company where Oguri worked, and though I wasn't under the illusion that an acquaintance with the editor of their publicity magazine meant I could clinch the deal there and then, it still gave me a definite point of entry. I was also confident that the low cost of our display cases, if not their actual quality, ought to be decisive.

As I entered the elevator on my way to see the chief of their sales promotion division, I became aware of a large man bearing down on me just as the door was about to close, so I pushed the "open" button in some haste. The large man stood before me, blurted out unceremoniously his amazement that I could possibly be me, and then grinned awkwardly with no attempt at the usual civilities. This smile gave a sudden boyishness to his face, as though the interval of nearly twenty years since we'd last met had suddenly fallen away.

"Hardly recognized you either," I said, and we both laughed, but after the exchange of a few words our elevator arrived at the third floor, where my contact worked. Oguri accompanied me as far as the door, and on parting invited me to drop in on him before I left, which naturally I agreed to do.

Once I'd worked out there was a good chance here of a large order for display cases, which took me about an hour, I left things at that. It was now around five o'clock and people in the publicity department were starting to go home. I spotted Oguri waving at me and went over to his part of the room, pointing out as I approached that only he seemed to be present now; and it was a fact that the separate area of the large room where the five magazine workers had desks was inhabited by him alone. This reminded me vaguely of the situation at MITI (the Ministry of International Trade and Industry) at the end of the day, when the "non-career" members of staff would depart promptly at five o'clock. (One bureau chief used to compare them to escaped rabbits, although he'd always tended to have one word too many on most subjects, so never looked as if he'd make it to undersecretary, and never did.) The "career" administrators, on the other hand—those who'd passed the qualifying exam and had both feet firmly on the promotional ladder—inevitably stayed behind. I reflected nostalgically that they must have an identical setup here, but Oguri soon dispelled that illusion. Yesterday had seen the final proofreading, and since they hadn't managed to get everything tidied up until one in the morning, he'd taken them all off to a bar where he had his own bottle of whisky. When solidly pissed he began thanking them sentimentally for all the hard work they'd done that month, slaving night and day, saying, in a burst of vainglory, he alone would turn up and do all the work himself. Despite a hangover which was nearly splitting his head open, he'd got into the office almost on time and had somehow struggled through the morning, but at noon he went off to a nearby restaurant to have the drink he was craving. This then led to a visit to the sickroom to have the

5

doctor look him over. The doctor was pretty much used to this sort of thing and gave him a vitamin injection, suggesting with a little leer that he could do with a good lie-down. Oguri did just that on a couch in the sickroom for an hour, after which he felt much better, and from then on had been up to his ears in various bits of work until a short time ago.

"I was thinking of indulging in some more hair of the same dog. How about yourself?"

"A good idea. An extremely good idea," I replied, thinking I could at last fulfill that earlier promise to drink with him, and at the same time find out something about running a publicity magazine. My company made domestic electrical goods, so we produced a promotional journal too, but the operation was entrusted to an outside source and the product was almost unbelievably boring. I'd been thinking for some time that something ought to be done about it.

Despite the fact that I'd agreed cheerfully enough, Oguri suddenly changed his whole attitude.

"Ah, there's one thing," he muttered to himself, taking on a grave, formal air. "I heard of your recent sad. . ."

But his words were interrupted at that point by an exotic shouting of his name from the doorway, performed by a young female voice. The expression on his face immediately changed again as he looked up, switching from the speciously solemn to radiant, superficial delight, remarkably like what happens to someone's face when a film is speeded up, and he replied gaily:

"Hi there, Mayo, how's things?"

All the remaining staff of the publicity department automatically looked up and focused their attention on this latest distraction, a tall young lady who was now approaching us at something close to a trot, wearing a bright red dress. Since the dress had these very thick white borders on the lapels and the pockets, the overall impression it gave was very like a spacesuit. Behind her came another girl wearing a dress of dark green silk, with a trailing scarf of the same color and material. What they both had in common, besides being extremely good-looking and dressed in this sophisticated way, was that they each carried a small case with them as well as the usual handbag.

"Darling, I'm absolutely starving," said Mayo to Oguri, having swift-

6

ly reached his side. "Been shooting since nine o'clock this morning; ten for me and ten for Yukari. Neither of us has had any breakfast, either. All we've had all day is just two teeny bottles of milk."

"Okay, don't worry," said Oguri, nodding sympathetically. "How about some noodles?"

"Oh, my. Noodles. I ask you," said Mayo, turning to the other girl and laughing.

"One bowl of noodles between the two of you is what the doctor orders," said Oguri with a look of feigned seriousness. "I'm sure you should be dieting. Mayo seems to have put on weight again. Carry on this way and the music halls will be crying out for you."

"Same old Oguri, I see; and the same old joke."

Oguri ignored this critical remark and went on, pointing at me:

"This is an old school friend of mine. Used to work at MITI, but now he's in. . . Come on, produce your card."

He then continued, addressing his remarks to me:

"They're both fashion models. The large one is Mayo Miyazawa. Best model for beer bottles in Japan. The other is Yukari Nonomiya. She hasn't made an appearance in our magazine yet."

"But Yukari's pretty tall as well, surely?" Mayo muttered, apparently irked by some hidden, unflattering meaning in that comment about beer bottles; but then her manner suddenly changed and she introduced herself to me in a ladylike fashion, producing a small visiting card. This was presumably something the modeling agency had made for its members, for Yukari handed over an identical one.

"Business must be pretty good if you can get to know gorgeous girls like this," I said to Oguri, as an appropriate piece of flattery.

"A bevy of beauties," he replied, using the obvious cliché, and then addressed himself to the two girls again. Mayo was still standing up, but Yukari had sat down after giving me her card and was fingering her scarf in a fairly affected way. He told them that we two were just about to go out and invited them to join us. The girls had no objections, and I was delighted with the idea, since I'd been much taken by Yukari's delicate looks ever since she'd entered the room. Her balanced, well-defined features had no unpleasant sharpness about them but—I imagine because of the whiteness of her skin—an aura of vague cloudiness much like a certain kind of photograph. I found myself likening her face to the color and texture of apple or pear blossom (perhaps the dark green of her dress suggested such botanical analogies), and was struck by the old-fashioned way my mind was working. However, although I certainly found her face attractive, I can't say I had any ambitions as yet in her direction, but was simply pleased at this welcome addition to a reunion with an old acquaintance.

When there is any possibility I may go out drinking I always leave my car in the company car park, and I had done so on this occasion. On hearing this (and we were now almost alone in the room) Oguri announced that here we could see the essential seriousness of the true civil servant, and this made the girls giggle. I suppose it was a slightly comical thing to have done, although I didn't see it as a sign of some basic bureaucratic streak deep down in my character. It showed the wrong kind of caution, perhaps, for a man going out to dine with a couple of good-looking girls, but I hadn't known I was going out with them anyway, had I?

Oguri slipped smartly into the front seat of the taxi, leaving me in the rear with Mayo on my right and Yukari on my left. At the first place we went to, a steak restaurant, Oguri sat next to Mayo and I sat next to Yukari. I appreciated the fact that he was trying to help me get off with Yukari, and was impressed by the unobtrusive skill with which he managed the seating arrangements to that end.

However, the girl in the green dress, though certainly not unfriendly, behaved simply in accordance with the normal demands of sociability and politeness. When they'd finished their melon dessert, the two girls glanced casually at each other and stood up. Now that we men had been left alone together I asked Oguri a question that had been troubling me for a while:

"Is there anything, you know, going on between you and Mayo?"

"I wish I could say there was—and with Yukari as well for that matter—but unfortunately there's nothing of the kind. Mustn't allow pleasure to interfere with business, must we?"

"A very upright sentiment, I must say."

"Well, that's the way the world goes," Oguri said, and laughed, but the smile then vanished and that specious solemnity which I'd observed before came back. "I hear that your wife has died."

"Yes," I said. I had married shortly after joining MITI, a marriage arranged by one of the bureau chiefs there, but my wife had died this February after a year's illness.

"I'm sorry," he said, and bowed his head, mumbling something I couldn't catch, then adding, "How long ago was it?"

"About three months."

"You must have had a pretty bad time."

"Well... Luckily there weren't any children. Lucky in that respect, anyway..."

I gave an account of the way things had been at home, and he nodded and finally replied:

"Ah well, inscrutable are the ways of heaven."

I found this weird remark oddly moving. A habit of using ancient saws and sayings in a slightly off-key manner (although you could say, I suppose, he got them more or less right most of the time) was one he'd had even at high school, and it had aroused much laughter at the time. During all those nearly twenty years, while I'd gone from college into government service and finally into a business company, while Oguri had done all kinds of jobs and ended up as the editor of a publicity magazine, while I'd married and lost my wife ... this habit of Oguri's had remained unchanged, and somehow served as a celebration of the fact that I had no children and as consolation for my wife's death. It was this I found moving, rather than the old-fashioned wisdom itself assuring me that misfortune could always be a blessing in disguise.

"I'd hoped there might be an opportunity to break your fast this evening, but then those two got in on the act..." he said in tones of some regret, then raised his eyes and looked straight at me. "Still, perhaps that's all to the good?" he added.

"Of course it is. Better than two men drinking alone, anyway," I replied cheerfully, which made Oguri go on with increasing zest:

"Yukari's taken to you, I can see that. Been noticing it for some time. As a model she's not in the top class, middling or a bit above I'd say. The same goes for Mayo. Still, you might try your luck there. Might be able to make out. Might even go the whole way."

"Do you reckon so?"

"Sure of it. And my judgment's never wrong in these things. Incidentally, she's got a university professor as a father: French literature or agricultural economy or something like that..."

"But there's some difference there, surely? Baudelaire and farming cooperatives don't have much in common. . ."

Since Oguri seemed a bit out of his depth in academic matters he switched the subject back from the father to the daughter, saying that although Mayo's name was merely assumed for modeling purposes, Yukari's was in fact her real one.

"I'm not absolutely certain about this, but I believe she lives alone in an apartment. Nice face, good figure. Voice not so good, I admit, but then heaven never combines all the virtues in one vessel. . ."

"Well, I like her voice. It's nice when a girl as pretty and delicate-looking as that has such a low, husky voice. Very attractive."

"You're generous in your praise."

"And you're grudging in yours."

As we two middle-aged men sat laughing at each other the girls came back from refurbishing their makeup.

"Hello, a change of bridal garments," said Oguri with his usual promptness; and indeed Yukari had removed her flowing scarf and put on large earrings, while Mayo had altered her appearance by turning up the lapels of her jacket. Still, I must admit I had no eyes for Mayo, who interested me hardly at all, but gazed instead at Yukari with passionate attention. In theory this combination of pink earrings with a dark green dress should have been unpleasantly vulgar, but I was surprised to find myself struck by the originality of the contrast, which suggests my obsession with Yukari had already begun, an immediate consequence of Oguri's encouragement.

"Those are very interesting earrings you have on," I said to Yukari, and she thanked me kindly, although still in no way that went beyond the call of politeness; so Oguri put in a word for me.

"You know, Mabuchi here's been going on about Yukari all the time you've been away. Lost in heartfelt admiration. Face, figure, and voice; the three main requisites all present in one object."

Oguri talked as if he were relaying gossip about someone who wasn't there, but it seemed to please Yukari, who smiled sweetly and thanked him for his kind if exaggerated words with a little cry of delight. As I listened to this husky squeal of hers, aimed at Oguri and not at me, I felt a sensual coyness within it which made me jealous.

"Well, where are we going next?" said Mayo, and Oguri asked her teasingly if she'd pay for him, whereupon I hurriedly took what I thought was a hint and said I'd be responsible for it this time. But Oguri told me importantly to leave it all to him, for he would take us to a place where they had real Spanish dancers all the way from Spain.

Oguri seemed to be a regular at this night spot and we were shown to excellent seats right up front. Oguri chattered to Mayo about the various doings of certain models, and I gave Yukari an account of the journey I'd made to Spain the year before. I still don't think I recall her behaving in any way unusual at that point either.

Then the lights grew even dimmer and the show began. The two girls took a keen interest in the penultimate dance, in particular in the wild hip swiveling of a male dancer right in front of them, whose antics made them gasp with excitement. So enthralled was Mayo that she even stood up and handed her white lace handkerchief to the young dark-haired Spaniard, as he bowed with sweat pouring down his brow. He kissed her hand in return, and when she sat down again she went on excitedly about how splendid the young man's thighs were, particularly that lovely rise of his buttocks, so different from the deficiencies of the Japanese male in that area. Yukari's eyes flashed as she passionately agreed with every word, while Oguri and I just sat there having our glasses constantly replenished with whisky and water.

Perhaps it was because the drink had already gone to his head, or because he insisted on switching to saké at the next place, a sushi restaurant I took them to, where he drank almost nonstop; anyway, Oguri started to behave as if he were trying to pick a fight or something with me. "Pick a fight" is quite the wrong way to describe it, I suppose, since he was in a very good mood, and it took the form of praising the way I'd once behaved in the past; but it still sounded as though he were getting at me.

He was listening to a painstaking account by Mayo of a drama she'd seen on TV the night before, taking the occasional gulp of saké and making the odd casual comment, when he turned away and began talking to me.

"Mabuchi, what do you think the idea of a 'citizen' can be said to mean in Japan nowadays?"

This sudden question required the kind of complex response I couldn't provide at that moment, but he continued on what seemed a quite different tack:

"Still, you were a damn fool. Should have stuck with the civil service till you were an undersecretary or something. Much better pay you'd have got; far better."

"I could hardly have counted on reaching such heights," I replied with a grin, and Mayo, who was just completing her lengthy account of last night's soap opera, put in:

"I do wish you'd be quiet a minute. I'm trying to talk to Yukari."

This rebuke made Oguri give a groan of what could have been dismay or even the prelude to some bad-tempered outburst; but he checked himself and merely ordered another bottle, returning to what he'd been saying. The story, as he told it, was that his friend Mabuchi had been obliged to resign from government service because he'd refused a transfer from MITI to the Ministry of Defense, an attitude typical of someone who'd come of age during the war and thus objected to war in principle and was prejudiced against armed forces of any kind. That sort of rebelliousness was ridiculous in a civil servant and showed what a fool Mabuchi was, but it was a foolish streak that he, Oguri, really liked and admired in him.

Such was the gist of what he said about me, but I insisted he'd got it all wrong, since although it was true I'd objected to being transferred to the Ministry of Defense, and had indeed refused to go, this had been done out of no lofty ideals of rebellion against the powers that be.

"Let's get the facts straight," I said. "First of all, though non-career civil servants have no retirement age, there is one for career bureaucrats. One has to stop working sometime; it's as inevitable as death."

"Of course I know that," said Oguri. "But you packed it in a bit early, didn't you? The reason you had to pull out was because you said you didn't want to go to the M. of D., and you paid for it in the way you got treated after that. Still, at the bottom of your heart, when you refused that transfer..."

"Look, let's drop this. Just when I'm trying to make it with Yukari you start on about me coming of age during the war, as if you're trying to broadcast how old I am."

This was meant to be a piece of amusing repartee on my part, but he only glared at me with drunken eyes and went on solemnly:

"Just a moment. What I see in that refusal of yours, right at the bottom of it . . . is the blood, the lineage, of a free citizen. . ."

I stared at him, since I'd no idea what he was on about. He responded to my look by saying:

"What was that story you told me, then, about your great-grandfather? One of the heroes of the people's rights movement, coming back late one afternoon from a cherry blossom viewing, attacked by a thug hired by the backs-to-the-wall opposition, consequently cut down, so dying with appropriate glory. . ."

"Gosh!" cried Yukari.

"How super!" said Mayo. "Just right for the Meiji centenary celebrations, too."

"Very appropriate," I said. "Very suitable. Look, it's true I did tell you something about my great-grandfather, but in the twenty years since then the whole thing's been transformed inside your head into some incredible romantic melodrama straight off the Kabuki stage. The truth of the matter is. . ."

The truth of the matter was, in fact, very different.

The Mabuchi family were landowners in a minor fief in northern Japan, the original ancestors having apparently come from the Ise area in the south. "Landowners" gives a slightly misleading impression, since basically the family existed by trade, such as saké brewing, or selling salt, tobacco, and products of that nature, and the woods and arable land had been acquired gradually as a consequence of these middleman activities. The Meiji Restoration took place during my great-great-grandfather's time, and the change of government saw an increase in the family wealth, so it looked as if we at least had done well out of the confusions of the times.

This very success, however, brought the envy and hatred of the local samurai families upon our heads. The leading families were what remained of important *daimyo*, or feudal lords, who had supported the Tokugawa shogunate for generations. Naturally their allegiance at the time of the Meiji Restoration was still to the defeated *bakufu* government, and thus the new Meiji government did not look at all kindly upon them. In those days samurai families all over the country were suffering great hardships, but these people had a particularly bad time of it, so bad they attempted a mass back-to-the-land movement, back to the wretched pieces of wilderness that had been apportioned to each household. What made matters worse was that they attempted to farm by the Ninomiya method, the experimental approach advocated by Sontoku Ninomiya in the mid-nineteenth century, which the fief tried for twenty years without any success whatsoever. This back-to-the-land idea had been adopted, as a last resort, by the leading clan elder, who was an impassioned devotee of that moralistic sage. Nothing came of it, but the useless enterprise certainly gives some indication of his unique character, as a man of influence, unfortunately, rather than as an agriculturist. His influence persisted even into the Meiji period, so that the region remained dominated by totally irrelevant ideas of loyalty to the clan and shogun system despite the fact that it was now quite dead.

Consequently, although a bank was built in the main town and rice granaries in the port some twenty-five miles away, they were controlled through and through by the samurai families and their antiquated notions of what should be done, and they could fix the price of rice just as they pleased and establish a virtual dictatorship in the area. Thus it was that Jukichi Mabuchi, my great-grandfather, set out to defy the feudal bases of the samurai system, and the Mabuchi family, which had already done so well out of the turmoil of the Restoration, was all the more hated by the "people of family" (as the samurai liked to think of themselves).

My great-grandfather became head of the household in the twelfth year of Meiji (1879) at the age of twenty-seven. Being a very active person with a passion for the new, he busied himself introducing the latest methods of rice farming and fruit cultivation, and with the improvement of livestock strains. It would have been fine if he could have expended his energies in that direction only, but in order to check the stagnating influence on the area's economy of the bank run by the samurai elder (with its motto of borrow cheap and lend high) he set up a rival bank with himself as president, providing more favorable terms for the merchant class. Obviously the "people of family" weren't going to take this lying down, particularly as Jukichi became the power behind the scenes of the local liberalization movement and was ensuring that people friendly to himself were elected as mayors and Diet representatives. Since the samurai families had managed to establish connections with the bureaucrats in office, there was bound to be constant conflict between them and my great-grandfather. For example, at the time of the second general election in 1892, the one notorious for its corruption and blatant interference with electoral procedures, a drunkard barged his way into my great-grandfather's campaign office and lunged at him with a spear, but the spear got stuck in the wainscoting, and while the drunk was struggling to pull it out my forebear was able to make good his escape on his stockinged feet. However, the really decisive struggle came over his plan to set up a rice exchange in the main town, which he hoped would break the monopoly of the rice granaries in the port town, by means of which the samurai had so far been able to control the price of rice at will. It was while he was returning one evening from a blossom-viewing expedition at a hot spring in the hills that he was set upon by some thugs, and his ricksha thrown into the river with him inside it; all this taking place some two months before his rice exchange office came into being (with Jukichi as president). When Great-grandfather finally managed to crawl home looking like a drowned rat, he claimed the bullyboys must be samurai (despite the fact that he'd been unable to see their faces in the dark) because they used the forms of language peculiar to such people.

So it wasn't surprising he should have come to the conclusion that he wasn't likely to die in his bed, and he was constantly telling people that no real man could expect to do so. But he did die in bed, of an illness, just two years after his rice exchange was set up, in the thirty-first year of Meiji (1898), when he was only forty-six and should have had many active years still to live. There was a rumor that hordes of samurai were going to disrupt his funeral, but nothing happened, although his wife returned home in such a state her legs gave way under her (out of relief, no doubt) and she remained squatting in the entrance hall for some length of time. On the day before his death he is said to have called his young eldest son (my grandfather) to his side and advised him to bring this feuding to an end, for "all the tiles torn from the family roof would never suffice."

When I reached this fairly cryptic point Oguri burst in:

"Meaning, of course, that if he himself had gone on living he'd certainly have continued the struggle by tearing the tiles off his own roof and hurling them at the enemy."

"Well, I suppose you might interpret it that way."

"Fight to the last roof tile. There would've been thousands of them with a house the size of the one you were born in, Mabuchi. Now, here we see the true Meiji spirit, the true spirit of nascent capitalism. . ."

"I'm not at all sure it meant any rebellion of the spirit of capitalism against things feudalistic. Maybe there's a bit of that, but basically it was just plain obstinacy on his part," I said, at which point Mayo made the irresponsible comment that, as a story, being cut down after cherry blossom viewing would have made a much better ending.

"Wasn't there something just like it in Kyushu or somewhere the other day? You remember . . . a local politician or some big-time gangster, and this hired killer. . ."

Oguri raised his hand as if to silence this misunderstanding, and almost scolded her:

"No, no, that's quite different. Mabuchi's family is one with a long history up north; a proper, respectable family. . . I seem to have got the story about that drunk during the election and the return from the cherry viewing mixed up somehow. Even so, Mabuchi. . ."

He seemed about to return to his former argument, but luckily Yukari broke in with the comment that she thought my great-grandfather was wonderful, a real man, and asked if any photographs of him had survived.

"Just two. Both, of course, studio portraits with him looking straight ahead, all stern and dignified. One of them's fairly large, and it's been framed and hung back home. He was quite good-looking, you know, with nice, rather friendly eyes. I suppose he grew his sideburns so black and long, plus a thick moustache, to offset the gentle impression his eyes gave."

I then told the story about the gold watches, prefacing it with the remark that Oguri probably wouldn't have heard it (as he certainly would not, for I'd been a student during the period before and after the defeat when most people were very hard up, and avoided any subject that might have suggested I came from a wealthy family). I decided to reveal this secret episode in my ancestor's life since I was aware that all three of them, Oguri, Yukari, even Mayo, had acquired an extremely heroic picture of the man. The atmosphere of awe I'd unwittingly created I found oppressive, and hoped this would dispel it.

However, the only one who saw the joke was Oguri—or, rather, Oguri and the man behind the sushi bar, who smiled as he listened to my account of Jukichi Mabuchi's foolishness—while the two girls, of course, were almost swooning over this romantic tale of true love in the Meiji era. Mayo had tears in her eyes as she murmured over and over how lovely it was and how he must have really loved her, while Yukari tilted her head a little to one side, enough to set her pink plastic earrings swaying, and said how marvelous he must have been at both work and love. That's what a real man was like, she said, and looked me straight in the eyes as she spoke.

At that moment I felt, for only a split second it's true, that this person being so fulsomely praised for his heroic exploits in love and work was actually myself, but soon remembered it was my great-grandfather she was admiring. Meanwhile the man behind the counter raised a modest doubt as to whether the acquiring of a dozen gold watches in such a cause was really all that "manly," and Oguri himself was oddly quiet and restrained, though he soon returned to his usual crudeness of expression:

"A bit different from his great-grandson, anyway. Mabuchi here may be all right at work, but so far as the romantic passion is concerned he's a complete washout . . . or so I gather, don't I? . . ."

He followed this up with a great bellow of laughter, and I found myself apprehensive about the way Yukari might react. I didn't want her to think I was some stick-in-the-mud totally indifferent to the "romantic passion," nor would I have been happy if she'd drawn the opposite conclusion and thought I went around sleeping with practically anybody. However, Yukari capped Oguri's laughter with the remark that she was sure sideburns, nice long ones, would suit me, an extraordinarily irrelevant response to what Oguri had just said. Still, it gave me a great deal of pleasure, being the first time she'd said anything that demonstrated some kind of interest in me as a person.

Mayo expressed some doubt about the suitability of sideburns, and Oguri added:

"Better not photograph him full on—his face couldn't take it. He looks all right from the side, though. Handsome in profile, the very opposite of me, don't you think? I've always thought so."

This attention now being paid to my features was slightly embarrassing so I said:

"I don't think I ought to grow sideburns since they'd probably be mostly gray. I've got enough gray hairs as it is."

Yukari chimed in that she thought gray hair like mine was very nice, which made Oguri burst out laughing again. He urged everyone to eat up since Mabuchi was paying for it, and then added to me:

"Fashion models eat a lot. You'd be surprised. All that stuff about them existing on Coke and instant noodles is a complete myth."

Both girls protested that was an awful thing to say, it really was, though they continued helping themselves to various good things, while showing a wise restraint over the more fattening foods. Oguri had ordered a glass of cold saké, since he was tired of drinking the warm stuff out of the traditional cup the size of a thimble, but the man got it wrong and brought glasses for all four of us. Mayo sipped slowly at hers but Yukari, under the impression it was water, knocked half of hers back in one gulp before realizing, with a little wriggle of her shoulders, that it was alcohol, although she didn't seem all that put out by the discovery. I admired the way models seemed not only to have voracious appetites but were pretty accomplished drinkers as well.

Oguri was now sitting with his glass in front of him, not drinking much and in some kind of daze.

"Subway . . . citizen . . . swimming pool. . . Of course."

Having said this once he said it again. I suppose he thought he was only mumbling to himself, though what he produced was more like a drunken bellow. Mayo's response was to ask for some rice balls with cucumber inside, but I asked him what he was talking about. At first he seemed not to know, although finally he said:

"Ah, I was thinking about something a bit odd that happened at work today, and I don't seem able to get it out of my head."

He spoke as if he were trying to recall some far-off event, which then seemed to come back to him, and he told me the following story at his usual brisk pace. After he'd had his little lie-down in the sickroom he'd gone back to the publicity department, where a half dozen men had drawn up their chairs in front of the boss's desk and were experimenting with word associations, hoping in this way to gain some helpful hint on how to run the winter advertising campaign. This was quite unconnected with Oguri's own work, but since he had nothing to do (or nothing in particular) he thought he'd join in.

Someone started off with "subway," which was immediately followed by "citizen" and then "swimming pool," at which point the boss made a sneering remark about the obviousness of their associative powers, saying he wanted something a bit more extravagant than that.

"I was taken aback, I can tell you," explained Oguri. "From subway to citizen is obvious enough, I suppose, but it seems a bit of a leap from there to swimming pool. But that was the man's response. No fool, I suppose. Knows what he's up to, although I couldn't make it out; and then I had five phone calls, one after the other, and four people came to see me. All go, I can tell you, and I thought I'd forgotten all about it and now suddenly I find myself thinking about it again. Still, it's not important, I suppose."

"Yes, but it's not all that strange, surely? I mean, the three words hang together. The subway is the form of transportation by which people go to work, and is thus a symbol of labor, whereas the swimming pool is a symbol of recreation for the same citizens."

"Well, that's probably it," said Oguri, as if he still wasn't satisfied in his own mind about it. "I just thought it a bit funny at the time."

"What does the word 'citizen' suggest to you, then?"

"The French Revolution."

"There's an orthodox response for you."

"That's because I did sociology at college. Still, you see, I didn't want to be accused of being pedantic so I was desperately trying to think of something else when someone said 'pool,' and the man reacted in that way and somehow I started vaguely letting my mind play with the subject—citizen, *citoyen*, that sort of thing—and what the word could be said to mean."

While he pondered this, and I pondered with him, Mayo made a totally irrelevant remark which produced a thick, drunken howl of laughter from Oguri. The place was getting crowded, so finally Oguri announced, in a surprisingly steady voice, that he was going to see Mayo home, and therefore. . .

The implication for me and Yukari was plain enough, and she seemed to have no objection as she looked at the three of us with sleepy eyes. I signed the check and stood up. The girl in the green dress also stood up, but a little slower than me, and then staggered and started to keel over in my direction. This gave me the illusion that I myself had stumbled and was falling forward into a meadow of green, so I automatically thrust out both arms and arrested her descent. Enveloped in a thin mist of saké and perfume I embraced this supple expanse of grass and held her unsteadily on her feet. Mayo gave a cry and Oguri said something. He then set upright a stool that had been knocked over.

"I'm sorry," said Yukari, continuing to lean against me as though about to pass out, "I must have got drunk." When I withdrew my arms a moment she looked as if she might slump down onto the floor, although she retained a firm enough grip on her small handbag. As I held her soft, lithe body, I said:

"That glass of cold saké must have been the last straw."

This cool, analytic statement of the situation was meant to cover the embarrassment our sudden physical intimacy had created. However, the attempt was completely foiled by two banal remarks, one from Oguri ("That's the style, but a bit more feeling this time") and another from Mayo ("Seems just the right size for you, Yukari").

This last remark was not intentionally obscene, I'm sure, being simply a reference to our respective heights. I was taller than Yukari and so didn't look comic holding her like that, which Mayo had suddenly realized on seeing us standing close together. Mayo, of course, was just standing there watching, but Oguri had cleverly curled the fingers of one of my hands around the handle of Yukari's small case, and thus I made my way, clumsily and slowly, supporting Yukari toward the door. As she stumbled heavily out into the night air she sighed with pleasure at its coolness, and Oguri stopped a taxi for us.

So it was that I sat in the taxi gazing at the pale blur of her face and growing excited as I fondled her small, soft hand. At this stage I was considering the possibility of taking the girl somewhere to spend the night, but what made me hesitate was the feeling that, this being the first time we'd met, perhaps it was slightly vulgar to rush things to a conclusion before various pertinent rituals, normal in these matters, had been observed.

As we approached her apartment Yukari gave the driver precise instructions as to its whereabouts, and finally the taxi came to a halt. I got out carrying her case, half hoping she might indicate she was in the mood for something by inviting me in for a cup of tea or whatever; but instead, once she too was out, she merely shook my hand briefly and thanked me, receiving her small case from my hands.

"Can you manage it? Or shall I see you as far as your front door?"

"No, that's all right. I can manage."

Since that was her attitude I said in as nonchalant a manner as possible:

"I'd like to see you again sometime."

"So would I. Phone me."

She gave me her number, and also the briefest of farewells, as if she were urging me to hurry on back into the taxi. I was not even granted any leisurely view of her disappearing down some dark lane, for by the time I'd told the driver where to go and written down her number in my little black notebook with its company crest, we were already some distance from the scene. The taxi driver, who seemed to be quite old, tried to engage me in conversation:

"Very nice-looking girl, sir."

"Is she?"

"She certainly is. I had a good look, I can tell you. A dancer?"

"No, she isn't," I replied with some emphasis, but then relented slightly and said he wasn't all that wrong. He seemed to assume that his customer was not in the mood for talk and said no more. I began to think about Yukari, realizing that if she hadn't needed to have her case carried for her, and could give such precise directions to the driver, and also keep a firm grip on her handbag when leaning against me in the sushi restaurant, perhaps she hadn't really been drunk at all. It could all have been part of some naive play she'd been making for me. If that were the case (and I couldn't be sure, of course) then I'd made a serious mistake in not having been more positive just now; but I reflected that her giving me her phone number still let me in with a chance. So, thinking back over the events of the evening—the sight of her neck which that scarf showed to such good advantage, pear blossom, Spanish songs and dances, Oguri's opinion of my leaving government service, his ideas about citizenship, and so on—I began to have a suspicion that the girl in the green dress had been attracted to me because of my great-grand-father. In fact when I thought about this Meiji melodrama of rights and liberty and the new ringing out the old and the romance of the twelve gold watches, I supposed it wasn't strange that a girl of her age should be moved by it, considering how popular the crude coloring of Meiji prints seemed to have become again recently. However, I soon dismissed that idea, recalling the sepia photograph, its ancient oval shape against a white background, of Jukichi Mabuchi back home, and think-ing how totally different that dignified gentleman was when compared with Eisuke Mabuchi of the present generation. So Eisuke Mabuchi lit a cigarette, and thought about Mayo's remark about size, grinning wryly. It was a fact that most models were very tall, and obviously it was important for them that a man should be tall as well, but surely she could have chosen a slightly less crude word to express that inno-cent fact. There must be something wrong with Oguri if he could fall in love (as he clearly had) with a girl who talked like that; and as I noted this mental criticism of my old acquaintance, I seem to have as-sumed that the girl I'd fallen in love with could never possibly talk in that vulgar way.

However, having registered this criticism, my expression gradually changed, as the wry, ironical grin left my face to be replaced by a look of simple lust. I began to think about the question of size, the size of mine and the size of Yukari's, imagining how they would combine together. I was once again aware of my vulgarity in taking things to this sudden conclusion without the preceding rituals, even if only in my imagination. Yet one thing I never imagined was how dramatically my life was to be changed by this evening's encounter with Yukari, nor how comically fate would amuse itself with me as a result.

2

Tsuru Kaneko greeted me in the entrance hall when I got home, and told me nothing important had happened during my absence. The tailor had brought some material for me to consider, somebody had come from the neighborhood association asking for a contribution, and two bottles of local saké had been sent by a local politician back home who'd decided (totally on his own initiative) that I should run for mayor. So, as she said, nothing worth mentioning had taken place, and I decided a typical day in my life must be much like a typical day in Oguri's, glancing up at the stopped hands of the clock hanging there on the wall. I'd brought it here from my family's house in the country; my dead wife had had a peculiar affection for the thing, which she referred to as an antique (using the English word to add a touch of class, I imagine), and before she became ill she'd invariably taken it to be repaired every time it broke down. Now, however, for almost a year its two hands had remained motionless together near the quarter past three mark.

Tsuru used the arrival of this present of local saké to point out that the brewer was a distant relation of the man who'd sent it. This was news to me, as well as information about which I felt total indifference, but I thought I should keep her company for a while so had her pour out some tea for me in the living room. As always it tasted quite unlike anything I got at the office or elsewhere.

This woman, now in her early fifties, had previously been in domestic service at our house up north. Since my mother had been prone to illness, my brother, sister, and I had each had a maid to look after us, and in my case, up until my second year at junior high school when she got married, everything was done for me by Tsuru, who cleaned my room, tidied away my bedding, did my laundry, and polished my shoes. She was then a girl with nice, gentle eyes, a slightly overlarge mouth, and a pale complexion, but not very talkative. She married a man from Kobe and went to live there, but he was killed during the war, and since she didn't get on at all well with her mother-in-law she returned home, helping out with the silk weaving in her parents' cottage and occasionally coming to our house to work. Finally, when I went off to college in Tokyo (just after the war when there was a shortage of decent lodgings), my father bought this house and asked Tsuru to go with me to cook and generally take care of things. The original idea was she should stay until I graduated, but since I could never find anyone else she just sort of stayed on. Even after I married she remained because it seemed impossible to find a suitable maid, and remain she had ever since. Of course one could always say she was the one who needed to stay since she had nowhere else to go. Immediately after I'd passed my civil service exams there was talk about her remarrying as her relations had found her a possible match, but she wasn't much taken with the offer, declined it, and never received another. I suppose I ought to add that, as far as myself and my family were concerned, we had no interest whatsoever in finding her a suitable marriage partner.

Despite the fact that she came, as it were, with the house, Tsuru got on perfectly well with my wife. I don't suppose either of them could have been called intelligent women, but they were neither of them fools. No doubt, given the difficulty of finding domestic help, my wife was delighted to have this maid who not only could (and did) do everything but had an almost feudal attitude toward her work, and I expect Tsuru was happy to remain in a place where she was already at home and taken good care of, and where she need have no worries about the future. Tsuru taught my wife a good deal about my tastes in food (although, except for one or two occasions each week when my wife prepared some elaborate meal, all the cooking was left to her), and for Tsuru, born as she was in a weaver's cottage in the north, this provided an excellent opportunity to learn how to speak and behave properly from a daughter of one of our more distinguished, even if now impoverished, commercial families. She took the opportunity, and had even managed to lose her thick northern accent over the past ten years, an astonishing feat considering her age. My wife showed considerable zeal in her reeducation, but there could be little doubt that it achieved this grand measure of success because Tsuru herself was determined it should do so. She was, in fact, the ideal student. I can remember one occasion (I think it was around the time I was being urged—or rather told—to go to the Ministry of Defense, or just a little before) when I observed her glance up at me in a way that was exactly like my wife, and I experienced a sense of shock, almost horror, at the transformation that had gradually taken place.

"I met Oguri tonight. You know, he was at school with me. Came here once or twice, although that was some time ago."

Tsuru thought about the matter a while, then said:

"He's that tall gentleman, I believe. He borrowed some money from you and never paid it back."

"Didn't he? I'd forgotten about that." As I replied, it struck me that Tsuru had quite a barbed tongue when she chose, and so I decided not to tell her what Oguri had said about her. This was when we'd been in the steak restaurant and he'd been offering me his condolences, saying how hard life could be for a widower with no children to help in any way, and how lucky I was to have a maid who could do everything for me.

"Tsuru still with you, is she? Frankly I can't work out why any man should want to get married when he has the ideal servant."

Of course this wasn't the kind of remark one would want to pass on to a woman, and Oguri had in fact made it when Yukari and Mayo were away doing their makeup. The only other time he'd mentioned her was to offer the conventional expression of his regards, followed by sober reflections on how old she must be now. Given her slightly caustic remark about him, I felt I could only talk about Oguri as a man who had (or so she implied) been devious about paying back the money he owed me, and show her I wasn't one to be taken for a ride.

"Well, at least he stood me a pretty good meal tonight. He's working on publicity in a beer company. Has section head status, so the expense account provides, you know..."

Tsuru made no relevant reply to this statement, so I was obliged to change the subject. I talked about my great-grandfather's watches and how I'd told the story to Oguri and the two fashion models, and how mortified I'd been by the remarkable enthusiasm it had aroused in the two girls.

Tsuru smiled very slowly and said:

"Of course they were just teasing you."

"Teasing me?"

"Yes, because they'd like you to buy them watches as well, and they wanted to see if you'd be able to work out what they meant."

Having solved that puzzle to her own satisfaction she pointed to two cardboard boxes under the alcove shelves, each of which contained a large bottle of saké.

"I opened them for you."

I stretched out my arm and pulled one box toward me, and took the bottle out of the box. It seemed to have some sort of gold leaf mixed in with the saké, for when I gripped it by the neck and shook it some dubious, minute, oblong and diamond shapes swirled about in the thin amber liquid, raising an ominous, evil-looking blizzard there. I was now urged to inspect the suit material, which had been placed on top of the alcove shelves, but I couldn't be bothered and said I'd have a good look at it in the light of day on Sunday. So I put the naked bottle of saké back where I'd got it from, and then noticed a cheap magazine beside one of the cushions.

I picked this up and looked at the double-page color photograph at which it lay open. It was of a middle-aged man, the star presumably of numerous gangster or *yakuza* movies, lying in a vaguely suggestive pose on some startlingly green and fresh-looking tatami matting, adorned with tattoos and a smug-stern expression on his face. The way he was lolling there not only carried a large hint of sexual promise, but had a heavy tension about it that seemed to extend to the two slightly outsize dice he held in his right hand. His eyes, smoldering with provocation and a kind of intimidatory bluster, were fixed firmly on the reader, and the overall impression was of a sullen obscenity. I looked at it for a while, then closed the magazine.

"So they still have film magazines," I said.

"Yes. After all, the cinema is more interesting than television," Tsuru replied, sliding the magazine toward her in some embarrassment.

"Well, that may be."

"Oh certainly. Television is only about normal, humdrum things."

"I suppose so. Movies are on a larger scale, of course," I agreed, with a mild sense that this conversation seemed to be confusing movies and movie magazines, but otherwise thinking nothing much about it, perhaps because another thought had come into my head.

Before I married, whenever I'd come home late Tsuru had always sat up waiting for me in the living room just as she had tonight (although I confess the only reading matter I can recall was either the evening paper or some respectable women's magazine), but when I was married she would always wait in the maid's room, even though my wife would normally be already asleep in our bedroom. Now, once again, she had moved back into the living room to wait for me, and I had a strange sense of having journeyed back in time and yet also having not returned, much like looking at a clock that's exactly as it was twelve hours ago though one knows twelve hours have passed. It struck me as odd that, still only in my forties, I should be brooding on the passage of time, and as ludicrous that it should be recorded for me by something as trivial as this minor alteration in the ecology of my household.

I drank my tea and stood up.

"Will you be working in your study now, sir?"

I was aware that since I'd joined my present company the amount of reading I did had declined, but that couldn't be helped. I shook my head. Then, as I was leaving the room, she said something else.

"I really do think it would be a good idea if you spent the night somewhere occasionally; then you could go straight off to the office from there."

This was something that Tsuru had repeated like a cheerful if admonitory refrain about once a month ever since my wife had gone into the hospital, usually adding a few significant remarks like "After all, men are different." Whenever she spoke like this a number of generous little wrinkles would appear good-humoredly at the corners of her eyes, an expression of tolerant virtue exactly like that time she'd caught me smoking when I was twelve years old. At first I'd been astonished that a servant who had got on so well with my wife and worked so hard for her (visiting her so loyally in the hospital, too) should have casually encouraged me in sexual betrayal; but by this time I felt no shock whatsoever, simply smiling and going upstairs.

27

3

Three days later I rang up Yukari, listened to the bell ring twenty-four times, then gave up and left the glass and metal confines of the public phone booth. I'd felt certain qualms about ringing up a woman on the company phone. It was lunchtime and, although it was raining, quite a lot of people were wandering about. As I made my way to a restaurant I began to wonder if I hadn't written the wrong number down in my notebook, or perhaps she'd deliberately given me a false one; but, after some time, in fact after I'd eaten my spaghetti and drunk my coffee, I changed my mind and came to the conclusion there was nothing strange about someone who worked being out. Anyway, I decided to phone again just to make sure, but she still wasn't in. This time I thought I'd try contacting her through the modeling agency, and was greeted by a very grandmotherly voice, which was then succeeded by an even more ancient one, though neither seemed to know where Yukari might be. The day after that I rang her apartment again and, after waiting a considerable length of time, I finally heard Yukari's sleepy voice at the other end, but she expressed no joy at my invitation to go out somewhere that evening, merely saying she was much too tired to be able to see me.

I phoned her again three days later, having decided that, this being the third attempt, if she turned me down now I would stop bothering. Today, however, the phone was answered almost as soon as it began to ring, and she said in a completely carefree voice:

"I'm awfully sorry I've made you ring so many times, and I'm afraid today's no good either. There's this appointment I just have to keep. Well, it's not really an appointment. I mean it's not work, really. Still, I've got to go out."

She then gave me an account of the shopping she'd just done, of the dress and the accessories she'd bought, the various shoes she'd tried on ... all this information delivered at great speed yet still taking an awfully long time. Finally she said:

"Oh my, just look at the time. Must fly. Bye now."

The receiver was put down hastily before I'd had time to get a word in edgeways, and I interpreted the perfunctory clunk of the phone at the other end as an overt expression of the fact that this girl had no intention at all of going out with me. Thus when I left the phone booth my smile of disappointment may well have looked reasonably cheerful, since I felt at least that some kind of decision had been made for me. After all, the girl was much too young for me to have an affair with.

At the time I genuinely thought so, but then about ten days later, one Saturday afternoon, I was in an area near where she lived and I thought I'd try ringing her from a phone outside a cheap tempura shop. It was a red phone, the kind that are placed quite openly in front of various stores, and I never liked using them because passersby could overhear what you were saying, but I'd been unable to find anywhere else to park my car. As I stood there dialing her number and trying to keep my face away from the stench of cheap frying oil issuing from the shop, it occurred to me how very inconvenient a country Japan had become for romantic involvements. As far as my resolution about giving up on the third unsuccessful attempt was concerned, I'd been able to convince myself some days before that of my three attempts one had taken place when she wasn't in and so did not count, and yet I'd been so chronically busy at work I hadn't had time to make my final wager. Still, my mind had been dominated by the idea that if I drew back now I wouldn't look much of a man compared with my great-grandfather, and there was also the fact that I inevitably thought about Yukari with some passion once or twice every day. My deliberately coming to her part of town to phone her was an indication of the obsessive nature of my feelings (which I wouldn't want to deny), and yet, while I was listening to the phone ringing in her apartment, there was also this negative feeling that I'd rather she were out than have her put me off again for the third time in a row.

She was in. This time, however, she spoke in a calm, leisurely, friendly fashion, seeming very pleased to hear from me and saying she'd been waiting for me to get in touch for ages. She promptly accepted my invitation to dinner that evening, and asked me to come and collect her, giving me swift and precise instructions how to get there; but when she heard I was close by she became flustered and asked me to give

29

her half an hour to get the place tidied up. Naturally I knew thirty minutes wouldn't be enough, so, having swiftly got clear of that tempura takeaway, I first ascertained where her apartment was (it was above a tatami-weaving workshop, reached by a narrow staircase at the back of the shop), then went for a leisurely stroll around the neighborhood, eventually arriving back at her apartment just as she'd switched off the vacuum cleaner.

"Oh, and I haven't done my makeup or changed yet. Still, you can come in," she said, and smiled at me.

She was wearing a light sweater and skirt and, not surprisingly I suppose, in the light of day her face seemed much plainer and less shapely than it had at night, lacking any eye shadow or false eyelashes or lipstick. The person standing before me was no fashion model but an ordinary twenty-two-year-old girl, certainly with features that were well out of the ordinary, but still very clean and healthy-looking. On my way here I'd been considering kissing her as soon as we got inside, but now this seemed hardly an appropriate thing to do.

The apartment consisted of two rooms: a main room about twelve feet square, and a dining-kitchen. I sat down at the small table in the kitchen and drank some Coke and talked to Yukari who was in the next room doing her makeup. She was seated on a low stool in front of a dresser mirror, and one of the side leaves of the mirror prevented me from seeing her face. At first she made a conscious effort to keep her legs properly together, but as she became absorbed in her makeup ritual, first her left leg drifted to one side of the stool, and then the right one gradually disappeared around the other. As I looked about me I was impressed by the packed array of electrical appliances she'd somehow managed to get into this tiny kitchen, including the inevitable electric rice cooker, refrigerator, and toaster, but also a mixer, a warm air heater which she hadn't yet tidied away even though it was the end of May, and the very latest in microwave ovens.

"Ah, I see you've got one of our refrigerators. Much obliged, madam."

"Oh, is it? I suppose it is," she replied, ambiguously concealed behind her mirror, and casually bringing her knees together again. That room would no doubt have a television and stereo, but I couldn't see it all, only the uncarpeted wooden floor and a small double bed under a red bedcover. Between the dresser mirror and the bed I noticed a pile of foreign fashion magazines which I imagined she used as reference works in the performance of her trade. The one on top of the pile was the French edition of *Vogue*, and there was another copy of the same magazine, the most recent April number, on the dining table, from the cover of which a Scandinavian girl wearing a black and white blouse over her soft, plump shoulders looked out at me in a meaningful way. Right beside it was a rectangular digital clock with two windows in its face, the one on the left showing an unchanging 3 while the one opposite moved from 25 to 26 to 27, the square white shape constantly adding one more number to its sum with only the faintest of sounds. I gazed at this as if I were seeing a clock without hands for the very first time, and reflected that it was about time my own company changed over to digital clocks.

Still, what most attracted my attention was a poster on the wall of the cramped kitchen. It was a kind that had become fashionable recently, made not so much for advertising purposes as for interior decoration, a picture of a leading actress done in *ukiyoe* pastiche. The main emphasis was on the upper half of her charming body, with its elaborate tattoo of dark, scattered cherry blossoms extending from her back over her shoulders and down her upper arms. This lady *yakuza* (an underworld boss, no doubt), with a cut across her cheek from which the blood dripped down, was dramatically posed against an old tiled temple wall on which a number of votive cards had been randomly affixed. The dagger in her hand was streaked with blood, witness to the gory goings-on that must have celebrated the conclusion of this obviously sensational film. The fact that the scattered votive cards had been used to show the title of the film, the name of the director, and so on was an additional subtle touch.

"That's an interesting poster you have here," I said.

"Great, isn't it? I think it's rather super," came Yukari's voice from behind the mirror.

"There's something about her eyes that reminds me a bit of you."

"Really?"

"Pretty cute for a fashion model to stick something like this on the wall."

"Well, I do sometimes model kimono, too. Only very occasionally, though. Shall I show you some photos of me in one of the magazines? A kimono's awfully hard to look good in."

"Your figure's better suited to Western clothes. I thought so from the moment I saw you."

This piece of flattery had the required effect and she gave a pleased little laugh.

"Would you like something to read? Do you like comics?"

"Can't say I do very much."

Basically I suppose I could say I frown on posters of that kind, and particularly disapprove of openly displaying such things on the wall of a room. Crude vulgarity of that degree is a direct challenge to any decent way of life which values dignity, honor, and decorum; or, if one doesn't want to go that far, it reflects a state of mind that is just itching to destroy the social order. But as I looked at this poster I had no such thoughts. It simply interested me that this girl should have that poster on her wall, and I also felt it suited her, was just what she needed to bring a feeling of change, of something different, of relaxation, into her life. This doesn't mean I thought of Yukari as some crazy, way-out person, for what the *yakuza* movie poster indicated to me was not eccentricity but youth, a straightforward expression of the difference in our ages.

But it would be false to put the matter as simply as that, because my response was not straightforward. What I felt in Yukari's room, in addition to the clumsy tensions the situation aroused, was an uplifting, almost floating sense of relaxation. This may sound a bit funny from a man who has only traveled overseas on official business, but it had much in common with sensations experienced on going abroad, a general feeling of release from the constrictions of the responsible mind; something I'd felt in other situations, too.

I remember, for example, a very similar feeling when, back in my home town, I'd been to visit the lady who ran a local inn-*cum*-restaurant (and who I'm now aware must have been my father's mistress), where I used to drink tea and play cards. It was this same lady who'd arranged, as a present to celebrate my passing the university entrance exam, that I should sleep with a young and very obedient geisha. This was my first taste of such pleasures and I would have been happy to repeat the experience, but no matter how many hints I might drop, nor how much I might assure her I would pay next time, she merely laughed and refused to arrange anything else. I imagine she'd probably confessed the matter to my father and been roundly scolded by him. However, what I want to stress here is the sense of emotional relaxation just talking to her in her office or laughing around with the geisha there used to give me. When I sat in the tiny room with its two or three samisen hanging on the wall I felt as if I'd actually escaped from my home and from the town itself, and it was strange how the poster on Yukari's kitchen wall seemed to affect me in much the same way as the samisen hanging on that other wall so long ago.

I also felt the same sense of release when I was in the studio of a painter I'd grown friendly with while I was a university student. This was a large room, some twenty-four by fifteen feet in size, with a floor of plain wooden boards and numerous unframed surrealistic paintings of his own on the walls. I had no particular interest in painting itself, but just enjoyed sitting in a broken-down wicker chair amid the reek of turpentine, looking at the various paint smears on the walls and furniture, an experience I found so soothing that for one longish period of time I used to visit regularly once a week. Mostly I would drop in when out for a walk, and if this were at night I'd often miss the last train and have to walk back the distance of two stations. He was also well read in certain ways, had spent two years in Paris, and was a skilled raconteur who liked someone to talk to. Whether he had polished his skills in another respect while in Paris I don't know, but he was always living with different women and that provided an additional source of interest. In fact the reason we stopped seeing each other was, when the third woman I'd seen there (I have no idea how many there may have been before) ran out on him, he jumped to the conclusion that I was the other man involved. I found the whole business completely ridiculous, so the visits came to an end. Since this all happened when I was preparing in earnest for the civil service exams, my visits hadn't been that frequent for a while anyway.

Still, the impression that remained most vividly in my mind was not so much of the paint smears on the walls and the furniture, nor of the three women who'd lived with him, but of a fairly tall, narrow bookcase which was next to the battered wicker chair. On the bottom shelf there were large art books, the paintings of Picasso, Dali, Ernst, photographs of Roman erotic sculpture, and so on. On the next shelf were more art books, mainly biographies of painters and suchlike, and on the next were works on history and anthropology, and some novels. The top shelf, however, had no books; instead there were three mortuary tablets with inscriptions in gold lettering on a black background, plus a hand-bell which was fairly dented and blackened with age. The bell had been placed on a small red cushion with gold tacking threads hanging from its four corners like cat's whiskers. It lay on its side, covered in dust, with its wooden clapper protruding and, although it was grimy with years of handling, one could just make out a red and white striped pattern on this clapper.

I realize now he had never been able to escape completely from the formal, decorous life of his parents and ancestors, no matter how hard he may have tried, and these objects were symbolic, laughable reminders of that fact. At the time, however, being young and simple, and also having a powerful hatred for the trappings of the same Buddhist gloom that had accompanied my own northern upbringing, I felt a real thrill at seeing these mortuary tablets set immediately above erotic works of art in this combined bookcase and Buddha shelf. I interpreted their presence as being in some ill-defined way an indication of contempt for bourgeois order, and I'm sure I made a number of fatuous comments on this subject from the vantage point of that creaking wicker chair. I admit it's a bit peculiar that someone who was so attracted by that kind of thing should have ended up as a civil servant, but the human heart is full of contradictions and contrarieties, never more so than during one's youth, and it may well be that my association with this painter who changed his "wives" so frequently was the impetus required to turn me into a bureaucrat at MITI. And now, on an afternoon more than twenty years later, I sat beneath the gaudy portrait of a girl boss of the underworld, this passionate psalm in praise of being outside the framework of society. Once more I let my contradictory desires, to belong and not belong, wage war within me, experiencing the old longing to opt out and the fear of doing so, until I brought the matter to a lame conclusion by reflecting platitudinously that people don't change very much no matter how old they become. I don't mean to imply I worked things out in that conscious way at the time, for I was too occupied with whether we should go to a movie, since it was a bit too early to have dinner yet, and whether we should have Western or Chinese food, to concern myself with any analysis of these feelings.

My plan was that first we should go and see some fairly innocuous film which would make no great emotional demands, then have dinner, then a few drinks, proceed to some suitable place—or, if she objected, I would see her home—and so sleep with her. I'd already just about decided on the cinema, the restaurant, and the hotel I would take her to later on; and I suppose it was my concern over the disparity in our ages that made me ask Yukari her opinion (on the first two items), but she only made the vaguest of replies since she was totally absorbed in her makeup operations; and so time passed.

"Well, that's finished. Now I'm going to change," said Yukari in a cheerful shriek, just as I was lighting my third cigarette.

"Ah, this I must see," I said, and stood up, but the husky voice from behind the mirror replied that she couldn't allow me to look yet and I must wait till she changed, and then she'd let me.

"You won't look, will you? Promise? I don't think I can trust you. I'm sure you'll try to peep so I'm going to close the door, all right?"

I agreed and sat down on my chair again and waited.

It was strangely quiet. I was surprised it could be as quiet as this in Tokyo. She hadn't closed the door to her room all that efficiently (which may have been on purpose, I don't know), and there was a fairly large gap through which I could hear her taking her things off one by one, a much more emphatically erotic sound than if the door had been wide open. The fact that I thought I could hear the rustling sound as she slid off her stockings probably only indicates how the lack of a visual object will stimulate the imagination to more vigorous activity, and now I was seeing Yukari as she approached stage by stage the state of total nudity, pricking up my ears in the silence that this perverse, usually clamorous town had decided to preserve for me, forever it seemed, and smoking my cigarette.

In an even deeper silence Yukari must have been putting on her going-out clothes, and then finally she started talking to herself in some confusion as to which accessories she should wear. On hearing this I let out a great cloud of cigarette smoke, accompanying it with something like a sigh, which shows, I think, just how much I'd been affected by this brief but profound sequence of stimuli. I felt in fact that I'd been reduced to a complete bundle of nerves.

Then the door slid open and there she was dressed up to the nines, ready to go out except for her shoes. She smiled at me and, as she did so, the neighborhood sounds seemed to start up instantly again. First there was a strained, expressionless voice from a nearby street announcing he would exchange your old newspapers and magazines for cheap toilet paper, and this apparently set off a whole series of other noises, the wild revving of a motorbike, a car's loud horn, a child crying and its mother's scolding voice, and all the other harsh hubbub of the town. As this dusty commotion seemed to be forcing its way into the room above the tatami workshop I said:

"You look terrific."

I was telling no lie. The extremely brief dress she had on was of some luxurious material that might have been silk, or cotton, or even wool, with a bold, traditional pattern of black and white, and it was beautiful. The full, wide sleeves with dramatically tight cuffs and the belt of a similar material provided a very effective emphasis. She wore a gold pendant made of four linked diamond shapes which hung almost as far as her belt, and that harmonized with the gold clasp of her white handbag and the gold of her earrings in a stunning combination. What particularly caught the eye was the bold fringe of the dress: thick black strings hanging sparsely from the hem of the very brief mini-skirt, a direct provocation, it seemed, to thrust them aside.

"That takes one aback a bit, I must say. It looks like the stringy apron thing Sumo wrestlers wear dangling down their legs."

"Sumo wrestler, indeed. This is called a fringe, if you must know."

Yukari smiled at me as she made this rebuke, and then, with an innocent look on her face, she straddled her legs slightly and wiggled so that the fringe swayed about. For a moment I had the illusion I'd become a fashion photographer.

Naturally she chose high-heeled shoes of white enamel with gold ornamentation to match her handbag and earrings. As she was putting her shoes on I said:

"Wait a sec. I wonder if I've left anything smoldering?" and I took off my shoes again, which made Yukari tease me:

"You *are* an awful worrier, like some old man."

I went back into the kitchen, but my cigarettes had been carefully stubbed out. Having come this far, however, I thought I'd better have a look around to make sure everything else was all right, and so I went unceremoniously into the other room, where I noted through the frosted glass of the window that she'd left her bedding quilt hanging over the rail outside to air in the sun.

"Now look at this, for heaven's sake," I said, and Yukari came back into the room muttering something under her breath. I opened the window vigorously and laid my hand on the dark quilt with its chrysanthemum pattern picked out in white, but the fashion model in all her finery said sharply that she would do it and took hold as well. I said just as briskly that *I* would, but Yukari wasn't prepared to let me and, flushed with embarrassment, she seized hold of the quilt not only with her free right hand but also with her left, in which she was still holding her handbag, and tried to wrest it away from me by sheer brute force. I started laughing in a silly kind of way. I found this display of strength by a mere slip of a girl aimed at me, a grown man, positively heroic, so all I could do was laugh. But, as I stood there laughing nonchalantly, Yukari was gaining possession of the quilt, and in order to reverse the process I began pulling it back in some haste. This only stirred her to greater efforts, and then me as well. Our eccentric tug of war made us both pause and smile slightly, but neither was prepared to give in. So the struggle continued, compounded of one part pure tomfoolery, one part killer instinct, and one part simply not knowing how to put an end to it, and, as it went on, beads of sweat began to stand out on Yukari's brow and cheeks. A smell of mingled perfume, sweat, and quilt started to fill the room, and this seemed to spur on my fighting spirit. I became determined to win, and so my contest with the girl with the light blue eye shadow and the pink flushed face reached its consummation. With one enormous heave I dragged the quilt toward the bed, and so pulled it out of Yukari's left hand. She dropped her handbag, spilling out keys and small change that clattered on the wooden floor. But this now meant both her hands were free, so she was able to pull back again with redoubled strength. I somehow stumbled and let go of the quilt, which fell to Yukari's side with myself on top of it, the girl in the gorgeous attire with the perspiring face giving a high-pitched groan and half collapsing as well... So it was that this crumpled quilt alone became our nuptial couch.

After a long while she said:

"The window's been open all the time. Look."

But she made no particular move to get up and close it. Her hand-bag still lay open in a corner by the bedding cupboard.

"Yes, this is, apparently, something that causes great concern to the Public Telephone Corporation," I replied.

"In what way?"

"Well, there's one of their operatives shinning up a telephone pole in the lawful pursuit of his trade, and it just so happens he gets this glimpse... Can we be glimpsed?"

"Oh dear."

"His curiosity inflamed, he leans forward to get a better ... and so falls."

"He must hurt himself, then."

"That is exactly the point. He injures himself, and all such injuries are then classified as those encountered in the proper course of duty. The compensation paid out is enormous..."

"Oh come off it. I'm not going to swallow that."

"The absolute truth, believe me. The president of the corporation gave out this information in reply to questions in the House of Representatives."

"You're having me on, you liar."

And so, wrapped around by the laughter and the scent of the girl, I appear to have dropped off to sleep again, aware as I dozed fitfully of the pleasant softness of her naked thigh resting lightly on my own. Finally I heard her mutter:

"Looks like I've got a run in my stocking."

"All right, I'll buy you another pair."

Then, after another pause:

"Oh, my fringe is all wet."

Right in front of my eyes appeared her gorgeous dress, and as I gazed at it I decided it was either wool or some new kind of fabric.

"It looks very expensive. Must cost a lot to replace something like that."

"You're pretty mean, aren't you?" and she gave me a good prod on the top of the nose with her forefinger to show her disapproval. She went on to explain that of course it would cost the earth to buy anything like that in a shop, but if she asked the magazine people direct she could always get the clothes she'd modeled herself quite cheaply, usually for less than half the real price. Even so, she didn't tell me what she'd paid for it, but said it should be all right if she had it dry-cleaned, and maybe it wouldn't even require that: information clearly meant to set my mind at rest.

Naturally I wasn't concerned at that moment with questions of clothes getting crumpled or wet, nor even with the fact that I'd failed to take any contraceptive precautions. I just lay there looking around the room, which had, as I'd imagined, a splendid stereo set against the wall with fashion magazines and exotic-looking record sleeves piled on it, and also a sofa and a triangular whatnot for ornaments in the corner with a ridiculously large white teddy bear and an onyx vase with no flowers in it, and then on the bare floorboards an electric iron which had been left there upright with its metallic face reflecting my discarded trousers. . .

That's what I saw, but what was I thinking? I was thinking thoughts of a mainly idle kind, namely how strange it would be for a MITI official to have an affair with a fashion model. Since this also appeared to be something undesirable for the editor of a brewer's publicity magazine, how lucky it was that I happened to be a head of department in an electrical goods company . . . simple thoughts which reflected the complete satisfaction I was feeling at the moment. I suppose I'd already realized, though not in any precise way, that I would henceforth be responsible for the rent of Yukari's apartment each month; but it had certainly not crossed my mind in any form that I might end up marrying this girl.

4

One Friday toward the end of August I left the house, first making sure I had an umbrella since a minor typhoon was said to be approaching; which meant that, as I drove tight-lipped through the morning rush, the short black object was rolling about in the narrow space between the back seat and the rear window. As soon as I'd parked I phoned Yukari to tell her I wouldn't be able to see her that evening because of a farewell gathering for a man going to Southeast Asia which had suddenly come up.

I'd thought she'd still be in bed, but she soon answered and, having heard what I had to say, replied in an unconcerned voice:

"But that fits in just fine with me. We're shooting until eight o'clock, all pantalons, would you believe it? And I'm having this hairstyle that should be real fun. I'm dying to show it to you. Why not come around nine?"

She spoke at her usual rattling pace, and while I was humming and hawing and not being sure I could make it she said she'd see me then, and so decided the matter by herself. It was clear to me she wanted her apartment rent today, and although a hot, humid day like this wasn't the kind I would choose for visiting a woman, I felt it would be a bit hard on her if I didn't deliver the money, so somehow I managed to get away and arrived at her apartment a bit later than the appointed time, around half past nine.

She wasn't back yet. I let myself in with the key she'd given me, and stood my wet umbrella in a corner of the tiny entrance hall. Since early evening the wind had got up and it was now blowing hard, with heavy rain. I switched on the light and saw that the room was impeccably tidy. The only sign of disorder was on the small dining table: a milk saucepan and a large glass, both with white sediment at the bottom; also a small plate with one leftover wafer biscuit next to the glass. I had a look at the *yakuza* movie poster and then at the digital clock just as it was changing from 9:29 to 9:30, placing beneath it an envelope with the money for the rent inside. I opened the window a bit, and the cool feel of the air was pleasant, but it provided no more than a momentary respite from the humid heat so I went into the bathroom and had a shower.

Whether it was because I felt nice and fresh after washing away the sweat or because of the sense of freedom in walking about stark-naked I don't know, but I had a sudden desire to eat something and stretched my hand out to the leftover wafer. Since it had been exposed all day to this hothouse humidity, however, it was soggy and tasted nothing at all like it looked. I grimaced, and then lay down on the bed, and although I could feel a soft, slightly irritating lump under my back which seemed to be Yukari's negligee, I dropped off to sleep enveloped in the sweet scent of a young girl.

I think it was the sound of the telephone that must have woken me up, and when I came to I saw Yukari was sitting on the bed answering it. I could feel the soft roundness of her thigh resting against my left shoulder, but such was my drowsiness it took me some time to work out that the telephone must have rung just as she got back. If Yukari had been speaking in a more animated manner I might have assumed she herself had rung up somebody on her return. Not only did she speak in a low, restrained voice, but she said very little, her responses being limited to murmurs of agreement, or muttered thanks, or reserved, brief statements of doubt. This made me convinced it must be from another man, and I strained to catch his voice but couldn't manage to do so. When I laid my face on her lap and started to tickle her by wiggling my nose and lips, she briskly unzipped her skirt and slipped it off while still continuing this long conversation. Finally it came to an end.

"I'm sorry I'm so late. Look, do you mind if we have the light on? I want you to see my hair."

"We can do all that later."

In the darkness her black lips moved in her white face saying she was starving, but she didn't resist me.

Eventually I asked who the man was.

"Ah, so we're getting all jealous, are we? Well, let's say he's a camera . . . a camera enthusiast. He runs his own small business. I met him at a photo outing; you know the sort of thing, when a camera club takes a model to a park or a reservoir or something and they all have a good time taking photos. Stop it. That tickles. I didn't give him my phone number. He must have got it from the agency. They are so stupid. They're not supposed to do things like that. Such a nuisance."

She moved her hips slightly and then cried out in obvious disgust:

"Ugh, there's something here. Something funny."

Finally she gave a wild shriek and said:

"Look at that: a wafer. Now who left that here? Who's been eating wafers in my bed?"

"Ah, I see."

"You see nothing."

"I was always being told off about eating rice crackers in bed by. . ." Having got that far it would have looked odd if I'd stopped so I continued: ". . . my dead wife."

"Weird sort of memories you have."

I chuckled at that and so she went on:

"Used to get crumbs in the bed, I suppose?"

"That's right," I replied, and laughed again. As I ceased laughing Yukari leaned heavily over me.

"So you've been keeping it secret from me, haven't you?"

This, however, was spoken with no trace of anger. I took hold of her nicely shaped buttocks in both hands and said:

"I have no secrets, I can assure you. Why should I? I don't mention things that don't matter, but you can't call that having secrets."

"Yes. The official reply."

I smiled at this in the darkness although she couldn't see, and then she spoke as if she were going to ask me something, but seemed to change her mind, saying there was no point in asking anyway. Having decided there was no point she then did so, still lying heavily on me:

"Someone must be looking after you, you're always so neat and tidy. Have you been deceiving me?"

I shifted sideways and tipped her off, explaining that an old woman servant looked after me. The fashion model showed little interest in this, being much more concerned about whether she'd mussed up her hair or not. Muttering that she'd had nothing to eat and there was nothing in the place so she'd just have to make do with rice, tea, and

42

pickles she supposed, she got out of bed. I called after her retreating white figure that there was an envelope under the clock, and she thanked me in her customary brief and casual way.

She didn't allow me to sleep, however. While she was preparing her snack and then eating it, she confessed to me as if it were a matter of major import that there was a chance she might be going to appear on television. It seemed the editor of a fashion magazine had recommended her to a drinking companion of his who worked, he said, as a "TV director," and was probably in some sort of assistant capacity in some program or other. I said this was great, although the situation as she related it was of so nebulous a character one could draw no sort of conclusion about its outcome. Still, I was pleased to see her showing such enthusiasm at the prospect of appearing on television, since I judged this indicated she didn't have marriage on her mind. I had, naturally, been keeping quiet (up until that slip just now) about the fact I was in a state of bachelorhood, for I thought it would be inexpedient to put the idea of living with me into her head. I was genuinely terrified at the thought of remarriage, particularly to a fashion model, for I assumed it would be the death of me in more ways than one. But the very mistake of mentioning my dead wife may well have meant that, deep down, I was already imagining being married to her even then.

A powerful splashing came from the bathroom, which was Yukari having a shower. I smiled at the thought that she must have been so hungry she'd eaten before showering, and then I turned over in bed with my face to the wall and closed my eyes. At that moment Yukari let out a short scream, and I looked in the direction of the kitchen but could only see darkness. The bathroom door opened with a great clatter.

"What's up?" I asked.

"A power failure, I think. There's a flashlight in the bottom right of the cupboard. Get it for me, will you?"

The first few of these words had been partly drowned by the noise of the shower, but halfway through she turned it off and the rest were fairly roared at me. I got up and opened the cupboard door, but this was the first time I'd ever done so and I'd no idea where anything was. I searched about with my hands, but only came across things that felt

43

either like soft bundles of something, piles of magazines, or shoe boxes. While doing this I had three exchanges of questions and answers with Yukari in the bathroom, and then at last realized that what I'd thought was a tea container had a switch in the middle of it. I pushed the switch, producing a surprisingly dazzling light which transformed the contents of the cupboard in its bright circle. It revealed a confusion of objects, two of which particularly attracted my attention. The first was a pile of four biscuit tins, empty I supposed, placed right at the back of the cupboard immediately behind the flashlight. The other was a toy koala bear. This was right at the back, too, where it must have fallen down, but it had lost its black nose so it took me some time to work out what kind of animal it was.

"Ah, it's on again," said Yukari, and when I looked around the light in the kitchen was back.

"Just the very moment I found it, too," I said, switching off the flashlight with some regret. Yet when I got back into bed again and closed my eyes, the melancholy image of that unhappy animal persisted in my mind. I laughed at myself for being concerned about something like that, but the image wouldn't go away. Even when I followed Yukari's example and was taking a shower, I could still see the sad-foolish face of the beast on the wall of the all-white bathroom. So it wasn't strange that, when I walked into the kitchen with a towel around my waist, I should suddenly ask her about that bear.

After a moment's hesitation a dubious look came over her face:

"Oh that," she said, and laughed.

It seemed the little boy in the tatami shop had been fooling about and pulled the nose off, and she'd always been meaning to stick the thing back on again but somehow never got around to it.

"Burn it," I said. "It's so damn pathetic like that."

"Be even more pathetic to burn it."

"Maybe so."

"Yes it would. And I like the way you order me about. 'Burn it.' You sound like you're my father or my..." I was vaguely expecting the word "mother" to follow, and felt genuinely wounded when the word she produced was one that established our relationship in a way not to my liking: "... or my old man or something..."

"Okay. So I'm not in a position to talk to you like that."

I might well be her patron or even master, but I was damned if I was going to be her "old man."

"All right, then. I'll buy you another one. A much bigger one. It looks as if I'll be going to Australia next month," I added, trying to appease her. It seemed to work immediately since she cheered up again.

"Not just a koala bear. I want an opal as well," she said, speaking very sweetly; but then adding in a mock sulky voice: "You never told *me* you were going anywhere."

I promised to buy both the koala and the opal, asking her in return to mend the bear in the cupboard as quickly as she could. Yukari was in a good mood now and promised to do just that, so I rattled on gaily, teasing her in order to get away from the subject of my secretiveness:

"I saw something else in there. All that talk about nothing to eat, but you seem to have enough tins of biscuits. Or are they all empty? You must eat an awful lot of them."

"Biscuits?" she said in a confused, vacant way, and then burst out laughing, and went on laughing.

"Mayo asked me to look after those. They're just full of film negatives. So bad luck, you're wrong again."

"Really? I never realized fashion models kept the negatives of their photos. That's interesting."

"No, no. They're not Mayo's. Gen asked her to look after them."

"So they're pictures of a model called Gen?"

"Oh, of course they're not. You're hopeless; you don't understand a thing."

This sharp rebuke seemed to ignore the question of how incompetent her account of things had been; anyway, she went on to say there was a young photographer called Gen Kaizuka, and those biscuit tins were full of negatives of his own pictures. The biggest kind of tin was best since there was room to fit in a desiccant at the side, but smaller ones didn't have that space so they weren't much use. That was why he asked all his relations and friends to hang on to any biscuit tins they might have. They were miles better than any of the special boxes you could buy in the shops for keeping negatives in. That was what Yukari said.

The principal reflection this information aroused in me was a solid doubt as to whether that previous telephone conversation really had been held with some dotard who ran his own small business. Wasn't it more likely that she'd been talking to this young man? But I didn't voice that doubt.

"Specializes in female photographs, does he? You know. . ."

"Female photographs! Really, is that all you can think about?"

"I don't mean just nudes. Well, fashion, things like that. . ."

"No, they're more kind of social. Marches, demos, strikes—things in society."

"Does he make a living doing that?"

"Scrapes along, I suppose. But he's going to start really making it soon. Of course, he's not exactly what you might call handsome. Still, he's very attractive in his way."

"Ah?"

"That's why Mayo. . ."

"So that's it," I cried. "He's Mayo's lover?"

My face must have taken on a complex expression if it was reflecting my mixed feelings adequately. I was certainly relieved to hear he had no special relationship with Yukari, but felt like blaming that fool Oguri for dithering about; for look what had happened, when he ought to have been carrying things to some swift conclusion like myself.

Yukari gave a large, thoughtful nod in response to my statement, but then said:

"Still, they're not exactly lovers. Just good friends, although there was a time when they must have been pretty close. That Mayo, you know she says the crudest things. I get really amazed sometimes."

"The crudest things?"

"Like he's really enormous."

She looked me straight in the eyes with total insouciance as she said this. No longer made up, her face looked ingenuous and ordinary, an appropriate condition for calm, objective discussion of so sensitive a subject. Even so, I was quite startled, but I calmed myself, and laughed an affected, unreal laugh:

"Well, well, lucky boy. Makes me feel quite envious. But hold on a moment. Since you're actually looking after the negatives this suggests some sort of intimacy with you as well, doesn't it?"

"It's just because there's nothing of that sort at all that I'm looking after them for him."

The logic behind this statement apparently was that, with him rushing all over the place shooting riots and clashes of various kinds, there was always the possibility that the Criminal Investigation Bureau might demand he hand over these negatives as material relevant to their work; and the demand could come at any time so he might be caught napping. Obviously it would be best to disperse them in various hideouts, although Mayo's place would be no good since she knew him too well and they'd soon work that out. Someone like Yukari, on the other hand, whom he'd only met twice, should be all right.

"Naturally," I nodded, indicating my grasp of the argument, and lighting a cigarette. "Even so, he does seem to have overdone it a bit, surely? I can't think of any good reason why he has to be all that worried..."

"Well, he says it's pretty dangerous stuff. The police are, well, you know, they're really awful..." Yukari passed on this opinion (straight from Kaizuka, no doubt) with a grave and solemn look.

"Surely he's being a bit neurotic about this? No matter how much time the police have on their hands, they're hardly likely to start investigating the female connections of a not yet up-and-coming photographer."

"But it seems that just isn't so. They are really wicked, and crafty, too," she said quite seriously, but then her eyes smiled and she added: "Or so she says. I guess the fact that Mayo is scared to death of just about everything may have something to do with it."

It seemed that Mayo, despite her physical size, was frightened of most things. If she heard thunder, even in a good, safe concrete building, she'd turn desperately pale. She always refused to cross the street at any other point than a proper pedestrian crossing, and once a little puppy dog someone was carrying barked at her and she went absolutely rigid with fear and just couldn't move. The mere idea of the cops bursting in and ordering her to hand over those negatives was too much for her, too unbearable for words, or so Yukari said. Her imitation of Mayo being frightened by the puppy dog was so good, so true to life (although naturally I hadn't seen the "life" it was true to), that the whole story seemed to have a very genuine ring to it. In fact I found her performance so amusing I stopped bothering about whether the photographer's anxiety had been excessive or not.

"Now, you've got to have a good look at my hair," she suddenly said. I knew what that meant so I praised it copiously, although I couldn't see for the life of me how it was anything but hopelessly inappropriate since she was wearing a *yukata*. She paid little attention to my remarks, however, apparently absorbed in some more serious question.

"I want a much bigger one. Really enormous. As big as this," she burst out, extending her arms and indicating a size of a yard or so. This shook me for a moment, but then I saw what she was talking about.

"Ah, the koala bear? Do they have them as big as that? I'll get one if they do."

"Make sure you have a really good look, because I've seen one that big in a magazine."

This was a color photograph of some film actress just back from her honeymoon in Australia getting off a plane with a huge koala in her arms. Yukari had been particularly impressed that the husband was carrying a variety of objects, but the actress had just the bear and her handbag. That was really nice.

"Right. I'll see if I can find one."

"And an opal too. Just the stone will do."

"Right."

As I put on my shirt and suit I was thinking how I was going to be pretty busy on this trip and might only have time to buy her an ordinary koala bear. Yukari was explaining about the merits and demerits of various opals and what I had to look for. I just kept quiet and nodded at times, but I can't say I was paying all that much attention.

The trip to Australia was supposed to have been undertaken by one of our directors, but since he'd fallen ill the thing had been passed on to me. It appeared this illness was going to cause some shake-up of personnel in the company. When I'd first joined, one of the conditions was that eventually I'd be given a place on the board, and it now looked as if I could expect that to happen quite quickly, promotion next spring having become a real, if surprising, possibility. If that happened, perhaps I'd be able to let her have a bit more than just the money for the rent.

I'd just reached this point in my ruminations when Yukari, as she was seeing me out, asked if it would be all right to phone sometimes. By that she meant could she ring me at the office, and I said she could providing she kept it short. So I put on my shoes, but quite forgot about my umbrella, probably because it had stopped raining by then, and also because I was debating in my own mind the way I should respond, in particular the tone of voice I should adopt, when Yukari phoned me at the office.

Still, the thing that had really bothered me that evening was those biscuit tins, as I realized when I got home, for the very first thing I saw when I entered the living room was an identical one on the table, the same gold color with the same blue lines, although this one seemed somewhat smaller than those others had been.

"What's that doing there?" I demanded of Tsuru in a voice unintentionally harsher than my normal manner of speech, and this seemed to upset her for she assumed a rigid expression and said:

"It's for shirt buttons. . ."

She opened the lid and showed me the contents: a pincushion, some thread, a small pair of black scissors, and so on. I nodded (indeed there were three of my shirts lying there on the tatami), and was surprised to realize how disturbed I'd been by Yukari's cupboard, which had presumably aroused not just a feeling of incongruity but of real weirdness. Here, after all, was this ordinary metal box, the kind often sent in summer or before New Year as a gesture of esteem and obligation from house A to house B (and then probably sent on direct from house B to house C because house B already had enough of such things on its hands); a solid symbol of calm, quiet, boring everyday life. And now it had been transformed—four of them had. Four of them had been packed full of vivid, violent images of contorted faces, streams of blood, rocks being hurled about, and the backs of people fleeing for their lives, and all of these images were uncannily back to front, with black as white and white as black. What could be more inappropriate, then, than to have encountered these disturbing objects in a young girl's room where I'd gone to seek the opposite of what they implied, desiring not confrontation with reality but a breathing space apart from it, an asylum of rest, a place of escape? The thought was a painful one . . . and then if one allowed feelings of jealousy to combine with it? But I hurriedly rejected that idea. It was nothing at all really, I decided, as I sat down.

5

Although the next day was Saturday, as soon as I got to the office I was told to leave for Osaka right away, which I promptly did. The Osaka branch had committed some gross and witless blunder, and running around trying to pick up the pieces was a very intricate and thankless task. I was there until the morning of the following Tuesday and then took the plane back, but the minute I arrived there was a conference followed by a reception, during which I was horribly conscious all the time of the unpressed state of my trousers. I didn't manage to get home until ten o'clock that evening.

I'd telephoned Tsuru only twice and very briefly on the company phone during my absence, but she knew what she was up to and had dealt with this sort of thing before so I'd had no particular worries about her. In fact she'd managed everything at home all right, as I'd imagined she would, but as she came out into the entrance hall to greet me and receive my bundle of dirty laundry (the only present I'd brought back for her), she made this astonishing remark:

"I thought perhaps you might be staying with Miss Yukari tonight."

This astonishing remark did not actually astonish me (until later), and I replied in a perfectly normal tone of voice:

"No. I'm absolutely worn out."

That, of course, was a perfect giveaway, but things had still not got through to me as I sat down and began taking off my shoes. However, just as I was starting to take off my left shoe I got the feeling that her remark was a bit odd, and by the time I'd fully removed that shoe the feeling of oddness had become powerful and oppressive. But, probably because I was tired, it still didn't sink in until I'd walked two or three paces and was glancing sideways at the broken clock, when finally intellect triumphed over fatigue. It was as if some recollection of my dead wife, via the medium of her beloved antique, had stirred somewhere in the murky depths of my unconscious and stimulated my mind to action. I stopped and called out:

"Oi!"

"Yes," said Tsuru, smiling slightly at me. Frankly it would be impossible to say that Tsuru was good-looking. She was also in her fifties, so the main effect of this smile as it gradually spread across her fairly crude features was to create a striking increase in the wrinkles at the corners of her eyes.

"Knew about it, did you?"

"Yes."

"It sort of shows?"

"Well, yes, one can sort of tell. . ."

In fact this veiled claim to intuitional powers on her part was something of a lie, although one would never have guessed it to look at her. The strange thing is I didn't feel any natural relief that I'd been caught out by Tsuru and not by my dead wife (that would have been much too simpleminded a response) but only a generalized awe at the superior abilities of women to sniff out secrets; and this feeling then extended to the particular case of Yukari. I started wondering what would happen if I began to have an affair with another woman, and had the awful defeatist feeling that no matter how hard I might try to hide it from her she was bound to find out. It was, I suppose, some measure of the seriousness and depth of my desire to marry Yukari, even at that early stage, that I'd already clearly reached the point of worrying about being unable to conceal future infidelities from her.

I went into the living room, and there were the letters and newspapers that had come during my absence neatly stacked on top of the alcove shelves. Next to them was some black object, but I turned my back on it and sat down without having time to notice it was the umbrella I'd left somewhere and been slightly concerned about. I think I didn't recognize that small object as an umbrella probably because the notion of an umbrella as something long and stick-like with a handle that could dangle from one's arm was still firmly fixed in my mind, although I'd been using the folding type for ages.

Tsuru brought in the tea with a slight grin still on her face in place of her usual expressionless mask. After I'd praised the quality of the tea, I asked the obvious question:

"How come you knew?"

Tsuru didn't answer that it was her female intuition, but said instead:

51

"Because I met Miss Yukari on Sunday last."

"Well, well."

"Such a very lovely young lady. And then, of course, being the daughter of a professor, a wonderful person too, I thought..."

"Oh, really?..."

In an attempt to cover my embarrassment and confusion I stood up and switched on the air conditioner. Then I took up the questioning again after I'd sat down.

"But how did you manage to meet her?"

She looked toward the umbrella, and at last the whole thing became clear to me. I turned around to look at it.

"So that was the reason?"

Tsuru nodded firmly, and happily explained what had happened.

Heavy rain had fallen in Tokyo all day Sunday and there seemed little chance of it letting up on Monday either. Yukari was rather anxious about my umbrella and telephoned the house (I suspect she was in fact using the umbrella as a pretext for a good long chat). Tsuru answered the phone and explained that I had left for Osaka the previous day on business, at the same time introducing herself as the maid and saying she could always go and collect anything belonging to her master. Yukari herself was just about to leave for a department store to do some shopping, so she said she'd meet her there. They agreed on a time and place, and Yukari described the clothes she'd be wearing.

This in itself struck me as all very unusual, but Tsuru went on to say something that really shook me.

"I got this poster at the same time. I suppose it will be all right if I put it up on the wall in the kitchen?"

"Ah, a poster?" I said, not catching on yet.

"Yes. I've been a great fan for years. I kept looking at it so much that Miss Yukari was kind enough to say she'd let me have it."

"You mean...? You mean you went to the apartment? Above the tatami shop?"

"Yes, sir."

"Aaah, ah..." I gave a long sigh culminating in a groan. Why on earth, I marveled, did this sort of thing have to happen? And yet when I heard why, it all seemed natural enough. They met at the department store as planned, but Yukari, although she'd brought her own umbrella, had forgotten to bring the umbrella in question, namely mine. So the two of them drifted from one floor to another, had tea together, then finally went off to the apartment, where Tsuru prepared Yukari's evening meal for her and was asked to join her since she didn't like to eat it on her own. After that they watched TV until relatively late. Since I appeared to be aghast at this information Tsuru said:

"I beg your pardon, Master Eisuke, if I have forgotten my place and gone too far."

She leaned forward reverentially, showing a head of hair in which there was a good deal of gray.

"No, of course not. I don't think you've gone too far. It just seems a funny sort of thing to have happened."

I wasn't, in fact, quite sure what to say, or even what to think. Still, finally I decided all it amounted to was that my maid had learned I had a woman, and since there was no possibility whatsoever of her telling tales to my nonexistent wife, I had nothing really to worry about. Having come to this conclusion, I began to find my bewilderment of only a moment before itself unintelligible, for I realized I was much better off now that I had nothing to hide. The one thing I did find rather annoying was that up to now my relationship with Yukari had been something concerning just the two of us, but, because of an umbrella, it had suddenly become public property, even if the sole person who represented this "public" was a weaver's daughter from the north who'd lost her husband and turned into an aged domestic servant. So I sat with my cheek resting on my hand and puffing a cigarette, watched over by the eyes of a rather wrinkled public dressed in a new pin-striped *yukata*, reflecting that my great-grandfather had had a mistress, as had my grandfather and, so it seems, my father, and there was nothing odd about my having one (although my simply paying her rent could hardly be called keeping a mistress on the grand scale, and the word "mistress" itself seemed almost comically inappropriate). If one also considered the fact that, in my case, I had no wife, the whole thing seemed only too natural—or so I told myself.

As Tsuru poured some more hot water into the teapot she said, in a kind of compromise mumble which could have been addressed to me or merely to herself:

"Certainly a most charming and agreeable young lady."

I nodded in silent consent and so, as she placed my cup of tea before me, she muttered again:

"Lovely white complexion. Very ladylike."

I nodded once more, maintaining the same silence; and yet, as I sipped my tea, I reflected that my dead wife's complexion hadn't been all that good; she'd been rather dark in fact, and this observation led me on to thoughts of that clock, and I was brooding about whether it wasn't perhaps about time I got rid of the thing, when Tsuru spoke again:

"Master Eisuke, why not have everything made right, once and for all?"

"Well, yes. . ." I replied vaguely. "Still, you know, no one really wants to fiddle about with a bit of old rubbish like that. . . Even our local watchmaker would probably take one look and say no."

Tsuru had sat in what seemed like startled silence while I was speaking, and although she didn't actually laugh she seemed to be amused by something. Finally what she'd really been talking about got through to me.

"Now look," I said. "That really is going too far."

This rebuke made Tsuru lower her head in humble apology, but there was almost no anger in my voice and I imagine Tsuru herself was well aware that this was only a conventional reproof on my part. She'd probably counted on only being mildly rebuffed when she'd made her decision to speak her mind in the first place. So she lowered her head again, making a brief, simply verbal apology this time, and asked me if I would take my bath, in an obvious attempt to change the subject.

"Okay. I'll get in right away," I said, but in fact I didn't, since I thought I should add a few more words about Yukari. These were offered as an appeasement to my loyal servant, but I ought to have just kept quiet. All it meant was that as I adopted the role of benevolent, understanding master, I appeared to be eager to get back to the original subject. No doubt that was how Tsuru understood it.

"Well, first of all," I said, "it's like this. . ."

Tsuru settled down to hear my explanation, but I immediately found trouble starting. I did, in fact, first want to explain that her idea of having "everything made right"—meaning I should make an honest woman of Yukari—didn't actually apply in this case, because I didn't look upon

54

Yukari as a "mistress" whom I could turn into an "honest woman." Yukari and I were lovers, and so Tsuru's idea of "rightness" was irrelevant in our case. Still, I didn't say that; firstly because it would look as if I were scolding her again, and secondly because perhaps it implied I was being a bit too casual in my attitude toward Yukari. The whole question needed more thinking out. Then there was one other thing that gave me pause, which was that Yukari might well have told Tsuru I was paying the rent of her apartment, in which case my classification of the relationship would look very suspect. I did, in fact, blush as I thought about this, perhaps because I was feeling ashamed of my own insistence on considering a woman who was, in effect, my "kept woman" or "mistress" as my lover. This made me flustered and so, pretending to be unaware that I was blushing, I said to Tsuru:

"One problem is, well, she's a model."

"Is she indeed?"

"You see, Tsuru, modeling isn't a respectable profession," I said, and grinned, but Tsuru remained perfectly serious.

"Surely nowadays it is just as respectable as working in an office?" she retorted, making a move to stand up. "Superior work to that, I should have thought. Only nice-looking and charming young ladies can do it."

"Look," I said. "The fact is that . . . well, it's a sort of underworld, you know. It's a very dodgy profession, as are all the people in it. It's like being some kind of *yakuza*."

That was a mistake. In fact I needn't have said anything, for Tsuru had already made her move back toward the kitchen, indicating that the discussion was over as far as she was concerned. And if I'd wanted to say something, then it should have been that she was just a girl I was having a casual affair with and of course I had no intention of marrying her. For some reason, however, I didn't find myself saying anything like that, and what I did say raised only an amused response from Tsuru, who turned around and remarked:

"What very old-fashioned ideas you have on the subject. Why, even in the country they don't think like that any more."

She spoke quite cheerfully and smiled as she did so. By "the country" she was actually referring to my elder brother and his wife back

55

home up north. It was a habit of mine to express consternation, sometimes even disgust, at the hidebound, antiquated nature of their attitudes to a variety of things. I must say Tsuru's reply made me laugh as well.

"Okay, then. But she's hopeless at housework. Can't cook and things like that."

Once again I had chosen exactly the wrong thing to say. This time Tsuru did not turn around, keeping her back to me as she said:

"You have me to do all that. It will be no different from when your first wife was here."

Having made this parting shot she left the room.

I thought I might have a look at the mail lying there on the shelf, but found I couldn't be bothered so instead I just lay down with my head pillowed on my arm and started to wonder why I hadn't felt particularly annoyed about Tsuru's "going too far." But there was no real mystery about it, and the answer came out pat soon enough. Tsuru was a loyal servant who was constantly concerned about her master, and everything she'd done, her meeting with Yukari, her suggestion that I do the decent thing and make an honest woman of her, had been entirely on my behalf. I felt complete confidence in this judgment, having what I saw as corroborative evidence of its truth.

During the whole long period Tsuru had served me, this was only the second occasion on which she had not (as she put it) "known her place." The other occasion was when I'd refused the transfer to the Ministry of Defense. My dead wife didn't approve of my behavior and said so fairly often, going on about it in a petty, niggling way which didn't amuse me much. One Sunday afternoon when the whole business was beginning to prey on my mind I went out for a stroll around the block and met Tsuru walking along with her shopping basket. She approached me with a determined look on her face as if whatever she had to say must have been the result of long rumination, hesitated a little, and said:

"I will do my best to bring Mrs. Mabuchi round so there is no need, Master Eisuke, for you to be anxious about her. I am sure she will be all right. . ."

She bowed in a shamefaced way after this outburst (to which I made no reply) and then entered the local vegetable shop and began inspecting various radishes. Even if the statement itself wasn't strikingly clear, I thought the import certainly was. It meant she approved of my refusal to go to the Ministry of Defense and was urging me to persist in my resolve. As I stood by the concrete telegraph pole in front of the shoe shop, watching the back of my sole ally in the act of handling some giant white radish, I confess I was much moved, and it does seem that from then on I acquired the habit of interpreting everything Tsuru did as an expression of her strong sense of loyalty. Now, as I lay with my head resting on my arm, I recalled the scene in front of the vegetable shop, reliving my excited feelings of that time. Frankly I was much moved again, and just as frankly I must admit the reason I hadn't got angry at the suggestion I should marry Yukari was because I thought there was a lot to be said for it. My reflections on a true servant's loyalty and so forth were merely a way of giving form, of giving plausibility, to my own desire to do just that.

Having arrived at this positive state of mind I was all the more surprised to experience a sudden doubt. With only a few months gone since the funeral, it was surely a little premature to urge remarriage upon me? The feeling of surprise this aroused was enough to make me sit up. Was it possible to bear a grudge against someone with whom she'd been on such good terms for so long and for whom she'd apparently had such respect? Well, obviously it was, or seemed to be; and just as obviously the answer was that there was only one real master for Tsuru, and that was me. She entered the room again as I reached this conclusion.

That weekend I met Yukari and naturally we talked about Tsuru, with the result that certain discrepancies appeared between their two accounts of what had happened. When Yukari had got to the department store and found she'd forgotten the umbrella, she'd simply apologized and expected to leave things like that, but it was Tsuru who'd insisted on returning with her to pick it up. Again Yukari had simply meant to hand the umbrella over at the door, but Tsuru had begged for just a glass of water, and so naturally she had to let her in and provide her with tea. Similarly, when Tsuru had suggested she prepare dinner she was already standing in readiness at the sink. The woman seemed to have been a bit too domineering by half, yet that, I assumed, was the way a maid would treat someone whom she thought of not as her master's lover but merely as a kept woman. All I could do was laugh.

Yukari had another thin slice of fish and then said:

"I suppose she wanted to have a good look at the apartment."

"Probably that was it."

"Did I pass the test, do you think?"

I wasn't too happy about that phrase. Pass what test for what? But I decided to make no remark that might lead into deeper waters.

"She said nothing about the apartment, but she was very flattering about you. Very good-looking and refined, she said."

"Still, it does look as though nothing's going on."

"Nothing's going on?"

"Between you and Tsuru."

"Not very likely, is it? Did you think there was?"

"Just a bit."

She hunched her shoulders slightly as she laughed, then had another sip of saké. That evening we were sitting in a Japanese-style restaurant, and Yukari was wearing a kimono for the occasion, a fine-textured crepe (I think) dyed in Okinawan style, with a plain, light blue sash. I whispered my compliments on this tasteful combination, which presumably made her feel shy for she produced an interesting gesture. She moved the palm of her right hand up near her mouth, not covering it in the traditional gesture of modesty and giving a silly giggle, but instead flapping it slightly. At the same time she produced a "huh" sound which was more or less a half-snorted and half-gasped, deprecatory, semi-scornful, and yet quite formal dismissal of the compliment. I realized she must have learned this exotic gesture from a foreign model, which turned out to be almost the case, for the girl who must have taught her this new form of etiquette was a Eurasian of Turkish and Japanese parentage. This I assumed because Yukari immediately began a tirade against her, saying it was an absurd affectation in someone who was half Japanese to behave as if she were a European. I, however, was unable to feel displeasure at the unjustified aping of foreign ways—I was feeling perfectly delighted by it, in fact, probably because all the people in the restaurant (which was now pretty crowded) were obviously conscious of Yukari and kept stealing glances in our direction. I felt inordinately proud of being able to bring a girl like Yukari to a place where I was a regular customer.

Eventually we got back to the original question of my relationship with Tsuru.

"Maybe Tsuru's visit was meant to relieve your suspicions in that quarter."

Yukari made no response to this lighthearted remark, but spoke instead with some feeling:

"It must be awfully useful having someone like that, a servant who's really good at cooking. She made me all sorts of nice things; much nicer than this." She prodded the pot of rice and savories with her chopsticks. "Next time let's have our date at your house instead of a restaurant."

I received these remarks with considerable reserve, a purely reflex response, perhaps, to some subconscious danger signal that this talk about Tsuru's cooking was a way of hinting at marriage. The automatic nature of that suspicion does indicate, I suppose, how much the idea of marriage was on my mind. I tried to evade the issue by turning it into a joke, saying it just wouldn't feel right at home, helping myself to saké since Yukari (not being properly trained in that respect) had failed to pour me any. I then lowered my voice and added:

"It would cease to be a proper affair and so our affair would cease to be proper."

This had a striking effect on Yukari. She giggled with such delight one would almost have believed she'd made the joke herself and was reveling in the pleasure it had caused. Her reaction satisfied me that she wasn't contemplating marriage, and although that set my mind at ease to some extent, I felt a dispirited gloom at the same time, something very close to disappointment or even to a mild despair.

Back in bed above the tatami shop we again spoke about Tsuru.

"Ah yes, there's this other funny thing she said. Told me I ought to marry you. Said she'd look after all the housework. Didn't matter at all how bad you might be at it."

I suppose what made me finally say this was some aftereffect of that powerful feeling of regret I'd experienced in the restaurant. Of course, my motives in saying this were dual, although perhaps not intentionally so. One of my aims was certainly to give the question of marriage an airing, but the other was to consider it only as "a funny thing," thereby taking the edge off any discussion that might ensue.

Yukari's response was, I thought, very ambiguous. She simply said: "There's the generation gap for you."

I found this ambiguous because I couldn't be sure if she was referring to the gap between Tsuru's old-fashioned ideas and those of us young people, or if it wasn't the gap between my age and Yukari's. Anyway, she gave a lengthy, if fairly silent, laugh after she said this, which made her nipples tremble beneath my fingertips. As I enjoyed this sensitive wobbling I reflected that one thing could certainly be gathered from her remark: her total indifference to the suggestion of marriage itself.

Still, there could be no doubt that the idea of having an efficient, faithful servant really attracted Yukari for, after we'd finished, she said:

"You know Tsuru's like one of those . . . what do you call it? Living cultural properties or human national treasures. That sort of thing. A living treasure, a real treasure . . . something quite, quite special."

Yukari spoke this last sentence with the upper middle class Tokyo drawl which she otherwise hardly ever used. As I listened I thought how much she sounded like a middle-aged lady who'd been absolutely tormented, my dear, by servant problems for years, and I teased her about it. Surprisingly she was positively fierce in her response.

"No I do not, so there. Anyway, once I start appearing on television I'll just have to have a servant. Won't be able to manage without. It won't be any laughing matter, believe me."

This did not lead, however, to any detailed description of her future television appearance, but became a series of third-hand accounts of the various troubles numerous models had encountered over servants.

The following week I was too busy to see her, so it must have been after an interval of nearly a fortnight that we met again. This time she sat in her kitchen beneath the blank white space of wall where the poster had been, and spoke to me in tones of great seriousness, quite different from her usual manner, on a subject of major importance.

"I'll probably be going for a marriage interview. Just have to go, I suppose. I don't really know."

It was quite clear that this was no pretense or some kind of joke. I muttered vaguely in reply, asking if it were true, and when I saw the large, solemn nod she gave I suddenly found the whole thing irresistibly funny and burst out laughing.

"Please don't laugh. Please don't. You really shouldn't."

Yukari explained in an awkward, embarrassed way that her parents, who up to now had simply let her do exactly as she pleased, had suddenly begun to urge marriage on her almost incessantly, and just last week her mother had come home with a proposal and was reacting very positively toward it. Yukari herself said she hated old-fashioned things like arranged marriages, and anyway she had no intention of getting married for the time being, but she'd not been able to persuade her mother, who had insisted that she should at least go to the interview and give it a try, since she could always refuse if she didn't like the man. She also said that if, on the other hand, there was some other man Yukari was in love with, then she should go right ahead and marry him. Her mother kept up this two-pronged attack with such persistence that in the end her eyes had filled with tears, and Yukari was so taken aback she hastily said she didn't have any lover, which only made things worse because she'd thus cast away a major reason for refusing the interview. Anyway, she really hated this kind of formal seeing and being seen, because she was sure the man would like her and become horribly enthusiastic, which would make it all the more awkward.

"I suppose so. Fall head over heels, I shouldn't wonder," I chimed in with equal seriousness. "Still, why should your parents suddenly be in such a hurry about this?"

I asked her if she had a younger sister, for it often happened that an older sister had to get married earlier than she wanted because she was holding up the chances of the younger, but Yukari only had a younger brother. She also explained that her parents tended to have crazes about things, sudden enthusiasms which would die away as quickly as they'd arisen. Her mother's craze for batik and then for needlepoint had been just like that, her father's announcing he wanted to go abroad had been of the same remarkable abruptness, and now she supposed the two of them had been smitten by an identical craze to get her married. Since her brother had entered college that spring they had nothing to worry over, so it was her marriage that was to occupy them instead. The way Yukari was now talking about it you'd have thought she was some third party indifferently gazing on.

"Perhaps your father's under some obligation to somebody, and the marriage is being imposed from outside?"

"Could be, although Mother says that's not so. He's always tended to suck up to people like that. He's crazy about people with power; authoritarianism they call it, don't they?"

I found myself grinning at this scathing judgment, and Yukari felt inspired to tell me various stories of the behind-the-scenes power struggles at his university. During all this she broke off from time to time to wonder what she should do, at first as a kind of joke with her arms folded in a parody of the puzzled, serious thinker, but gradually the former note of genuine seriousness, even pathos, came back into her voice. Yet I had no bright suggestions to make.

"Probably the best thing is just not to take it too seriously. Just put in an appearance, you know, for the sake of your parents."

Having now encouraged her to go to this interview I did, of course, mean to add that she could say afterward she didn't like the man and so refuse, but Yukari butted in before I got that far in an apparently frolicsome style:

"Okay then, and if he's not all that bad, why, we'll get married straight away." She looked at me with mischievous eyes, deliberately provoking me.

"That's it. Not a bad idea," I replied, casually disposing of the possibility by nonchalantly acknowledging it; but I then began to have a nagging suspicion that she might already have seen those inevitable appurtenances of the arranged marriage, a photograph and *curriculum vitae*, and even been attracted to the man.

"Anyway, what's he like?" I said with an even more determined attempt at nonchalance.

It transpired that he was thirty-three years old, a graduate in commerce from a first-rate private university, and already a section chief in an up-and-coming electrical goods maker that was in pretty stiff competition with my own company. He was also rather handsome, although he did look a bit like a roasted peanut. I responded to this in the same casual manner as before.

"Ah-hah, a business rival. Must be very bright to have become a section chief at the age of thirty-three."

This casual praise concealed envy of the unknown man's youth, plus contempt for the fact that he hadn't graduated from a national university (in particular for not having graduated from mine).

"Show me a photograph of the peanut," I said.

"You really want to see it? Whatever for? Now why would you want to see something like that? Perverse tastes you seem to have. Anyway, I sent it back."

As she said this the combination of her malicious smile, her provocative eyes, and husky voice so affected me that the roasted peanut became transformed into a being of exceptional, even fabulous beauty, and I felt real pangs of jealousy. With a sensation of dull gloom in my heart I told myself that at some time in the future I'd have to let Yukari go and this might well be much sooner than I imagined. I was also thinking of ways of talking Yukari out of the match, such as suggesting that a handsome devil like that who'd remained a bachelor until he was thirty-three must be a raving homosexual, but it seemed mean and cowardly to try to scare her off in that way, and I hesitated. While I was hesitating she said something really odd.

"Why don't you have a try yourself?"

I wasn't able to understand the implications of this, so I could only gape in reply. Was she seriously suggesting I should look for a partner in the same way as herself? Then I saw what she meant.

"Between me and you?"

Yukari nodded and then smiled in a way that put me nervously on my guard.

"I'm sure Mum and Dad will soon lose their enthusiasm for this. The main thing is to get through the danger period somehow or other. After all, they did say I ought to marry my lover if I had one, didn't they? So my marriage interview doesn't have to be with that man, but could just as well be with you. They'd be awfully pleased, I'm quite certain. Absolutely."

"Yes, but you know, how would we behave?"

"Like complete and utter strangers. That's pretty obvious, surely?"

"Of course if we weren't there'd be no need to arrange a meeting between us, would there? Still, in practical terms, how do we arrange this coming together in the first place?"

"You could become a fan of mine."

"A fan?"

"Well, we'd make out you'd seen a picture of me in a magazine when you were at the bank or the barber's, and you'd been instantly smitten. Love at first sight. Desperate languishments, so you get in touch with the publisher and find out that this is the lovely Miss Yukari Nonomiya ... and where do we go from there?"

"That would be easy enough," I said, having grasped her suggestion. "I ask an acquaintance of mine, a teacher at your father's university, and he intercedes for me. Thus a formal meeting is arranged between us." Having got this far I started laughing, a long peal of laughter that kept interrupting my next words. "Still, since we've already performed ... on numerous occasions ... what should come some time after our first meeting ... even after the wedding itself ... it does seem..."

My laughter prevented me from saying what it seemed like.

"Well, if you put it like that, I suppose we have really."

I found this answer quite hilarious, as well as her idea itself when I pondered it, such a beautiful example of that narcissism which one finds so appropriate in a fashion model. I also had to admit there was something splendid about the plan, very much like attending the funeral of someone who was still alive, a deception that impishly trampled on all those contracts, forms, and stipulations that bind societies together. I saw this eccentric plan that Yukari's mind had labored to bring forth, this formal marriage interview between two people who'd been sleeping together for some time, as a fiction of considerable ingenuity. This was how a practical joke should be—cheerful, ingenious, and directed against the social world and its ideas of order. I could enjoy this as a more innocent, more ridiculous blasphemy than those black mortuary tablets and the bell set above the erotica in the corner of that painter's studio, and I blessed the good fortune that had made this priceless woman a part of my life.

"I wish you'd stop laughing in that silly way, I really do."

Yukari shook my knee with her small hand, and I nodded and wiped away my tears and said:

"Let's ignore all that formal stuff and start off with our nuptial bliss."
Yukari gave me a large, slow wink (one more skill learned from that Eurasian girl, I assumed) and headed for the shower.

Two hours later, just as I was leaving, I said:
"I shouldn't bother too much about all those things we said."
"I guess not. It doesn't mean much anyway," she replied, sounding as if she really couldn't have cared less about it.

6

Two days later I'd just finished dinner at home with Tsuru. It was my custom to eat with Tsuru in the living room when I dined at home. When I was out Tsuru apparently made do with whatever happened to be around, and she ate in the kitchen with the *yakuza* lady on the wall as her companion. I watched TV with her for half an hour and then went upstairs to do some reading, but this only involved skimming through a few articles on management theory, which I found extremely dull. Since there is a tradition (as I'd been assured when I first joined my company) that ex–government officials have little grasp of such matters as interest rates and taxes, I'd done some solid reading on that sort of thing in those early days. I was thinking how even that was preferable to the dreary stuff I had to cast my eyes over now, when I heard the front doorbell ring, giving a somewhat more portentous sound than usual. Tsuru apparently answered it, for I could hear the low voice of the visitor, and Tsuru's louder, higher-pitched voice in reply. From this I sensed a visitor of some importance, and prepared myself for the occasion, closing my book and my notebook.

Tsuru came up the stairs much more slowly and solemnly than was customary. She stopped in front of my study door, called my name, and then came in with a tense expression on her face:

"This gentleman is here to see you."

I looked at the card she gave me, on which the visitor's title of professor in the faculty of arts of a certain private university was printed in small type on the right-hand side, and in large type in the center his name: Yujiro Nonomiya. I took a large gulp of breath.

"Any similarity?" I asked.

"With Miss Yukari, do you mean, sir?"

"Yes."

"None whatsoever. She must take after her mother, perhaps?"

I muttered something vague in reply, although I really wanted to ask myself out loud why on earth he'd come here, but thought I could hardly do so in front of the maid.

"Is the guest room tidy?"

"Yes. Shall I show him in there?"

I nodded silently, watched her leave and, in order to calm myself, smoked a cigarette and thought about the tactics I might employ, but since I didn't know what he'd come about exactly there was nothing practical I could think of. I did think about ringing Yukari up to ask what the situation was, but somehow felt it would be an odd thing to do and decided not to.

After what I felt was an appropriate interval I got up, and as I was descending the stairs I saw Tsuru disappear into the living room, having first given me a casual glance of no particular import. As I entered the guest room a tall, dark-suited, excessively thin man, without glasses and in his fifties, got up from an easy chair.

"I must apologize for disturbing you at this late hour," he said in greeting.

Here, I felt, was a typically smooth university professor, although of a more cheerful, friendly character than the cold intellectual type I'd envisaged. This reassured me a little, and I urged him to sit down again. As we made the usual preliminary polite exchanges about it still being remarkably warm although we were already in September, I came to the conclusion that his face bore a certain resemblance to a goat. All that Yukari seemed to have inherited from him was his height and pale complexion, though naturally the father's was pretty much sullied by age. The one thing that might have suggested the parent of a fashion model was that he had his initials embroidered on the breast pocket of his shirt, the Y done in a pinkish red and the N in a pale blue.

The professor praised the small Umehara on the wall behind him as being representative of that period when the painter's use of oils had been at its most precise. I replied that even an Umehara meant little if it was as small as that, but he maintained that a "thumbnail" (using the trade name for the size) of that artist and period would be of considerable value. In fact I'd received the painting when I was working on the Coal Board from the president of a mining company, his secretary having delivered it as a wedding present, casually enclosed in an ordinary cardboard box, on the morning of the day I was married.

When Tsuru had brought in the tea and retired again, Professor Nonomiya changed the tone of the conversation.

"Well, as you have probably realized, I am the father of Yukari Nonomiya, and. . ."

As soon as he began on this track I brought into action the speech I'd been planning on the way downstairs.

"Yes, of course. Your name is, obviously, one with which I have been well acquainted. However, I feel I must insist that the relationship between myself and Yukari is of a totally private nature, meaning, shall we say, that we know each other as friends, and although naturally there is nothing, well, shady or, er, underhand that we need to hide from the world at large, we see no need to publicize or make public our relationship in any way. Our relationship being of this nature I must confess that, if I may be excused this manner of speaking, I had no intention of requesting that I be allowed to associate with any members of Yukari's family in any form whatsoever. . ."

I'd given this address in precise, clear accents, in very much the style adopted at a committee meeting when a matter of some importance is being stated. I'd prepared all this in my head on the assumption that he'd come in a belligerent mood, and would either order me to get my hands off his daughter or (though I realized it was most unlikely) attempt to extort information about what was going on or even some form of financial compensation. So I thought the smart thing to do was to take a pretty tough line from the start.

Professor Nonomiya's response to this showed a remarkable quickwittedness, a swift ability to adjust to circumstances I had not seen rivaled in either commercial or government circles.

"Well, well, this is most welcome, I must say," he said, smiling with what seemed an innocent delight in my words, and showing a set of teeth that he must have got on the cheap since they were far too white. He continued:

"I confess myself in intense agreement with your frank mode of expression, which we may call modern and European in style, and which is also very much shared by myself. As you yourself are well aware, Yukari did not even complete her courses at junior college, and although this could be put down to the demands that her career as a fashion model were making upon her, I fear I must add that her overall academic

record has only been an indifferent one. Her personal appearance—
due to some hereditary mutation, no doubt—is perhaps something in
her favor, but her school record is poor. However, I do pride myself
that, if we ignore the various formal grades she received and judge her
as a person, as a woman—and if we think in terms of her basic grasp
of life, her attitudes, sensibilities, and so on—then I think I can say she
is, well, not bad, not bad at all; although obviously I have always been
dogged by an uncertainty concerning the validity of these feelings of
mine, since they may well be nothing but fond prejudice on a parent's
part. Still, having discovered she has chosen a man of your way of thinking as her closest intimate, although I would not wish to claim that this
must inevitably indicate my intuitions concerning her have all been
vindicated, yet I do feel something of that kind has been shown to be
the case... A parent's foolishness, you may well say, and you are
welcome to laugh at such fondness."

Since I assumed he hardly expected me to accept this invitation to
laugh, I remained silent. So the professor continued:

"In fact, I must admit that your rational approach to the question
is the correct one. My own feelings are indeed identical to yours, as
I am bound to confess. However, what in practical terms occurs from
now on presents, I believe, certain knotty problems. We must realize,
surely, that we are living in a society whose attitudes and customs are,
fundamentally, very Japanese, Oriental, pre-modern; or, to give a certain dignity and also precision to the matter, shall we define our present situation as being intermediate between a pre-modern and an anti-
modern state of society? Now, I must also admit that one's view of the
merits or otherwise of this very Japanese, Oriental, pre-modern quasi
anti-modern situation will vary with individual obsessions and concerns,
depending upon taste, grasp of the world at large, and whatever set
of values one may have. Still, let us set aside for the moment such complex matters as the validity of taste as a basis for argument and the
nature of the value judgment, and consider this instead as a practical
question for, like it or not, this is the kind of society, the kind of situation, in which we are living... We are obliged, surely, to recognize that
this is the case."

At this point I quite automatically gave a large nod in agreement,
realizing as I did so that I was behaving just like a student listening

to a lecture in the front row of the classroom, and worrying that if things continued like this the issue would be dominated totally by my opponent's methods and opinions. As he spoke he held a cigarette in his right hand, toying with it as if it were a piece of chalk and making no attempt at all to light it. This aroused a certain irritation in me. But the professor went on:

"This being the case I have to confess that I myself have made considerable adjustments to the customs and expectations of the world about me at various times during my life. This must, I feel, be viewed as something unavoidable; not only unavoidable but, indeed, natural. I can see no objection to using that term. On New Year's Day we naturally partake of the traditional foods and drinks, for these seem more natural than, say, ham and eggs and coffee. Consequently I trust you will view this desire on my part to make the acquaintance of a friend of my daughter, not as some troublesome impertinence, but in the same light as you would consider those other natural forms of behavior. Or am I asking too much?"

Before, however, giving me any time to reply to this question he had launched into another:

"Incidentally, Mr. Mabuchi, which high school did you attend?"

As it happened, one of my teachers at high school, a German teacher, had been in his class at junior high school, and he then told me various eccentric stories about him, which were so ludicrous and alien to that teacher's character as I'd known it that I could hardly help laughing.

The result of this chatter was, firstly, a relaxation of the atmosphere and, secondly, a feeling on my part of a certain, if only mild, respect for the classmate of a person who'd given me my first painful moments in German. I felt fairly sure a man of this kind would hardly stoop to using the amorous inclinations of his daughter to extort anything from me. Still, the main result was a definite change in my viewpoint. Up to that moment I'd been considering my relationship with Yukari from the complacent position of a middle-aged man who felt free to do much as he liked, but suddenly I began to feel I was seeing things with the eyes of a sexually inexperienced boy; or, at least, I began to feel some embarrassment, perhaps even shame, at sitting here in front of a man whose daughter I'd been sleeping with on the sly. Naturally I was still pretty nonchalant on the surface as I puffed my cigarette and exposed

70

the source of this German teacher's nickname. I also encouraged myself with the thought that Yukari's dad looked about the same age as our managing director so there could only be about ten years between us. Then I had another thought: he was a professor at a second-rate private university, and a professor of foreign languages at that. After all, anybody who had been through a literary department in an old-style university was bound to be thick, idle, and ignorant. These reflections cheered me up quite a lot.

Eventually Professor Nonomiya changed his approach very slightly and said:

"Oh yes, by the way, I hesitate to meddle in an area that should perhaps be out of bounds to me, but I gather that my daughter is receiving each month the rent for her apartment from you. I was wondering just how I should consider the nature of payments of that kind?"

This really did take me by surprise, and I could only express my astonishment that he knew about it. Professor Nonomiya smiled at this and went on:

"Well, women are dreadful chatterboxes, to be sure. However, let me say that ever since I heard of the matter, I had been hoping I might be able to be on such terms with you as would enable me to ask a question of this kind. Naturally, if you object to the question, you are quite at liberty to refuse to reply. It is, of course, rather absurd that a father should meddle in matters of this kind, but, then, we are living in Japan, are we not?"

The very casual nature of these remarks deprived me of any escape route and I was obliged to answer. I muttered a few ambiguous words to give myself time, since I'd no idea how I was going to explain the obvious contradiction between the term "friend" and the fact of my paying her apartment rent, and I had to work something out in double-quick time. Some indication of the panic-stricken confusion of my psychological state at that moment can be gathered from the fact that it didn't even cross my mind to ask him what account Yukari had given of the "nature of payments of that kind." Instead I just blundered on, my face growing red as I spoke:

"Well, this is a particularly delicate question which is extremely awkward to explain. However, if I may put the matter frankly..."

"By all means, by all means."

"When an unmarried man and woman are on terms of intimacy, it is proper for them—in Japan today—to go to a hotel, I believe. As far as my own inclinations are concerned I should prefer to do that. I'd feel happier in myself if it were so. That is, to speak in rather pretentious terms, I would feel I was escaping from the everyday social world and that my consequent behavior existed in a separate area of its own. However, your daughter ... Yukari, that is ... always objects to the idea. Consequently the expense of the hotel is spared, and so, for that reason..."

"Ah, I see," said the professor, taking this information in his stride (or so his face indicated) and adding calmly: "You are, in fact, making savings."

"In fact making savings?"

"The phrase means nothing to you? Really? Only one very small difference in terms of years between the generations, yet such is the result; a phenomenon often seen in backward countries, I believe. The European method of calculating generations in terms of thirty years is quite misleading in this country, where they should rather be measured in units of ten years or sometimes even less. That is my own theory of the matter, anyway. Very well. I shall explain. What I mean is the habit of feeling one wants to eat an ice cream but judges it a waste of money to eat one, so one considers the money not spent on the ice cream as money that has been, and should be, saved. The same can be done with beer. People often used to talk of making savings in the past, and the principle seems the same in your case."

"Well, I suppose you could say that, now you come to mention it," I replied rather dejectedly. My love affair with Yukari was turning into something wretchedly characterless and non-erotic, something downright banal, and the thought depressed me.

"In that case, then," said the professor, "the payments are being made on a basis of comradely equality?"

"Yes. After all, with payments as small as those..." I'd wanted to say it was impossible to "keep" any woman with that fiddling amount of money, but the professor interrupted me with ease and fluency:

"That is certainly a load off my mind, and makes it much easier for me to give voice to the following request, for thus I can think in terms of marriage. Would you, I ask, get married?"

"Get married?"

"Yes, I mean get married."

"To Yukari?... Your daughter?"

Although I was certainly surprised by this request, the important thing was that it made me smile. It was a cheerful smile. I confess I'd been much shaken by this proposition from the goat-faced professor, but obviously he wasn't out to extort anything from me since he seemed to have the same benevolent concern for my future as Tsuru. This put my mind at rest. Why I should have seen this request to marry his daughter as an act of goodwill and why it should have put my mind at rest is another question, and could presumably be answered by saying that in my unconscious mind I did genuinely want to marry the girl.

However, I did, in fact, reject Professor Nonomiya's offer, explaining as politely as possible that I'd no intention of remarrying for the time being. He nodded in generous acceptance of my position.

"Forgive me, I have gone too far. I had intended not so much to ask you to marry my daughter but—how shall I put it?—simply to hope you would, as it were, keep the question of marriage in mind. The truth is that I believe a person of your social status will be obliged, sooner or later, to marry again and settle down. Bourgeois society inevitably makes such demands. If you remain celibate as now, you would not, as you would in Europe, be accused of pederasty, since fortunately our cultural attitudes are not of that kind; but you would be equally inconvenienced by different forms of rumor, such as the suggestion that you were carrying on with your secretary and suchlike."

"But surely..." I began to reply, yet the professor pressed on in determined tones:

"But surely you would, without question. The world may be relatively tolerant in that respect toward artists and writers; in fact it is arguable that a certain amount of scandal of that nature may well be desirable in such figures, even *de rigueur*. However, in the case, for example, of a university professor..."

"But surely there have been distinguished scholars who've remained unmarried?"

"There have been, and quite a number; whether one could say a great many or merely a considerable number I am not sure, but they have certainly been reasonably numerous. However, I am afraid that someone outside the profession could have very little inkling how much such independence has cost them in terms of real human suffering. Superficially a university teacher may seem to be someone different from an ordinary member of the public; but, believe me, his is certainly no free existence above the struggle, for struggle he must, and the stares and glances of this world are something he must always bear in mind. The academic world or, more precisely, the formal assemblies of his immediate colleagues, such as senate and faculty meetings, all create a society, a representative form of society at large, which constantly exerts pressure on him."

He'd become quite melancholy as he made these remarks, which were heavy with an odd pathos. I couldn't help feeling sorry for him at what I imagined was the loss of face he'd suffered when it became known his daughter was a fashion model.

"I'm sure it's not really all that bad. . ." I blurted out, which was presumably some attempt to comfort him. He was looking very sad and lonely about the eyes and nose, a dolefulness that made him look even more like a goat, reduced to gloomy silence for a while. But then he cheered up again.

"My implication is that, if you are to lead an harmonious social life, you will shortly be obliged to give the question of remarriage your serious attention. When you do so I should like Yukari to be considered . . . as one of the possible candidates. Given what has already taken place I do not see how that could be thought an unnatural thing for you to do."

Although I flinched somewhat at his "what has already taken place" form of euphemism, I replied:

"Well, yes, I understand your import, but I must stress that, at this moment, I have no intention whatsoever. . ."

Whereupon he interrupted me again and said in a sanctimonious, even unctuous voice:

"Of course—a very natural response from a widower who still wears the garments of mourning. I myself have been spared any such experience, but I feel I can say that I appreciate and even endorse such sentiments. I regret now that my own behavior may have appeared insinuating, intrusive, even ill-mannered; and yet—how shall I put it?—through the, er, medium of my daughter I feel I have gained a friend

74

in yourself; and if, in my position as a friend, I suggest you contemplate the question of remarriage, I believe my suggestion will not appear as one that is totally unreasonable."

He smiled at this point, with that smile which a teacher will bestow on a student who has done well and can do even better; and then went on:

"If, therefore, in the future, things should turn out as I suggest they will, then I merely hope and trust Yukari will be borne in mind; no more than that."

I found myself impelled to give a nod and grunt of assent, which made Professor Nonomiya lower his head respectfully and voice his thanks, then draw an envelope out of his inside pocket and lay it before me, saying it was for my information. I wondered what it might be, and took up the envelope with some misgiving, discovering there was some ordinary notepaper and also something much thicker inside. The thick paper was a photocopy of his family register, and the ordinary paper contained a painstaking outline, written by hand with a thick-nibbed pen, of the *curricula vitae* of Yujiro Nonomiya, Kyoko (his wife), Yukari, and Shin'ichi (her younger brother). For example, at the end of the section devoted to Yujiro Nonomiya (54 years of age) his publications were listed. These included *An Introduction to the History of Western Art*; *Beauty and Technology*; and *Culture from the Rococo to Cubism*; and under "translations" there were some seven or eight books on art by such authors as Clive Bell and Herbert Read. These dozen or so books, with two or three exceptions, had been brought out by publishers I'd never heard of, and I realized the professor's standing in the literary world couldn't have been very high. It's odd that the mild contempt this aroused in me made me feel I could handle him now, dumbfounded though I'd been so far by the variety and deviousness of his approach. As I glanced through the records of his children, noting that Yukari's academic career had come to an end when she quit a two-year junior college halfway through, and that her brother had entered a good Christian college which had only been set up after the war, I smiled and said:

"I'd assumed we were talking about the future in purely general terms, but it does seem to have come very close and imminent all of a sudden."

"You are, of course, quite right to say so. I regret I have a reputation for rushing into things regardless."

He seemed to have been put out slightly by an admission that I felt I'd wrung from him, and this cheered me up some more so I thought I'd try to put him down again, but from a different angle.

"There's another major factor in that Yukari herself has never shown, either by her words or behavior, that she has any desire to marry me."

This sharply delivered remark, however, didn't so much floor him as ensure that we return to the original subject, and the professor began to speak in tones of heartfelt pathos, even of restrained agony:

"That is exactly the point, the whole problem. I personally believe that, in her heart of hearts, Yukari herself desires marriage with you. I am, naturally, speaking of what is going on in her . . . let us say subconscious. However, she herself, in her conscious mind, is not yet properly aware of that."

"A pretty odd way of putting it, I must say. If you insist on making things as complex as. . ."

"I regret to say that the poor child has been placed in this 'odd,' this 'complex,' situation quite contrary to any desire or will of her own," the professor replied in funereal tones.

"Are you implying, sir, that it's I who have placed her in this situation?"

"By no means; certainly not. What has imposed this situation on Yukari is the profoundly critical cultural condition of contemporary Japan."

I could only register a startled silence in response to this.

"The truth, as I see it, is that you and Yukari have been attempting to construct a relationship, from the point of view of one free man and one free woman, that will be a free yet lasting expression of love, an intimate relationship which does not see marriage as one of its preconditions. However, such a new form of human relationship cannot, I feel, be established on an antiquated, Japanese basis. It is quite impossible; impossible because the essential condition of the system of cultural attitudes and responses must prove your undoing. Perhaps it would be possible to use the larger term 'tradition' and say that it will actually prevent you from doing what you are seeking to perform. Naturally an intellect of your caliber will possess the skills and abilities whereby to evade and endure the harsher consequences of this. We intellectuals in backward countries possess such techniques, and as a typical example I might cite the cases of intellectuals in the various countries of Latin America. Now, however that might be, is it reasonable, is it sensible, to expect to find such wisdom in a present-day Japanese fashion model? No, it surely is not; as her father I find this eminently regrettable, but also see it as a fact one must simply accept. Now, what comes first into Yukari's own mind as the natural solution to this situation is the idea of marriage to yourself. However, she has been taught by you that your relationship is a free one based upon free love, and not only does she love this teacher who has taught her such ideas but profoundly respects him as well. Thus her subconscious forbids that the idea of marriage should ever take on a conscious form. Now, another method of solving the problem is open to her, and that is. . ."

"To separate?" I said without thinking (no doubt an expression of my subconscious desire not to let Yukari go).

"No. There can be no question of that, since she is in love with you," he said, casually rejecting my suggestion. "Yukari is thinking, as a second best measure, of becoming your mistress in the formal sense of being what is traditionally known as 'the number two,' thereby achieving some kind of reconciliation with Japanese customs and ideas."

"A number two?" I mumbled obscurely, thinking how clumsy I was at sounding surprised. Of course it was a kind of playacting on my part, and I wasn't all that concerned how bad my performance was either. But there's also the fact that I'd been genuinely surprised, at least to the extent that I needed to say something in reply; which accounts, I think, for the parrot-like nature of it.

"Quite so," said Professor Nonomiya with a casual nod. "It is for that very reason she receives from you something for which she has no real need—namely the rent of her apartment—in an attempt to give some semblance of concrete actuality to this role of number two which she desires to assume . . . although naturally I am speaking of what concerns the unconscious regions of her mind. That is the case, don't you agree? Similarly I see your own motive—once again, of course, I am talking in terms of unconscious motivation—in providing such symbolic money as stemming from a desire to establish a stability in your relationship which can only be achieved in such a pre-modern social configuration, resulting in the transfer of rent money each month. That, at least, is how I judge the situation."

"Your account is so eminently lucid I feel it can only be taken with several large grains of salt," I said in a low voice. His method of advancing his argument was so much more offbeat and dubious than anything I'd yet come across in either MITI or my present company that I'd no idea how to respond; although I did also feel that if one were to attempt to talk about sexual relationships maybe this was the only way to do it. I was, I must admit, only half doubtful, not totally so. Or, to put it another way, I was half prepared to take what he said seriously, even seeing it as somehow relevant to the truth of the situation; but only because such unverifiable rubbish about Yukari's unconscious mind was welcome, flattering news in that it said quite plainly she wanted to marry me.

Her father, however, smiled at my response, admitting this was simply his own interpretation of the matter, and asking me what my interpretation of paying Yukari's rent might be; then saying no more. It was clear he had total confidence in his own theories and was only asking me my "interpretation" out of courtesy. This smug academic confidence probably stimulated me more than anything else, and I began to feel that if I didn't take him down a peg or two I was never going to get anywhere. This required a sudden change of approach.

"I wonder if perhaps there isn't some particular reason why you should recently have become so concerned to marry your daughter off? I was told, just the other day, in fact, you are constantly demanding that she attend marriage interviews and suchlike. I felt there must be something behind this, and my suspicion is today confirmed by this very frank, direct recommendation aimed at me. I am obliged to conclude there must be some other, major factor at work here of which I'm still unaware..."

"You are quite right. There is," he replied instantly. "This other factor is Yukari's own recent posture. As her lover you would not, I think,

78

be aware of this, probably because you are not adequately distanced from her to notice. But I am in a position to observe, and this is true even more so of her mother. Recently she gives the impression of being somehow disturbed, lacking in a proper balance. . . I am unable to find any precise words to describe it, but that is how it seems to me. This has aroused an anxiety in me, and I have been wondering if marriage might not be the answer. So, after various tribulations, I finally heard your name mentioned, and thus. . . Well, it is a parent's obsessive concern, no doubt. . ." He smiled, showing his excessively white teeth. "Your own suspicions seem to me perfectly justified, given my sudden appearance at this late hour. You will, I believe, be assured of the validity of such statements as I have made from a perusal of the family register and other documentation that I shall leave with you. In this regard— although I have, of course, no intention of doing anything of a similar nature myself—you may have my affairs investigated to whatever degree you may think fit. I have no objection at all, and you may do so at your own discretion."

Having made this statement with ponderous good grace, he stood up, and then appeared to remember something else:

"Ah yes. These may be considered as another version of my visiting card. If you should ever have the leisure to cast your eye over them. . ."

So saying, he took two books out of the cloth in which they'd been wrapped. They were *Culture from the Rococo to Cubism* and *An Introduction to the History of Western Art,* the former having a painting by Watteau or somebody on the cover, while the other was a paperback which had something odd about its title, probably because the print was all out of alignment. I thanked him ceremoniously, and while I was wondering if courtesy demanded I should ask him to sign them, he sped out of the room. He stopped, however, a brief moment in front of the broken clock, saying that it had considerable interest as an "*objet,*" and then apologized for the length of his stay, bending his long, thin body in a low bow and departing.

Tsuru didn't dash out of her room into the entrance hall until after I'd closed and locked the front door behind him and was looking vaguely at the clock, stopped, as always, at a quarter past three.

"Has the gentleman already left, then?" she asked, rather as if she

79

were speaking to herself. Then she suggested I take a bath, but I said I'd do so later. I was thinking first of telephoning Yukari to find out what was going on. I told Tsuru to switch the phone over to the one upstairs in my room.

Since I had this device on the telephone it was odd that I'd never once called Yukari from the house, and as I dialed her number I reflected I'd not even done so after Tsuru had found out all about us. I suppose I may have refrained from doing so out of a sense of duty toward my dead wife, but I'd still come to no conclusion about this when Yukari answered at the other end.

She listened to my account of the evening with exclamations of amazement, delivered in a tone of voice that didn't in fact sound all that surprised. When I ended she said:

"He does get completely carried away at times. Usually he's perfectly calm, but when anything really important comes up he seems to get all sort of excited."

This critical judgment on her father was followed by her admitting that she had, in fact, mentioned my name the very day before, as a way of getting out of going to the marriage interview. Presumably her father, on hearing this and after (or without) consulting her mother, had decided to pay me a visit. I didn't bring up the question of the rent payments, in order to spare her feelings; and she made no mention of it herself.

"In that case I can just about see why he came. Still, I find the whole thing a bit off-putting."

"Off-putting?" echoed Yukari, and started giggling, which made me laugh as well.

"Yes. I mean I don't know what I should do. After all, I can't think of many precedents for this situation. I don't mean there aren't lots of examples of two people like us, only in our case it's your father who seems enthusiastic and not the couple involved. Including you on the list of possible candidates when I consider remarriage was such a vague idea there wasn't really anything I could say. Maybe it's because he sometimes teaches art theory at college, but I find his basic premises so wild, yet the logic-chopping he supports them with so rigorous, I just can't handle him."

"Can't you?"

"No, I can't. His arguments are absurdly eccentric, but the logic itself seems to hold together."

"Now you say so, I remember Mother often complains he argues about odd things sometimes and comes to really weird conclusions."

Yukari then gave me a lengthy account of some daft theory her father had about the connection between athlete's foot and the saving habit, urging my agreement when she finished:

"There you are. That's really odd, isn't it?"

"It is. It's weird. I understand how your mother must feel," I agreed, but in a dull and melancholy tone which was obviously much too elegiac a way to greet the end of a funny story. My meeting with Professor Nonomiya must have had some real effect on my psychic disposition to make me so nervous and depressed.

After a short while I said:

"Anyway, you don't want to get married to me, do you?"

I don't know why I let such a pointed question escape me, for it's the sort of carelessness I'm normally never guilty of. I suppose it must have been because I was undergoing some kind of mental or emotional relapse, as I've already suggested.

Yukari, who usually responded with almost chronic promptness to anything I said, did not reply to this. Her silence continued for some time. I also remained silent at my end of the line, my heart full of an unrest that was both ominous and yet not at all ominous at the same time, waiting for her reply. Finally a brief answer dropped into that silence.

"There seems to have been some big misunderstanding."

"Some misunderstanding? What do you mean?"

Still the unrest, now a kind of thumping, continued inside me as I asked her to explain. I knew I was doing the wrong thing, that this could only lead to heaven knows what, and whatever it was it was going to be something horribly important.

She replied: "I've always thought a proposal would have been much more romantic."

Besides making me feel relieved this remark also struck me with horror (such contradictions are one aspect of the human heart), and I shouted out wildly:

"Now look here, Yukari!"

"But it's true. That's what I was really thinking."

This was said in a certain dreamy, lyrical tone, but was soon transformed into her usual cheerful, sportive vein:

"Well, reality's a different matter, I suppose..."

I found myself groaning at her remark, but she didn't seem to interpret this as the reaction of a man struggling with bewilderment and confusion, but more of someone trying to conceal some happy embarrassment. Her silence confirmed that she'd understood my response in that way, so I hurriedly added:

"Of course, since things haven't boiled down to that yet..."

This inelegant way of putting it seemed to imply my feelings would eventually boil down to that, or had already done so, and I was simply hesitating to put them into precise words. What made it worse was that her interpreting them like this couldn't be called a simple error; indeed there was a sense in which she could be said to have read my feelings correctly. The whole thing was very muddled, and I suppose at least half my mind was occupied by the thought that this girl was in love with me, and I felt extremely, almost awesomely happy.

"What an awful way to say it: 'things haven't boiled down'... It's just like..."

"Like talking about some personnel problem at work?"

"That's right. Of course, it is a question of personnel in a way. A very personal personnel problem..."

This witty remark of hers gave her peculiar delight, and she appeared to have doubled up with side-splitting mirth, complaining of the pain in her stomach and repeating the phrase with obvious glee. As I listened to her peals of laughter I felt I was at last beginning to gain a grasp of the situation. Quite simply, if I allowed things to drag on like this I could end up marrying a fashion model. Besides the fact that I probably wouldn't be able to stand the physical strain, I was also aware that once the anniversary of my first wife's death was over there were bound to be marriage proposals from other quarters which would be instantly preferable to this one. Surely there was no need to be carried away by the persuasions of my mistress's father (I didn't want to go so far as to call this a plot hatched between the two of them) and feel obliged to make an honest woman of her. What could be the objection to carrying on exactly as we were now?

It was in this critical, reflective state of mind that I listened to Yukari's laughter, and when it was finally over I said:

"Anyway, we'll go into all this when I get back. Still, you know, I can't help thinking it might be better for you in many ways if we just split up now. Let's see how it goes. . ."

This enormous hint of separation, delivered, I admit, in a light tone of voice, seemed to make no impression at all.

"Marriage would be okay, but you can't just rush into a second one, can you?" she said with her normal irrepressible cheerfulness.

"Why not?"

"Because of the wedding dress. You only wear white when it's the first time. In a second marriage you can have any color you like. When Liz got married the fifth time she had orange, and Bébé was in red."

As I was pondering the obvious implication that she was indeed thinking in terms of marriage, Yukari seemed to misinterpret my silence as some form of ignorance and gave me scholarly footnotes on B.B. and Liz. She then explained that on the day I was due to get back from Australia she'd be away on location in the sand dunes of the Japan Sea coast and wouldn't be back until late that day after the shooting was over.

"Maybe we'll meet at Haneda, then?" I said.

"Not a chance of that," she said, finally ringing off with her usual "Bye now," which showed no sign of uncertainty, nothing to distinguish it from the way she always spoke, and that made me feel unhappy. I did, in fact, determine to put an end to all talk of this marriage. Obviously to marry a girl whose sole concern during a discussion of the problem was what color her wedding dress should be was simply asking for trouble. It would be a disaster; not the sixty-year famine which a bad wife is traditionally said to bring a man, but a good hundred years of it.

It was a decision that was bound to cause me pain; and it did. However, it wasn't all that difficult to convince myself this was inevitable, something that simply had to be done. I entered the bath with the pleasant feeling that at last everything had been settled, and as I was relaxing in the tub I found myself whistling some of the songs we used to sing in the dorm back in my high school days.

Still, the following day, although I was busy with my departure for

Australia on the day after, I put in a hasty telephone call to the president of a certain public corporation, making an appointment to see him the same day to arrange my forthcoming remarriage.

The truth is that, after I'd taken my bath and was reading a book and drinking my nightcap, I was suddenly overtaken by feelings of regret at the thought that I'd have to say goodbye to Yukari some day. I started to remember the white blur of her face in the darkness, her slim, resilient, energetic thighs, the constant moistness of her eager body. Not only that, however; indeed not even principally that, for her main attraction for me was something that mattered much more: the fact that when I was in her company I could taste a sense of freedom, the joy of feeling released from the constrictive cage that otherwise seemed to enclose my days. If I let her go now I'd be like the man who threw away a priceless pearl, knowing he'd never find another like it. Even if I were to acquire the daughter of some director of a high-class bank, or the niece of the president of some company that was even higher than high class, and even if this superior wife with these superior connections were neither some unfortunate whom no one would choose to marry nor some widow, could she possibly be superior to Yukari as a woman? If such a woman existed, surely she wouldn't want to marry some minor executive (due to be promoted next spring to the board perhaps) in a company that was still not much more than second grade. The idea was absurd. No woman of that kind would even look at me.

I was aware of becoming flushed with drink, and could laugh to some extent at the erotic fantasies it had encouraged, and the "ideas" thereby produced. But these were fantasies I was to find I couldn't escape from, even in the light of day next morning.

The go-between for my first marriage was a man who'd ended his career at MITI as a bureau chief and become the vice-president of a public corporation. He was now the president of a different public corporation. I was shown into the spacious, luxurious presidential office where a man in his mid-sixties, dressed in a beautifully tailored double-breasted suit, was idly leafing through a catalog of Korean pottery. He was now quite unrecognizable as that bureau chief so involved in his work as to seem a walking example of "indifference to personal appearance." The president made some imperialistic joke about the pottery he was looking at.

"Well, Mabuchi, are you getting on all right where you are now?" he then asked in a rather anxious voice. He seemed to be under some misapprehension that I'd come to complain about my work and wanted to move elsewhere.

"When I spoke of a personal matter, sir, I didn't mean my work but my domestic situation."

"Ah, so someone has produced a suggestion?"

The president had soon worked out I was talking about a possible marriage. Probably he felt some kind of pique at having been bypassed in the matter, or even envy of the person who'd produced whatever suggestion it might be. The president was a firm believer in marriage being determined by the inclinations of almost anyone other than the two people principally involved. My first marriage had been of that kind—as, I suddenly came to realize, my second was turning out to be as well.

"Yes. The father of the person concerned."

"Interesting. So the father's taken a fancy to you? Not a common happening these days, surely?"

His envy vanished with this supposedly neat remark. It was in some sense a misunderstanding of the situation, but I could only explain the affair in such a way as to leave that misapprehension basically intact, and naturally I didn't touch on the complexities of the apartment rent problem. Thus the president was inclined to view the matter exclusively as some man-to-man relationship between myself and Professor Nonomiya, and he endeavored to see everything along those lines.

"What is your own standpoint with regard to all this?"

"Well, I can hardly claim to have my own standpoint as yet. I was merely hoping to hear your own opinion, sir, and thus be able to use it as a main point of reference."

This was a lie, of course, but it seemed to please him.

"Mabuchi, you've certainly grown highly skilled at keeping your distance from a problem, and moving slowly all around it. A pity you didn't have the same foresight and wisdom in the past."

This was a very belated dig at the fact I'd not consulted him when refusing the transfer to the Ministry of Defense. I thought it was surely a bit late in the day, particularly since he'd never expressed any displeasure or dissatisfaction over the matter before.

"Exactly," I said with humility.

"You haven't seen Mayama yet?" he said, asking a question whose answer was as obvious to him as it was to me. Mayama was a favorite, bright-eyed protégé of his who'd been promoted as far as undersecretary and then left MITI to become a director of the company where I was now working. He was, indeed, the managing director at this moment. I don't really need to add that I'd joined the company because of his presence there. I replied that there was an order of doing things, and also he wouldn't be back from America until tomorrow or the day after.

"Always busy as usual I see. Well, let's do it like this. Leave the question of whether the go-between should be Mayama or your company president to me. I'll talk to Mayama about it and then decide."

I was well acquainted with his habit of leaving out various stages in any argument or series of statements he put forward, as if he found it unbearable to give a slow, complete account of the process of his ideas. Presumably the fact that a man of his intelligence, who'd worked in the ministry as personnel director and head of the secretariat, should never have been promoted to undersecretary could be put down to this oblique manner of speaking, or perhaps to his habit of showing quite openly on his face what he thought of someone who was unable to grasp what he was implying. That was at least a widely circulated rumor. I was also aware that if I asked him to act as go-between himself he wouldn't give the real answer that it would do my career no good at all, but would rather brusquely insist that to undertake the same service as he'd previously done for me, before my former wife had been dead a year, was something a decent respect toward her must forbid. So I simply remained silent and bowed my head in acknowledgment of what he'd said and in thanks for what he would now do for me.

The next morning I hired a car to take myself and my two pieces of baggage out to the airport, having decided beforehand to call in on my parents-in-law on the way there. The house, hidden behind tall hedges, was just as noisy, with the TV blaring, as it had been the night before when I telephoned. Both of them seemed to be pretty hard of hearing, and their only amusements in life were going for walks, television, and playing games of *go* in which the wife was just about able to make a contest of it by receiving a handsome handicap.

After being shown into the living room I knelt and paid my respects. My father-in-law, also kneeling there upright and proper and wearing a black, unlined kimono, abruptly drove my mother-in-law from the room with a few brusque words of command, having apparently guessed I'd come to talk about the question of marrying again. Despite the racket from the television I was able to provide a description of the situation in somewhat greater detail than the one I'd given the president, and in the same way I refrained from expressing any viewpoint of my own but merely asked for my father-in-law's opinion, which he gave with remarkable promptness.

"My congratulations, Eisuke. I was thinking it was about time I should be saying something myself. We at this end have no objection whatsoever, and merely hope that you'll stay on the same friendly terms with us as before. You'd probably be well advised to have the wedding before the year is out."

Having made this statement in a reasonably solemn if overloud voice, he then smoothed his bald pate with his left palm and changed his tone somewhat.

"If she's a model she must be a nice-looking girl. Eh? I'll bet she is. Just about the right age difference for a second marriage. Still, being the daughter of an Eng. Lit. man, there is a slight question of how bright she is. That's the only problem as I see it."

"Ah, well," I said.

"Of course, our daughter was hardly one we could be all that proud of in that respect."

He laughed, and said he hoped he might be invited to the reception. He particularly wanted to get a good look at this lovely young girl, he said, giving an even larger hoot of laughter; so loud, in fact, that it actually drowned the roar of the TV. Eventually he called his wife back in again and (naturally) my mother-in-law had no objection to make either.

As I was leaving she asked after Tsuru. This brought memories of Tsuru back, and my mother-in-law became quite absorbed in her reflections on how lucky I was to have a maid like Tsuru, and how much she wished she had one, she was really quite envious, it would be such a help, and how the two of them had been doing without a maid, it was all such a business.

Luckily my father-in-law produced a joke relevant to my immediate purposes ("Don't need to bring us back a kangaroo from Australia. Just find a maid suitable for an elderly couple instead. No kangaroo required."), and I was able to take my leave, get into my car, and head for the airport.

Soon after we'd left Haneda a late lunch was served, and then an early dinner between Hong Kong and Manila. Sitting next to me was an American who said he was going to Manila on business, but luckily he didn't seem inclined to talk all that much. I'd become slightly fuddled by my pre-meal whiskies and had also probably overeaten slightly, so I soon dozed off and, in fact, spent the flight alternately dozing and reading, although I confess I didn't feel like devoting much attention to the book I'd brought with me. It was by a foreign journalist who, under the guise of writing fulsome praise of the Japanese economic miracle, was, in fact, simply flattering the latent fears his readers had about this, and stimulating their anti-Japanese sentiments; hardly the book for a trip of this sort. However, in an illustrated magazine the stewardess had given me I found an advertisement for a securities company which had a girl like Yukari in it (it was a very poor photograph), and thus the majority of these uneventful hours above the clouds were spent in thoughts of Yukari and imaginings of the days when we would be together. Naturally I also considered, to some extent, the various arrangements that would have to be made for the marriage. I'd have to speak to our managing director as soon as I got back and then ring up Oguri or something, since it would look a bit strange if the man who'd introduced us found himself confronted without prior warning by a wedding invitation. As it turned out, however, there was no need to make that phone call, for by complete accident I met him at Manila Airport.

When I stepped out of the plane at Manila into the velvet darkness and the sweltering heat, I regretted not having remained behind on the aircraft. This was partly due to the heat, but the main reason was that I remembered how nasty the duty free shop in the transit lounge had been some years ago, all they had on sale being local products such as Philippine cigars and some "artless" (or, to be brutally frank, barbaric) pieces of native handicraft, crude trays, boxes, and ornaments made of wood. I'd found them distinctly unattractive, feeling that in these primitive objects all the poverty and wretchedness of Asia was on blatant display, for everyone to see. I found myself wincing at the thought of going through that again, but it would have looked a bit odd if I'd retraced my footsteps so, accepting the inevitable, I caught up with the other transit passengers ahead of me, overtook them, and hurried on into the efficiently air-conditioned lounge. As I entered the gray darkness of the cool hall I felt a definite relief, and yet I didn't sit down to rest on one of the low chairs placed here and there but kept right on toward the one bright area in that gray space, the duty free shop, as if urged onward by the dread of what I was to see: the cigars and bits of woodwork, especially those objects whose manufacture had presumably been handed straight down by primitive man. Gazing at the piles of hideously carved and hideously colored artifacts, much as they had been those years before, the specialist term "Asian modes of production" came into my head as it had then. A man in a grubby technicolor shirt addressed me in Philippine English, attempting to sell me a wooden monkey. I walked off, saying curtly that I wasn't interested.

Immediately afterward, however, I came across some glass cases in which there were cameras, transistor radios, transistor TVs; and it cheered me up a good deal to realize they were all of Japanese make, although I smiled rather bitterly when I saw that none of my own company's products were among them. This new sense of well-being was probably not so much related to my present existence as an electrical goods manufacturer, but more to the government official in the field of international trade that I'd once been.

I continued strolling about the dimly lit hall among people loitering like myself and others seated and waiting. There were swarms of Japanese, each with his camera. There was also a white couple I particularly noted since both were of a remarkable ugliness, and yet the little girl the husband was holding was really very pretty. Maybe she was an adopted child. Finally I saw three empty chairs lined up side by side, and sat down in the middle one. The long, low bamboo chair was very pleasantly cool. So I sat there, smoking, taking it easy and yet with my ears pricked in constant readiness to listen for the English-language announcements, experiencing that peculiar tenseness which I'd endured in exactly the same way in every airport lounge I'd ever sat in.

Eventually there was an announcement saying the scheduled departure time of my flight had been delayed thirty minutes for maintenance reasons. This caused a slight murmur and bustle in the large hall, and I myself stood up and yawned, but immediately sat down again. At that moment a tall man approached me.

"Oi," he said, and for a moment I thought it might be the American who'd been sitting next to me on the plane, for it had never crossed my mind I might meet Oguri in a place like this.

As editor of his company's publicity magazine he'd been traveling around Southeast Asia, and had just come from Thailand. He said his flight had been delayed too. I gave him a brief account of my own business trip.

"Do they have a bar around here?" I asked.

Oguri had sat down in the chair next to mine with a glass in his hand. He held the glass up.

"Do you mean this?" he said, and gave me the glass full of yellow liquid. "I haven't touched it yet. Still, it's certainly not alcohol."

I felt the pleasant coldness on my fingers and palm, and looked at the glass in the dim, concealed light which seemed to fall like specks of dust, observing the cloudy, dew-covered surface of the glass and the thick yellow fruit juice with its texture like finely patterned lace. Oguri got up slowly again and went off toward the bright lights of the duty free shop, to receive another glass of the same from a Philippine waiter. So two former classmates went through the motions of toasting each other in cold orange juice.

"It's been a long time," said Oguri.

"A very long time. Since we always seem to be just missing each other, it's a bit odd we should meet here of all places."

"One lucky moment in a thousand years, as the saying goes," said Oguri, retaining even in Manila his habit of speaking words of proverbial wisdom that always somehow missed the mark. In this case the conventional phrase referring to a chance in a lifetime seemed hardly relevant to this accidental, idle encounter which promised nothing and meant nothing but was merely surprising. Still, it was the persistence of the habit and its being out of place in this setting that made me burst out laughing, and Oguri himself laughed in return, apparently well pleased with himself as he ruefully shook his head.

"When was the last time we met?" he asked.

"You remember, surely? We went out with Yukari and Mayo. . ."

"Ah, that's right. We went to see the Spanish dancers, and that fool Mayo went crazy over that young Spaniard."

"Yes, that was a bit annoying."

"You can say that again. After all, as Japanese men, we could hardly, could we. . . ?" Oguri laid great stress on this dilemma, and then burst into loud laughter. I joined in for a while, but became serious again.

"By the way, there's something I have to tell you. I'm getting married."

"Are you? Well done. What's she like?"

"Someone you know."

This produced only a questioning look, and when I said it was Yukari I provoked a similarly surprised silence, though admittedly of very short duration. It was quite clear to me how very unusual, even eccentric, my second marriage must seem to an objective observer. I was also made briefly aware that, although my superiors and my father-in-law may have given their assent to my remarrying, this was no more than an acceptance of the principle of remarriage and indicated nothing about their attitude toward marrying Yukari, since they in fact knew nothing about her. Neither, really, did I. I swallowed my breath, being suddenly overtaken by a complex emotion, one of confusion and fear mixed with excitement and joy in almost equal proportions. It was like visiting a town for the first time, when you wake in the strange hotel next morning and open the window, surprised (and also not surprised) to see the streets spread out, small and far away with all their distant life, experiencing a sweet, almost luxurious anxiety about what might lie in wait there.

"I had been hearing the occasional rumor. Still, I didn't imagine marriage. . . May I offer my congratulations."

Oguri had been mumbling halfheartedly at first, but these last words were delivered with considerable solemnity, something I took him to task for.

"You don't really have to be so surprised, do you? Look, you're making me go all shy and embarrassed."

"You're hardly of an age for that, so I suggest you stop," said Oguri, sharply altering his tone immediately and returning to his normal bland and mischievous level. "First of all, let's admit that the middle-aged man's dream of taking a young girl to wife and educating her to conform to his tastes is a perfectly commonplace one and no cause for astonishment. What is extraordinarily rare, however, is the appearance on the scene of someone who actually puts it into practice."

"Which means, in fact, that you really are astonished?"

"Well, you never know, she might make a surprisingly good wife . . . although I'm sorry to keep harping on the element of surprise."

"Tsuru has agreed to do all the housework," I found myself saying as if making excuses for what I was doing.

"I see. So she'll have a good drill sergeant to instruct her. Still. . ." Oguri hesitated.

"Still what?" I asked him.

"No, I was just thinking how much more interesting this would have been if you were still a civil servant."

"It would provide greater amusement?"

"Certainly it would. Look, if you are going to marry a fashion model you must expect people to be amused. You can't be so soft as to insist that people must not be amused, because they certainly will be. Don't you ever read women's weekly magazines?"

He laughed and drank up his orange juice. His voice had been friendly enough, but I felt something about his lowered eyes and his expression in the dim half-light that implied a definite, if perhaps only slight, malevolence, a grudge against the man who'd had the good fortune to suffer the sad loss of his wife. Feeling shaken by this revelation I raised my glass to my lips and said nothing, while Oguri repeated again even more regretfully:

"It's a pity; truly a great pity. If only you hadn't done it. What a marvelous combination that would have been, a marriage of extremes, the bureaucrat and the fashion model."

Obviously I couldn't let a remark like that go without comment, and I put forward the argument that the civil service wasn't as special a trade as people seemed to think, and that most likely being a fashion model, although I knew little about it, wasn't all that peculiar either; and yet I didn't have much confidence in what I was saying. I was interrupted by an announcement in English, to which Oguri quite literally inclined his ear with head cocked to one side and an expression of pro-

92

found seriousness on his face, finally saying it appeared to have nothing to do with either of us, but in a tone that seemed to demand I take some responsibility for deciding so. He then launched into an exposition of why the bureaucrat and the fashion model were poles apart from each other.

Generally speaking, bureaucrats were men and models were women. Certainly there were women bureaucrats but they served little purpose, and the same applied to models, for although male models existed they were inevitably very feminine in appearance and not worth looking at. Another major point of difference was that a bureaucrat increased in dignity and worth as he grew older, but the model was always at her peak when she was young. From whatever angle one considered them they were the exact opposite of each other, and thus the phrase "poles apart" was the appropriate one. Naturally an argument carried out in such cheerful, frivolous terms should more properly be considered a joke rather than a theory, and his conclusion was ordinary enough:

"Well, it's certainly of great interest, particularly when I think how a mere whim of mine has led to all this."

"Yes, that was a very chic way of expressing your condolences."

"It was a practical and material way of expressing such condolences," he said pompously, and then: "That was the thing, you see. That story about the gold watches. That went down really big. When I thought about it later it struck me that the gold watch was the perfect symbol for your great-grandfather."

"In what way?"

"A symbol of the people's rights movement. The idea of rights is central to your modern citizen, and your modern citizen's motto is surely the same as Franklin's: 'Time is golden.'"

"You're a bit out there, surely?" I protested. "What Franklin actually said was 'Time is money,' but for Jukichi Mabuchi time was a watch, a trinket to comfort his mistress in her illness. In Franklin's case Time meant that time during which one makes money or investigates lightning, both of which could be seen as offerings made to his God. But for my ancestors there was no consciousness of this God or of Time either, but just a general swamp of muddling through. For all those myriads of gods there could be no Time, and that, surely, is what pantheism is all about. So a watch becomes a mistress's toy. Anyway, my great-grandfather was probably no modern citizen. Not even a citizen for that matter..."

"Even so, what I said is roughly true. You shouldn't be so modest about him. After all, there's no need to be all that precise..."

"No, you're wrong, quite wrong. There was no such thing as a citizen in Japan then, and there aren't any today either, are there?"

Having given him this good piece of my mind I added:

"Well, it's your subject, and I know nothing about it."

The sociology graduate replied that his subject was not the citizen but beer, although it did seem the citizen drank the beer, which was perhaps not to the point. Then another announcement in English began, making the already quiet hall much quieter, announcing the departure of the flight to Sydney. About half the transit passengers in the lounge made quite a bustle as they stood up. I stood up, too.

"I wonder when my plane's going to take off?" said Oguri with a sigh, getting up with me.

"Well, cheers. Come to the wedding. Still haven't fixed the time or place yet, though," I said, and started walking.

"Thanks. Make sure you serve champagne. In all my experience it seems to be the finest cure for a hangover," he said as he walked along with me, adding what was presumably meant to be the last word in today's discussion: "We certainly chose a most peculiar place to meet." He faltered slightly, so I thought I would say it for him:

"And you heard the most peculiar news?"

"No. I'm afraid I brought up a most peculiar subject. The citizen! What a thing to talk about, particularly when one isn't drunk. To talk about the citizen when sober..."

We'd now come to the exit for the transit passengers and our conversation was brought to an end. We waved cheerfully at each other, and I went out into the indigo night of Manila Airport.

When I got off the plane at Haneda with an enormous cuddly koala bear, everybody, even the customs officials, smiled equally at me and the bear, or maybe in the proportion of seven smiles at the toy animal and three at the man in his forties who was holding it. No doubt the thirty percent of smiles directed at me implied not only amusement at the fact that I was obliged to embrace the beast in this public manner (it had seemed extravagant to buy a suitcase just to put the toy in) but also a certain criticism of my lacking the wit to have the thing sent by post. (I'd decided a leisurely voyage for it by sea mail would have resulted in such a delay that Yukari would be seriously displeased.) But I imagine the main motive was a sympathy for the parental indulgence my possessing this object indicated. I smiled back at these kindly folk, imagining their amazement if they found out this was no display of a father's fondness, but a present I'd bought for a mistress some twenty years younger than myself, one whom I was shortly to make an honest woman of; and also from a sense of pleasure at the feeling that I was, in some obscure way, making a smart, even striking gesture of repudiation of the everyday world and its commonplace values.

Since I couldn't take the koala bear to work with me, I dropped in at Yukari's place expecting to leave the toy there for when she came back, but in fact she'd just arrived home from her modeling trip and was delighted with the two presents, the bear and the opal.

"Look, I've got something awfully nice, too," she said proudly, and she spread out a pure white wedding dress, which she'd modeled and liked so much she'd got them to let her have it cheap. So, without any definite statements being made, I found our wedding had become an accepted fact of life, something I'd just "drifted into" as they say.

The wedding and reception were held toward the end of November in a hotel in the center of Tokyo, on a day that was unlucky according to Buddhist superstition and thus avoided by most people. It was all on a very small scale, and the attention of the comparatively few guests was completely focused on what Yukari was wearing. The wedding dress she'd acquired through the benevolence of a fashion magazine ("in radiant village maiden style" was the caption in the magazine where it appeared) was highly praised in particular, and I heard whispers that she really did look like a teenage girl. My elder brother and his wife gazed on all this with patent delight, as if they were attending some fashion show. I'd phoned him on the night of my return from Australia expecting he would have gruff, unfriendly words to say, but at some point in time this crusty, hidebound traditionalist seemed to have been totally corrupted by the poison of popular culture, and he complimented me by saying I must be cutting an important figure in the world if I was able to marry a fashion model (his voice showing no trace whatsoever of irony) and wondering if news of the wedding might appear in the weeklies. This went on for some time since he had to keep explaining everything (without bothering to put his hand over the receiver) to his wife at his side, whose enthusiasm was such that eventually she could no longer restrain herself from coming to the phone and announcing the titles of the magazines they took, wondering if Yukari's photo had appeared in any of them, and if she wasn't perhaps that lovely girl with the large beauty spot near her eyebrow (she wasn't), among various other things. After giving the appropriate responses to all this I had her change back to my brother to make sure he really approved, and he maintained that since everyone was in favor he didn't himself feel it was too early to put an end to my celibate existence.

Our go-between was not the company president but the managing director. As soon as I'd got back to work I'd gone to seek his advice. After a lengthy two-minute silence he said:

"You know, I think perhaps I ought to act as go-between, don't you, Mabuchi?"

Obviously all I could do was express my heartfelt hope that he'd do me the honor, which meant the managing director had to explain the situation to our president, and I had to phone the president of the public corporation asking him to explain to our president what had happened about the question of the go-between. On the day itself, the president of the public corporation didn't attend since he was suffering from gout, sending a long telegram of good wishes instead, but our president was there and provided us with a very, very long congratulatory address.

Since I was getting married for the second time, I was probably able to view things with a more objective eye than on the first occasion, and I must admit there were a good many things about this wedding with which I wasn't in the least content. I spent the whole time in a state of uncertainty as to whether I'd been right to wear formal morning dress or not, with the bride in this village maiden getup. I was pretty much taken aback by the general grubbiness of the presiding Shinto priest's robes and his habit of sniffing and snuffling all the way through. Then there was the food. The consommé was much too thick and bitter. The lobster was passable (it never tastes much like anything anyway), but the roast beef was tough and heavy. I'd asked Oguri to act as M.C.

at the reception but, owing to his hangover and having again had a bit too much to drink, all he could produce was a string of frivolous jocularities.

Despite all this everyone seemed perfectly satisfied. The main reason was the frequency with which Yukari disappeared to change her clothes and hairstyle, giving perhaps an excessive air of bustle and to-ing and fro-ing to the proceedings, but also providing plenty to feast the eye on. All other things apart, the flair with which she wore the clothes and never wavered in the least with all eyes focused on her certainly showed the experience of a professional. There was an additional interest for everyone in that two magazine photographers were present, constantly taking pictures all over the place. Yukari's younger brother was also at work with his own camera and the whole scene was remarkably lively. Although he was only a student at a Christian college his long hair made him entirely indistinguishable from the other two, and most people seemed to think he was one of them.

All that, however, was more or less according to plan, or at least to what I'd imagined might happen, but with the closing addresses from representatives of the two families things took a slightly unexpected turn. My elder brother's speech was crude and blunt, but what stole the whole show was the address given by Professor Nonomiya, much to my surprise.

At the beginning of his address Yukari's father picked out a few words from our president's congratulatory speech and said what a powerful impression they had made on him.

"I have not made this remark," he continued, "in the hope that my daughter's husband will receive a raise in salary" (some laughter) "although, of course, that may have been a minor part of my intention."

This produced a great burst of laughter, and even the president beamed affably.

"However, let me state that my principal aim was to indicate my feelings at the time, which were that I was being privileged to hear words of a truly profound wisdom concerning marriage, one of the major events in any human life."

By such cunning switches of tone he soon gained full control of his audience, and he went on with a fairly high-powered discourse, though never overlooking the demands of the vulgar by inserting humorous remarks at various apposite points. Each time there was a general roar of laughter at these jokes I was particularly struck by the way Mrs. Nonomiya, a lady only a few years older than myself, would look rejoicingly at her husband's face, and also by the specious expression of gravity the professor himself maintained. The speeches preceding this had all been very tedious. Our managing director's words had been uniformly dull, and our president's congratulatory address had been even more so, although this could be seen as unavoidable. The remarks of a member of the Diet Upper House (acting in his capacity as youthful intimate of the public corporation president), those of the president of our subsidiary company, and also those of Mayo had been no more than a succession of long-winded, pointless chatter, while the fashion magazine editor had simply muttered one or two words and then bowed, so it wasn't surprising the professor's speech should have shone in such company. Even so, he certainly gave the impression of doing the job professionally, showing the skill of a man who earns his bread by talking; which may be gauged by the fact that even I found myself half persuaded that our president's dreary remarks showed "a profound wisdom." Thus when he ended there was a prolonged round of applause, and while Oguri was announcing the formal ending to these proceedings our president went over to the professor and, face glowing red, offered to shake him by the hand.

We decided not to go on any honeymoon, because I had to go to South Korea on a business trip which had been arranged some time before. The managing director had offered, half out of politeness and half in jest, to take my place, but naturally I'd refused. So we spent that night in the same hotel where the reception had been held, and next morning I handed Yukari over to Tsuru, who'd come to the hotel to collect her, while I set off for the airport.

Our newly married life was uneventful. Tsuru took good care of the bride and Yukari herself seemed to be really very competent at handling her servant. She certainly adopted a more dependent tone with Tsuru than my first wife had done, perpetually asking her advice, but this seemed, in a young wife of twenty-three entering a house where the maid was already in residence, more natural than any unreal attempt to order her around. There was also no sign of Tsuru taking advantage of this. So I didn't have to worry about what was going on at home, and could instead get on with my work and attend the end-of-year parties (only another form of work anyway), where I knew I was bound to become the butt of drunken wit about the nights passed in the company of my young wife.

Yukari kept on with her modeling, although there weren't many calls on her time made by the agency. Yukari explained, even without being asked, that now she was married the magazines for young people wouldn't be able to use her. I began in fact to wonder whether she hadn't always had just as many "rest days" in the past, but was hardly concerned about it. Obviously it would be stupid for any husband, no matter how efficient and reliable a maid he might have, to hope his wife would be out all day and express dissatisfaction because she wasn't.

But Yukari was still pretty busy. There was all the fiddling business of the season, the end-of-year gifts and the New Year cards to be sent (I gave her the names and addresses); and although we weren't in any position to make major alterations to the house, there was quite a lot of rearrangement to be done inside with furniture and decorations and so on. This took the form of Yukari consulting with Tsuru, and then I would agree to most things when they were already a *fait accompli*. The result was only different curtains and new chair covers in the guest room, but the house now had a completely different air, a place in which a young bride was living. The antique clock, however, remained in position in the hallway despite my proposal that it should be got rid of, since Yukari took a strange liking to it, although she had the two unmoving hands removed because she insisted it looked smarter and more fashionable that way. The poster of the *yakuza* lady on the kitchen wall was taken down by Tsuru and apparently used to ornament her own room.

I had already sent my former wife's furniture and other belongings back to her home as her parents had suggested I should. Yukari herself brought very little furniture with her, just a dressing table, a wardrobe, a chest of drawers, and one or two other bits and pieces. I didn't have her bed brought over, partly in order to spare the expense of removal, and also because it wouldn't match mine, deciding instead to use my dead wife's which was the other half of the twin set. The rest of the things above the tatami shop were simply disposed of. The bedcovers and so on were all replaced after consultation with Tsuru. Yukari brought almost none of the various electrical appliances she possessed either. Tsuru found this very strange and asked her why, to which she replied that it wouldn't be right to use anything that wasn't made by my company. This response aroused Tsuru's admiration since she assumed it must indicate great depths of loyalty on my part toward my employers. I was fairly deficient in that quality, and the whole thing only made me laugh.

Consequently my new life was not all that startlingly new, and I found this itself a source of satisfaction. A middle-aged man appreciates novelty only in the context of some quiet continuity, and I felt both had been conveniently imposed on me in the form of Tsuru, representing continuity, and Yukari as the freshness of the new. I considered things were going very well for me, and one day in the middle of December when I was entertaining a young section chief from MITI— not, on this occasion, to ask anything of him but simply to play mah jong—he said:

"How's life then? Glad you remarried, I suppose?"

Although I replied that I wished I'd done it ages ago and meant my reply to be a casual joke, it wasn't in the least untrue. The various disasters I'd foreseen had certainly not taken place; indeed I would occasionally reflect how wrong I'd been on that score.

It was ironical, therefore, that when I returned home that very evening I should have tasted my first experience of disappointment and displeasure with Yukari. Tsuru came out to welcome me home, and then Yukari came down the stairs saying she'd suddenly been asked to do some modeling tomorrow for a March number and so she'd decided to go to bed early. Despite this resolve she seemed to be staying up an awfully long time, so eventually I glanced into the bedroom and saw she was pruning her new false eyelashes, snipping off every other individual lash (or each one in three) with a small pair of scissors. She said if she used them just as they were it would make her look like a black-eyed badger. I concurred with this remark, sitting down on the bed as I did so, and was then disconcerted to notice that the scissors she was using were, in fact, mine, the tiny pair I used for trimming the hairs inside my nostrils. I took Yukari to task for this, but she was quite unmoved, maintaining they were just right and she was sure I didn't mind, and if I did I oughtn't to, concentrating entirely on her careful snipping of the false eyelashes.

This was the very first time I'd ever compared Yukari with my former wife and found her wanting. She would never have done anything like this (not surprisingly since she'd never used false eyelashes, or even eye shadow for that matter) and if she'd been told off she would have stopped immediately. I said nothing more, but simply swallowed my annoyance. From the object which Yukari held in her left hand, like a tiny, delicate, and flexibly rounded comb, the black lashes fell one by one, dropping softly onto her vermilion skirt. I stood up and returned to my study next door.

By any standards this could only be seen as the mildest of contretemps, but since it was the sole unpleasant experience of those early days of my marriage it has remained fresh in my memory. Those early days were truly very early and soon over, for five days after the scissors incident Yukari's grandmother suddenly appeared on the scene, and that was the end of our brief period of quiet happiness.

On that day I was due to return early from the office, and Yukari was going to cook (under Tsuru's supervision, of course) a tempura dinner for the first time in her life. In fact somehow or other I didn't manage to get away until late, and I also got caught in a traffic jam, so when I finally rang the front doorbell it must have been almost seven o'clock. Tsuru came to let me in, but she looked different from usual, nervous and anxious about something and not smiling as she usually did.

"What's up, Tsuru? Something gone wrong with the tempura?" I asked, but received only a vague, evasive reply.

It was then I became aware of a peculiar stillness and silence in the house. I couldn't hear the sound of the television, and there was no trace at all of the distinctive smell of tempura frying. It was very much like the atmosphere of a house where it has been accepted, for some reason or other, that dinner is not going to be cooked that night.

I found myself feeling hungry and looked automatically at the hall clock, but since it didn't even have hands on its face now, the gesture served no purpose. I glanced down at my wristwatch and asked Tsuru what had happened, but all she could say was that Yukari had come home about an hour ago and immediately gone upstairs and shut herself in her room. She hadn't come down since, and when Tsuru had called out to her she'd expressed nothing but apparent irritation. She had no idea what could possibly have caused this, although something must have happened to be sure. I told her to hurry up and get some food ready, and meanwhile I went upstairs and opened the bedroom door.

At first I couldn't see Yukari anywhere, because there was only a dim light from the bedside lamps and Yukari was crouched down in the dark space between the twin beds. Even though the door had been opened she made not the slightest movement.

"What's wrong, Yukari?" I asked, and finally she turned her face in my direction and, after a long interval, stood up. As she did so something slipped off her lap onto the floor, crumbling onto the carpet like snow, or ashes.

"Look. Like a poncho," Yukari said in a strangely shrill voice.

"A poncho?" As I echoed her words I pressed the switch by the door and the ceiling light came on. Yukari looked dazzled by it. Certainly what she had on was similar to a South American cloak, for she'd taken her pink bedcover (which made a pair with my light blue one) and cut a large, crude circle out of the middle of it, and it was this she'd whimsically placed over her head. The central portion of the bedcover had originally consisted of a symmetrical embroidery of flowers in lilac, green, and white thread, and now the torn blossoms and leaves and stems formed a ragged, playful border about Yukari's slender neck. A pair of heavy scissors with jagged blades produced a silver shining at her feet where they'd been thrown. The circular piece of the bedcover that had been cut out and fallen onto the carpet had then, it seemed, been chopped into tiny fragments by the same scissors. Amid these cuttings her false eyelashes had fallen like two small combs, but these had been left unscathed.

"Have you had enough of being a wife then? Do you want to go back to your apartment above the tatami shop?" coldly asked the middle-aged husband.

The young wife replied with the same expressionless face:

"That's right. I've had enough. I've just about had enough of everything."

This was delivered in a voice that was quiet at first, but ended in something like a scream.

"Stop shouting like that. Tsuru will hear you," I warned her, and then sat down on the bed with the pale blue cover, picking up the scissors and putting them out of reach. Yukari crouched down again, wrapping her arms around her knees. I looked down at the line of her shoulders and asked her:

"Don't you get on well with Tsuru?"

Yukari shook her head, so that wasn't it.

"Something unpleasant happened at work?"

"Uh-uh." It wasn't that.

"Then what has happened?"

No reply.

"If it's something I've done, then. . ." But I didn't complete the sentence, instead jogging her back with my left knee. "If you just keep quiet all the time how can I be expected to understand?"

"Switch off the light, please," she said quietly.

"Okay."

I went to the door and flicked the switch off, and as the light changed into darkness I was prepared to hear some confession about another man. Perhaps it was because I was much older than her, but the fact is I'd never been very confident about my wife's faithfulness, feeling right from the start that some young man was bound to appear on the scene sometime. She was in a rather special profession, and I had made her my "mistress" first, and there was also that comment of Tsuru's about making an honest woman of her, so I had the illusion at times of a crowd of fantasy figures, all men, standing there behind Yukari. Obviously this was something that bothered me, but I'd always been careful not to torment myself with such imaginings.

I went back and sat on the bed again, and Yukari started to say something but then fell silent, and finally began an account of how she'd asked a jeweler's to set my Australian opal in a ring, but the woman doing it was really fussy about getting it right and it still wasn't done yet.

"Hardly matters all that much, does it?"

"Well, you know what that kind of woman's like, all obstinate and round, and tough as an old boot. She says she was slim enough when she was young, but now that she's all fat her husband says the marriage was a swindle."

103

I smiled dutifully at this apparent attempt to be cheerful, but I was still waiting for her to get on to the subject of the other man.

"Still, she says it'll definitely be ready next week."

"Good. Next week. That's fine, then. That stone certainly cost enough. A man from the embassy took me to a place. But you don't want to worry too much if it's ready next week or not."

There was a short pause after that, then Yukari said:

"You won't be angry, will you? You won't be angry? I'll be really miserable if you are. I was so amazed, I could hardly believe it."

"I won't be angry. Just tell me what happened."

"We'd better not have any children."

"Well, we won't for the time being. We've already discussed that."

"Not just for the time being. Never. Absolutely never. Things get inherited, you see."

These remarks had been made in a comparatively melancholy tone, but she then brightened up and spoke quite normally as if referring to the weather:

"You know, my grandmother's a murderess."

In situations of this kind people tend to respond in a stereotyped way, as I did.

"That's a stupid lie," I shouted, although I should point out that at the time I didn't think Yukari was lying. Of course I didn't feel convinced she was confessing the truth either. I suppose I was just too astounded at first for reflections of that kind.

Yukari replied in a perfunctory way that she'd thought so too at first, and I could clearly sense the desperation in her voice. I knew it was the truth and that I must have the courage to accept all she was going to tell me as true also. Even so, I repeated my accusation that it was a lie, of course it was a lie, with a gradually weakening sense of regret that it actually wasn't one.

"It's not a lie," said Yukari as if she were assuring herself of the fact; she then leaned her back against her own bed, thereby facing in my direction in the dim light, and gave me a long, disordered, and halting account of what had taken place. This is the gist of what she said.

Early that afternoon Yukari had gone to a department store with Tsuru. She'd then left Tsuru in the food section and gone to a different department store about her ring. After that she went to the hairdresser, and then decided she would take a taxi and pay her parents a visit since she hadn't seen them for some time.

There, however, she encountered a woman who seemed to be fairly old, but of strangely youthful appearance. On ringing the doorbell she heard what she assumed was her mother's voice coming from inside. Since the voice had inquired in not very refined language whether it was Father or Kyoko it was strange she'd thought this was her mother, since the latter always referred to Yukari's father as "Papa" and not "Father," and spoke in a very proper middle-class Tokyo accent. Even more obviously, Kyoko was Yukari's mother's name, and she could hardly have been inquiring if the person at the door was herself. Still, Yukari didn't suspect it might be someone else but simply announced her own name in a voice almost as loud as the one within. That voice then bellowed back that the door was unlocked.

At this point Yukari had her first suspicion, finding it strange that her mother hadn't locked the door, since she usually made a great point of doing so. There was also a feeling somewhere at the back of her mind that her mother had called out her name in a slightly vulgar and abnormal way. However, she opened the door and went in, to find, sprawled on two cushions watching some TV drama, this woman she'd never seen before. She was wearing an Oshima kimono with a matching *haori* jacket over it; a pearl ring glittered on the third finger of her right hand; and her sash (expensive-looking, like her kimono, but striped, probably Shoso-in) was loosened, as if she were lounging about in her own living room.

When Yukari entered the room the old woman stood up lightly. She had her hair, in which there were threads of white here and there, swept back into a bun and held together by a small tortoiseshell comb; yet, despite the old-fashioned nature of her hairstyle and general appearance, her complexion was healthy and comparatively youthful. Yukari did, in fact, get the feeling at that moment she had seen her before, but she'd no idea where.

The old woman offered her one of the cushions to sit on, and said:
"Well, you've certainly grown, Yukari. Turned into a real good-looker, too. And I hear you've got hold of a pretty grand husband for yourself as well, haven't you?"

This was spoken in a very friendly voice, and Yukari was sufficiently caught up in the spirit of it to sit down promptly without any of the usual polite formalities.

"Kyoko's just popped out to the shops for a minute. Young Shin went off skiing three days back."

After this reference to Yukari's younger brother, Shin'ichi, she went on:

"Don't you recognize me, then? I'm Granny. I'm just back from prison."

She maintained the same friendly, cheerful tone of voice, and Yukari didn't actually take in the significance of the word "prison," thinking somehow it referred to a foreign country. She even misinterpreted the word "granny" as the way you might refer to any old lady you knew who wasn't an actual grandmother. So as Yukari sat there trying her hardest to puzzle out who this might be, the only interpretation that occurred to her was she might be some kind of very distant relation. What mainly led her to this conclusion was that she didn't look the sort of person who should be in the living room of a university professor.

Still, Yukari had to say something, and since the old woman had said she'd got back from somewhere, and since she also assumed this distant relation must live at some distance, she decided she must have just come from abroad.

"Did you arrive at Haneda today?"

"Haneda?" echoed the old woman. "Of course not. Didn't come by plane, now, did I? Bound to be Ueno Station, seeing I've come back from the Tochigi Women's Prison, isn't it?"

"Oh, was it Tochigi? I thought you must have been abroad."

Yukari still hadn't caught on, and the old woman threw her right fist into the air, opening the fingers swiftly in a gesture of histrionic despair at human stupidity.

"Oh, for God's sake, Yukari, haven't you been listening to a word I've been saying? I'm your granny, your mum's mum, the one who's been away in the country, in prison, the clink, the pen, and I've finally got out, haven't I?"

At this point Yukari claims to have given a little scream, but isn't clear if she really did or not. Anyway, she was so astonished she certainly felt like screaming, being now convinced of the truth of what she'd heard. She could recall when she was very small how there'd been a grandmother who made just that gesture with her right hand when she felt awkward or confused, and she was quite sure her mother had told her that it was her own mother. Still, at some period, when she was eight or nine, that granny suddenly stopped coming to see them, and when she asked her mother why, the latter had said with a stern expression that she'd gone a long, long way away, and Yukari had understood in the way children do that she mustn't ask about her any more. Although there would have been the odd occasion when something may have reminded her of this vanished grandmother, it could have made little impression since she couldn't recall anything now.

Now here was someone just out of prison sitting in the living room of Yukari's home. As she thought about this it did seem that her face was at least something like the one she thought she could remember, and then that vague impression suddenly became clear and fitted perfectly onto the person before her, and she seemed not to have changed in the least over those ten years and more.

Having made this discovery Yukari became confused, then panic-stricken, by the thought that this was virtually the first time she'd met her grandmother (she had only been a child before) and that she'd have to trot out the polite nothings which etiquette demanded and which she herself disliked so much and felt so incompetent at doing. It was strange that she didn't seem disturbed by the fact that she was face to face with an ex-jailbird.

"What, I am wondering, was the reason why you paid your visit to that place?" she asked with painstaking politeness. This was, indeed, the question she felt most concerned about, and she was given a speedy reply.

"Well, just had to go, didn't I? Didn't have to find reasons. I'd killed somebody and got put away for thirteen years."

"Oh my, that must have seemed an awfully long time."

"Well, it felt long, and it also felt quite short too," the old woman said, and closed her eyes. "Just like Urashima, you know."

This mention of the fairy-tale character, the young fisherman who spends a brief, happy day in the undersea palace of the Dragon King and returns home to find many years have passed and all is changed, seemed to remind her of the treasure chest the hero brought back with him.

"Brought back some dried gourd shavings for Kyoko. Just a little present. You can have some of hers. It's a Tochigi speciality."

"Yes," said Yukari, bowing her head in thanks, and then, with some trepidation, asking: "I suppose it was, er, rather terrifying?"

The old woman seemed a little puzzled by this, but soon replied with a friendly, calm expression on her face:

"Well, you get carried away, you see. Don't really know what you're doing. . . Still, if there'd been a more understanding judge on the bench I reckon I'd have got off a good bit lighter. My defense lawyer was no good either. I was just unlucky, real unlucky. You see, when I picked up the razor. . ."

"Oh, you used a razor?" Yukari gave quite a shriek, and the old woman in the matching Oshima adjusted the comb in her hair lightly and clicked her tongue with impatience, giving a deep sigh.

"So Kyoko's told you nothing, has she? Always was absentminded. That was her trouble. Never used to talk much either, and would shut up like a clam about the funniest things. You know, there was one time, must have been the autumn of the year the war ended, when. . ."

But this tale of Yukari's mother's youth was never to be completed, for at that point the front doorbell rang. As Yukari got up to go and answer it her grandmother bawled out in the same manner as before, whereupon Mrs. Nonomiya came dashing in as if she'd literally run into the house, which she probably had. So this woman in her forties stood at the entrance to the living room with her shopping basket in her hand, and immediately proceeded to introduce the two, glaring at her mother as she did so.

"This is your grandmother. She's been living in Hokkaido for a long time, and is now paying one of her rare visits to Tokyo."

She wasn't allowed to go on any longer in that vein, since Yukari's grandmother made a huge dismissive gesture, waving her right hand in front of her face.

"Oh, don't bother with all that. I've told her everything. Besides, I *am* an ex-jailbird, so why not say I am? I'm a murderess. All right, it's the truth. Say I killed the husband I'd separated from, for that's what happened. You may hide something under a thick layer of lies, but that layer is easily stripped off."

"Mother!" Kyoko said softly, and then knelt down with her shopping basket on her knees. This refusal to put the basket down, holding it absentmindedly not upright but on its side, was presumably the result of shock. Consequently most of the contents tumbled out: spring onions wrapped in a thin sheet of newspaper and tied with a rubber band, some tofu in a transparent container, a wrapped-up packet of sliced meat, three or four large mushrooms (these were unwrapped), and some devil's-tongue noodles also in a transparent container. One of the mushrooms rolled over the floor and knocked softly against Yukari's foot.

"Ah, having sukiyaki for dinner, are we?" Yukari's grandmother said, and picked up one of the mushrooms. "Kyoko, you'd be better off doing it in red wine," she advised her, and then turned to Yukari. "We used to have a birthday party once a month; the people whose birthday was that month and all the 'grade ones' could go to it. It was with the staff as well, you see. Held it in the gym. Wanted to be sure it would all be fair and square so we used to draw lots to see who'd sit at which table. I don't know why, but I always seemed to sit at the warden's table."

"Mother!" said Kyoko with a sort of groan.

"What's up now? It's a true story, isn't it? Anyway, the warden was a man round about fifty and not at all bad-looking, so the others got pretty jealous, I can tell you."

"You had sukiyaki at these birthday parties?"

Her simple question had cost Yukari an enormous effort to ask. This talk about eating sukiyaki sitting on the bare boards of the gym had made her, at long last, suddenly aware of the fact that her grandmother genuinely was a murderess. Up to that point it had all seemed as if it might still be some appalling joke or a dream in extremely bad taste.

Grandmother continued with this tale of the prison sukiyaki party in the cheerful tones of a small boy just back from summer camp recounting his experiences. Of course this could just have been that the old woman was doing her best to make it all seem not too awful and depressing. Meanwhile Yukari's mother said nothing, very, very slowly collecting the objects that had fallen on the tatami and putting them back in the basket. While Yukari was handing her the spring onions, her grandmother said:

"Once I was really disgusted, though. Maybe it was because they didn't have proper spring onions, but, anyway, they used ordinary ones, the big, round kind. Someone said it was foreign-style sukiyaki, just like what you get in Japanese restaurants in France or somewhere. Oh yes, that reminds me, there was this girl who used to start fires. I mean that's what she was in for, arson. Well, usually that sort of person is a bit funny in the head and ugly to go with it, but she was really well up on all sorts of things and nice-looking, too, lovely white skin just like Yukari. . ."

This aroused further perturbations in Yukari's mother, it seems, for she swiftly gathered up the devil's-tongue noodles, put her shopping basket briskly to one side, and suggested in a very calm, gentle voice that she was sure they all had a great deal to talk about, but it would be very exhausting to do so all in one session, and she was sure she must be tired so wouldn't she rather go upstairs and have a little lie-down? Grandmother's response to this plan was a totally unconcealed, indeed pronounced, grimace.

"Are you saying I mustn't talk to Yukari? Kyoko, I may be a woman who has killed her own husband, but does that mean I'm not to speak to my own granddaughter?"

This protest was followed by others, such as that it had been nasty of her to keep the whole thing a complete secret from Yukari, and it had been very degrading not being allowed to send letters direct from the prison but always to some other address. And then what about the kimono she'd brought for her to wear when she left prison? Admittedly it was of very good quality, and she wasn't complaining about that, but it stank of mothballs; all of which only went to show how cold and unfeeling her daughter was. This harsh criticism was accompanied at first by what seemed to be a light smile about her lips, but at some point it had become bitterly serious for finally she cried out:

"Look, I'll tell you this. I haven't had a new kimono for over ten years," after which she began weeping openly. This made Yukari's mother, as if determined not to be left behind, burst into tears as well and rush off into the kitchen. The television had remained on during all this, and the program had now changed to one about musical children, a great number of whom were taking turns to play the violin in an equally execrable manner. Yukari felt she was observing some painful, oppressive, terrible dream.

"Please, Granny, don't cry. Please," she managed to say, trying to comfort her, but then the whole thing became unbearable and she left the house without another word to either of them and caught a taxi home.

"Yes, all right," I said. "But I still don't see why you should have got so upset."

I was playing for time by feigning ignorance, since I knew perfectly well this could be absolutely disastrous for all of us. But although I was aghast at what I'd heard, I still had no clear picture of what form the disaster might take; and so, as was my habit when in conference, I attempted to gain knowledge of the main substance by the astute asking of pertinent questions. The darkness provided by the inadequate lighting created an excellent cover for this scheme, making my questions seem innocent of any ulterior motive.

"Can't see what I'm so upset about?" she said feebly, but then with a sudden burst of energy added: "Look. I'm the granddaughter of a murderess. I'm her real granddaughter."

"Well?..."

"I'm of the same blood as her."

"Yes. That's right."

"The mother of my mother was convicted of murder. She killed somebody. With a razor."

"Well, yes. That's how it was."

"Then it's something to be upset about, isn't it? It's going to make everything very difficult."

"I don't think so," I promptly replied.

"You don't think so?"

"I don't. After all, I didn't marry your grandmother."

On hearing this Yukari gave a surprisingly cheerful laugh, but it was only short and ended nervously. I went on:

"For a start, she doesn't sound exactly my type."

This time Yukari really howled with laughter:

111

"Oh don't. Please don't make me laugh like that. Please. It really hurts."

It is gratifying for a middle-aged husband to see his young wife's hysteria brought to an end.

"Let's have some light on the subject," I said, and switched on the ceiling light. Then I promptly removed the bedcover with the crude circle in its center from about my wife. As I cast the pink cloth onto the red carpet I asked her if she was cold, and she stared up at me with a look of unwavering, steadfast, fawning affection. I turned on the oil stove and sat down beside her.

"Still," she said, hesitantly and anxiously.

"Still what?" I asked. "Go on."

"I didn't know anything about it. Honestly, I really didn't."

"I'm sure you didn't. I believe you. That's how it seems to me."

"I really didn't."

"I know."

I realized this was the first time in her life she'd experienced genuine anxiety about what might lie in store for her, something unknown and yet related to her existence in a fantastic, unspeakable way, as if she'd suddenly felt that one step ahead of her darkness lay in wait, or that hell gaped open just under the thin floorboards on which she was treading. But I said nothing of this.

"I really didn't," she insisted again, and then, in a casual voice as if talking to herself, she touched on the heart of the matter. "But Mother must have known. So did Father."

"They could hardly have not known," I said, in as lighthearted a way as possible. "That's obvious."

"Is it?"

"Certainly it is. They knew she'd be released before the year was out and that's why they were in such a rush about things."

"Marriage?"

"Yes."

"In that case you've been swindled, haven't you?" she said, very forcefully, almost as if she were accusing me of something. But then she spoke feebly again: "That's really awful."

I confess I shared her opinion, and I felt that Professor Nonomiya's behavior had been unpardonable, but the important thing at the moment was to console Yukari and keep her calm.

"Still, what does it matter? The result would have been the same, anyway. In fact I've done well out of it, marrying my lovely bride earlier than I might have done."

This generous remark of mine was accompanied by a suspicion in one part of my mind that I'd put the problem on a very simple, naive level, and I felt embarrassed by my own words, no doubt conscious of the significant degree of untruth in them. Yukari, however, showed no embarrassment. I suppose she was in no position to enjoy the luxury of such feelings. Instead, as she picked up the scraps of cloth from the carpet, she said slowly:

"I just felt in a sort of daze. I didn't have any idea what I was doing. Don't they call this sort of thing fraudulent marriage? It's criminal, isn't it?"

"That's a slight exaggeration. It's not what you'd call an actual crime. Of course, it is connected with a real crime," I said, and smiled. "I never thought of investigating your mother's side. No doubt you didn't think of finding out about it either."

"Not really." Yukari seemed on the verge of tears. She then crawled about on the carpet and retrieved something from under the bed. It was the large koala bear, and I had her sit on my knee holding it.

"I was so miserable and depressed I just threw it away," she explained. "There, there, did it hurt?" she said, addressing the brown beast as she stroked it. "I thought about cutting it up with the scissors, but it would have been such a waste so I didn't."

"My goodness."

"Ooh, I'm sorry. Did it hurt you then? Did it hurt?"

I'd felt a definite frisson of terror at these words, thinking a granddaughter who'd contemplated cutting up her cuddly toy with a pair of scissors did seem to have blood in common with a grandmother who had cut her husband about with a razor. I didn't voice these sentiments, naturally enough. I'd been twice to Tochigi as our company factory was there, but I'd heard nothing about a women's prison. Still, I had acquired the famous local product, dried gourd shavings, as a present and brought some back with me and believed we still had some of it left. I didn't mention that, either. And still the killer's grand-daughter, unaware of my shudder of fear (or perhaps only too aware of it?), sat on my knee and went on stroking her inanimate beast, speaking sweet nothings to it all the while.

"Do you forgive me?" she asked (me, not the bear), and in reply I slipped my hand under her skirt.

"I told you I didn't care, didn't I? Although I must admit I don't think I want to spend too much time in the company of that resolute lady. By the way, what's your grandmother's name?"

"Her name? Do stop that, it tickles. Well it's . . . oh, I don't know. Her surname is Nabeshima. We used to call her Granny Nabeshima."

"Ah."

"Honestly I didn't know. I really didn't."

"I know that."

I was thinking I could easily check up on the name through the family register, when Tsuru announced from halfway up the stairs that dinner was ready. I ordered Yukari not to mention one word of this, on any account, to Tsuru.

"Anyway, better wash your face. Although you don't seem to have been crying."

Since Tsuru was waiting on us we could hardly talk about the grandmother, so we talked about the food instead. The tempura tasted fine, perhaps because I was so hungry, and I had two bowls of rice with it. Yukari had three, but then her rice bowl was smaller than mine. As I drank my tea and watched her eating her third helping of rice, I congratulated myself on having suffered the misfortune of marrying the granddaughter of a murderess. It seemed at that moment the one piece of good fortune I'd encountered amid all the bad luck that had followed my leaving government service.

7

That evening I felt perfectly satisfied with my performance in calming Yukari's hysteria, and that was the only aspect of the situation I really thought about; but next morning I finally became nervously aware how very serious the whole business was. My wife's grandmother was a murderess. My wife was the granddaughter of a killer. On top of that, it was not some distant event which had taken place in the previous century, but only a dozen or so years ago when Yukari herself wasn't all that small. Her grandmother had slashed her husband (from whom she was separated) to death with a razor. This was something contemporary, not yet absorbed into history, and it felt horribly real and present as if I myself had been splattered by the great spurts of blood that flew about. I was convinced nothing worse could have happened to me. Indeed, I would have felt much happier if I'd married a descendant of one of those famous Jezebels of the early modern era, such as "Night Storm" Okinu or Oden Takahashi, since at least I should have felt at a proper remove from their sensational acts. In fact I regretted I'd not been afflicted with something of that kind instead, for it would only have meant a murderess's great-great-granddaughter in the family, and they'd also done their carving about when they were decently young.

Such were my reflections as I stood in my dressing gown and washed my face, cleaned my teeth, and started to shave. The dressing gown I was wearing wasn't the stolid British style my former wife had bought for me, but one Yukari had chosen in some extreme attempt to make me look youthful, and even my safety razor was different now, the latest and handiest model, which Yukari had urged on me when we'd been out shopping together. Whether it was because I was grimacing, lost deep in thought, I don't know, but I managed to cut myself on the chin and a thin trickle of blood flowed from the wound. This made me grimace all the more, and I wet my finger with saliva and dabbed it on the cut, but the bleeding didn't stop. I tore a square inch or so off the paper kept in the toilet and stuck it over the wound; and as I watched the bloodstain immediately well through the middle of the paper, I encouraged myself with the thought that, whatever I was suffering, it was nothing like what her grandmother's husband must have gone through. This simple thought was then replaced by a more complex one, namely that Yukari's mother was the child born of the union of the killer *and* the killed. I found this bewildering, probably, I think, because I found I'd been, as it were, cut in half, one part of me pertaining to the murdered and the other to the murderer.

Normally I only have one cup of tea for breakfast, but today I had another, straight, without milk or sugar. I glanced over the political headlines, and while I was reading the economic news a little more scrupulously (in the time it normally takes to drink one cup of tea) I began to wonder about that prison sentence. Surely a good dozen years for that sort of murder was much too long? A normal murder usually only led to a ten-year sentence (perhaps fifteen years for special cases), and since nowadays the prisons were desperately overcrowded, people were continually being given early release. There was something funny about being in for more than ten years. I closed my eyes and brooded on the subject. It must have been a special kind of murder, one of horrendous savagery no doubt, but since I'd no idea what had actually happened, all I could do was experience a form of fear and trembling and a desire to use the toilet.

As I sat quite still in the small white room I rebuked myself for failing to investigate the mother's side of the family. This was a massive error on my part, something for which there was no excuse whatsoever; but since I hadn't even thought about Yukari's mother's parents, there wasn't really anything practical that I'd overlooked. Come to think of it, I knew nothing at all about the professor's father either; and no doubt I hadn't felt the need to make such inquiries since I'd assumed Yukari's family must be all right precisely because he was a university professor. Anyway, even if I had looked at her grandmother's family register it wouldn't have had "Criminal Offenses: One (murder)" recorded on it, and if I had employed a private detective agency to investigate I very much doubt if they'd have done it competently enough to discover anything. Even if the remarkable had happened and the private eye had been conscientious and capable and cleverly sniffed out the whole business, would I really have given up the idea of marriage? I suppose I might have felt I just couldn't avoid doing so, but one can always argue this way or that, and I'm fairly certain I could just as easily have ended up deciding to marry her as not. It was all six of one and half a dozen of the other and, anyway, it was done now and what mattered was to think of appropriate countermeasures. So in this positive frame of mind I pulled out an extra length of toilet paper.

It seemed clear that the first thing to do was get detailed, preferably definitive, information concerning the murder itself. I assumed Yukari's parents wouldn't be all that helpful over this but try instead to cloak the whole thing in ambiguity, providing me only with such information as would inform me about nothing. I'd have to investigate this from a quite different angle, I thought, and I imagine that somewhere behind my decision lay a desire of some sort to avoid any immediate meeting with Professor Nonomiya. Ever since he'd urged the idea of marriage to his daughter with such skill and forcefulness, I'd become apprehensive of his peculiar form of logic, being uncomfortably aware that if I responded to him again in the same incompetent manner something really terrible might happen.

Of course, since I had been, if not deliberately deceived over the matter of Granny Nabeshima, at least passively deprived of the truth, I certainly felt like indulging in a few mildly cynical statements in his presence and at his expense. I'd already thought a number of times it would cheer me up considerably to do so. However, unless I was very careful about it, I might find the whole thing rebounding on my own head, and as I dabbed myself carefully with the paper I decided it would be wiser to leave my little revenge until some later date, or even not bother with it at all.

The next important aspect of the case was that it must be kept quite secret from the outside world. Last night I'd told Yukari with powerful emphasis that she must speak to nobody about this and not breathe a word to Tsuru, and my young wife had nodded away for dear life like a little schoolgirl determined to find favor with her teacher. It was quite impossible I would let slip any word on the subject (although obviously I'd have to be very careful while making my investigations), and my parents-in-law would presumably keep their mouths shut, as they had done so far. The person who worried me was the culprit herself,

Granny Nabeshima, who might well talk and, gathering from what Yukari had said, the danger of her so doing seemed considerable. If the secret did get out, then, it being a small world, the rumor would circulate until eventually it might come to the notice of people at work. In fact there was no "might" about it. It was bound to happen.

I was thinking I'd better make Yukari contact her parents right away to tell that granny to hold her tongue, when suddenly I was struck by an amazing insight. Here was something that had happened only a dozen or so years ago, and among Professor Nonomiya's university colleagues there must be those who had attended his marriage and would certainly know his wife's maiden name. They would have worked out what had happened as soon as they saw the newspaper report, and obviously they'd have talked about it to others. . . Why, the whole thing must be public knowledge at his university, but it was being kept as a joint secret there!

On further consideration this seemed more and more likely. When I'd first met him the professor had spoken in a very dejected way about the pressure imposed by those symbols of the outside world, the senate and faculty meetings, and I'd mistakenly assumed he was talking about something connected with his daughter's being a fashion model; yet surely what he was giving vent to was his doleful recollections of the bitterness he'd had to suffer because his mother-in-law had committed murder. By extension, therefore, wouldn't people who knew about this now be considering me some benighted wretch who'd had the misfortune to marry the daughter of this unhappy man? In fact, one of the trustees of the university plus a professor and a professor emeritus had been present at our wedding reception, sitting together at the side of the main guest table to my immediate right, drinking away and constantly praising Yukari's beauty in very loud voices (maybe because they were all three hard of hearing); but inside weren't they perhaps feeling sorry for me, even laughing at me, for being such a softheaded fool?

This thought produced a cold shudder, running right through me while I still dabbed away at the cut, reducing me to a state of frozen immobility for a moment; but I took up the dabbing again, tearing off more strips of paper, and arrived at the conclusion that it was impossible to be too careful over this question of protecting the secret. So I flushed the toilet and then found myself breathing a deep sigh, a sound that echoed sadly about the small white room, as if this essential melancholy was the only true conclusion I would ever reach.

My chin seemed to have stopped bleeding, so I removed the last piece of paper and returned to the living room, where Yukari was sitting in front of the gas fire with a bright red dressing gown draped across her shoulders, reading the other newspaper (the one that wasn't about economics). She always got up somewhat later than me, and after she'd seen me off would go back to bed again. Apparently this second session was particularly good, no doubt because she was still young. She raised her pale face and smiled. Her lips, without their makeup, were a leaden color, but they wished me a cheerful good morning. I wished her the same and asked if she'd slept well. She said she had, but was still sleepy.

I hung about for a while enjoying the pleasant warmth of the gas fire when normally I would have been on my way. One reason was that I was feeling so highly strung this morning I thought it would be wiser not to take the car, for if I did I might do something awful. Another was that the traffic was always so bad nowadays it was quicker to go by train, and whenever I made this decision I found I still had a certain amount of time to spare. I smoked a cigarette, and while I was doing so Tsuru came in with some hot milk for Yukari which she placed beside her. Yukari gratefully acknowledged this by drawing Tsuru's attention to one of the stories in the paper.

"Tsuru, isn't this awful?" she said.

"What is, madam?"

"A whole household murdered. Twenty-two-year-old man murders family of three and the cat as well."

"What? The cat too?" Our maid frowned. "The poor thing. Surely he didn't have to kill the cat as well?"

"Well, must be mad, I suppose," Yukari said.

"He certainly must be. A lunatic undoubtedly." Tsuru thus gave her own irresponsible confirmation of Yukari's analysis.

As I listened to this normal, humdrum breakfast conversation, typical of a normal, humdrum household, I was too struck by one aspect of it to notice the oddity of feeling sorry for the cat but not for the people. What I'd found more remarkable was that, despite what had occurred yesterday, Yukari had apparently so completely forgotten her grandmother's crime as to be able to chatter away cheerfully about this newspaper item. I was astonished at the speed with which she could forget such things.

Yukari tried a sip of the milk, holding the cup with the little finger of her right hand angled nicely upward, and said in an even more rollicking voice:

"What a really awful thing to do, I must say. Shooting a cat with a pistol, well honestly. . ."

"Dreadful," said Tsuru, chiming in with sad solemnity and an expression of deep pain on her face.

As Tsuru stood up to leave the room I felt a slight irritation in my throat and coughed lightly to clear it. I then stubbed out my cigarette in the ashtray.

"Well," I said. This was merely an indication I was about to go upstairs to change, but Yukari suddenly made a very odd face and gave a little cry as if she'd been reminded of something. Tsuru, who was just about to enter the kitchen, looked back and asked if there was anything wrong, but Yukari hastily assured her there was not, nothing at all.

I myself was ascending the stairs at a much more leisurely pace than usual. This was because I was absorbed in the discovery I'd just made about my real motives for wanting to conceal the fact that my wife's grandmother was a murderess. I had realized I was doing so for the greater happiness of society, my reasons being as follows. First there was my social rank and status to be considered. Personally I would find it slightly ludicrous to describe myself as a member of the elite, although it wouldn't be in the least strange if someone else described me in such terms. Anyway, with somebody in my social position, should it be discovered some loathsome criminal were a close relative of that respectable person, considerable surprise, even shock, would be experienced by all. Now, I realize this could be to the benefit of certain people, gratifying personal feelings of animosity toward me. Even so, its overall effect on what we wish to be a cheerful, happy, healthy world would be to create an atmosphere of unease and unpleasantness. At least it would be an additional impetus to incline society in that undesirable direction. By this I mean it would undermine our trust in society; the shock would leave a reverberation of doubt in people's hearts and minds.

Should repeated shocks of this kind occur, people might easily come to suspect, say, a company president (or even a permanent undersecretary) of having a grandfather who was a master thief, or his (or the other's) father of being a child rapist, or even the company president himself (or the permanent undersecretary) of being a pyromaniac of perverse inclination, perhaps of hidden cannibalistic tendencies. Once doubt had been sown, any belief could spring up, with the result that it would be hard to spend one's days in an agreeably calm state of mind. Productivity would fall off, with a consequent derangement of social order. Clearly if one's first reaction to someone was to think of him as a possible criminal, or the possible relation of a criminal, then one of the basic conditions for mutual trust in civil society would not be met. The wheels of society would cease to function, fall into disuse, decay and finally crumble away. Consequently my attempt to protect the secret of Granny Nabeshima was an effort to stave off impending social confusion, and most certainly did not arise from any merely personal and egotistic desires or motives... Well, I suppose there may have been an element of that, but only an extremely small amount, which one needn't take into consideration at the moment.

That was about the point I'd reached when I entered the bedroom. I put on my shirt, and was just pulling on my trousers when Yukari came in and glared at me.

"What was all that about, that 'little cough' of yours?" she said in an unpleasant, harsh voice she was trying unsuccessfully to control.

I didn't like the sound of that at all. In fact I liked it so little I began to think Oguri's derogatory opinion of her voice had been justified. Still, I restrained myself and said:

"My little cough?"

"Yes, your little cough. Go on like that and Tsuru will soon notice."

"Of course she won't. She may be reliable and all that, but she's hardly very observant. Don't worry, it's all right. No need to bother about her."

After this casual denial (I couldn't be bothered to point out I'd made my little cough because I had a frog in my throat) I did up my shirt buttons and put on my cuff links. Yukari then casually handed me a tie which, from my point of view, couldn't possibly go with the suit I had on.

"Wouldn't surprise me if she's noticed something already. I mean, I was hysterical yesterday, wasn't I? She'll put two and two together. . . Still, it'll probably be all right. . ." She said this in a gloomy voice, as if she'd been trying to think something out and hadn't managed it. "I don't know, perhaps it might be better to get in first and tell her everything?"

"No, that's no good. I said that's no good. You might think it's an interesting combination, but it's a bit too fancy for me. I'm not an actor, you know. Give me the one with the stripes."

"Oh but that's so dull, so boring. . ."

"There's no need to 'get in first.' None at all. If the worst comes to the worst I'll tell Tsuru myself. What did you have to start talking about that newspaper story for anyway? Be a bit more careful, can't you? Try to consider my position a little."

This rebuke made Yukari sulk and pout, and the thought did cross my mind that a genuinely beautiful girl would have still looked attractive even like that.

Yukari held up my jacket for me in a slightly brutal manner and said:

"Well, I didn't mean to, did I? It just happened. That sort of thing's bound to, isn't it? The whole thing's like a bad dream anyway, so it's not surprising I forget sometimes, is it?"

That was her explanation, and it was certainly true most dreams tend to be forgotten quickly enough and leave no trace; and as I stood there with my back to her and slid my arms into the sleeves of my jacket, I gave a silent nod of acceptance. Unfortunately, however, this was no dream but fact, and I wondered how long I was going to be hagridden by this nightmarish reality, frowning at the thought since fortunately Yukari couldn't see my face. As I did so I had the feeling that the business was beginning to obsess me, that an urgent desire to wade in and solve the problem was surging up in me, a feeling of individual responsibility and steadfast purpose, a belief that the matter must be put right, must be properly straightened out and neatly tidied away; which was probably one aspect, the major one no doubt, of that bureaucratic mentality Oguri had talked about. Anyway, I told Yukari to call her parents right away and have them make her grandmother keep her mouth shut; then I went into my study and took the copy of Yukari's family register out of one of the drawers.

Round about lunchtime I telephoned a journalist acquaintance of mine from a phone booth outside the company building. I'd got to know him while working for MITI, and I can remember playing mah jong with him either at some journalists' club or his company's place, where we were waited on hand and foot by some nice-looking secretaries who brought us drinks and towels. It had struck me while I was being buffeted in the rush hour train that it would be safer to entrust this business to him rather than to any of the journalists I knew who'd been with me at school.

At the time I'd known him he'd been working on the trade and industrial pages, but he was now transferred to the economics section, and when I rang up he still hadn't arrived at his office. I tried again after lunch, but once more the same young(?) man answered saying, with no attempt at an apology, that he'd just gone out for a moment. I was just asking him if he wouldn't mind telling him to ring me back, when the man in question turned up—whether because he'd just arrived or just been out for a moment, I don't know. After some brief words of salutation I asked him if he could possibly help out a friend of mine who wanted some information about a murder committed twelve years or so ago. I said I couldn't say anything more precise than that, but assured him there was nothing funny about it and he wouldn't be inconvenienced in any way.

"Don't see why not. Okay. Providing we've got the material on it here."

He'd agreed easily enough, so I told him the culprit was one Utako Nabeshima, wondering if that would be enough for him to go on.

"I'll give it a go, anyway," he replied in a practical and very reporter-like way.

Surprisingly, a large envelope with the newspaper's name on it came within less than two hours. I was leading a brainstorming session aimed at selling a new product of ours when a girl from reception arrived with the missive. Since this was the last of these sessions, we had a small celebration afterward with beer and a packaged meal, although I couldn't relax and enjoy it, being desperate to see what was in the envelope. When we eventually broke up I went to a nearby coffee shop and opened it to find that all it contained was photocopies of two short newspaper articles (one of eight lines and the other of ten). Attached to them with a pin was a scrap of paper with a message scrawled in pencil apologizing for the lack of information, saying their files weren't as complete as they should be and it had taken place before the boom in weeklies, so this was all he could find out.

Both articles gave the same information, namely the date and time of the crime, the assailant's name, age (48), address, and employment (unemployed), and the victim's name, age (62), address, and employment (company director); but, apart from that, all they said was that a woman had entered the house of her estranged husband and seriously wounded him with a razor. Assuming he had died the next day I wondered if there were any articles about that, but maybe there hadn't been any, or perhaps they just weren't in the paper's files. There was a photo of Utako Nabeshima with her name in Gothic print beneath it, but because of the Xerox copy it was just a blotchy, oval smudge.

As I held the two bits of paper in my hand I felt an enormous despondency. Nothing at all had been clarified, everything remaining in its former ambiguous state. Still, since I now had the date when the two articles had appeared I could also investigate other newspaper reports of the period. Unfortunately the papers of that time had so few pages I couldn't hope to find much. I suppose it was only natural I should have regretted that, but, as I gradually came to realize, this was in fact the one saving grace of the whole affair. My despondency gave way to a rising sense of well-being. After all, thanks to the small scale of the media at that time, here was this momentous, world-shaking incident (as I saw it) which the world at large had treated as an event worthy of no more attention than it had been given. Once I'd grasped this I felt much easier, pouring contempt on my own naive reflections of the morning about crime and social stability, and assuring myself there had been no need to treat the affair with that degree of seriousness. There had always been crimes and criminals since way back, and yet society tended to be uninterested and forgetful and went on ticking away quite peacefully. The one thing I did have to be grateful about, the silver lining to the black cloud, was that Utako Nabeshima had at least committed her murder before the mass circulation weeklies had really got going; and I *was* grateful.

This calm state of mind didn't last long. I put the sheets of Xerox paper in my breast pocket, and each time I moved I could sense the harsh, threatening rustle they made in the vicinity of my heart, a dry, unfeeling sound which announced unceasingly that there enclosed in my pocket was crime, a criminal existence, and as I walked the streets, busy now with preparations for the New Year holiday, that smudgy, small, oval photo lodged in there took on the appearance of a gaping wound, a pool of blood, or even a corpse lying huddled face down on the floor.

I decided not to show the material to Yukari. I couldn't see any point in showing her something as inconclusive as that, so I put it in the drawer together with the copy of her family register. I had a department store send the journalist a bottle of whisky, and also rang him up again to express my thanks. When I reflected how he had no idea I was married to the granddaughter of Utako Nabeshima I felt just a tiny bit proud of myself for having so skillfully taken my first step in social deception. For some reason it was very much like that pleasurable feeling when one receives too much change from a salesgirl whose face and tone of voice are not to one's liking.

At New Year I'd been in the habit of visiting my in-laws, and would have done the same this year except I was still officially in mourning for my first wife, and so I just sent Yukari by herself to pay her parents a formal call. As an excuse, of course, it was perfectly adequate, but the truth was I had no desire to meet the professor, and although this meant passing the holiday with no decorations and none of the traditional food, I was more than glad to have been spared that encounter. With the passage of time my general ill-disposition toward my father-in-law had grown into a powerful antipathy. There was something truly nasty about the betrayal of faith implicit in his proceeding with his daughter's match while concealing the facts about her grandmother, particularly in that the betrayal itself had been carried out with skill, as witness the cunning manner in which he'd created alibis for himself, such as giving me full permission to investigate everything about him to my heart's content, and only asking me to consider his daughter as just one of the possibilities should I ever think of remarriage, and so on. All this really got on my nerves when I thought about it. Thus, by the New Year holiday period, I'd come to the conclusion that Professor Nonomiya was a typical cowardly intellectual whom I loathed and despised.

Only a very short time had passed, however, before I began to experience a certain fellow feeling toward him, even something like sympathy. On the afternoon of January 3 Yukari had gone alone to her parents' house to deliver her New Year greetings, and I was relaxing at home thinking how much nicer this was than last year when I'd been pestered by a constant influx of guests. I sat in my study reading a book or arranging my newspaper cuttings, wondering if next year I shouldn't tell the people at work I was going away to a hot spring or some other lie so that I might enjoy this untroubled privacy again.

When it got dark I went downstairs and had some herring roe (one thing I really love, which Tsuru had prepared specially for me) and started drinking saké, which I rarely touch, while Tsuru sat nearby watching TV and warming the saké for me, occasionally getting up to go into the kitchen to prepare dinner. It was to this restrained domestic scene that Yukari returned, transforming all about her as an exotic guest will do when visiting a house plunged deep in mourning. She was wearing a large patterned Oshima kimono of a uniform indigo, with a *haori* coat over it of white crepe patterned in red and indigo, and a sash of *yuzen* printed silk, and she was like a winter peony, changing that room into something brilliant, exotic, and gay. Much of this brilliance was no doubt helped by her striking makeup, for she'd drawn her eyebrows thin and rising upward like those of a Chinese girl, and her light eye shadow was the same indigo shade as her kimono.

Yukari told me about her brother's skiing trip, drinking out of my saké cup as she did so, and then giggling as she remembered something and asked:

"Apparently they didn't have pinball before the war?"

"No, there was some. Nothing like it is today, of course."

"Did you ever play?"

"Before the war? Must have done. Anyway, what's all this about?"

"Well, Granny Nabeshima said the only thing that hadn't changed in Tokyo was that pinball was just as popular as it had ever been, and then. . ." Since Tsuru had come in while she was saying this she felt obliged to add a footnote for her sake: "Granny Nabeshima is my mother's mother, you see."

Personally I thought she'd have done better not to tell Tsuru she had a grandmother on her mother's side, and I was particularly wor-

126

ried that it must be pretty clear her granny had been living for some time in an area where there were no pinball parlors (which would have to be a pretty exceptional area in this country), but Yukari went on smiling in a completely unperturbed way, giving us an account of Professor Nonomiya's remarkable theories concerning the game. According to him, the extraordinary postwar boom in pinball was a reflection of the popular notion of why the war had been lost. As the common people saw it, Japan had been defeated by American technology, and although this might be an oversimplified and superficial view of the matter, it could not be maintained that it was basically incorrect. This was a source of great bitterness to the Japanese people, and as a form of psychological compensation all were seized by an irresistible desire to handle machinery of no matter what kind, and so the prewar amusement of pinball or *pachinko* came to serve that function. What began as a kind of spiritual retaliation to ease the humiliation of defeat was later to be transformed and reappear as a passion for playing about with cars and stereos and computers. But such toys cost money and the habit of pinball-pushing was already ingrained, with the result that one could say a deep-rooted bitterness concerning the Pacific War still persisted over a wide area, since the obsession with pinball remained just as before.

"I see," I said, breathing a deep sigh and then chuckling to myself, while Tsuru sat looking puzzled since she hadn't been able to take in the whole argument. "In that case, of course, you could also argue that the pinball passion has been the driving force behind the postwar economic boom. A very Father-like conclusion."

The word "Father" had come off my tongue perfectly naturally, and yet it was a long time since I'd referred to Professor Nonomiya in that way.

Yukari poured me out some saké and said:

"That's him. Technology . . . the machine . . . all his old favorites."

This made her giggle again, and when Tsuru made the perfectly inoffensive remark that it was what one would expect of a university professor, I found it tremendously funny and roared with laughter, thereby swallowing some of the saké the wrong way; and as Yukari stroked and patted me on the back I was feeling in a rather generous mood toward him. I thought of the poor hack, this outcast from reality who only had the wit to dream up these futile, vain, fatheaded, worthless theories, and what he must really have gone through, what absurd, appalling pangs, when he'd found himself in the position of having a wife whose mother had suddenly committed murder and been sent away to prison. And this had been going on for over a decade now, years of long, uninterrupted worry and anxiety. I felt sorry for him. I sympathized with him. I even began to consider him as my benefactor again, somebody I should rather thank for obliging me to take the plunge and marry Yukari, whom I'd been wanting to marry for some time anyway. (I also had the rather sly idea Yukari might become a more dutiful wife now that she had her grandmother's shadow looming in the background.) There was this feeling of intimacy, of oneness, for were we not companions in suffering, he on account of his wife's mother, me on account of my wife's grandmother, comrades in grief and tribulation?

Even so, I still bore a real grudge because of the bad luck of the draw from which I felt I'd suffered, and this had to be directed at somebody; so deep inside I began to feel strongly critical of Yukari's grandmother, as if she'd become a substitute target for my wrath in place of the professor. Judging from what Yukari's mother was like I had to assume Mrs. Nabeshima had been brought up in a decent household, so what possible reason could she have for murdering someone, particularly at that age? If she'd done it when young I might have sympathized a little. No doubt all sorts of things had happened, but no matter what they might have been she ought to have put up with it and tried to control herself, just hung on until she'd calmed down a bit, and then Professor Nonomiya and myself needn't have been inconvenienced in this way. I blamed her for it, and as I gave vent to these complaints inside my head an image of the old lady's unknown face also appeared in there, an image even more blurred than the oval smudge I'd seen.

The truth is she was already causing me a great deal of trouble, for I was growing more gloomily conscious in various ways of the existence of crime, especially of murder, and so my days passed in dismal reflections. I began to feel my marriage had been a mistake, and I regretted it enough to start thinking about divorce, not in any practical terms but just as something I vaguely imagined, although when I was once dreaming about this I suddenly found myself thinking that, after we had separated, there was a pretty even chance I might myself get killed. The picture that came into my mind just then was of the *yakuza* lady in the poster, whose face seemed to have become strikingly like Yukari's.

So when I saw an advertisement for a magazine that had an article entitled "All One Hundred Million of Us Are Criminals" and felt I simply had to read it, it was, of course, a direct result of the state of mind I was in. The article was of such unintelligible obscurity I couldn't work out what it was trying to say, but the title itself had an effect on me, leaving an ominous and lasting impression, making me feel that human actions all tended to have something potentially criminal about them even if they weren't actual crimes. For example, when I now found myself wanting to argue with a taxi driver, which happened often enough, I was aware of the feeling that if I let things go too far it might well end up with one of us murdering the other. This was true of any form of quarrel, and even if the quarrel didn't attain properly murderous proportions you still only needed a bit of bad luck with a casual blow and that could result in murder too. I also recalled the way I'd behaved when I refused the transfer to the Ministry of Defense. When the personnel director had called me before him and urged (in fact told) me to go, my very first impulse—if I may be allowed to exaggerate slightly —had been a desire to take hold of this plump and smiling man and thump him. In practice I responded with a pleasant good humor in no way inferior to his own, but this still probably indicates a sufficient criminal tendency within me. In fact I don't even need to talk about a criminal "tendency," since I have examples of what are more like criminal acts. That picture I received from the Kyushu mine owner could conceivably be seen as a genuine wedding present, and even if one accepts that all those oysters the young man from the steel company deposited at my house early one morning (saying he just happened to have brought them back with him from his house in Hiroshima) were only consumed in various appetizing dishes which kept us going for a week because it would have been a shame to let them go bad, then what about the case of the fertilizer manufacturer? I had handled their documentation in a manner they obviously liked, for there was a phone call from the president's secretary saying I could drop in at the menswear department of a certain store any time and there I'd find a suit made of the very best material all ready and waiting for me. If that wasn't a bribe it was something perilously close to it.

Such thoughts and the psychological burden they brought with them were truly appalling, so it would be fair to say the suffering the murderess Utako Nabeshima had imposed on me was profound, and my mental distress ensured I came genuinely to hate her. The fact that I was quite unable to respond to the humorous account Yukari gave of the admittedly crazy succession of eccentric remarks her grandmother had uttered when she took her to a department store in the middle of January must also be put down to this state of mind.

The final upshot was that I became seriously critical of the behavior of the criminal's former husband and victim. This may have been a result of the various devices I found I'd been able to employ when undergoing an imaginary assault from Yukari of a similar nature, but I really felt his response to an attack by a mere woman had been pathetic. After all, when a woman comes at you waving a sharp instrument about, all you need do is strike her smartly on the wrist and knock the weapon out of her hand, pick it up yourself and threaten her with it, and then gradually calm her down, nice and slowly... I'd spent some time pondering these imaginary actions.

Then, one night in early February, I again found myself reproaching Mrs. Nabeshima's former husband for his ineptitude, demanding why he'd been so hopelessly clumsy, for it was his idleness that had got us all into this mess. Surely he knew that if someone comes at you with a razor held in an underhand grip all you have to do is bring your own hand smartly down . . . when Yukari burst out laughing.

"What do you think you're up to? Having a sword fight or something?"

I realized I had ended up acting out this duel between granny and grandpa, although I could hardly tell Yukari, so I said it was nothing. Yukari was already in bed, having completed all the various things she did to her face, and I'd just got out of the bath and was sitting on the edge of my bed smoking a cigarette. I'd been vaguely listening to Yukari's account of her day, how she had fittings for three dresses and then went on to her parents' house, and that must have been the point at which I'd started wondering again at the rotten incompetence of Granny's former husband.

"It's awful, going on like that. . ." she grumbled, and then: "Oh yes, the day before yesterday Granny moved into a modern apartment. Well, it's only one room and a kitchen."

"You mean she's not going to live with them?"

I switched off the ceiling light and got into my own bed. Yukari gave a little cry of discontent and I told her to come over into mine. Even the dim light of the bedside lamp was enough to give me a good view, out of the corner of my eye, of Yukari transferring herself, naked from the waist down, to my bed. Then the warm, resilient body was next to mine, and said:

"She says Father doesn't like her there. She says she feels unwanted, like an adopted child. Well, I suppose that must have affected the way they all feel. Looks like Father's been thinking about it for quite a long time, since he paid the first deposit on the apartment last autumn."

"Did he indeed?" I said, feeling absolutely furious inside. It was totally unforgivable that his right hand should have been urging on his daughter's marriage and concealing the existence of his mother-in-law, while his left hand was buying an apartment for the ex-criminal to live in. It made my blood boil, as proof of which Yukari whispered in my ear:

"You are rough tonight. Do it more gently, can't you?"

According to further information Yukari gave me in bed, when her grandmother had left her husband and returned to her parents' home, taking her daughter—Yukari's mother—with her, she had received a certain number of stock market shares and so on from him, but just around the time her daughter married the professor (no doubt a mere lecturer at the time) her parents both died, and then she was swindled out of her capital by some crook and became really hard up. As a result, she made the occasional visit to her former husband to sponge off him, and it was on one of these occasions something took place that led to the crime. All she had left was the house, which the Nonomiyas took charge of while she was in prison, renting it out until it was bought up by the city council as part of some land redevelopment scheme. The money gained from this was used to buy the two-room apartment. Since Yukari had given me an edited version of her mother's account (and hers was the only one I had), there were a number of doubtful facts that I'd have preferred to have clarified, but, even so, one thing that was crystal clear was that the apartment was being got ready as early as last autumn.

When Yukari had returned to her own bed I said quite casually it must be very lonely for an old person to live by herself, wondering if there wasn't some suitable family she might live with, and insisting that at least she ought to have a maid to look after her. These few remarks, plus a mild rebuking of the professor's lack of filial concern, were merely a way of letting off steam and nothing more. If they were anything more, then they were an expression of a sudden upsurge of relief on hearing that Utako Nabeshima had moved from the professor's house to a small apartment. Now that this had happened a considerable distance had opened between me and the murderess, and I felt a cheerful reassurance that this ex-criminal, this antisocial element, had been set at some definitive remove from myself.

"Still, must have been an awful position for your father, a constant source of gloom to have to live like that with an old woman with a past. Even so, you know. . ."

I was just getting into my stride, but Yukari only responded with a few sleepy grunts, so I reluctantly turned off the bedside light.

8

I got home on the evening of March 3 at about nine o'clock. A number of minor things had kept coming up which I couldn't put off to the next day as I was going away on a business trip for three days. I'd wanted to get home earlier because it was the Dolls Festival, but since we were only a small household of three with no children I wasn't particularly concerned, and had told them to start without me if I wasn't back by seven.

The dolls and various things that went with them had been given us by my former wife's family on the occasion of my first marriage. Although I'd been able to send her furniture and other belongings back after she died, since luckily they had space for them in the storehouse, they'd asked me to keep the dolls and put them on display on the appropriate days each year if I didn't mind. They said it was too exhausting for an old couple like them to have to set them out and then wrap them all up again and put them away. I was happy to do so since Yukari would be pleased and the dolls themselves were of excellent workmanship, as that old trade official, my former father-in-law, boasted when I saw him on the anniversary of my first wife's death in February. Now that the anniversary was over, marking an end to the year of prescribed mourning, both I and Yukari felt we could relax and enjoy this festival as if it were a kind of delayed New Year celebration. So when I left for work that morning Yukari was all dressed and ready to start arranging the dolls on their stand. This should properly have been done on the eve of the festival, but Yukari had insisted on doing it herself, even though she was fully occupied with modeling work on the first and second, and she'd been so looking forward to it we decided it could all be done on the actual day.

When I got back that night I thought it a bit strange that only Yukari, wearing a bright yellow dress of some knitted material, should have come out into the hallway to greet me. Usually Tsuru came out first, and then Yukari would appear some time later. Yukari seemed to have had quite a few drinks and she slumped rather than knelt beneath the handless clock and smiled at me.

"Here," she said. "Granny's come. . ."

This, presumably, is what's meant by a bolt from the blue, and I was too astonished to be able to speak. It is still a mystery to me why I didn't let my briefcase fall from my nerveless grasp. I just stood there, overcoat still on, briefcase still in hand, while Yukari rattled away:

"She said she couldn't stand being there all alone in that apartment, particularly with today being the third of March, it was simply more than she could bear, almost driving her crazy, so she rang me up. After all, she's always had such a cheerful festival with everyone singing and laughing these past few years in prison and. . ."

"Whoah," I said in a low groan, thrusting my left hand out to stop her rattling on. She hadn't been talking in a particularly loud voice, nor had it been a low voice either, and I was worried Tsuru might overhear. Yukari didn't seem in the least bothered.

"It's okay about Tsuru. She's asleep."

I felt too surprised again to make any reply.

"She's drunk too much, and now she's having a nice little nap in the living room. We've both been working like slaves. First getting the stand up, and then putting the cloth over it and the dolls out, and going down to the flower shop, and then all the cooking. . ."

"All right, all right, I'm with you," I said and sighed; whether I was sighing at Granny for forcing her way in here, or in grief at Tsuru's intoxication, or just at the way Yukari went on and on, I don't know. It didn't silence her, though.

"Well, it's very easy to get drunk on just a little after all that. It soon goes to your head. She hadn't been drinking a lot at all. Then, of course, Granny had been talking. . ."

"About what?"

"About everything, all of it, to Tsuru."

This made me click my tongue in exasperation, but I hadn't the energy to cry out. I turned and sat down on the wooden step that leads up from the stone floor to the tatami part of the hall, put my briefcase down to one side, and honestly felt like just sitting there and doing nothing for a long time; but such indulgences aren't allowed, so I slowly started taking off my shoes.

"It just couldn't be helped. It just all seemed to come out in a flash," said Yukari from behind me.

"It's all right. It's done now, anyway. Just have to think out where to go from here," I said quietly, not really having the mental leisure to consider how disastrous the whole thing had been.

I then heard a voice (one I hadn't heard before and which had some kind of resemblance to my wife's) cheerfully urging Yukari to stop messing about and introduce her lord and master to her. Yukari shouted out a high-pitched assent, and while I was taking off my overcoat I was full of complex reactions to the impression I now received of being some kind of visitor in Granny Nabeshima's own home.

Next to the living room there was another, slightly smaller room, and normally I went through it when passing from the hallway into the living room. Today, however, Yukari took me around by way of the kitchen, obviously because access via that room was blocked by the dolls set up in there. As I was led along this different, narrower route I reflected that last year, being just after the funeral, there hadn't been any Dolls Festival celebrations and so the dolls hadn't seen the light of day for two years. This cheered me up a little since I didn't like to think of them stuck away perpetually in the dark, and gave me a certain courage as I faced the prospect of meeting Granny Nabeshima. Things had gone this far so what did it matter now?

The former jailbird was sitting with the red cloth of the doll stand— a graduated series of shelves like steps—behind her. Her face was sweating slightly, probably the combined effect of the gas fire and the drink, but she sat straight and rigid enough. She appeared to be wearing (although I'm not all that well up on these things) an Oshima kimono and Shoso-in sash, presumably the same she had on when Yukari first met her. As I entered the room she slipped neatly off her cushion onto the tatami and smiled at me. This well-executed courtesy and her appearance in general had surprisingly nothing ex-criminal about it, as if she'd been totally unaffected by her long stay in prison. The person sitting there before me could only be, by any standards, the rather refined wife of a company director, bank manager, or doctor, an old lady who seemed a perfectly appropriate visitor on this day, calm, relaxed, and dignified, just right for the dolls representing the imperial court of days gone by which were displayed behind her. She certainly looked more in keeping with them than either Yukari or I did.

I knelt down, placed my hands on the tatami, and bowed to her, introducing myself and thanking her for taking the trouble to visit us when by rights we should have gone to her. These totally conventional phrases rolled quite naturally off my tongue, and as I was ceremoniously mouthing them I even felt sufficiently relaxed to be able to reflect that Yukari looked much more like her grandmother than her mother. As she was in her sixties her complexion naturally wasn't white (she may even have been dark), and so it lacked that soft, misty quality which Yukari's had, her face being also covered with tiny wrinkles and tending to sag. Her hair was almost completely gray, although her eyebrows were a bit peculiar since she seemed to have lost half of them, the remaining halves being black and bushy and the lost portions drawn in with a thin, reddish brown eye pencil, which provided an odd sort of contrast. However, given these striking differences, the long, well-shaped neck, the large, wide eyes, and in particular the high nose and neatly formed mouth indicated the blood relationship with Yukari, and she must certainly have been very good-looking when young.

Utako Nabeshima responded in the same vein as myself, bowing low and expressing the proper formal sentiments, saying how delighted she was that her granddaughter had been received as the bride of so splendid a person as myself, and begging my forgiveness for this sudden, troublesome visitation, also praising the splendor of the dolls on display and remarking how well they must express the courteous consideration of my former good lady's household, for which she had no adequate words to express her admiration. She spoke a little too fast, although showing sufficient care about what she was saying, occasionally twiddling the shiny ring on her right hand as she did so. The voice and manner of speaking weren't up to the standard of her appearance, though still not such as could actually be called vulgar. I was producing a few polite nothings in reply to this, but my efforts were soon brought to an end, since Tsuru (who'd been lying asleep under a white blanket next to the table) began moving about and then struggled to sit up.

"Oh look, Tsuru's woken up at last," said Yukari.

The maid immediately sat up in a proper position and began apologizing for having failed to greet me. She accompanied these words with what was meant to be a humble bow, but since she was unable to stop this obeisance at a suitable point she ended up giving her head a severe crack on the table, producing a large bang and making the glasses and plates jump about. Naturally this made me laugh, and Yukari and her grandmother joined in without restraint, creating what amounted to an uproar, so Tsuru could only cry out in embarrassment and hide her now even redder and hotter face behind her large hands (I'd never noticed how large they were before), leaning forward onto the tatami and literally curling up with shame. This again brought her shoulder or arm into contact with the edge of the table, sliding it some way toward me, so that the objects on it (glasses, plates, saucers, chopsticks, saké flasks and cups) produced their varied sounds again and thus another session of gay laughter.

If Tsuru had gone on sleeping I imagine the evening would have passed quite peacefully and uneventfully, and my life would have continued along its normal, quiet, humdrum path. At least there seems a very good likelihood that might have happened. However, now that the maid, who had served me loyally, courteously, and silently for decades, had behaved in this manner, everything started to go wrong. As the laughter continued, the whole atmosphere of the room became lighthearted and comical. Yukari went to Tsuru's side, heaved her about to get her back on her knees, and then tried to make her stand up.

"Come on, then. Get up. It's all right, there's nothing to be ashamed about. We're all family here. Come on, have another drink."

While Yukari was busy encouraging her, Granny was convulsed with tremendous laughter, at the end of which she said, "Snap out of it, Tsuru," in very familiar tones, much as if she were talking to someone she'd known since primary school, or perhaps even one of her cell-mates.

"How long have I been asleep, madam—five or ten minutes?" asked the person being helped to her feet.

Yukari only leaned her head histrionically to one side, pondering the question with an exaggeratedly ironical look in her eyes, and didn't reply. This was done by Utako Nabeshima, laughing jovially:

"Must have been a bit longer than that, I'd say. You snored quite a bit. Even ground your teeth once or twice."

She went on in a tone of mysterious liveliness:

"Still, how about a drink for the master of the house?"

She reached out her hand toward the red tray at my side. I had a look at it myself and noticed that, next to the bottle of traditional white saké used to celebrate the day, there was one of Napoleon brandy which I'd been saving for a special occasion, and it was already open. Since Tsuru wouldn't have known you were supposed to sip brandy slowly, it wasn't surprising she'd soon got drunk. You couldn't really blame her, I thought, and started drinking myself. The other three did as well, but we confined ourselves to the saké until Granny decided to have a brandy and water, and then the other two followed suit. Thus this elegant and formal occasion, which admittedly hadn't been all that scrupulously formal or elegant up to then but had still certainly been normal, was swiftly transformed into a confused revel in which all restraint was cast aside.

Since Tsuru remained sitting and made no move to get up, Yukari went off to the kitchen to prepare some food for me.

"I beg your pardon, madam," said Tsuru apologetically, but both Yukari and Granny told her not to worry, Granny pointing out that "the girl's still young so leave her to it." Tsuru seemed to take heart from this, giving Yukari cooking instructions while she went on drinking, and eventually a meal of thick clam soup, turbo cooked in the shell, and *chirashi zushi* was placed before me.

Utako sang a snatch of an old song which she presumably thought relevant to the occasion as she filled my cup with sweet white saké.

"Nothing like the old Dolls Festival, I always say. It's really lovely, that sushi is. Plenty of egg in it; lots of prawns. Wonderful cook she is, Miss Tsuru; really is."

I took up this praise by making a suitable comment on Tsuru's excellence as a cook, but Granny Utako didn't bother with this, going straight to the heart of the great matter at issue.

"Now in prison they never put any prawns in it, only dried sardines. Only a teeny little bit of egg as well. Plenty of dried gourd shavings, of course, seeing as that's the region for it, Tochigi."

Mysteriously, Yukari and Tsuru were listening with apparent composure to all this, much as if they were hearing traveler's tales from somebody just back from Hong Kong or Hawaii. It seemed all I could do was go along with them.

"I have actually been to Tochigi," I said. "Our company's factory is there."

I spoke in a perfectly ordinary voice simply to keep the casual tone of the conversation going, and the fact is I didn't feel there was anything strange about it myself.

"You don't say so? Well, what an amazing coincidence having something in common like that," Utako replied happily.

"It's nice with eel," said Yukari.

"With crab, too. . ." Tsuru chimed in.

I assumed the subject would now move naturally in the direction of generalized talk about food, but Granny Utako immediately steered it back toward the prison again.

"Not a hope of anything like that; not a chance. No turbo and no clams either. For the Dolls Festival, too. Still, it was lucky it fell in March, I'll tell you that. Really lucky. The food always got better in March, you see, and plenty of it. Treats all the time. Ham for lunch, and a raw egg to put on your rice at supper. We used to wonder whether the prison wouldn't go bankrupt if they went on like that, and we did have a good old laugh about it."

"But why in March?" asked Yukari.

"Because the new fiscal year begins in April," I explained instead. "They have to use up all the budget during March."

Yukari didn't seem fully satisfied with this, and Utako shook her head; not in disagreement, however, but in admiration.

"There you are. He knows everything. Just as I thought."

I found her admiration slightly excessive and wanted to point out I had never actually been to prison myself, but she went on:

"That's what happens when you've been in the civil service."

This put me at my ease again, but she soon produced another odd remark to provide further concern and anxiety.

"Civil servants are supposed to be good at singing. Now you're in a bit of a mellow mood, how about giving us one?"

While I was failing to reply to this Tsuru revealed that some years ago I'd been in the habit of humming traditional ballads in the bath. This gave everybody a good laugh, which I joined in, and so the problem was bypassed for the time being. In fact I had taken lessons in *kouta*, beginning about six months or so after I'd turned down the transfer to the Ministry of Defense and was in two minds about what I was going to do with myself, but I decided I wasn't likely to be much good at it so I gave up within less than two months. While I continued smiling at the amusement that Tsuru's disclosure had given, inside I was wondering what could have got into her this evening since I'd never heard her talking in that way before. Still, it seemed that Utako Nabeshima wasn't thinking of civil servants being good at things like *kouta* but at singing sentimental popular songs.

According to her, some president or chief administrator from the Monopoly Corporation or somewhere like it had visited the prison with five or six artists to give a performance for the prisoners. I was unable to believe that anyone could actually *want* to do something as weird as that, and could only assume he meant to stand for the Upper House in a few years' time and this was part of his warming-up campaign (he must have been calculating that most of his audience would have got their vote back by then). Anyway, the concert had a tremendous effect on the prisoners, not because of the quality of the artists, who were uniformly dull, but because the president or chief administrator had told them the story of his life, such a pathetic tale of woe they all felt sorry for him and burst into tears. After that, to accordion accompaniment, he sang them the song "Weep Not, My Sister," which had them all weeping again.

"He was such a wonderful gentleman. Lost most of his hair, but still very handsome. He told us he'd managed to struggle on despite all his troubles, and said we must never give in, so that started us all blubbering again. So good at singing; lovely rich, deep voice he had."

As she gave these fond recollections her voice was somewhat restrained and sad and she brushed away a heartfelt tear, but she soon started knocking back the brandy and water again. I reflected on the odd things that could result from an election, and as I was feeling a bit hot I took off my jacket and tie. Then I said I would go and have a look at the dolls, and stood up. The fact is I was getting fairly cheesed off just sitting there and looking at the touching sight of our sad granny.

"That's a good idea," said Yukari, "seeing all the trouble we took arranging them."

The dolls were arranged on eight shelves, the thick red cloth on which they were set giving off a strong smell of mothballs. On the bottom shelf were two small children playing cat's cradle, a baby member of the imperial court crawling about on its belly, a variety of different sizes of wooden *kokeshi* and other dolls; and this motley collection, which Tsuru always looked after, had been added to by objects belonging to Yukari, including the large koala bear which looked like a monster in this context, and a Negro cherub holding a sky-blue candle (presumably of some religious significance) which she'd received when modeling at a department store. It was a combination of cherub, candlestick, and money box, for in its back, just underneath its small, light blue wings, was a horizontal slot for putting coins in. The other shelves had the traditional dolls and their furniture, although I noticed the second shelf, where the three tipplers were, was crowded not only with the customary three-striped rice cakes, but also a flower pot with two sprays of peach blossom in it, so that the three of them seemed horribly cramped as they performed their separate functions of weeping, laughing, and getting angry. Finally, right at the top where the toy emperor and empress in all their regalia should be close together in smiling harmony, it looked as if some other couple had elbowed their way in on the act, for Yukari had placed another pair of dolls she'd received from her mother, wooden ones wearing kimono, in front and between them.

"That's funny," I said. "The big dolls have the husband on the right, but the little ones have him on the left."

"That's right. We compromised," answered Yukari as she poured out some more brandy and water for herself and the other two. She explained she'd wanted to put the man on the left and the woman on the right, but Tsuru had objected it should be the other way around, and not until late afternoon when Granny arrived did they reach a solution. Granny said that Tsuru's arrangement was the traditional one, but the order had in fact been reversed sometime before the war, and so they compromised by having one couple in the old style and the other in the new.

"In the past they were always like that, all of them, weren't they, Mrs. Nabeshima?" said Tsuru.

"Of course they were. Only natural," replied Granny in obvious accord, and I reflected that the imperial couple must have brought these two into their present state of harmony. I tried to recall how we had arranged the dolls two years ago, but couldn't for the life of me remember.

"I wonder why a custom lasting all those centuries should have been changed?" I wondered out loud.

Granny Utako turned to me, with her glass in her hand, and explained that it was to make them conform to the imperial portraits, information she'd gleaned from the prison warden.

"The imperial portraits?" echoed Yukari, and the three of us took turns explaining that this meant two photographs of Emperor Hirohito and his empress. At every school ceremony we'd always bowed low to these photographs, and they were usually kept very carefully in a special storehouse called the place of enshrinement by the school's main entrance. At this point Tsuru started a nasal intoning of the anthem for Empire Day about the holy mountain towering in the clouds, and although I assumed none of this could make any sense to Yukari I gave an impersonation of our headmaster putting on his white gloves to receive some Imperial Rescript on Education and raising it reverently above his head. While I was doing this, Granny Utako, who was sitting with her back to me, raised a hand (the one that didn't have a glass in it) to adjust the tortoiseshell comb in her hair, and as she did so revealed an arm that was surprisingly white and plump.

"Always had the emperor doll on the left in prison. Not surprising, seeing it was one of His Imperial Penal Institutions."

She said this indifferently enough, certainly without irony, although the words gave me a genuine shock of horror, so that I found myself gulping quite involuntarily and seemed rooted to the spot, smiling helplessly before the thick red cloth, in a thin cloud of camphor and insect repellent. This momentary paralysis perhaps resulted from my responding instinctively in two opposite ways to Granny's remark, and the imposed immobility was my unconscious way of trying to manage this contradictory state of mind. At least that's how it seems to me now.

The first idea that struck me on hearing about "His Imperial Penal Institutions" was the suspicion that our democratic state might still essentially be reigned over and controlled by the emperor just as it had been in the past, and this was a case in point, where a wretched member of the populace, having committed a wretched crime and being in the position of having to pay for it, received some kind of transient satisfaction from her awareness that the sentence was given in the emperor's name. The second thought was that such criminals, prisoners, or ex-criminals probably responded in a manner that in no way contradicted my first supposition although it was in complete opposition to it, for they accepted this "master" who was above them, be it the state, or society, or any other name by which you might like to call the system, and yet only with feelings of resentment, hatred, or perhaps of something that should more properly be called a hostile, negative gloom.

None of this was clarified in my mind at the time, not even to this inadequate degree, but was simply presented to me as a momentary, confused, and imprecise intuition. The very violence of the insight ensured that a foolish smile should play about my lips, and the gloom of this grin perhaps weighed upon me physically as well as spiritually, since I felt a sudden exhaustion and slumped down on the tatami.

"Oh dear, it's all gone to my head," said Granny Utako by my side, and she removed her *haori* coat and dabbed her nose with a small handkerchief.

"Shall I turn off the gas fire, Mrs. Nabeshima?" asked Tsuru.

"Why not loosen your sash?" said Yukari at the same time.

Utako indicated to the maid by a gesture of her hand that there was no need to do that, but she followed her granddaughter's advice with some hesitation and wiggling about, and as she gradually loosened her sash a large red purse appeared from the middle of it, and slowly fell out.

"I'll have that," said Yukari, swiftly pouncing on it. Granny narrowed her eyes and, just as if she were giving advice to a small granddaughter on whom she'd bestowed some pocket money, told her to be very careful with it when she went outside to play in the streets. This clever response put her in great good humor, and she went on to give her reminiscences of the prison bazaar.

Every year, on the second Sunday in November, stalls were set up in front of the prison main gate selling various bags, dolls, and other articles the prisoners had made. They also sold the flowers they'd grown in the prison flower beds. Policemen would come to control the crowds, but there was such a stampede to buy that some people were even injured, and because of the amount of shoplifting that went on the bazaar always made a loss. So invariably the next day the warden would have all the prisoners assemble and address them. He would bend his index finger (a sign that stood for the pickpocket and general pilfering trade) and rebuke them, saying they called themselves professionals and yet look at the way they let a lot of amateurs get away with murder. He always ended by telling them to look a bit sharp about it next time.

"We couldn't help grinning, of course. I mean, we couldn't help it, seeing he wasn't really telling us off, after all."

This odd tale certainly amused Yukari and Tsuru, but it had me in fits, rolling about and holding my sides. What could be richer than this, I felt, with the honest citizens stealing from the criminals, and the new criminals protected by the same law that put their victims behind bars. The total confusion of the concept of social order this implied seemed to me brilliantly summed up in that image. It was the perfect paradigm and provided me with some kind of release from the oppressive ideas that lay behind it. Thus, face flushed with wine, I laughed and laughed, and when that was over I realized I'd suddenly become drunk, so I called for whisky to be brought, rubbing the tears from my eyes with my knuckles.

"Well, Eisuke, you certainly have a good laugh when you decide to have one. Never stop. That's what the drink does for you, I suppose."

I brushed aside Granny's criticism and gulped down the whisky that Yukari had brought me.

"Right then. Now, how about a good old traditional ballad?" I said, although I'd not attempted one for years; and I sat up straight. It was no great success, however. I managed to struggle through the opening line about the first snow of winter falling on the island, but after that I lost the tune and couldn't even remember the words. Granny Utako, who had turned up her eyes in dismay at this, produced the set phrase she must have used at prison concerts when one of the performers had dried up:

"Hello, the sound seems to have broken down on this TV."

Yukari, however, comforted me by saying that *kouta* couldn't really be sung without an accompaniment, and Tsuru harked back to those years when my bath-time renditions had been really good, she said, and I gradually began to feel embarrassed. Then Yukari announced she would sing an anti-war protest song, and despite the fact she didn't know enough English to even start to read what was written on package labels, she sang a song of considerable length (though with lots of repetitions and refrains) in the original tongue. We all three clapped, and this time it was Tsuru's turn, so she gave us a Japanese folk song which she said had been a favorite of her dead husband, with her eyes shut tight and much shaking of her head, but very well performed. She could really sing.

"Terrific, Tsuru. I'd no idea you could sing like that. Marvelous," said Yukari, and I clapped and praised her as well, saying it was particularly commendable as she didn't need any bathroom acoustics. Granny Utako also added her own compliments, and then stood up.

"Well, now it's my turn."

Before she got down to it, however, she staggered over toward the dolls and pointed in the general direction of the little lanterns, saying:

"Nothing like this, of course, but they had lovely dolls there."

She was referring to the dolls displayed in the prison, speaking with her usual pride in the place even if she was having slight trouble with her tongue.

"Careful, Granny, those really belong to the former lady of this house."

"I know that, Yukari," she replied brusquely, sending me a friendly smile which was to assure me I had nothing to worry about.

"The dolls they had there were donated by a special dolls' wholesaler at Asakusabashi—forgotten the name—and they were so big; why, the face of the doll emperor was as big as a great big apple. The lanterns had two-hundred-watt bulbs inside them, and the minister of the left—or was it right?—which one of them's young? Anyway, he was really handsome, very young-looking, very spruce and sharp, a bit of a raffish *yakuza* type. He was the best of the men; must have been ten or eleven of them, but he was the pick of the lot. Once it disappeared, can't quite remember when, and there was a big stink about it. People said it must be a woman who was in for lifting, and they were dead right because it was her."

In reply to Yukari's question as to what "lifting" might be, she explained it meant theft, and the slang word seemed to bring back more instant memories and she became positively sentimental about the Dolls Festival in prison. A huge stand was put up in the gym, and the red cloth they used was a bit too bright in color and had holes where the insects had got at it. The dolls were very large, but their vestments weren't up to much, and if you looked closely at the workmanship of the furniture it left a lot to be desired. The only light was the naked bulbs hanging from the high, unceilinged roof and the ones inside the lanterns, so it wasn't very bright and you could see clouds of dust that had drifted upward glittering about the lights. Each year they cut off some branches from the big peach tree in a corner of the prison yard, and then arranged them in a strong bronze vase almost as large as an old-fashioned cooking pot; a week before the festival it was put in the warden's room in the warm, flowering in variegated blossoms of red and white.

So between two hundred and two hundred and thirty women prisoners sat down on thin matting spread over the floorboards, together with the warden and all his staff, a meal of *chirashi zushi*, a cake, and one piece of fruit before them, to enjoy this sadly splendid banquet. Murderesses, thieves, pickpockets, prostitutes, absconders, arsonists, swindlers, inflicters of grievous bodily harm, women with all kinds of past records and of various ages sat there and chattered and made merry and dined, looking up at the quiet, refined splendor of the imperial court; and, as they did so, surely they felt within them, like a vague mist rising, a concentrated hatred for this royal family in whose name they'd been set apart, confined, deprived of liberty, and so condemned to isolation and forced labor.

That, at least, was the picture forming in my own head as I listened to Granny Utako's words, but it was disturbed by encouraging applause from Yukari and Tsuru. I saw that Utako had turned her face in dramatic profile, and was bringing her fist up near her mouth. Obviously this was an impersonation of some singer seen on TV, the fist holding an imaginary microphone, so I also clapped my hands though I was a bit slow off the mark.

Still maintaining this theatrical pose, she said:

"The warden always used to do this at the festival, you know."

The words were spoken with feeling, like a schoolgirl with a crush on some particularly philanthropic headmaster. She faced around swiftly to her front (with a considerable stagger as she did so) and began a sentimental number about the rape blossoms blooming all along the riverbank while their boat glided in the spring. She sang completely out of tune, and wandered about in a manner that could hardly have been reminiscent of the good old warden, but was obviously the same imitation of this singer on TV (unless the warden's own performance had been influenced by recent viewing). Since she was now well and truly plastered she wobbled and staggered about a good deal, and her loosened sash began to slip downward. We looked at each other and laughed, and Yukari laughed so much she fell over, but Utako was quite indifferent to all this.

When the first verse was done I immediately burst in with loud applause, praising her performance and modestly condemning myself as clearly the worst singer in the house, since I felt it would be positively cruel to let her go on any longer. She seemed disappointed because she said she knew the words for the second and third verses as well, but she sat down entwined in the folds of her sash. In response to words of flattery from the other two she said they needn't expect her to stand them a drink for saying that and, as if to prove her point, she immediately poured herself a stiff brandy and water. At some stage the reddish brown half of her eyebrows had disappeared, leaving only the black, bushy parts. I knocked back the rest of my whisky, and said:

"Well, perhaps we ought to break up now. I'm off on a business trip tomorrow. Granny, it's late so you'd better stay here tonight."

Thus, cheerfully, not quite in the manner with which a department chief of an electrical goods manufacturer will announce the end of a company meeting, but something near it, I made my statement and stood up.

Next morning when I woke up I was astonished to find Yukari, all properly dressed, sitting on the edge of the bed. This had never happened before, and I could tell by the light filtering in through a gap in the curtains that she was absolutely worn out.

I asked her what on earth was wrong, and she replied she'd spent the whole night nursing Tsuru and Granny, who'd been vomiting and groaning all the time.

"You are awful, sleeping right through that foul racket. I've had a terrible time."

"I reckon so," I said drowsily and must have dropped off again, probably for quite a while, for instead of Tsuru's obsequious voice from the other side of the door advising me of the time, Yukari burst in roughly saying:

"Come on, get up. Breakfast's been ready ages."

I had a brisk, inadequate wash (the bowl seemed to have disappeared from the washroom), and then breakfasted in the kitchen instead of the living room where I normally ate. When that was over I stopped outside the maid's room and asked her how she was feeling. Tsuru apologized at inordinate length, so I merely laughed and told her to take care of herself. Then I went into the living room and directed words of consolation at the closed doors of the room in which the dolls were arranged.

"Gather you've had a pretty rough night of it. Didn't know a thing myself. Sorry about that," I said in as cheerful a voice as possible.

The words that came in response, inviting me to enter, were delivered in quiet tones which weren't so much meekly apologetic as gloomy, even dismal.

"That's all right," I said, "I'll take my leave of you here if I may. Time presses, you know."

I then turned to go, but was called back.

"Eisuke, there's a favor I'd like to ask of you, if you would be so kind. Only a small favor," she said in a feeble voice quite different from that of the night before, and she appeared to be making a move to get up. Inevitably (particularly as Yukari was egging me on) I opened the sliding doors.

Granny was sitting up there before the elegant and riotous confusion of the doll stand, with its red cloth, dolls, rice cakes, carriages, peach blossoms, koala bear, *kokeshi* dolls, etc., on the whitish bedding we have for guests, wearing a gauze nightdress. Her face was gray and drawn, and her head hung down as she looked at me unwaveringly.

"I know I'm just being a nuisance. . . I really shouldn't, because I've no right to . . . but it's so lonely in that apartment . . . having to go back there."

The weak pathos of this plea made me drop hurriedly to my knees, moved in some way since I made an ambiguous grunt which could easily have been interpreted as one of assent. She clearly took it that way since she nipped smartly out of bed, placed her hands on the wooden threshhold that separated the tatami of one room from that of the other, and bowed her head reverently in humble thanks.

"For heaven's sake, Granny, you don't have to do that," I said. "Anyway, rest up here for a day or two; at least until you feel better."

She lowered her head again and expressed her thanks, which only added to my confusion. There was nothing I could do about it now.

"You don't want to catch a cold on top of your hangover," I said, trying to be pleasantly jovial about it. "I've once done the same myself."

So the enfeebled old lady in her sixties crawled back into bed with Yukari's help. I noticed some newspaper had been spread out next to her pillow with a bowl placed on top, and although there was no trace of her having actually vomited into it there was still an unpleasant smell in the dolls' room.

9

I had assumed she'd leave after three nights at the most, but I seem to have been too optimistic. The first really decisive misfortune was that I'd gone away immediately on that business trip, for I returned five days later to be greeted at the door by Tsuru with the unsettling news that she'd gone with Granny the day before to collect her things from the apartment. Tsuru observed my expression carefully, and then lowered her voice.

"I'm extremely sorry, sir, but it just happened. Mrs. Yukari is such an amiable, kindhearted lady, you see. But please let Mrs. Nabeshima stay here, at least for the time being. You can't help feeling sorry for her."

Tsuru was very earnest, and I did my best to restrain my feelings of displeasure, making a vague grunt in reply which certainly wasn't meant to indicate any kind of assent. At the time I still hadn't realized I would just have to accept the situation.

Granny had made the room next to the living room into her own, and there she sat with her legs tucked into the electric *kotatsu*. A small chest of drawers, which had formerly been mine, had been taken out of the storeroom and put in one corner of the room with a portable TV placed on top. She was watching the television using an ear plug for the sound. There was a photograph in a small frame on the chest of drawers as well, placed leaning against the wall. She was wearing quite ordinary, everyday clothes, and I felt as I saw her sitting there with her back to me that she looked just like one of the family. I had the distinct impression that the whole business was already a *fait accompli*.

Speaking from my years of experience as a civil servant, once any situation or fact is accepted as truly "accomplished," then one must also accept that the context, or overall situation, has approved of that fact or condition and, whether one likes it or not, all one can do is await the passage and process of time. Nothing can be less likely to produce results than some careless expression of protest or opposition. This doesn't mean one will inevitably go along with the situation, but one won't actually oppose it until and unless one can grasp a proper opportunity to do so. One must be totally noncommittal, falling, as it were, gracefully between two imaginary stools. I'd come to this conclusion as soon as I caught a glimpse of Granny Utako in her ordinary clothes through the open sliding doors, realizing it was the only method I could adopt.

As soon as Granny was aware of my presence she left her *kotatsu* and edged herself on her knees toward the living room, placing her hands properly and bowing to me, a posture in which she looked remarkably small. So the little old lady explained to me (after I'd hastily adjusted my normal squat to a polite kneeling position) that she felt so sad and all alone in that apartment she would like to stay here a little longer, though she knew it would be a lot of trouble for us, and Yukari and Tsuru had been kind enough to suggest she might, and she had promised herself she would never again let alcohol pass her lips. . . She went on at considerable length in a voice of great pathos, her gray head bowed all the while, and (particularly since Tsuru was nearby) I could hardly say anything heartless to her.

"Come on, now, Granny; no need to treat me like a stranger," I said, smiling broadly, and even finally managing to break out in a generous burst of laughter. "Ah-hah, I see you've got that chest of drawers I used when I was a student. Tsuru got it out for you, I suppose? Well, certainly brings it all back."

After this spell of remembrance of things past I alluded to the real question at issue:

"Of course, I suppose it is still pretty cold."

This was just about the only level on which I could handle the subject, the implication here being she should push off when it got warmer. Her response was to say she'd passed all those years of cold winters in Tochigi with nothing you could really call heating, and so this sort of cold didn't really trouble her, although, yes, it was cold, certainly cold, and so on; an innocent exchange during which I cast my eyes about occasionally, catching sight of the photo next to the TV which was, indeed, that of a man, and realizing in a flash of insight that this must be the creature who had suffered that fate. Utako's estranged husband and victim had a long face, rather pansy-looking, but handsome enough for all that. The photo had been taken with him looking downward, the fingers of one hand pressed against his cheek, in pensive, slightly melancholy mood, and was obviously not of him during his later years but when he was still quite young. The old lady, in her well-worn, even shabby kimono made of some indeterminate material that looked like a compromise between common *meisen* silk and pongee, seemed quite unaware of the direction of my gaze but went on earnestly nodding away. She seemed to be interpreting my comments as ones that permitted her an optimistic view of the situation; and as things stood she was obviously quite right to do so.

While I was getting changed in the bedroom I could hear what sounded like Yukari's arrival, and very shortly she came upstairs. She said Granny was very pleased, and she herself was grateful for my kindness toward her, adding:

"Still, I wonder how long she thinks she's going to stay? Any idea?"

She knitted her brows as she said this, and I must say it seemed a very irresponsible question to be asking me, seeing it was exactly the question I wanted to put to her. However, being much older than her and having the dignity of a husband to maintain, I avoided any riposte of that kind, and made the ambiguous remark that it would be getting warmer soon. She replied:

"It really is an awful nuisance, but I couldn't see what I could do about it. After all, you can't help feeling sorry for her, and then when someone who's only really a stranger like Tsuru tells her not to go and says she'll get her things for her, well, you can't say you just don't want to be bothered with her, can you? Particularly if you're her granddaughter. There might have been an excuse if only this house had been a bit smaller."

Having criticized the excessive number of rooms in the house she went on to make the peculiar comment that it was all the fault of the television. What she meant by this was that on the evening of the morning after, Tsuru was still in bed sipping hot tea with a little dried plum in it, but Granny was already up and about, apparently quite recovered, putting back a hearty meal and even asking for second helpings, when unhappily the TV soon had her crawling back into bed. The trouble was that she'd seen a news item about a ninety-year-old woman living alone who'd died and not been discovered for three weeks. The next morning, indeed, she got hold of Tsuru and told her how envious she was of her being able to live together with a young person, a statement she repeated a number of times.

I found all this intensely depressing. Here was I thinking I wouldn't have to trouble myself with the problems of old age for at least another ten or twenty years, and now I was having the whole thing thrust down my throat. I blamed Professor Nonomiya for that selfish irresponsibility and disavowal of family obligations one finds in intellectuals of his ilk, and felt a very serious grudge against him. This was apparently shared by Yukari, for she said:

"I'm sorry. It's all Father's fault. You can't trust him." Then, as if suddenly remembering something, she added: "I had my watch stolen today."

"By your father?"

"For heaven's sake, of course not. What an awful thing to say, talking about my father like that."

"But you're the one who said it."

"No I didn't. I was going to say I'd just had my watch stolen when I met him today, and he started talking about Marie Antoinette."

"I don't think I'm quite following you."

It seemed that on the afternoon of this very day Yukari had been on the basement floor of a department store doing some shopping, and had taken a crowded elevator to the fifth floor. She was holding her handbag in her right hand, with a large plastic carrier bag she'd acquired in the food section dangling from her left wrist. On account of the scrimmage in the packed elevator, with people pushing and shoving, this carrier bag began drifting off in an odd direction and so her left arm was naturally obliged to extend sideways after it. She could no longer actually see her own forearm, but she was too worried about the fate of the food she had in that carrier bag to notice with any concern a slightly suspicious sensation about the region of her wrist. At the third floor quite a number of people got out, and some more again at the fourth, but it wasn't until the elevator girl was announcing what was for sale on the fifth floor that Yukari adjusted her grip on her left-hand baggage, and found her wristwatch had disappeared. She looked around the shiny floor of the elevator and inside her carrier bag, and by the time she knew for certain it wasn't there the elevator had arrived at the roof, as she was made aware by all the children squeaking away in the playground up there.

She'd just informed reception on the first floor about her watch and was leaving the store when she came across her father walking slowly through the throng outside. He was carrying a brown briefcase in his hand, and he stopped and greeted her.

"Well, hello there. How are things these days?" he said in a bland and relaxed manner, a good contrast to the agitated way in which Yukari told him she'd just had her watch stolen. The professor lent an inattentive ear to her account, and then said:

"Buy another one soon, I suppose. Marie Antoinette received fifty on the occasion of her wedding."

"Fifty?" said Yukari, not knowing whether to laugh or cry, since she really hadn't expected a name like that to appear so suddenly in a situation of this kind. Her father, however, merely rested his briefcase on the low guardrail along the side of the road in order to take the weight off his hands, and went on:

"At that period in history, the eighteenth century, only the aristocracy possessed clocks or other timepieces. It was a sort of plaything, a bauble."

"Still, even if she was a queen, surely she wouldn't want fifty of them?"

"Not a queen, an empress. It was what one might call a sign or indication of wealth and power. What was once an object of luxury has, of course, in our age of the common man, become a utility, a device that measures the working hours."

"So I suppose the thief who stole my watch just wanted to be a common man like everyone else?"

"Well, since it was a lady's watch, perhaps not," smiled the professor; then, putting on an obsequious air, he said: "I hear you're looking after Grandmother. I can't apologize too profoundly for the trouble we're putting you all to. Really don't know how to thank you. I must admit I've never been able to get on with her myself; all my fault, no doubt. Give my best wishes to Eisuke and to that lady help you have, what's her name, Tsuru, I believe. Am most apologetic about it. The trouble is there's so much going on at school these days, hardly get a moment to spare..."

He reeled off a long list of dismal complaints, saying he was completely at his wits' end with all the faculty meetings they seemed to be having every day recently, and if they couldn't hold their entrance examinations then the financial situation of the university would be dealt a severe blow, and these students nowadays were just a bunch of illiterates, didn't understand a thing, and he never seemed to get a chance to go and look at any paintings these days; at the end of which depressed lament he added he was thinking perhaps he ought to send money to cover Grandmother's living expenses each month.

"Sounds like he's expecting her to stay here permanently," I said, thinking it would be better not to go into the question in any detail now, but decide after cautious study of the ins and outs of what it would mean in real terms of profit and loss. Instead I offered a few critical remarks about how typical it was of him to start talking about Marie Antoinette on hearing his daughter had just been robbed.

"He says it's all the fault of one professor that the meetings go on for so long," Yukari giggled, and explained there was a very old professor who would grow restless around five o'clock and insist on asking the clerical staff if provision had been made for a packed meal to be served in the event of et cetera; and very reluctantly they would order dinner for all the teaching staff present. Once this had been ordered everyone began to feel in a mood to eat, and thus a faculty meeting that should have ended at 5:30 would drag on until six. Since it would look a bit strange to go home immediately after eating the dinner, they then spent another hour debating this and that just for the sake of appearances.

I couldn't express any surprise at this, since it seemed very much what one might expect to happen, and I began vaguely wondering if the old professor's wife wasn't ill and in the hospital, which would explain his concern about keeping things going until dinnertime. As I was lost in these thoughts, Yukari, who was sitting next to me on the bed, shook my knee and said in a wheedling voice:

"Buy me a watch, won't you? We models are working girls, you know."

"Um."

"What sort of reply is that? Don't want to, I suppose, even though it's the first time I've ever asked you to buy me one."

"Well, that may be so," I said, and she became horribly sulky, although naturally it was all just a form of play which goes on in the home of any newly married couple, particularly when there's a gap in years between them. Yukari was perfectly well aware of that. However, while I was absorbed in this amusement, I wondered if she was also aware that a suspicion had crossed my mind concerning the identity of whoever might have bought her the watch that had been stolen. Naturally I knew what to do with doubts of this kind, and had done so since before I was married. I simply thrust them away from me, crushed them to death, for it was wiser that neither of us should be concerned about the other's past, since, for a start, one was hardly likely to get a straight answer to any such questioning. So after a bit more sport and byplay on the subject, I promised I'd buy her one providing it was cheap. Yukari responded with slightly exaggerated feeling:

"Oh, a Piaget. How nice!"

"Come off it," I said severely. "Remember it's only a device to measure your working hours."

But then I suddenly became serious.

"Look, you'd better not mention anything about having your watch stolen to Granny, although I suppose you realize that already."

"Can't we talk about anything to do with crime, then?" she asked, glancing straight at me for a moment.

"I think not. We ought to be considerate about her feelings, you know. Things will work out better at home that way. Tell Tsuru as well."

"All right," said Yukari, and sighed. "Oh dear, worrying about things like that all the time, what an awful drag."

That sigh irritated me, so I shouted at her:

"What the hell do you mean? She's nothing to do with me, you know. She's your relative."

"I'm sorry," she said with a little shrug, but since she saw I was still genuinely annoyed she changed her tune to one of carefree amusement, and made what she considered a joke.

"That's pretty funny, don't you think?—her not liking the idea of dying alone. Maybe she feels she was at least there by Grandpa's side, taking good care of him when he died?"

The white face took on a coquettish air of bland innocence, as she gave me a long, sideways look with her azure-shadowed eyes.

I tried manfully to smile back understandingly at this quip, although I was in fact trying to grasp the meaning of the slight cold shudder I'd felt down my spine. I imagined it must be because I belonged to a generation that didn't believe in making tasteless jokes of that kind (always assuming they occurred to one in the first place), and so probably I'd felt a swift surge of regret at having married a member of a generation whose tastes varied so much from my own. But I let the joke pass.

"Anyway, for the time being we've just got to have her living here with us. Still, something's got to be done about that photograph. We can't have that."

"Photograph?"

"The one on top of the chest of drawers. Next to the TV. I'm sure it's her . . . her spouse."

Yukari's large eyes grew even larger.

"Wow," she cried. "The one she killed?"

"Don't talk so loud. Anyway, what do you think? Has Tsuru said anything about it?"

"No, nothing. The thing is, I did, in fact, ask Granny myself. She just sort of mumbled something, as if she was feeling shy, you know. So I just sort of thought. . ."

"What did you just sort of think?"

"That it must be an actor she had some sort of crush on." Her words slowly faded and tailed off at the end as she reached this absurd conclusion. I was taken aback by the sheer stupidity of the idea.

"Well, he's long and lean; pretty sexy-looking. You must take after that side of the family as far as sex goes."

Naturally Yukari responded in a fairly complex way to this straight talk. Perhaps I'd been a bit too blunt, but I feel it's a good thing with a young wife to give her the kind of short, sharp shock that will induce a proper awareness of the way things are. There hadn't been enough of that in my relationship with my former wife.

I went on: "I suppose that's her way of praying for the repose of his soul. I understand her wanting to preserve his memory and so on, but it's going to drive me crazy, I tell you. It'll be a constant reminder we're living with a killer in the house."

"That's right. Still, she doesn't burn incense before it or offer it water or anything like that. Do you think she's trying to spare our feelings?"

"Don't ask me. Anyway, you tell her. Suggest to her she ought to keep the photo hidden away somewhere and just bring it out when she prays."

"All right. Tomorrow morning," Yukari replied.

I stood up from the bed and said, as though to myself:

"Once it gets warmer they'll stop having news on TV about old people dying alone. People take down their shutters, open their windows. Not many houses left where you don't know something of what's going on inside."

10

One thing that did change completely with Granny Utako's presence in our house was the matter of flower arrangement. Naturally Yukari had no training whatsoever in the art, and Tsuru's efforts were mainly a few pretentious tricks picked up from watching my former wife's attempts and imitating aspects of them; but Granny was a properly trained student of the Ikenobo school, old-fashioned it's true, but she certainly knew how to get it right. In the alcove and on the alcove shelves the arrangements of pine and bunched camellia flowers, or a few roses and azaleas, had an authentic feel about them, as did her choice of vases, and this not only gave a sense of shape and purpose to that room but, mysteriously enough, to the whole house as well.

Thus it happened that the advent of this intruder ironically gave our newlywed domesticity an improved atmosphere, a sense of things coming properly together, even a kind of dignity. For example, I noticed sometime around mid-May that Tsuru had stopped referring to me in that slightly childish manner of "Master Eisuke," but now called me "the master." This was clearly Granny's influence, even if only a slight instance of it, showing that something my former wife had never even tried to correct in Tsuru had been rectified by Granny in a very short space of time. The way she behaved in general was similarly old-fashioned, and it would probably be true to say that these ancient habits had been preserved in her by the experience of prison life.

So it was that, when toward the end of April I announced I'd been promoted to the board of directors, not only did she congratulate me with words of solemn respect, but she also said:

"It's at times like this you really feel the lack of a Buddha shelf in this house, since you can't announce it properly."

Yukari agreed with this remark, saying she felt having a little shrine would be tremendously chic, while Granny went on to urge me at least to telephone my elder brother or something to announce the great news:

I protested in some embarrassment that it was just a plain directorship tacked on to my present job as head of the planning department, and since there were ten of us on the board it didn't seem worth making a song and dance about. But eventually I did take her advice, which turned out to be quite right because my brother back home was extremely pleased. It was at moments like this one could see how she tended to become the spiritual and moral center of the household, and from that point onward I endeavored to consult her whenever there was any question of sending messages of congratulation or condolence (among the events that required condolence, there were fortunately no instances of sudden death by misadventure), with the result that I became acutely aware how unstable my life had been up to now, with only a young wife in her twenties and a maid approaching sixty.

The one thing I deliberately didn't attempt to consult her about was any matter relating to money. This was unavoidable since, naturally enough, her grasp of present prices and money values was quite inadequate owing to that long blank period she had lived through. Right up to around May she was apparently famous in the neighborhood for the innocent amusement with which she'd exclaim at the prices of things even when she went out shopping with Tsuru, and they seemed to think she must have been living as some kind of recluse. Most of the flowers she used for arrangements could be picked in our garden, but on those rare occasions when she had to visit the flower shop she'd keep on mumbling complaints about the cost for some time afterward. Another thing that seemed to cause her a great deal of trouble, even distress, was the traffic, and she refused to cross the road anywhere except at a pedestrian crossing. Yukari and Tsuru had both told me of her response to an ambulance bearing down on her when she was on one of these areas of theoretical safety, which had been to turn quite pale and start screaming.

She organized her days as regularly as clockwork, and this strengthened the impression she gave of scrupulous integrity. Each morning she would wait until the maid was about before getting up herself (sometimes calling out to Tsuru on those occasions when she overslept), tidy away her bedding, perform her ablutions, and then take the framed photograph of her dead husband out of the chest of drawers and mutter something of a religious nature before it (Tsuru had happened to observe all this while busy in the room next door). When the weather was fine she would go into the garden and water the flowers and do a little weeding, always making quite sure she never missed any of her favorite TV programs. She would take breakfast together with Tsuru after I'd been seen off to the office, then the two of them would do the washing up and clean the house, watching television in the intervals of their work. Yukari would come downstairs and show her face just as I left, but normally went back to bed again.

After all this Granny would sit in front of the mirror and do her hair, and then do Tsuru's, who would have finished washing her face by then. While this was going on Yukari would make her own striking entrance, and after a combined breakfast and lunch she would have her hair done by Granny as well. Tsuru and Yukari marveled at her grasp of the hairdresser's art, which seemed superior even to her flower arrangement, and both said it must be because she was just naturally gifted and very clever with her hands.

This was how Granny usually spent the first part of her day, and she showed the same scrupulous observance of temporal regularity in such things as what time dinner should be, or when she should take a bath, or when to go to bed. Up to now I'd always said they should start dinner at seven even if I wasn't back by then, but normally they would wait thirty or forty minutes, and I'd often reproved them for this; but once Granny had come to live with us there was no more of that. Tsuru said it was because of the television, since on most evenings there was always some program at eight o'clock that she'd decided she didn't want to miss. There may have been something in that, if a person of such old-school beliefs as Utako insisted on starting dinner even when the master of the house still hadn't returned (naturally she was only doing what the master of the house had told them all to do, but even so). However, it seemed to me the main reason was that a strict sense of time observance had been imposed on her during her years in prison, and her obsessive punctuality was a leftover from that experience. There was also another possibility that one more acquired habit, of having nothing to look forward to except one's meals, persisted for her in my household as well.

Naturally I talked to Yukari about this, sometime around the middle of May, I think, in our bedroom one night.

"Still, Mother is really strict about being on time," she said. "I don't know, but maybe she was brought up that way by Granny?"

This was a straightforward contradiction of my view of the matter, and if it were a fact that Utako had been a model of punctuality before going to prison, then my assumptions must be all wrong.

"Come to think of it, though," Yukari went on, "she did say she wanted to buy a watch. She got all excited when we were in the clock section at the store the other day. Perhaps it's the influence of television. By the way, what's happened about my wristwatch?"

Thus the discussion went off at a quite unexpected tangent from the main subject.

Granny went out with Yukari and Tsuru to other places than the department store. She accompanied Tsuru to see the latter's favorite *yakuza* movies, and she told me with great pleasure how she thought she recognized the face of one of the actresses and was delighted to find out she was the one on the poster in Tsuru's room. Yukari once asked Tsuru how Granny responded to that inevitable scene which takes place outside the prison walls as people are greeted on their release, but Tsuru said she'd been too busy watching what was happening on the screen to notice her companion's reactions.

"She says she'll have a careful look next time, but I wonder. Tsuru is so crazy about the movies I doubt she'll be able to manage that."

I need hardly add that all three of us became more and more passionately interested in the nature of Granny's past life.

Granny Utako kept her promise to drink no more alcohol with great conscientiousness, even refusing the hot toddy that Yukari prepared for her when she'd caught a slight chill near the end of March because it had whisky in it; and, indeed, she was a quite different person in every way from the one I'd seen on the evening of the Dolls Festival. She crooned no more songs, nor did she speak of her life in prison, and never once touched on the subject of crime. This obvious effort she was making to be accepted as one of a normal household we naturally found very understandable, and also moving, and it ensured we behaved considerately toward her while inevitably deepening our curiosity about those things she never mentioned. Sometimes Tsuru and Yukari made apparently innocent attempts to get the talk going in that direction, but it seems Granny evaded them quite easily. Once I even tried myself

162

(this must have been just before the hot toddy episode, so sometime toward the end of March) when I was alone with her. The subject of our talk was heading that way, but this fairly direct attempt I made to pump her was entirely outsmarted.

I began to question the rightness of my own attitude and behavior. Obviously I could argue I had a natural duty as the head of the household to know the past histories of each member of it, but I was also ashamed to have to admit that my own interest in the question was hardly different from the type of scandalmongering one found in the women's weeklies, as was clearly the case with Tsuru and Yukari. I sympathized with her desire to have no one poking his or her nose into her past, and I made up my mind I would scrupulously refuse to question her on the subject or try to fool her into talking about it, and that the other two would do the same. Indeed we all three kept to this resolve quite well, I think, but again that naturally made our curiosity even more profound. The fact that Yukari should have shown an interest in Granny's reactions at the cinema was just one indication of the effect this repression of our desires was having on us.

Granny went out alone sometimes as well. On the seventeenth of each month she would leave in the morning wearing black, formal Japanese dress. She was, needless to say, going to visit the grave of her dead husband and victim. She did let slip on one occasion that on her return from this expedition she would call in to see a man who acted as a probation officer (he ran a shop that sold seals and stamps) and talk of her latest doings, thus taking care of her month's duties in one day. Since I never saw her in black formal dress I wasn't particularly affected by this, but apparently for Yukari and Tsuru seeing her off on those days and deliberately not asking her where she was going was a very moving experience, and they both began to be stirred by strange emotions. It wasn't only that she looked like the *grande dame* of some noble house as she set off, refined, dignified, imposing, but she also had something of a pensive sorrow about her more suited to a tragedy queen.

Gradually an odd idea began to take possession of Tsuru's mind, perhaps stimulated by the fact that she too had been obliged to wear mourning once this month. One evening at the beginning of May when I'd made one of my rare returns home by six o'clock I found that, just as rarely, Yukari had taken her grandmother on a visit back home. While I was still in the living room reading the newspaper, not having changed yet, Tsuru brought in the tea, poured me out a cup, then went on kneeling there and said:

"Why do you think, sir, that Mrs. Nabeshima did, well, you know?"

This was an obscure way of expressing herself, but she was asking a very central question. Obviously she must have been thinking about it a great deal, since her cheeks were quite red with the embarrassment of broaching the subject even this indirectly, and I began to wonder about Tsuru, idly imagining that this middle-aged maid of mine, despite the fact she was supposed to have been married, might well be still a virgin. But eventually I did reply to her.

"You mean why . . . that?"

"Yes."

"Why did she kill him? That's what you mean?"

"Yes."

"I don't know. I investigated it a bit, but couldn't find out anything specific. Some kind of *crime passionel*, maybe. Could always be quite wrong, of course. Hasn't she ever told you anything? I don't mean anything you may have got out of her, because of course you haven't, but, you know, just something she might have said?"

"No, sir, nothing at all. She does happen occasionally to talk about prison life. Just the other day when the mail came she said how nice it was to be able to open your own letters and not have to read them after it had been done by someone else; but then she looked at me as if she felt she'd said the wrong thing and smiled a bit ruefully. I said what a hard time she must have had, but she only went on to talk about what we'd be having for dinner that evening."

I was rather struck by the idea of the pleasure that reading letters that hadn't been through the hands of the censor would give, and I must have shown my interest, for this seemed to encourage Tsuru.

"I think perhaps there has been some mistake," she said.

I waited for her to continue.

"You often read about it in the papers, innocent people being found guilty."

"You mean she was sentenced for a crime she didn't commit?"

"Yes. The thought just seemed to cross my mind the day before yesterday, in the evening when I was doing the washing. After all, such a wonderful person like that, it's not possible she should do something as atrocious as to slay her husband."

"Um," I grunted. "That would be nice if it were true, but is it? Wouldn't she tell us herself if that were the case? And yet she hasn't said a thing about it. After all, the very first time Yukari met her she confessed quite openly that she'd killed her husband with a razor, didn't she?"

"That was not what she said to me, sir. She merely said she'd been sent to prison for murder. Of course, I was simply astonished, I was, which was why I started drinking, to calm myself down."

Tsuru started apologizing again for her behavior that night as if she found the mere memory embarrassing, but I stayed with the main question.

"All right, so you're suggesting she gave the name of the crime for which she was sent to prison, but she didn't say she'd actually committed it. In other words she was sent to prison for something she didn't actually do? Well, I don't know. Of course there do seem to be a lot of mistakes made in the courts. Of all the legal profession the judiciary are said to be the worst. . ."

I suppose one could claim that I'd made this quite unfounded and brash remark because I was an economics graduate and had a complex about graduates from faculties of jurisprudence, but I feel it was rather a matter of my having no real idea how to handle a maid who was caught up in a fantasy of this kind. I merely wanted to bring the discussion to an end, but Tsuru wasn't prepared to let that happen.

"That scar on the finger of her right hand; couldn't it have been caused by torture?"

I found myself literally boggling at this, and could only produce a few grunts and mumbles in reply, which made Tsuru even more overbearingly confident.

"She doesn't say anything because she is determined to bring no distress or trouble upon this house. A lady of the old school like her would do that, simply endure, simply and bravely put up with everything in silence. . ."

She screwed up her face as if she were about to burst into tears. I hadn't a clue what I could possibly say in reply, but luckily the man from the saké store arrived with a delivery and that brought the talk to a close.

As I lay on the tatami I started thinking about the subject. First of all, this kind of romantic fantasy was obviously the best and easiest way of reconciling the ordinary citizen to the existence of crime. It meant that crime did not actually exist, for all convicted criminals were in fact not guilty and thus peace and goodwill alone existed on earth. If you heard or read about a crime, you knew the charge was baseless, any indictment a result of torture, and verdicts of guilty mere miscarriages of justice; and so we were living in a positive utopia, a society in which not one single genuine criminal existed, a world full of virtuous people in which it was a genuine pleasure to live—that is, until you became the victim of a crime, or even turned into a criminal yourself.

As a reaction against this world I began to imagine what it would be like if I myself were murdered by Yukari for some reason or other and, after ten or twenty years had elapsed, she came each month to visit my grave, dressed in black and all the trappings of melancholy mourning. Naturally I didn't find the image very pleasant. I grimaced and shook my head as if trying to dislodge it, and then it was replaced, for reasons I cannot fathom, by another image of myself, an imprecise, blurred lantern slide of me grown old, wearing the morning coat I'd been obliged occasionally to put on while working at the Ministry of International Trade and Industry, walking among the gravestones.

I sat up in a pensive mood, and smoked a cigarette as I looked out at the small garden in the twilight. The evening birds were singing away, and while hearing their sounds, though not listening to them, I began to question this desire to see Utako's crime as only a false charge against her, wondering if it wasn't simply an example of some popular wisdom which attempted to justify the curiosity it felt toward the criminal act by turning it into an ethical concern with justice. It seemed to me more than likely such unconscious motives were at work, and the excitement with which newspapers revealed miscarriages of justice was presumably because they'd perceived or intuited the way their readers' minds worked. It then occurred to me that my maid's concern with the larger issues of justice wasn't something I could ever have much use for, so I merely smiled and decided to let the matter rest.

Since I hadn't gone along with her theory, Tsuru next whispered it to Yukari, who reported it all to me, apparently much amused.

"What a weird idea," she said, obviously not prepared to take it seriously. "After all, it's hardly likely, is it?"

I agreed, adding I wasn't unsympathetic to her desire to think like that; and then I went on to talk about the scar on the finger, since I'd been giving it careful scrutiny ever since Tsuru had mentioned it. Well, there was a small scar there all right, so she must have sustained some minor injury, but even the country police would hardly have deliberately injured people's fingers at that stage in our history, and it was almost unthinkable in postwar Tokyo that rough methods of that kind should be used.

"Even assuming there was some sort of coercion used," I said, "it would only have taken the form of, say, making her sit straight or kneel upright for a while."

"Well, that wouldn't have had much effect on Granny, because she can sit like that for one or two hours with no trouble," Yukari replied; which did mean, I assumed, that she agreed with me, and was in total accord with all my ideas on the matter. Imagine, then, my consternation when I discovered, in less than a month, Yukari had been converted to the belief that Utako had been falsely convicted.

In the middle of May I had to go for a few days to Taiwan on business, returning on the twentieth at about noon. I went straight from Haneda Airport to the office, and after tidying up two or three things I telephoned home. I just wanted to announce my safe arrival and also to arrange to have dinner alone with Yukari that evening, something we hadn't done for a long time. Up until the time Utako had come to live with us, Yukari and I had always eaten in the living room (on those occasions when I was home for dinner) and Tsuru had eaten alone in the kitchen. Still, we could hardly have Yukari's grandmother eat in the kitchen, and if we had her in with us Tsuru would feel left out of things, so we moved a larger table into the room and all four of us ate together. That was fine, but there were times when we looked back to those days when the two of us had been alone together, and we'd talked about going and eating out sometime, just the two of us, although up to now the opportunity hadn't presented itself.

167

While looking forward to meeting Yukari that evening, and clearing up the pile of papers in my in-tray, I had a visitor who brought with him a letter of introduction from my first wife's father. He said he was the president of some trading company of which I'd never heard. I had him shown into the reception room and, when I'd reached a natural breathing stage in my work, I went in to see him. He was a bald, greasy-looking man with a good deal of flesh on him, fairly old—just slightly younger than my former father-in-law, I thought, and the fact that the letter referred to him as an "old friend" seemed to imply my assumption was right. Presumably my ex-father-in-law must have established some kind of connection with him when he was working in the Ministry of Commerce and Industry. Perhaps he was feeling the cold because of his age, for he was wearing a three-piece suit although it was well on in May and very warm outside. Still, he wasn't all that badly dressed in fact, but his was the kind of face I have a distaste for, and that, combined with the sort of foxy dotard look he had, meant, quite simply, I wasn't much taken with him.

After a long apology about suddenly visiting without first inquiring after my convenience, the old man chattered about this and that for a good while and finally got down to business. I listened to this as if it were an appeal from some petitioner, always smiling and cheerfully considerate but only replying in the most ambiguous way. So he started all over again, repeating the same rigmarole, to which I replied in the same desultory manner which neither encouraged expectation nor absolutely forbade it. His next move was to invite me out to dinner with him that evening should I have the time to spare, which naturally I didn't and so declined, courteously of course, saying I had a previous engagement.

As soon as he'd left I passed his card to one of the planning department staff in order to have his company investigated; and then, to make sure, I rang up my former father-in-law.

He asked me how things had been in Taiwan, and I was interested to see that he knew about my visit, although apparently he'd rung me at home the day before yesterday and heard about it that way. What he'd rung me up about was the same thing as I was phoning him about now: today's visitor.

"I'm fairly certain he spent the war in Manchuria, so I must have met him at one of those prefectural association get-togethers. Can't be sure, though: getting a bit forgetful these days. He asked me if I knew of anybody in domestic electrical appliances, so I wrote that letter of introduction for him. Still, he's by no means an intimate of mine, so there's nothing for you to be concerned about there. That's about it, I think."

It was very much what I'd expected him to say, and he then reminisced about Chinese food in Taiwan toward the end of the war when he'd been sent there on Ministry of Munitions business. I kept things going a bit longer by comparing the food situations in Japan and Taiwan during the war.

I had arranged to meet Yukari at six o'clock in a hotel lobby. I left my heavy suitcase with the company janitor, saying I'd come back to collect it later, and set off a little earlier than I needed to. I'd walked from the subway station and just reached a main intersection near the hotel, where I was waiting at the crossing for the lights to change, when I noticed Yukari was standing exactly opposite me on the other side of the road. She must have arrived a little early, I assumed, and was taking a stroll in the May twilight. The young woman in the white dress with purple polka dots still hadn't noticed me even though there was now practically no traffic passing, and she stood there idly in a rather affected way. To her right was an old foreign couple, and behind them a group of women dressed as if they were just returning from some wedding reception, each holding a gift wrapped in identical red and white and talking constantly to each other about something.

I kept expecting her to notice me, but although she was facing in my direction she still maintained her rather prim, distant expression. I finally lost my patience and raised my hand when I saw she was looking intently at me, and then immediately her face broke into a smile of incredible sweetness, like a flower opening. Straight away she stepped smoothly out toward me, still smiling, and I let out a great shout of warning. A light brown limousine swept by on the other side of the road but, once it had passed, there was Yukari back on the edge of the sidewalk and still smiling at me. The lights at last turned green and Yukari and I met in the middle of the crossing, where she separated from the old foreign couple and the women returning from their wedding since she went back with me to the side from which she'd come.

As we walked toward the hotel she said:

"Fancy shouting like that!" remonstrating as she stared at me with her great big eyes.

This mild incident had made me feel extraordinarily happy. It seemed to me that she'd been prepared to risk death in her desire to meet me, such was the depth of the love she felt. So the delighted middle-aged husband said:

"Quite an assignation, Yukari; dicing with death."

"That's an exaggeration, that really is."

My feeling of happiness lasted a long time. Even though we were kept waiting ages for the elevator, this allowed me adequate time to boast about the gift I'd brought back from Taiwan (I didn't disclose what it was), and although the window table I thought I'd reserved hadn't been kept for me through some oversight, I remained full of good humor. We both read through the menu with great care, rather as if we were reading the Saturday evening newspaper, ordered the food and the wine, and then chatted about this and that. Yukari announced that her mother had paid us a visit during my absence, bringing her grandmother's favorite: boiled rice wrapped in fried tofu.

"Father may be sly, but Mother's worse," she said. "Father's like that because he's an intellectual, but you could hardly say the same about Mother, could you?"

This unpleasant remark gave me a certain amount of pleasure, since it seemed to indicate she'd detached herself completely from the Nonomiya household and was now entirely the wife of Eisuke Mabuchi. What had happened was that her mother had come bringing cash for Granny's living expenses and pocket money (her real reason for coming) and handed it over to Yukari, saying from next month onward the same amount would be paid direct into a bank account. Yukari asked me what she ought to have done, and I said she was right to have accepted it. She went on to complain that nothing for March and April had been included, and looked as if she were about to say more, but she changed her mind and started drinking her soup again.

Finally she said Oguri had telephoned. He'd had no particular reason for doing so, only he'd rung me at the office and heard I was in Taiwan, so he'd telephoned Yukari jokingly suggesting she must be lonely.

"Well, that was very kind of him, wasn't it?" I said.

"Still, I really think he wanted to find out about Mayo. He asked me if the rumor was true she was going to give up modeling. I really don't know why he couldn't just ask her himself."

We had now got on to the meat course, and as I ate my veal I remembered the telephone conversation with my former father-in-law. I mentioned this to Yukari since he said he'd phoned the house.

"Oh, I forgot about that!" she said, poking her tongue out slightly in a minor gesture of self-reproach, and not wasting the gesture by licking some gravy off her lips. I drank up my glass of wine, poured out another, and reminded her she was supposed to record all incoming calls in a memo book provided for that purpose and then read them out to me as soon as I got in touch (which was a repetition of the same instructions I'd given her just after we married). Yukari apologized and I returned to the subject of Mayo. Yukari had talked to Mayo about what Oguri had said and she'd laughed and explained he'd no doubt picked up the idea in the following way. Only the other day she'd said to one of the fashion photographers that it was probably more interesting working as a bar hostess than a model, and jokingly added that perhaps she'd be better off in a bar herself. It just so happened that this photographer's elder brother was an ex–film director (Yukari had even met him once) who also happened to be writing a series of gossipy articles for Oguri's magazine about what kind of food went best with saké.

"Well, that proves it. It certainly is a small world."

As I was nodding wisely at my remark, Yukari quite suddenly switched to a totally unconnected subject, saying she thought Granny's being sent up for murder was probably a case of wrongful conviction. Luckily she did have the wit to keep her voice down as she said this. So once again I found myself dumbfounded by her, but this didn't prevent her giving me a serious account of how she'd come to this conclusion.

She had learned to play cards ("flower cards") at the modeling agency, and quite recently she'd learned a new game which she was wild about. Yesterday she'd invited Mayo to come back home, and on the way she dropped in at a bookshop and bought a pack of cards, and they'd played at home for quite a long time. Eventually, after long persuasion, they'd managed to get Granny to join them, but before that she'd constantly told them not to laugh and shout so loud because they might disturb the neighbors. Most of this veiled criticism had been nervously addressed to Yukari, and only showed how much she was concerned with respectability and what other people might say. This was particularly noticeable, however, when Mayo had given a loud shriek and Granny had put her finger to her lips and told her to shush. Such was her discomfort she shrugged her shoulders as if giving them up for lost, and then on at least two occasions she rebuked Tsuru in a very stern manner, glaring at her and shifting her seat ostentatiously.

After this detailed account of last night's proceedings, Yukari took her glass in her hand and said:

"Do you understand what I'm trying to say?"

"Yes, I do. You're saying it's simply impossible that someone as concerned with old-fashioned values and wondering what the neighbors will say (to wit a very moral person) should have killed her husband. You're suggesting there is something odd about an evil murderess going to pray each month at the grave of her victim in commemoration of the day on which he died. This is, therefore, a case of someone being falsely accused and convicted. The true villain is somewhere else, a man or a woman, alive or dead, and. . ."

"That's right. Exactly," said Yukari, who was still holding her wine glass in her hand without raising it to her lips.

"Well, I wonder," I said, and had another piece of veal, some vegetable, and then another sip of wine.

"Something wrong with it?"

"Maybe. What you say makes perfectly good sense, but if you consider it from a slightly different angle then you could argue it's precisely because she is that sort of person that she was able to commit that kind of crime."

"Could you?"

"Yes."

I explained that a concern with keeping up appearances and worrying about what other people might say was a form of ethical consciousness, but a person with such moralistic inclinations tended to de-

172

mand moral behavior even more rigorously of other people. If these other people showed no concern for the social appearances that meant so much to Granny and behaved in such a way as to cause her public humiliation, then it was certainly likely she'd feel very angry.

Yukari nodded: "That's why we were told off, then. Not just me but Mayo and Tsuru too."

"That is true to some extent, although you weren't being rebuked so much as cautioned or advised." I hesitated to say the next words but finally added: "In the case of real anger an admonition wouldn't be enough. It would take a more violent form."

"Well, you know, come to think of it, when she's arranging flowers she looks quite terrifying cutting the stems and branches and things."

This could hardly be taken as serious evidence in establishing the guilt of a murderess, but as I drank my wine I felt satisfied with myself in having at least got my argument quite conclusively through to her. But, inexplicably, she soon said:

"I think the real criminal was a man, and that Granny just took his place."

"Took his place?"

"Yes. Almost certainly he'd have been her young lover—well, no need to be young, of course—anyway, her lover, and he did the actual killing. That's why she took the blame on herself."

"You mean she confessed to his crime?"

"Seems likely, doesn't it?"

I happened to glance at her face and saw she was actually serious; indeed it might be more correct to say she looked positively grave. I realized her statement was probably a mixture of the invidious influences exercised upon Yukari by romantic novels and films, and Tsuru's obsession with the *yakuza* type. It was probably a fantasy the two of them had dreamed up together last night after Granny had gone to bed. I was aghast, although this didn't seem the time to go into the matter since I had to order dessert first.

After a while, however, I went back to the subject and asked her to see it from my point of view. The first step in my refutation of her theory was the one I'd used previously against Tsuru, namely that if she was innocent it was odd she'd said nothing about it to anyone. Yukari's reply was that she was still covering up for her lover, and she seemed disinclined to accept my argument. So I moved on to my second point, which was that the business of taking the blame for someone else's crime might work in the *yakuza* world since the assumption there was that the police had no desire whatsoever to discover the real criminal; but in the case of honest, decent people they certainly had that desire and it was hardly thinkable they'd swallow a deception of that sort. This seemed to have a definite effect on Yukari, and clearly she was wavering, but her response was of the "Really?" or "Just can't believe it" kind, and she persisted stubbornly in her belief.

I began to think of breaking the news to her that I'd acquired actual newspaper accounts of the crime, although I realized she would be angry with me for not showing them to her before. No amount of talk on my part about wanting to protect, out of pure kindness, my young wife from a shock like that would convince her that I wasn't being merely secretive and scornful of her, so I decided to keep quiet. There was also the awareness that any criticism she might make of my behavior could well be justified, so I told myself I would, sometime in the very near future, show her the photocopies, claiming they were something I'd only recently come by. For the time being I decided to make my third point.

"What do your parents think about this business?"

The question immediately made Yukari despondent. Professor and Mrs. Nonomiya had never put forward the idea Granny might not be guilty, and their constant efforts to evade the subject made it only too clear they were quite convinced she was.

"Which means, surely, she must have done it?"

"Well, I'm not really in a position to ask, am I? I can't go into all the details just like that. It's not a very nice subject for a start, anyway. Still, I just think the way she behaved when we were playing cards last night. . ."

This was a desperate attempt to get the subject back onto safer ground, but since she realized it wouldn't work she simply started to sulk.

"Okay. Then the best thing is to find out properly. Ask your mother. That's the best way."

After that it was time for coffee and *gâteau*, but the cake was too sweet and there was too much of it, though I didn't say anything, since what was supposed to have been a pleasant evening out had already had a damper thrown over it by Granny Utako, and I didn't want to add to the bad mood we were both in. Yukari remained silent for some time after she'd finished her dessert, then smiled slightly and stood up. I smoked a cigarette and reflected that it had been a mistake to let Granny stay with us, although there was nothing I could have done to prevent it on that first night. This turned my thoughts in the direction of the Dolls Festival, wondering why they should celebrate it in a women's prison. I was pretty sure they didn't celebrate the Boys Festival on the fifth of May in men's prisons, with those military dolls on display and all the old lags eating rice cake wrapped in oak leaves and gazing at the things. These foolish reflections engaged me quite seriously until I began to feel quite annoyed by the unfairness of such different treatment.

Yukari was away a remarkably long time, and when she came back she said with a shamefaced expression:

"You were right, she said. Lucky we didn't bet on it."

I couldn't work out what she meant, and she explained she'd telephoned her mother.

"You phoned her? On a public telephone?"

"Don't worry. It was all right." She waved her hand and said there were three phones right at the end of the passage and not a soul around so she'd suddenly decided to ring home. Mother had been all het up at first when she'd asked about Granny, saying they had three people from the university there and she had her hands full and couldn't she ring back about it some other time. This may have been genuinely true but it sounded to Yukari as if she were just trying to wriggle out of it again, so she forced her to give straight answers to her questions, begging her just to tell her if Granny had taken the blame for someone else's crime or had really done it herself. All she wanted, she said, was a simple answer of yes or no. This was given her by her mother, who said yes, she really had done it, and no, she wasn't covering up for someone else. When Yukari pressed the point again she gave the same answers.

Yukari gave a deep sigh:

"Well, Tsuru's going to be really disappointed when she hears this."

Obviously she was expressing her own despondence, and I muttered the odd remark about that being just the way it went, which served neither as consolation nor even as wisdom. Outside the window the deep blue-black of night extended, and reflected in the dark mirror of the plate glass were the waiters pushing wagons about and stopping before the guests' tables, pouring alcohol over puddings and ice cream and setting light to it, so that the flames flashed and trembled in the night. As I gazed at their reflections Yukari was looking at one of the actual wagons.

"I wish I'd had one of those instead," she said, virtually to herself.

"Why don't you order one?" Suddenly I was satisfied and happy again. The meal had been good, as had the wine. The business in Taiwan seemed to have gone well. There was no good reason why I shouldn't consider my position with the company as fixed and settled. My young wife had not only grown to admire and respect my ways of thinking about life and the world in general, but she was so fond of me that when she had seen me standing by the roadside she'd made straight for me, heedless of danger, like a dog when it sees its master. I smiled languidly. The sense of happiness and well-being I'd experienced before seemed to have doubled in intensity.

Still, what probably caused me most satisfaction was another aspect of this evening. I'd always felt that I alone had been struggling so far with these knotty problems of crime and society and the relationship of the criminal to us ordinary citizens, but now it seemed both Yukari and Tsuru had become aware of these questions as well (even if only at this late stage and in surely the vaguest possible way) and were beginning to share my burden. That was why they'd leaped to the nonsensical conclusion that Granny wasn't guilty of her crime, a preposterous solution which they'd soon realize was of no help whatsoever; and now they were going to find themselves in real trouble. So as I watched the flames reflected in the black window of the hotel restaurant, inwardly scoffing at the two deluded women and also pitying their plight, at the same time I felt heartened that I'd obtained two companions in misfortune, enjoying that silent delight of the precursor, the pioneer, the pathfinder, the trailblazer, the man who observes others treading the same path he has already traveled, and yet decides to mention nothing of it to them. That, at least, is the way I think I felt; or let's say it would be difficult to maintain I didn't feel something like that, as proof of

which I can offer the fact that I then said to Yukari in a cheerful voice:
"I think you'd better tell Tsuru as soon as possible."

The next morning I met Mayama, our managing director, in the corridor and told him about the old man in the three-piece suit and what he'd had to say and what I'd learned by having his company investigated. He gave his immediate and unreserved approval of the way I was handling the situation. Mayama was in the habit of classifying everything under three categories, A, B, and C; and the C classification was for matters on which he was only prepared to give thirty seconds of his thought.

A few days later the old man suddenly descended upon us again, this time bringing with him some joker in his fifties who was considerably shorter than me and yet looked as if he must have weighed almost twice as much. This Tomokichi Murata said he was a general dealer in domestic electrical goods and claimed to know three people on our staff, starting with the managing director. I felt skeptical as to the degree of intimacy he'd achieved with them, and assumed he probably just knew their names. Murata was, in complete contrast to his companion, a rather flashy dresser obviously doing his best to look young, and he had the friendly behavior to go with his wide, indiscreet tie, keeping up a perpetual smiling and beaming from beginning to end. Presumably that must have been his role, since he'd nothing whatever to say about the issue at hand, but seemed to pay much more attention to two or three landscape photographs (all of the same village with apricot trees in blossom) which our president had taken and which were hanging on the walls of the reception room. Photography was our president's main interest in life, and it turned out that it was also Murata's hobby, for the old man twice made jokes about it during the conversation.

My intention was to put a gradual damper on the proposal that the old man was making. I said it was a very interesting project, but I doubted if our company really had the capacity to see it through, and we would need to study it a while before committing ourselves in any way. Obviously he must have gathered we didn't want anything to do with it, but he still persisted in inviting me out to dinner again, just the three of us, tonight or tomorrow. I was particularly conscious of the fact that Murata seemed to be paying even closer attention to the views of the apricot trees as this subject was raised, and I replied that

I was fully occupied on both evenings. The old man seemed to realize there was no point in extending any further invitations. My assumption was that the matter was now closed and they knew I thought so, although both Murata and the old man looked very unconcerned as they took their leave.

Certainly as far as that evening was concerned I hadn't been lying when I said I had a previous engagement, since I'd invited out three of the mainstays of the Ministry of Finance. Thus I got home horribly drunk and late at night, mumbling a few cheerful quips to Tsuru as she let me in, and making my way upstairs to the bedroom, which I found to my surprise had so many things scattered all over the floor there was hardly space to stand in. In the dim light I happened to tread on a cardboard box which sent me staggering toward the bed. I just about managed to cling to the bed, but then sat down on a pile of foreign magazines which immediately gave way beneath me, and I let out a deep sigh.

The noise must have woken Yukari since she apologized from the shelter of her bed in a very sleepy voice, saying it was all right for me to switch on the light. I stood up and stretched my hand out toward the wall switch, and a dazzling light poured down from the ceiling, illuminating a melancholy litter, scattered higgledy-piggledy on the carpet, of handbags of various sizes, packets of Kleenex, round boxes for hats and square boxes for shoes, drawers removed from the chest of drawers and just left there, a box of chocolates, an iron, odd gloves, some coat hangers, a koala bear (the noseless one), and boots with newspaper stuffed inside them. This mass of objects had been piled together in small heaps in places and a kind of apology for a path had been cleared from the doorway to the bed. It was so ludicrously narrow that the scene was dominated by its absurdity and I felt my irritation gradually subsiding. So the man who'd been flat on his backside addressed the woman who lay curled up beneath her bedcover like a kitten:

"What is all this?"

Yukari covered her eyes with her hands to shield them from the light and squinted at me between her fingers, giving a lengthy, serious account of things. Her voice, however, gradually took on a languorous note, and finally she began giggling and returned to her normal chatterbox style. Her legs were now stretched out quite straight beneath the bedcover.

This is what had happened. That afternoon Mayo had brought the photographer Kaizuka to the house in order to pick up the negatives of those demo photos he'd once left with her. Yukari had started to search as soon as she'd had the phone call from Mayo saying they were coming, but she just couldn't find those empty biscuit tins anywhere. After they'd arrived the two of them had waited ages, listening to the stereo and watching television, but Yukari was still unable to unearth the things, so finally when Mayo and Kaizuka began playing cards she just gave up looking and joined in. They left late that afternoon, saying they'd come back in two or three days' time, and she had started looking again, becoming so exhausted she'd gone to bed without even taking a bath.

I sat on the edge of my bed and laughed. My right foot was resting on a fairly large pile of foreign fashion magazines, and in front of my left foot was a brightly patterned, small round object for keeping stockings in. This was fully unzipped and I saw it contained no stockings but was packed full of bits of material. Seeing I was in a good mood, Yukari herself was quite relaxed now, so she repeated her account of all the trouble she'd had looking for the empty biscuit tins with all those negatives inside.

"Well, bound to turn up sometime, just where you didn't expect to find them."

This irresponsible remark afforded Yukari no comfort.

"That's exactly what won't do. He suddenly seems to need them now." Then she remembered something. "Tell you what. I've found something you should enjoy. Look, give me that. No, not that; the one next to it."

After much severe finger pointing from Yukari I finally managed to lay my hands on what she wanted. It was an old magazine, and on its dusty front cover Yukari, much thinner than she was now, with a face like a boy's, was smiling clumsily at me.

"My first photo as a model," she explained, adding that for a whole month after this magazine had appeared she couldn't go into a bookshop, or even see someone carrying a copy of it on the train, without feeling unbearably embarrassed.

"There's some more inside, on three pages somewhere in the middle. Ought to be a marker, isn't there? I can't stand them, just like souvenir photos. Of course I was absolutely hopeless then."

The reasons she gave were that, first of all, she didn't know how to stand or how to look, and she didn't know how to make up properly, and she also had the bad luck to get a hairdresser who had no idea what she was doing. Secondly, they had this photographer who'd just come back from Paris, where he'd picked up a new method for getting the models in the right mood, which consisted in the occasional fondling of their tits and waists, but at which he was quite astonishingly incompetent. The third reason was. . .

But I found these three early photographs, because of her obvious tension and nervousness, ones of enormous charm, with that something about them which most stimulates and attracts a man. I felt aggrieved I'd never seen her when she looked like this, that we'd never met at that time, and jokingly I told her so.

"My, my, you say the sweetest things," she said, hiding her face with her hands, not because her eyes were dazzled, but as a way of showing her skepticism and teasing me as well.

"It's true, I'm telling you. I'm telling you the truth," I said, vowing my seriousness, and adding: "Why didn't that slob Oguri introduce us then?"

As if to testify to the sincerity of my feelings I gave the round stocking bag in front of me a light kick, and surprisingly the exotically patterned red, white, and green object flew up into the air and landed on Yukari's bed. That was only the container, however, for the contents were all dispersed from its zip opening, twenty or thirty small square pieces of cloth of different bright colors scattering excitingly all over the place. I had a feeling I'd seen some of this neatly cut up material before, and realized Yukari had been keeping the leftover material from her dresses in this tidy way.

I laughed happily. The extraordinary mess of the bedroom was something one could only laugh about, and now that I'd added this further confusion to the chaos I felt I wasn't simply abandoning the concept of order but making a definite rebellion against it. This filled me with happiness, with intoxicating delight. It may have been, of course, that in this mild disorder in one small room I'd seen a premonition of some major disturbance yet to come. But, added to this, even dominating it, was a simple sense of joy, a knowledge that the doubts I'd entertained about Yukari's relationship with this young photographer had been shown to be completely unfounded, since she took him so lightly she couldn't even remember where she'd put the things he'd entrusted to her. Not only was my jealousy without cause, but I felt that her innocence (in that youthful portrait) and her surprising scrupulousness (in the way she kept those scraps of cloth) had been demonstrated in a magic display as those brilliant colors were all scattered about the room.

Since I went on laughing, Yukari, who'd taken her hands from her face, warned me:

"We'll be told off for disturbing the neighbors."

Her face, which still had its makeup on, looked very drowsy.

"In that case we might as well produce some really disturbing sounds," I said, starting to undress quickly.

Yukari smiled: "All right, but go and wash your hands first. I'll bet they're filthy. And bring a damp towel for me at the same time. . ."

Her voice didn't sound in the least sleepy now.

11

Gen Kaizuka came to visit us the following Sunday (by himself this time), and by then his empty biscuit tins had been found. Yukari had thought she'd put them away somewhere in our bedroom, but in fact they were right at the back of the cupboard in Granny's room.

Kaizuka was a young man taller than me, just about the same height as Oguri I should think, and his features were what might be called handsome; the most striking thing about him, however, was his brilliant white teeth. He was wearing a brand-new jacket and trousers to go with his teeth, or so it seemed, though in fact he'd been taking shots of the riot police entering a certain private university that morning and had been completely soaked by the spray from a water cannon, so he'd gone straight to a department store to get a new set of clothes.

"I'd been thinking of buying some anyway," he said, smiling apologetically.

"Do you mean you got a completely new set, underwear and all?" asked Yukari immediately, a peculiar sort of question which made Kaizuka blush. I could tell by the way he turned red that he had a delicate skin.

I was much amused by this exchange as I puffed away at my cigarette, and it continued with what was presumably half-jesting advice from Yukari.

"It must be awfully dangerous with all those stones flying about. Never know when you're going to get hit, do you? You ought to wear a helmet."

"I do wear a helmet. Like to see it?"

So he produced a helmet from the cloth-wrapped bundle he had with him. It was made of a slightly rusty-looking metal, and he said it was U.S. Army issue he'd acquired through some irregular channel.

"Must have been pretty expensive," I said as I picked up the heavy, solid, and slightly damp object with both hands.

Kaizuka looked shamefaced again:

"Everyone pulls my leg about it. They say I'm the best helmeted photographer in the country, and start nudging each other whenever I put it on. They all wear those plastic ones which are just for show, and then go where it's really dangerous. I call that reckless."

Meanwhile Yukari had taken hold of the helmet with great care, as if she were handling some expensive Western antique, and after giving it a good all-round scrutiny which seemed finally to satisfy her curiosity, she went out into the passage and called her grandmother.

"Granny, come here. I've got an American helmet to show you."

As Granny made her entrance Tsuru also appeared with tea and cakes, and both of them handled gingerly what they called the "tin hat." The young man then put on the helmet for us, and with the brown strap (made a darker color by the water cannon) biting into his cheeks, he talked about that morning's disturbances. He spoke in a very calm way about his experiences, and although he was inevitably on the side of the students his grasp of things seemed pretty objective to me. I confess I felt well disposed toward him, even going so far as to think more highly of Yukari for having young friends of this caliber. While he was talking about the riot police Tsuru withdrew, but Granny took off her slippers and folded her legs underneath her on the sofa, smiling and nodding while she listened, which showed she too had taken a fancy to him.

During a pause, Yukari asked him when he had bought his watch, and since an interest was being shown in something other than his helmet he took off his large wristwatch with its red dial and showed it to her. It was a peculiar mixture of vulgar pomp and rustic crudity, and the red strap was twice as wide as the watch itself.

"It's a hippie watch. Dead cheap. Keeps pretty good time, though."

"That's a bit funny, surely: a hippie watch?"

"What's funny?"

"Oh, I don't know; just funny."

Yukari didn't attempt to expand on this remark, but tried the watch instead against her wrist.

"Um, not bad. I bet Shin will want one of these. Probably got one already, though."

She went on to speak about the hippie affectations of her younger brother, Shin'ichi, the Christian college student. The watch was now in the hands of Granny Utako, and she didn't just try it against her wrist but slipped it on and did up the buckle. Since the size of the strap matched the thickness of Kaizuka's arm the watch merely dangled from her left wrist, glittering as it slid about as if she had on handcuffs.

The young man, drinking his tea, got in a swift compliment before Yukari and I managed to:

"It really suits you, you know, Granny."

I'd been thinking of Kaizuka as someone in a constant state of semi-embarrassment, and was interested to see how easily he could pay compliments to a person he hardly knew. He finished his tea, took off his helmet, and said:

"You know, when you've got that watch on like that, it looks exactly like you're wearing. . ."

I was reduced to a panic by this since I was convinced he was going to say "handcuffs," but all he said was "a bracelet," so I calmed down again.

"Perhaps I ought to get one of these?" said Yukari, looking mischievously at me, an obvious dig at the fact that I hadn't bought her a watch yet. But Granny burst in sententiously:

"Well, really, and you've already got a nice watch too."

This prompted an immediate response from Yukari:

"No I haven't. I had it stolen in the department store by some pickpocket. In the elevator."

She sat there totally unconcerned, as if unaware of her own slip of the tongue and my discomfort, but more surprising still was the cool, calm way in which Granny, that red watch still handcuffed to her wrist, replied:

"Did you, now? I didn't know a thing about it. Well, it just goes to show you can't be too careful these days. The world is full of really wicked people."

This critical attitude toward the criminal shook me rather, because I couldn't work out if she spoke with any awareness that she was a criminal herself. In fact it shook my confidence in my own ideas on the subject, although I tried not to show this in my actual behavior, for it seemed to imply (although this was, of course, unthinkable) that maybe she mightn't be a murderess after all, and perhaps she had been wrongfully convicted. This was only the very smallest of doubts, naturally, but it added to an overall confusion and loss of confidence already brought on by the cheerful, unconcerned way in which she'd spoken.

Still, she wasn't the only one who seemed unconcerned. Yukari, having forgotten my firm admonitions to the contrary, was now giving elaborate details of the theft. Granny kept nodding enthusiastically, returning the red watch to the photographer, who put it on again and said:

"Well, you're lucky in some ways to have got away with just that and no real damage done. Petty thieves these days can be pretty violent."

Here was another remark that one could hardly call inoffensive, even if unintentionally so, and I was put nervously on edge again. But a glance at Granny's face showed what appeared to be calm indifference, though there was no way of knowing what kind of suffering she might be enduring inside, as I assumed she must be. I felt I had to change the subject quickly, and although I was aware this might seem rather abrupt I decided to do so by saying:

"By the way, Kaizuka, do you only take these documentary-type photos? The reason I ask is that our president, only an enthusiastic amateur of course, concentrates entirely on landscapes—you know the sort of thing, the old village with the apricot trees in bloom. . ."

Kaizuka responded well to this lead and gave us quite a long account of what he'd done, including his background and upbringing, which reinforced the already favorable impression I had of him since he showed a good understanding of social values, in the sense of knowing how to get on with other people.

He'd become interested in photography at high school, and when he joined the faculty of commerce at a private university he became a member of the photographic club and played an enthusiastic role in it. He must have got a good reputation for himself, because the following year he was asked by one of his seniors, who worked as an assistant to a photographer famous for his landscapes, if he wouldn't take over for him while he was busy with his final exams. Kaizuka leaped at the opportunity to do this very indifferently paid work, not for the free travel but because he wanted to acquire professional skills and techniques. For some time he'd been thinking more in terms of becoming a photographer than joining some business company, and this seemed the perfect opportunity to make a definite choice. So for a bit more than a year, once or twice each month, he would go on field trips, and had seen most of those landscapes that are thought worth photographing.

"I should think I almost certainly went to that village with the apricot trees you mentioned. The one I remember, probably the same one, had a lot of storehouses with white walls."

"That's right, lots of white walls."

"I'm sure it's the same. The pictures we took appeared in a magazine and made lots of amateur photographers rush off to the same place."

Kaizuka talked about the village with his usual enthusiasm for a while, then returned to his *curriculum vitae*.

Some little while after the apricot blossoms had fallen, in fact just about the time the irises were coming into bloom, disturbances started at his university and he found himself being gradually drawn into the struggle. His work as an assistant to the landscape photographer ceased automatically when the great man succumbed to some illness, and he himself was spending nearly all his time at the university anyway. Perhaps as a reaction to all that lyrical work on the "beauty of Japan," he began to find what really interested him was taking pictures of striking students. He managed to sell some of these to the weekly magazines, with the help of another member of the photography club who'd graduated and was working in journalism. This meant he'd almost become a professional, specializing in social problems. His student life, which had consisted almost entirely of strikes and photographs, eventually came to an end when the disturbances settled down enough to allow him to graduate, and he decided not to take a job anywhere but live off the proceeds of his pictures instead. This he had managed to do, although it had meant large economies in his life-style.

"It's a tricky kind of business—dangerous really. I've got nobody pushing for me, no big noise looking after me, but I'm just about making it on my own. Well, half making it perhaps," Kaizuka concluded, flashing his teeth.

I could imagine from what he'd said just how dangerous a way of life it must be, how risky and uncertain; but he looked very calm and composed about it and that made me share his apparent lack of anxiety.

"Of course, unless you've had plenty of experience you wouldn't be all that smart at running away, would you?" said Yukari, and I put in a similar joke saying it would become pretty exhausting once he'd got a bit older and physical debilitation set in.

Granny Utako, still sitting erect, listened to all this with apparent pleasure, but once the exchange of pleasantries was over, Kaizuka's expression changed slightly and he asked me a very pointed question which I had some trouble replying to.

"What do you feel about the anti-establishment riots going on in the universities now?"

I gave a fairly lengthy answer which was all verbal obfuscation and said virtually nothing. Kaizuka went quite red at this, as if himself ashamed of having induced it, and then said apologetically:

"I hope you won't think I'm rude, but I was hoping to hear the actual opinion of someone like yourself."

This was certainly said in all politeness, but it did mean he wasn't going to be fobbed off with my previous spiel, and the question still required an answer.

Yukari asked if we'd like some beer, and I said we would, after which I replied to Kaizuka in the following way:

"I'm not sure I really have an opinion I could state easily, just like that. However, let's put the question another way and ask if I would join in these anti-establishment doings if I were myself a student now. Of course, the assumption itself makes any reply I give virtually meaningless, but, anyway, assuming I was a student I doubt very much if I would actually take part. My first reason is that, as you'll have gathered from the fact that I used to be a civil servant, I am very much an establishment person myself. I'm not quite sure how to put this, but perhaps I should say I prefer to do things that have a more obviously direct usefulness. By that I mean that if it's decided society as a whole requires some basic alterations in its structure, then the universities are the very last places I would start with. If society were to change, then maybe the universities would change with society, or equally they might not. But to maintain that society as a whole would change because the universities had changed seems to me an absurd idea, something that simply couldn't happen."

Kaizuka nodded quietly at this and said:

"I can't say I don't follow the last part of your argument, although there is one small point I disagree with because I feel any attempt to change society must take the form of an engagement in those immediate issues that are closest to one as an individual. Still, the real question, as I see it, is in the first part, about your being an establishment person."

Yukari brought in beer and cheese. We two men drank beer while Yukari had a nominal sip at hers and Granny slowly ate some cheese.

I replied: "I can't see any question there at all, although there might be something to discuss in the rest of what I said. The fact is I just am an establishment person. That's what I am. Look at my career. I started as a bureaucrat in MITI, and a career civil servant at that. I'm now on the board of a company that makes domestic electrical goods. Nobody who's a company director, even if he's only a small fish like me, can possibly be said to be anti-establishment, surely? It simply wouldn't make sense, particularly as the very fact that I'm working in this company now makes it all too clear how solidly I have the government establishment behind me. This is the way it goes. Someone leaves MITI and goes into private enterprise, right? Now, whether this rumor is true or not I can't be sure, but the rumor is that in such a case the government is prepared to give you three chances—that is, they'll look after you on three occasions. So, you enter one business and if you make a mess of it you have another two goes left. That only applies to career bureaucrats: non-career bureaucrats only get one chance. Semi-career bureaucrats—those who passed the qualifying exam but only after they'd actually joined MITI—are given two. Now, I don't want to argue about the rights and wrongs of that, but just to point out the degree to which I personally am being taken care of, and consequently there's no possible chance I could ever be. . ."

I don't really know why I should have given this suspect inside dope, for which I had no evidence, certainly no proof, to a young man I was meeting for the first time. It may be I'd decided I could talk freely to him since he looked so calm and sensible, or perhaps I felt this exposure of my own position, indeed this boasting of my own wickedness, was a good way to ensure the discussion wouldn't drag on much longer. I'd given my point of view in a very relaxed manner, and Kaizuka had grinned at several points while he drank his beer.

Then Granny butted in:

"Does that mean you'll become director of another two companies?"

"That's what I was wondering," said Yukari.

"Can't say," I replied. "Maybe, in some sort of watchdog role; though I assume that doesn't mean I'll be made a security guard." This raised a laugh, and I went on: "Still, there is the question of how long I'll stay in my present company. Becoming a director makes it even more problematic."

Yukari looked as if she'd like some further explanation, and Granny asked me directly why that was so.

"Well, in a company the size of ours," I replied, "although admittedly it may well be the same in much larger organizations, it's the president alone who finally decides who will, and who won't, be members of the board. So it's all right when you haven't yet become one, but once you have and you then lose your place, well, unless you're remarkably thick-skinned, it becomes a pretty unpleasant place to be. You have to get out. That's why all the directors spend so much time sucking up to the president, so that he won't give them the shove next time. . ."

"Then you ought to try and keep in his good books by being mad about photography. Gen can teach you," Yukari said jokingly.

"Maybe you're right," I said. "They'd have to be only landscapes. I don't think pictures of strikes and riots would go down all that big."

They all laughed. As I looked at their laughing faces I thought how nice it would be if I had beautiful white teeth like Kaizuka's and not my own filthy ones the color of cheese. They were even yellower than Granny's. I swallowed my beer slowly, holding it a while in my mouth in the hope that it might make them a bit cleaner.

"Well, I just wonder," said the youth.

"About establishment man?"

"That's right."

I waved the hand that wasn't holding a glass and told him to forget about it, but this denial of mine led to Kaizuka conducting his confrontation from a totally unexpected quarter.

"Still, considering the fact that you were unable to remain in MITI because you refused to go to the Ministry of Defense, I wonder if it's possible to say so with such confidence. Isn't it rather that you've lived on the surface as if you were a true establishment man, as everybody seems obliged to do to some extent nowadays, and yet inside, right in your heart of hearts. . ."

"How did you manage to hear that particular piece of gossip?"

"I told him," said Yukari. "Shouldn't I have? I mean, I thought it was a rather neat thing to have done. Well, wasn't it?"

She turned to her grandmother and appealed to her. Granny responded with a nod of deep approval, either because she really thought so or because she felt Yukari's chatterbox nature should be apologized for in some way.

"That's right," she said quite seriously. "That's how a man should behave, all clean and open. That's the spirit I admire."

This was becoming really embarrassing.

"Well, that's very kind. I'd offer you a drink, Granny, only you've given up alcohol."

I was trying to bluff my way out, but Kaizuka persisted, perhaps in an attempt to take some of the blame off Yukari.

"Mayo told me as well," he said, adding: "I'm sorry if I've butted in on something that's none of my business."

"No, of course not. It's not a matter of any importance. It's certainly no secret. Still, I'm not at all sure it was an anti-establishment gesture, as you seem to assume; not sure at all. It is true I refused to go to the Ministry of Defense, but I don't think there was any kind of ideological motive behind my decision. Something much more simple than that. Namely, I just didn't want to go. Didn't like the idea, that's all. Again, I don't want you to get the wrong impression about this. I wasn't ordered to go. I didn't receive some order I stamped my feet and protested about. It doesn't work like that. You just receive unofficial notification from the director of personnel asking you if you wouldn't mind going somewhere or other; and sometimes people indicate they're not happy with the idea. I don't say it happens all the time, or even very often; but it does happen occasionally. Most people wouldn't do that sort of thing, of course, but if there were no possibility of it happening then there'd be no point in holding any sort of prior consultation at all, would there?"

"Prior consultation?" said Kaizuka, who seemed to have lost confidence in his ideas.

"Naturally. Just putting out a few feelers, that sort of thing. Bureaucracy works like that."

He nodded, but he didn't look as if he was really with me.

"Still, if you do refuse, you certainly pay for it, don't you? They take it out on you, surely? All this business about putting out a few feelers is just a formality. If you don't do what they say, then. . ."

"That's not so," I replied. "Although things could be like that, perhaps, with non-career staff; but career civil servants have a very strong sense of being in the same boat, *esprit de corps* if you like, and they are very, very careful about each other, because the setup is arranged to make them behave like that. Even when I began stalling about the personnel director's proposal the atmosphere was still extremely cooperative and friendly, a sense of both of us wanting to work things out. And as things progressed there was never any particular incident that happened, no confrontation, no confusion, but everything going along quite smoothly and easily. I'm sorry if this is going to disappoint you all, but I don't myself think that had anything much to do with my being chucked out of MITI."

"Well, I don't know, it really does seem. . ."

"It looks as if I'm telling a lie? It's the truth, anyway."

"No, I certainly don't think you're lying," said Kaizuka hurriedly. "I just think that for someone who had the courage of his convictions you're admirably modest about it."

"Thank you. Thank you for turning me into a figure of such heroic proportions."

I made a slight bow to Kaizuka and refilled his glass, also filling Yukari's at her request. It was not an unpleasant feeling being praised by a young man as reliable as he seemed to be, even if the praise was based on a misunderstanding. I was particularly pleased because he belonged to a quite different world and had nothing to gain or lose by his remarks.

"Honestly, I'm not trying to flatter you," Kaizuka said shyly, and looked as if he was going to say some more, but I just stayed silent and drank my beer, showing by my rather distant expression as I nodded two or three times that I wanted the conversation to end there and then. The truth is I hadn't yet related half of the business, but I didn't feel up to giving the detailed account that this complex, ambiguous affair required. I was also slightly regretting the fact that I'd already confessed a bit too much to someone toward whom I had no obligation of any kind.

Granny Utako had probably read the situation since she asked him in a very leisurely way about the village of the apricot trees, and the three of them got into one of those discursive, time-wasting discussions (in which I didn't join) about the relative merits of apricot and apple blossom, about methods of preserving apricots and plums, and so on. When this casual chatter had reached a natural interval, the young photographer turned to me again and, after a moment's hesitation, said:

"Still, you know. . ."

"Oh, not that again," I said, but as my voice didn't sound the least bit out of temper he must have felt it was all right to go on.

"Afraid it is. There's just one slight question still bothering me. That is . . . you're quite sure you don't mind?"

"No, not at all. Go on."

"I was just wondering why someone as courageous, as tough-minded, as yourself doesn't, you know, in the case of Grandmother here, exercise. . . I mean, you have quite a lot of influence."

I didn't see at all what he was getting at, so I just muttered:

"Exercise? Well, yes. Important, I suppose. Of course I'm not in the house all that much so my influence. . . Don't know much about it either. Still, she doesn't seem to be suffering specially from lack of exercise, does she?"

This question wasn't directed at anyone in particular, but Granny mumbled something I couldn't catch and Yukari seemed slightly mystified, so I realized I must have got hold of the wrong end of the stick, although when and in what way I couldn't fathom. Kaizuka straightened me out, however, in a very serious, even fatuous way.

"No, I didn't mean that kind of exercise. I meant exercising your influence, your authority, on her behalf to protest against the injustice she's suffered. I was wondering why you didn't do that?"

In the short silence that followed I heard Yukari give a little gasp, and this seemed to stimulate me into some kind of response.

"Kaizuka, who told you about that? Not Yukari again?"

He blushed immediately and said:

"No, it was Miss Tsuru. Just as I was leaving the other day. . . Sorry. Have I said the wrong thing again? I always seem to be putting my foot in it. Perhaps I'd better. . . ?"

He looked questioningly at me and Yukari, although he kept his eyes away from Granny. Yukari said absolutely nothing, and she had the palms of her hands pressed tight against her cheeks and her head lowered as if to indicate that this was absolutely forbidden territory. I, on the other hand, answered in as relaxed a manner as I could muster:

"Well, there's nothing much to be done about it now. I can't say I'm pleased you know about this. In fact you oughtn't to know, but since you do. . . I don't personally care how much my own history is pried into, but when it starts to go beyond that. . ."

Kaizuka was clearly wavering at this point, but he still kept on with insensitive persistence:

"What does that mean? After all, since she wasn't guilty of. . ."

"Oh please, Gen," said Yukari, trying to stop him.

"Wait a minute, Kaizuka," I said, at which point Granny Utako raised herself slightly on the sofa and, with a totally expressionless face, lowered first her right foot, and then her left foot, very, very slowly. When it seemed she'd finally got both her slippers on, I said:

"That's a good idea, I think, Granny. Perhaps you ought to go into the other room."

Granny, however, after slowly looking around at all three of us, said quietly:

"For some while now I've felt from time to time there's been a little misapprehension about me. Still, since I've never heard properly what this was it would have been a little strange if I'd spoken out, wouldn't it? So I've just kept quiet. This seems a very good opportunity, so I think I might as well tell you the whole story, and have it all out."

Yukari and Kaizuka were so flabbergasted as to be quite silenced. I had decided I must courageously accept the inevitable, and so I said with great gravity:

"If you feel like that, then perhaps it would be the best thing to do. I think Tsuru should be called."

As I signaled to Yukari with a glance, Granny indicated that she agreed. My wife left the room with a stern, almost terrified look on her face, and Kaizuka shifted about awkwardly in his chair, standing up when Yukari reappeared with Tsuru.

"I think I really must leave now," he said, almost shouting.

I made no attempt to stop him, but Granny, both hands placed neatly on her lap, said in a remarkably unruffled voice:

"There's no need for you to go. I don't mind at all. Stay if you wish."

He sat down again slowly as if he felt it would be a serious breach of manners to decline her offer, and also probably because his curiosity held him back. I assured myself, smiling a little bitterly inside, that it hardly mattered if there was an increase or decrease of one or two in the audience, since it wasn't likely to be written up for the weeklies.

Tsuru sat on a small stool in a corner of the room, and Granny, her hands still neatly on her lap, turned to her and said:

"You know, it was very kind of you to think so, but it wasn't a false charge at all."

Tsuru mumbled a little, then paused a while, then finally plucked up the courage to ask her if it was really true. Granny replied that it really was true, it really was, and added the mysterious remark that it was the barber; whereupon she screwed up her face and burst into tears, still talking about the barber. All four of us had no idea how we should react except by shifting uncomfortably about and offering words of consolation. Yukari was searching for a handkerchief but didn't have one to give her, and there wasn't one in my trouser pocket either. The one Kaizuka had was all crumpled and filthy and he only produced it very tentatively. Yukari gave this handkerchief to Granny, who gripped it tight in her hand but made no attempt to wipe her eyes with it. She continued sobbing as she told her story, a fragmentary account which leaped from one point to another and all over the place; but an organized summary of it would read as follows.

Utako had married a man who owned three smallish buildings at Shimbashi in central Tokyo as well as a number of houses near their own which he rented out. Quite soon after they were married she came to accept the fact that he was constantly sleeping with other women and had a regular mistress. However, in the tenth year or so of their marriage, he decided to set up a new mistress in one of his rented houses, which was right behind their own house, and this really made her angry; so she decided she would stand no more of it and went back to her parents' house, taking her daughter (Yukari's mother) with her. This made her husband immediately sorry for what he'd done and desperate to have her back (at least that's what she said), and then he started grumbling and complaining when she refused to return, saying that at least he ought to have the child. The quarreling dragged on for three years until they were finally officially separated. At the time her father's business was going well, and her elder brother, to whom she was very close, was still alive, and her return home caused no problems of any kind. But then, right at the end of the war, her brother and his family were killed in the bombing, her father became ill when the war had just ended, and so the fortunes of the Nabeshima household took an acute turn for the worse amid all the confusion and distress of that period. Even though she tried to keep her father's business going there wasn't much a woman could do, so she found herself living off and eating into the family assets and capital. Nor could she find her daughter a suitable husband to marry into the family and get the business going again. It looked as if they were doomed to poverty, for money simply refused to come near them.

Having decided there was nothing she could do to keep the Nabeshima name alive, she allowed her daughter to marry a lecturer at a private university ("Is that how it happened?" cried Yukari at this point). Then her father died at the end of a long illness and her mother, no doubt worn out from nursing him, went soon after. Now she was quite alone and all she had to live on was the income from her stocks and shares, making up the rest by selling off houses previously leased, as well as the family land. Since the house she had was large she also began to rent out some of the rooms. While she was managing somehow like this she was swindled out of the remaining family land by some shady character (this part of the tale wasn't clear at all, but I received the impression that, as she was approaching fifty, this deception had been accomplished by some powerful exercise of masculine charm), and suddenly she was finding it very difficult even to get by. She still managed to struggle along, selling off stocks and trying to sell her home, although she could never find a suitable buyer; then she scrounged off her married daughter whose husband had now been promoted to assistant professor, though naturally he had very little to spare. Finally she made up her mind to go to her estranged husband and borrow (in fact receive) money from him.

Clearly this would seem a pretty impertinent request to make of him, but she felt there was something to be said on her side, particularly

195

since when they'd divorced twenty years ago she'd received no separation money whatsoever. One reason for this was that a woman's legal rights in such matters weren't recognized before the war; also she was the one who'd insisted on the separation taking place; and, finally, her family hadn't needed money at the time. She also felt she'd brought their daughter up all by herself with no assistance from him, and it was perfectly reasonable she should receive some portion of the cost of raising and educating her now.

Her ex-husband had become an old, gray-haired man somewhat over sixty, but he agreed to see her, behaved pleasantly, and gave her exactly half the sum she asked for. She'd heard occasional rumors that he'd married his mistress, making an honest woman of her, but then the woman had died and now he was enjoying a carefree bachelor life again. Utako's own conviction was that something was going on between him and the maid who brought in the tea, a woman in her thirties.

Two months later she went to sponge off him again, again receiving half the sum she asked for. However, on the next occasion, and then the next, the maid refused to show her in, saying he was out. She thought of just giving up, but necessity insisted otherwise; so one day when she'd just gone out to the local shops, dressed in her everyday clothes, it suddenly occurred to her to go all the way to his house, determined this time to barge her way in. She arrived there exhausted, only to be told once more he was out. She was not going to be turned away, however, so she said she'd just come in and wait, stepping uninvited into the house. She went straight to the living room, and just as she was about to enter a voice inside inquired:

"Oi, has she gone?"

It was her ex-husband's voice, and she felt furious. Not only did it make her furious but it seemed to exert an immediate, irresistible attraction. The maid tried to stop her, shouting she mustn't go in there and holding her arms out wide to prevent it. This really got on Utako's nerves, and she glared at her and asked her to stand aside. Granny realized humble petitioning would get her nowhere and only threats would serve her now, and she suddenly remembered that by peculiar chance she happened to have a cutthroat razor with her. Just as she'd been passing the barbershop one of the people working there had come rushing out and called to her, then given her the razor. It was one she had left at the shop a week ago to have sharpened, but when she'd called for it the day before it hadn't been ready.

Utako insisted over and over again she had only meant to use it to threaten and not to kill. She had no intention of killing anyone, but she felt she just had to remove this nuisance of a woman from her path or she wouldn't be able to see her ex-husband. She still felt, despite what she'd heard him just say, that if she met him face-to-face she would soon manage to get the money out of him. That thought alone was enough to produce considerable inner tension, and it also seems certain that other factors—sexual jealousy aimed at the maid combined with a contempt for her as a member of the lower classes, and the fact that this had been her home and she had forced her way into it as a stranger—must have come together to produce an extraordinary level of emotional turmoil.

"You'd better let me pass. I've got this."

She dug deep into her shopping basket and produced the long, black, oblong case. The maid, however, didn't seem to understand what it was. This really irritated Granny, and in her impatience she took the razor out of the case, quickly threw the case aside, and then slowly eased the silver blade out of the handle. The maid let out a piercing shriek like a whistle, and sat down abruptly on the floor. At this point the door to the living room slid open and the gray-haired old man, wearing a thick kimono over his nightdress, dashed out at her. From then on she remembered nothing except that when she was at last aware of things again her ex-husband was lying soaked in blood, fallen across a vase of flowers in the corner of the room, and her own feet were wet with the water from the overturned vase.

We all heaved a deep sigh, rather like people who've just finished eating an oversize dinner. Granny pointed to the scar on the index and middle fingers of her right hand.

"There, you see."

"That's what it was," said Yukari, while Tsuru nodded silently.

"There was no need for anything like that to happen," said Granny as if lamenting someone else's misfortune. "There really wasn't, was there?"

This didn't receive the assent it seemed to require, for no one answered.

197

"Was there?" she said, and this time she wept.

When she had stopped weeping, Kaizuka addressed some remarks to me rather than her:

"Surely extenuating circumstances should've been taken into account in that case? That's accidental homicide. I don't suppose you could go so far as to claim it was an act of self-defense, but even so..."

"Well, yes, maybe," I said, not wishing to commit myself. According to her description of the trial (which had come earlier on in her haphazard account) the defense had stressed that very point, but the main witness, the employee at the barbershop, said he'd given her the razor not on the actual day itself as she insisted, but on the day before that. Consequently the killing was not judged as accidental or as something done on the spur of the moment, but as premeditated murder planned some time in advance. Granny obviously felt bitter toward the man from the barbershop, although she blamed her lawyer's incompetence more than anything else.

Yukari and Tsuru produced a stream of innocuous consolatory remarks, saying it had all happened ages ago and it was all over now and bygones were bygones. Kaizuka maintained we should appeal to have the trial reopened and the charge changed from murder to accidental homicide, but the two women showed little interest in this for, as they saw it, when all was said and done, she had actually killed somebody. I made no response at all, my own unexpressed view being that there was little chance of any retrial for so minor a distinction.

Granny started talking about her visits to his grave, complaining how very small the temple grounds had become, with a kindergarten and an apartment block they'd put up there. She still went on about "the barber" as well, although this could have been taken in two ways, implying either that the murder wouldn't have taken place if only he hadn't returned the razor then, or that if he hadn't told a lie she would have received a much lighter sentence.

"Still," Tsuru said, "since you are going every month to his grave to pray for him, I'm sure eventually his soul will be able to rest in peace. After all, it must have been very unpleasant for him to go through that kind of experience."

"Yes, it must have really hurt," said Yukari, wincing as she did so.

This seemed a pretty peculiar thing for them both to join forces about and emphasize, and I wondered how Granny was responding to it, although I couldn't work that out at all. Her face was tearstained and swollen, but her expression itself had hardly changed.

Kaizuka chose that moment to add his own contribution.

"Cuts from any kind of sharp instrument really sting," he said, and proceeded to tell us in detail how he once cut himself with a penknife in a handicraft class at primary school. I don't know if he'd suddenly forgotten where he was and whom he was with, or whether this was some crude, incompetent attempt to change the subject. I suspect he himself didn't really know either. I suppose we'd been so worked up by the murder story we were all a bit queer in the head.

While he was still talking about his penknife trauma I interrupted him:

"More than ten years is still a very long time. Nowadays the most one would spend in prison would be ten years, and if you were lucky you could be released after about five."

I wanted at least to get some distance away from the actual killing, and at the same time I rather wanted to have a doubt cleared up which had been bothering me for quite a while; so my remark was really directed at Granny. Yukari then asked Tsuru to bring another bottle of beer, and as she was about to stand up Granny produced another astonishing statement delivered in her matter-of-fact way. She replied to me by nodding and then said:

"Yes. It was because of the jailbreak. They kept me in longer because of that."

Tsuru sat back weakly in her chair again; Yukari cried out "Wow!"; Kaizuka's mouth gaped open; and all stared unblinkingly at her. No doubt I behaved in a similar fashion.

More detailed information revealed, however, that she'd not sawn through the bars of her cell with a file somehow smuggled in to her, nor had she dug a tunnel under the prison walls and escaped; for she hadn't, in fact, escaped herself, nor had anyone else done so in such a spectacular way. What had happened was they'd been on a prison picnic and one of the prisoners had run away, Granny aiding and abetting her escape by telling a minor lie. Modern prisons for women seem to be astonishingly free compared with those of the past (or compared with the image the general public still have of them), and twice a year, in autumn and spring, the prisoners would go on an outing in a fleet of buses. Everybody went, except those who required special custody, and naturally they weren't handcuffed together. It was on the second of these picnics that Granny was asked by a fellow prisoner to cover up for her since she wanted to make a break for it. Although she was due out next month she said she just had to see her little girl's face, and that kind of appeal was one Granny could hardly refuse, so she decided she'd do what she asked. When assembly time came round she stood in front of the one public toilet, asking whoever was inside if she'd finished yet and telling her to hurry up. She kept this farce up for an hour (thus giving the other adequate time to escape), with the result that a fifteen-year sentence which she could have expected to be reduced by five years eventually ended up as thirteen, three extra years for that one hour's work.

We were all delighted by this story of the "jailbreak." Granny herself began to smile as she remembered, running through the story again for us, this time with vivid pieces of mime, such as banging on the toilet door, to aid our imaginations. This led to a flood of other questions about a variety of subjects, probably as a reaction to the repressions and restraints we'd imposed on ourselves when the talk had been about the actual murder.

Kaizuka asked if the woman had escaped successfully, but it seemed she was arrested at home the same night. Yukari was worried she might have been caught before she'd been able to see her child's face, but there had been no need for concern since, in fact, she had no children, and she'd run away because she was desperate to sleep with a man.

Kaizuka responded in cynical disappointment to this, but Tsuru replied pretentiously in a very quiet, sentimental voice that it was bound to be so since that was a woman's karma; although she went on to say sympathetically that Mrs. Nabeshima had certainly suffered through the transgressions of another.

"That's because you're too kind, Granny. You're too good, and she took advantage of your goodness," Yukari added.

"Not really," said her grandmother. "I thought it must be something like that she was after." She paused a little, then went on: "I also felt I wouldn't mind if I got no remission at all. That was a part of it. Fifteen years is the sentence for murder. I thought if I stayed for the full fifteen years then I'd have received my punishment in full as well, and that was just and proper as it should be. I thought I'd feel easier in my mind about it, because I would have paid back all the debt I owed. When I'd paid back all my debt then I could return to the world with nothing to fear. Also, of course, she'd asked me to do it. Once you've been asked to do anything then you have a duty toward that person. It's a question of honor, too, because you've been trusted. That's very important, that sense of duty."

There was quite a long silence after that. Finally Kaizuka leaned his head slightly to one side in some puzzlement and said:

"I suppose it is possible to think like that."

"Maybe so," said Yukari in a more ambiguous response than Kaizuka's veiled skepticism, while Tsuru simply nodded in agreement as if her emotions were too great to be expressed, and she looked at Granny with profound respect.

I wasn't sure if these various reactions, from skepticism to deep emotion, applied to Granny's remarkably optimistic theories about the nature, meaning, and effect of the penal system, or her opinions on the part duty should play in our lives; but when I think about it now I assume they were vaguely directed at both, for both could certainly have been included under the ancient concept of duty (Granny's "debt" being a "duty" she owed to the soul of her murdered husband and to society in general), and so they were responding to that, either with distrust or with admiration. At the time, however, I was only interested in the latter remarks about duty. I felt Granny had given us this detailed account of her crime from the same motive that had made her help a fellow prisoner who was planning to escape. It was from her sense of duty, a duty that, in this case, she felt toward me. Kaizuka had blamed me for not appealing for a retrial and, because she had this duty toward me, Utako had endured the shame of exposing her past in order to show there had never been any grounds for such a demand on anyone's part, and this implied criticism of me was unfounded. I couldn't be certain, of course, but at least at the time it seemed likely, perhaps more than likely. There was nothing else she could have done, for her sense of duty was so firmly rooted it had to take some outward form, and always would.

As these vague ideas drifted through my mind I looked with equal vagueness at her. She was still squatting on the sofa with her eyes closed, presumably because she was tired after having talked so much. I also noticed that Tsuru was still looking at her with eyes full of fervent respect, and as I did so I at last realized that this respect was not for the grandmother of her master's wife, but was more a form of worship of Utako Nabeshima as a person in her own right. This in itself was a surprising discovery, but there was another, worthy of even more surprise, a thought that only rose slowly to the surface of my mind. It had at last got through to me that the one who'd mentioned this to Kaizuka was Tsuru, although the old Tsuru would never (to my knowledge) have breathed a word about the secrets of her master's household to any outsider.

12

From June onward the atmosphere in our house changed, or so it seems looking back at it now, for I can find various indications of the fact that things were changing or had already done so. And yet I remained in a very carefree, untroubled state of mind, perhaps because I was deliberately trying not to be fully conscious of things that I'd noticed, or of which I was at least half aware.

First of all, Granny Utako started talking about prison life from time to time. Still, since she had already confessed so much to all of us, and Kaizuka as well, I could see nothing odd in that; in fact it would have seemed much stranger if she'd gone on concealing anything. It appeared quite natural, with nothing immodest or imprudent about it. Indeed I rather admired her discretion in not mulling over the details of the crime itself again. Also, her recollections of prison life were only certain pleasant memories of the past thirteen years, such as the games of volleyball they used to play, and the various gossipings about whether this pair of inmates or that were lesbians or not; and she only touched on such things briefly and occasionally. When she'd been talking about the lesbians, both Yukari and I would have liked to hear more, but she had nothing very specific to say. In fact she was rather boring on the subject, and I gathered homosexual love held no interest for her at all.

The thing she seemed really quite fanatic about was food, so inevitably we all became reasonably well up on the various menus provided in the Tochigi Women's Prison, where April offered a marked contrast to the junketings of March, due to the new fiscal year, although the really bad period was the four months from May through August. Since that was the season we were now in, she kept wondering aloud whether she oughtn't to go and pay them a visit and take something nice to eat with her. I myself had heard her say this on two or three occasions, and all three of us had agreed it was a very good idea, since one can hardly object to a charitable project of that kind, particularly when there seems little danger of its actually being carried out. Utako was delighted when she heard we all agreed with the idea, and she started thinking about what she should take, finally deciding sushi would be better than sandwiches, but a thermos of hot saké wouldn't be right since it would be a betrayal of His Excellency the Warden's trust and concern. In this prison it seemed former inmates were allowed to use the night watchman's room when visiting, which was very convenient for meeting an old comrade, for here they could sit together and eat the various good things that had been brought.

One problem was we didn't possess in our house the appropriate kind of wooden box for taking this gift of food in. So she went off to a department store, but was absolutely astounded by the prices (not only of the three-tiered genuine lacquer sort but the two-tiered Bakelite ones as well). She began to wonder if something cheaper couldn't be found, or if her daughter Kyoko mightn't have one, and consequently didn't buy anything. In this manner the plan seemed to be dying a natural death, yet only a few days passed before it was revived again.

"We never ever had iced tofu," she muttered one day, her voice trembling with pathos, and the plan to visit Tochigi was taken up once more; although the impression I got wasn't so much of the gloom of the past when she'd been deprived of cold tofu, but of happiness concerning the present in which it was available.

We'd had this for dinner one Saturday toward the end of June, and the following day at Sunday lunch (a combined breakfast and lunch for Yukari and me) Granny was eating her *somen* when she happened to mention the kind of cold noodles they'd had at Tochigi:

"If only they'd had a decent sauce to dip it in it would have been quite nice, I should think. Everybody used to say so."

"Everybody," of course, meant the prisoners in Tochigi, and I was just grasping the fact that this was no statement of nationwide opinion when Yukari started to giggle.

"I'm sorry, really, but it is funny. It's like the way people go on about the war—you know, having to eat dumplings made out of noodle fragments and rolling cigarettes in pages torn out of dictionaries. When Granny talks about Tochigi it sounds just like that to me."

This started us all off on a passionate discussion of the availability of food during and after the war. Since Yukari couldn't join in she expressed an almost pantomimic petulance, saying she was going into the garden, which she did, clattering off in her wooden-soled sandals. This didn't affect us, however, for on we went, smiling ruefully at one another, with our more than twenty-year-old tales of rice and vegetable porridge and Occupation Army Issue corn soup, very much as if the three of us had been in prison together and were enjoying reminiscences of that time. While we were doing so the front doorbell rang and Tsuru got up to answer it; she returned saying that a Mr. Murata was here who said he happened to be in the neighborhood and thought he would just drop in to pay his respects.

At first I had no idea who this might be, but after I'd gazed at his visiting card a while it dawned on me that Tomokichi Murata was the joker claiming to be a wholesale dealer whom the old man in the three-piece suit had brought to see me.

"Is he alone?"

"Yes, sir."

I gave an expressionless nod, and told her to show him into the guest room.

When I entered the room Murata, who appeared only to have just sat down, stood up and smiled cheerfully at me. This was the way one expects a close acquaintance to behave when making an ironical display of good manners, and I was sufficiently influenced by it to give a cheerful, casual greeting in reply, behaving much more informally than I'd done when at the office. Today he was more sober-suited than he'd been on that occasion.

After repeating the obvious lie which Tsuru had already relayed to me about just happening to be in the neighborhood, he deposited a long, thin cardboard box on the table, saying it was just a small token of his whatever. The box was made of a very solid white cardboard, and had "by appointment" stamped on it in gold letters of very antique script.

"Ah, I see," I said.

"Yes. It's a whisky specially prepared for the court."

"Well, well, what a splendid gift."

As I offered my thanks I took the bottle out of its box. It was a special whisky produced by a Japanese firm, and the shape of the bottle and the design of the label were both remarkably uncouth.

"Well, it certainly has a distinct air of the auspicious about it," I said.

"Yes. I confess I'm much taken with it myself. I hope you find it suits your taste."

After that we discussed this year's weather, both of us agreeing entirely with what the other said. Murata went on to praise my house, and I was endlessly self-deprecatory in reply. We'd just about reached the point where I was expecting him at any moment to tell me what he'd come about, when I heard a sudden voice at my back. This was Yukari at the door bringing in the tea, but she made her greeting to my guest with a greater show of energy and charm than usual.

"Good afternoon, Mr. Murata. It's been a long time since we last met."

The man looked up and half rose in his surprise, gasping out her name in a manner that suggested a degree of intimacy in the past, a familiarity I'd have much preferred not to know about, although I now feel it may be possible I misheard what he said and that it was of a perfectly innocent nature.

"Do you two know each other?" I asked.

Yukari was maintaining a deliberate, poised calm before us two astonished men, and after she'd set down the tea and cakes she repeated her greeting to Murata, slightly more formally this time, which seemed to allow him to collect his wits. He and Yukari then clarified the situation by indulging in memories of the good old days. What transpired from this was that some distinguished gents, devotees of the photographic art, had hired Yukari and Mayo from the modeling agency to do some outdoor photography, and thus they had met each other. After that, four or five of them had sometimes had dinner together or gone bowling. As I listened to this conversation in which the names of men I didn't know and of models other than Mayo appeared with some frequency, I began to wonder if their relationship had been quite as innocent as they implied. However, at this point (and well beyond this point, indeed) I forbade myself to give any facial expression to whatever suspicions I might have had.

"You remember when that student at the bowling alley. . . ?" said Yukari, almost doubling up with laughter.

"Ah yes, of course," said Murata, and then explained to me. "Rather an awful experience. I'd just left the others to have a quiet Coke when four students approached Yukari and one of them asked her if she'd like to join them. She declined, saying she was with somebody, pointing me out to the student, who said they wouldn't mind her father joining in as well. Made me see red, I can tell you."

"Yes, very rude of him."

"Ghastly experience," said Murata, pretending "amusingly" to be much aggrieved even in retrospect, "particularly as I'd only taken up this energetic sport to regain my lost youth."

He then turned to Yukari and said:

"Still, remarkable you being Mr. Mabuchi's good lady. It certainly is a small world. I had heard a vague rumor that you'd married some 'big noise' in MITI, but that was, of course, a false report, since you've married a distinguished former government official."

"I really can't let you get away with that," I said. "I have never made a large noise in either capacity."

"Only my little joke, you know," he said rather stuffily.

I explained to Yukari I'd received a bottle of the whisky they seemed to favor in court circles, turning to Murata again and saying:

"Since I never made it very far up the civil service ladder, this is, in fact, the first time I've ever received a gift of this superior quality, as perhaps you may not realize?"

"Oh, really, well..."

"Yes, it really is, isn't it?" said Yukari, picking up the whisky and marching off with it while telling us to enjoy ourselves. This manner of taking her leave, despite the exotic impression her slightly vulgar culottes may have given, was an almost impeccable demonstration of how a young wife of good family is popularly supposed to behave. It even prompted Murata to stand up and bow as she went out.

"How many years ago was that, now, our little amateur photography get-together? Still, I was most impressed, I can tell you. Obviously one expects a model to be beautiful, but that refined charm was something rather special, I thought, showing the breeding one expects in the daughter of a university professor. Now, of course, with that definite poise which maturity gives, she's even more delightful."

After paying this compliment he completed the discussion by saying how remarkably fortuitous a meeting it was, which was presumably his way of summing up the matter. While I listened to him I felt the stirrings of a certain envy, for he'd known Yukari when she was just starting out as a fashion model, an aspect of her I only knew from those three photographs. This was, I suppose, a form of jealousy, even if only a very abstract one; but the suspicions I'd felt before and hoped to hide beneath a perpetually beaming exterior had now totally vanished. I'd decided that only a sick mind would imagine the relationship between Yukari and a man who'd been mistaken for her father as anything other than the ordinary one between an amateur photographer and a hired model—a comforting thought which seemed to be conveniently ignoring the fact that there was a considerable difference in years between Yukari and myself. One other comforting thing was that I'd automatically compared Yukari's and Murata's heights when he stood up to see her out of the room, and recalled Oguri's saying that models didn't like short men. It would be a bit like myself and Mayo (where no one could possibly say we seemed just the right size) and I found the idea wonderfully amusing.

What Murata had come about was the same proposition the bald dotard had put forward, and which he now, in complete contrast to his behavior before, urged on me with great enthusiasm. I had to acknowledge that he did his part with considerable skill, but I'd no intention of changing my mind. I thought the idea of getting color TVs on the market by using a completely different distribution system was a genuinely interesting one, but I didn't see how the low prices he was talking about could be achieved. He kept on persuasively for quite a while, but finally accepted my position.

"Right. In that case there seems no alternative but to drop the whole thing. Still, although we can bury this particular proposition here and now, I should like, if that's all right with you, to make use of this occasion to hope that I may be allowed to call on you again sometime— concerning other matters."

He bowed low and humbly as he said this, and naturally I made the conventional reply. I certainly didn't dream he would so misinterpret me as to come gate-crashing into my house again.

When I went with him to the hallway, Granny Utako was kneeling there with great decorum beneath our handless clock, arranging some hydrangeas. As soon as Murata saw her he also dropped to his knees and introduced himself, praising the way the flowers were being arranged. I remained standing, and as I observed Granny's response I felt slightly sorry for Murata. He was being completely taken in, for it could never have crossed his mind that this composed and refined lady was someone who'd only left prison some six months ago after serving a thirteen-year sentence for murder. Yukari also appeared from within, and Murata stood up and made the usual remarks about hoping the relationship would continue between us, leaving immediately afterward. I think I probably compared their respective heights at that moment too.

Granny seemed to have taken a liking to Murata, no doubt because he'd flattered her to her face, and at dinner she said what an affable person he was, with other words of praise. Yukari said she didn't know anything about what he might be doing now, but previously he'd been running two or three restaurants or cafes, and presumably his geniality was the result of being engaged in a business where the customer was always right.

"Of course," said Granny, "that must be the reason," and she nodded knowingly as if she felt that running a restaurant was a very high-class job to have.

Tsuru remained silent all this time, and although it's certainly not a maid's business to be regularly opening her mouth in situations of this kind, I thought I noticed from her expression that she hadn't liked what she'd seen.

"You don't seem to have much of an opinion of him, Tsuru. Of course, he is very different from young Kaizuka in a number of respects."

This teasing made Tsuru blush, which delighted everyone; then Granny added, as though making some innocuous, everyday remark:

"He's not much to look at as a man, but he looks a bit of a womanizer. He's the type."

Tsuru and Yukari expressed amused surprise, dissent, even giggling contempt at this, and naturally I joined in the laughter; but just for a very brief moment I felt I'd caught a glimpse of the crude, raw atmosphere of the prison with the women sizing up men of all sorts and conditions, from the male warders and other officials to those they only saw in photos in the weeklies. Granny's remark just now had all the weight of those years in jail behind it, an unconscious expression of the "wisdom" or at least the knowingness she'd gained over that long period of time. While I was thinking this I also said:

"Shame on you for saying he's not much to look at. Still, perhaps calling him a womanizer makes up for it."

But I didn't say the thing that was most on my mind: namely that in the three months Granny had been with us she'd never once made a remark that could have been considered "erotic," and the mild joke I'd just made to Tsuru about Kaizuka could hardly be thought of as giving her any sudden license to do so.

The real oddness of this fact was one I didn't have time to brood over, for we started talking about something else, and once dinner was over there were some papers I had to look through. There were to be a number of important committee meetings next week, and I had more than enough to occupy my mind. It was probably because I was so constantly occupied that when I heard a few days later that Murata had again visited the house when both Yukari and I were out, bringing another gift with him—this time a large fish, a black porgy, which he proceeded to prepare for cooking himself, spending a further thirty minutes in casual conversation with Granny before he left—I didn't pay any particular attention but simply wondered at the fact that there seemed to be a lot of men in this world with time on their hands. It didn't seem to worry me that he was bringing these gifts, maybe because bureaucrats are just used to getting such things. All I noticed, I suppose, was the response of the three women, Granny praising Murata more than she had previously, saying it was wonderful how well he could handle a kitchen knife seeing he was only an amateur; Yukari agreeing he must be very good with his hands; and Tsuru keeping her mouth shut firmly tight.

I suppose I first became partially aware that things at home had changed when Yukari's brother, Shin'ichi, got mixed up in one of those anti-establishment riots. It resulted in his receiving bruises on his left arm that would take a good month to heal. The establishment this riot was aimed at was not the usual university authorities but a certain religious body. Immediately before the war there'd been a grand unification of the Christian churches in accordance with government directives—merely one more aspect of the general intellectual repression that went on then—and this religious body had still persisted in an abbreviated form after the war. While the grand amalgamation was still in full flow, just before the end of the war, one of its leading lights had proclaimed that Shinto altars should be set up inside the churches, and had maintained in a book his new theory that the Trinitarian doctrine of God the Father, God the Son, and God the Holy Ghost should be so modified that it became four rather than three in one, the new number being made up by the inclusion of the Japanese emperor. (In fact no copy remains of this book, for the whole edition was burned to ashes when the bookbinder's warehouse was destroyed by bombing.) The rebellious students demanded that this organization be immediately disbanded. Since Shin'ichi was no believer (despite the fact he was a student at a Christian college) and naturally belonged to no church, it wasn't at all clear why he should have so passionately supported this issue. Be that as it may, he put on his black helmet with the gold cross on it, took up his stave or stick, and joined in with the other students as they occupied the third-floor offices of this religious body's building. Here for three days they subsisted on bread and instant noodles, until finally they were driven out by the riot police who'd been called in by the organization, and in the process Shin'ichi received some solid blows on his left arm.

We first heard about this when Tsuru happened to meet Yukari's mother at a subway station; this was followed by a telephone call from us and then a visit from Yukari which put us in possession of the whole story. Yukari said Shin'ichi looked very well and was indulging in energetic debate with his father. Professor Nonomiya argued that the overall tendency nowadays was for the churches to draw closer to each other, as was happening with Protestants and Catholics all over the world, and therefore it was only natural that the rifts between the various Protestant sects should grow less and even disappear. These remarks could be interpreted as putting the case against the students, and they seemed to annoy his wife, who said there was no reason for upsetting the boy with such arguments at a time like this. Here I should point out that I've been obliged to organize, even alter and enlarge, the confused account given me by Yukari, so I can't vouch for its total validity. If I may give one example of the problems I faced: with the question of the three in one becoming four in one, Yukari had hesitated, wondering if it mightn't be five in one or even seven in one. But I soon worked out the source for that final figure: at dinner quite recently we'd used a new flavoring at table to sprinkle on our food (some recent discovery of Tsuru's); it was called Seven in One Cayenne Peppers.

Naturally Granny Utako wasn't much concerned over the theological question of whether three people can exist in one, but she reacted strongly to the news that Shin'ichi had been beaten up by the riot police:

"Fancy that happening to young Shin, a good boy like that. There are some real nasty ones among the police, and that's a fact."

Thus what should have been a debate about the Catholic and Protestant faiths and the problems of church unification became wholly concerned with the trials of poor Shin'ichi, and then turned into a discussion focused on the vulgarity, nastiness, and violence of the police. The emotional atmosphere of the talk also became very high, if not actually heated, for reasons I'm not quite clear about; and though we tended to make light of Granny's attacks on the forces of law and order, it engendered rather bitter, unhappy feelings.

"Still, I can't see why a hippie dropout like young Shin should have to join in one of these political struggles anyway," I said, perhaps trying to move the subject away from this vilification of the police, but it only aroused a peculiar response from Yukari.

"He's said to have masses of girl friends."

The implication of this (assuming it was in answer to my remark) was the incredible logic that because a hippie dropout inevitably had masses of girl friends he was bound to take part in anti-establishment riots. Still, I didn't want to get myself into an argument so I just gave a little "Oh-oh" of surprise and interest, assuming something would develop from there. What did develop was another surprising remark from Granny.

"I don't suppose Shin knows anything about women, anyway." She said this with some confidence, implying, I soon gathered, by his not "knowing anything" that he was still a virgin.

This made Yukari smile; and Tsuru blush a few moments later.

"Really, Granny, the things you say. It's not like it was in the old days now, you know," said Yukari, taking the opposite point of view.

"Well, that's the way it looks to me."

"I wonder."

"I'm sure of it."

As I drank my tea I put in a few conciliatory words:

"It's the sort of question where it's safer not to leap to any generalized conclusion. Up to a certain point in time we can say, I think, that Granny's statement would be true, but it's also possible to say that, quite recently, something may have happened to alter that."

This was the tone I'd learned at committee meetings in MITI when an appropriate form of logic was required to satisfy both opposing parties and offend neither.

Yukari poured tea into her rice bowl. Granny and Tsuru were still eating. As I listened to the two old women chomping their pickles, I imagined a prison scene where each time the women prisoners saw some youth they would debate with passion whether he was still a virgin or not, and I was astonished to think that it was just such a ritual that had suddenly been enacted in my own house. I began to wonder slowly why I'd failed to foresee several months ago that subjects of this nature might soon come to dominate our dinner-table conversations, and I decided something must be done to stop this; but at that very moment of decision the telephone rang, a call from a young MITI official, and I forgot all about it.

Then, one morning a few days later, I entered the living room and saw displayed on the alcove shelves one of those boxes Granny had been wanting to take food in to the prisoners in Tochigi. This was obviously no modern product but a piece of good, solid, prewar workmanship, a three-tiered box of black lacquer. I opened the lid and saw there was nothing inside, but was pleasantly impressed by the sense of depth the bright red interior gave. I went out onto the wooden veranda to talk to Granny, who was in the garden.

"You bought one at last, I see. The price must have made your eyes pop out," I said to her, although I was well aware she would never have paid whatever it must have cost.

"Oh. Did you say something?" she said.

"Yes. Went to bed late last night and I'm still tired this morning. I wonder how Yukari manages to sleep so deeply."

"Ah, when I was young I was always sleepy; sleepy all day."

After this interplay I got back to the subject, and learned it was Murata who had brought it yesterday. Granny said happily she'd just let slip in his presence that she needed one, and it was so good of him to remember and be so thoughtful.

"I said I didn't know if it was all right for me to accept it or not and I should have to ask you first," she said, though making it perfectly clear she was desperate to have it.

"I suppose it's all right. Since I'm no longer a civil servant it won't look as if I've taken a bribe. Not that I would have worried about a thing like this in the old days, anyway," I said and smiled.

"Now you're all ready to go, Mrs. Nabeshima," said Tsuru from the living room.

"Not quite. First I'll have to fill it up with nice things and go and see young Shin."

In this manner the journey to Tochigi was decided. I talked about our factory in Tochigi, but Granny seemed to have no idea where it might be. Of course, I hadn't a clue where the women's prison was, either. I then asked her what Murata had come to see me about, but she said he hadn't come to see me.

"It wasn't Sunday, was it? He just said he'd come to bring this. Then we talked for about an hour or so, him and me and Yukari."

"Surely it was more like two hours?" put in Tsuru.

I found myself worrying slightly about something I knew was of no importance, and then Yukari came down wearing her dressing gown.

"Marvelous, isn't it? Don't you think so? So classical," she said happily.

Sometime during that day Granny wrote a long letter to the prison warden stating the date on which she wished to pay her visit and giving the names of the people she wanted to meet; and the next day with Tsuru's help she prepared enough *inari zushi* to fill the two bottom tiers of the box and set off for the Nonomiya house. Shin'ichi still had his left arm in a sling, but although he'd only just finished his lunch he had a wonderfully healthy appetite, and he said her *inari zushi* tasted quite different from anybody else's. Despite all this praise, however, she returned home in a very despondent mood, and while they were all watching television after dinner she started crying. When I got home around ten o'clock she brought her troubles to me and started sniveling again. The cause of this grief was that her daughter had scolded her for all the bad things she'd said about the police to Shin'ichi. As a mother no doubt she'd been worried her son might be stirred to more mischief by such inflammatory remarks, but from Granny's point of view it was as if her own daughter were supporting the villains who'd assaulted her grandson, or indeed as if she were exculpating the people who were Granny's own enemies.

"She's so heartless. Probably doesn't love even her own child," she sobbed.

It also seemed that my mother-in-law had become very worked up during the discussion, which resulted in her going so far as to bring up the unrelated subject of all the troubles she'd been obliged to go through during those thirteen years, and how much insult and reprobation the professor had endured. This was made worse by the fact that Shin'ichi, who naturally knew about his grandmother's past, put forward a new view of the matter by saying that he, on the contrary, set a high valuation on the crime as a rebellious act directed at the establishment, which upset his mother even more. The one bright spot in this day of gloom was that the professor wasn't home, being occupied with student disturbances at his own university, and thus the discussion was saved from plumbing further depths of obscurity.

Yukari had become quite fed up listening to all the various grumblings by the time I reached home, and Tsuru had gone off immediately to her own room once she'd passed Granny over to me. Unfortunately I was unable to say much to the point in my clumsy efforts to console her, because I was worried I might say something that looked as if I were befriending the police, and also because the fact is, of course, that being a civil servant is in many ways remarkably close to being a policeman. So I kept quiet mostly, eating three of the remaining *inari zushi*, although I ought to have had only two because they can be very fattening. They were really very good, though, the perfect food for summer with just the right amount of seasoning, and I couldn't stop. I washed the feast down with a cup of strong tea, and finally resorted to the emergency measure of giving her some sleeping pills, as I couldn't think what else to do.

While I was sipping a little cognac in our bedroom Yukari came in very quietly, having just seen Granny off to sleep. She apologized for what had happened in a very sweet way, and the sight of her so apologetic made her seem much more frail and charming than usual. I said I couldn't see that it was her fault, and truly I couldn't, but she was very gloomy and depressed and kept on saying how sorry she was. I finally put an end to this lament by telling her to give it a rest, for heaven's sake, and offered her some cognac.

As we both sat there silently drinking, I suddenly found the alcohol had gone to my head, and odd thoughts started to come into my fuddled mind, although the thoughts were, in fact, perfectly logical. For example, I admitted that there probably were a few, maybe quite a few, villains in the Japanese police, but why did that mean I had to sit there silently eating *inari zushi* and listening to an old woman's moans? I felt bitter about this because I was sure it would have tasted even nicer if I hadn't had that sort of thing to worry about while I was eating. Again, no doubt there had been theologians in this country who'd not had a proper grasp of the basic essentials of the Christian faith, and probably there still were, but did that mean I had to force my wife's grandmother to take sleeping pills and then be pestered by the slight worry that I might have given her an overdose? It then struck me that one cause of my troubles, a distant one admittedly, was the way food supplies were distributed to Japanese penal institutions. Well, all right, maybe there had to be some noticeable falling off in quality during the four months of May, June, July, and August, but surely there was no need to go to extremes in the Tochigi Women's Prison. Why did they have to put so much water in the soup? Why did the pat of margarine with the three slices of bread have to be so much smaller than during the other eight months? Why was the once-a-week treat of meat—either beef, pork, or whale (mostly whale)—only half the size of what it normally was (only one-third or even a quarter when compared with March)? And why did that have to result in my wife apologizing to me in that irritating way, and me having to try to comfort her and make her stop, saying "All right, all right" all the time, and getting that desperate feeling that perhaps it was her fault in some way and so start thinking my marriage had been a mistake and I never should have done it? I was angry at the terrible unfairness of it all, but I only had a very vague idea of what I should be angry about, having no object for my rage; until I realized my wrath was aimed at the fact that I myself existed within that complex, elaborate structure which we call society.

How nice it would be if society didn't exist. I sighed for a moment as I relished the bouquet of my cognac.

As I sighed so did Yukari, perhaps stimulated by me, as she lay there sprawled on the bed.

"I wonder why I have to go through all this misery because of something like that?" she said, which was exactly what I was thinking. She went on: "I blame my mother. You should just let old people say what they like and take no notice."

"You may be right," I said, "but she doesn't want young Shin to get mixed up in any more of these riots, I suppose."

This good word put in for her mother didn't deter Yukari, for she went on relentlessly:

"It's an awful thing when you have a mother who's just not very bright."

This was but one criticism among others, and the way she said it certainly seemed to imply that she, though her mother's daughter, should really be considered pretty bright herself. I started to speculate whether it might not be because she was so fond of her father that she was so hard on her mother; but if that were the case, then perhaps she'd grown intimate with me because I was nearly the same age as him; a thought I didn't find particularly pleasant.

13

On the day before the long-awaited journey to Tochigi, Granny went out with Tsuru to buy her ticket, the food that would fill her box when cooked, and some small gifts for the prison warden and others. Yukari remained behind alone, and after a session of skipping in the garden she was watching television when the doorbell rang. She went to see who it was, and there was a woman who may have been in her mid-thirties, or perhaps around forty, standing with a basket in each hand. She asked Yukari if she'd like to buy some carrot wine. She was dressed neatly in a bluish woolen kimono, was not so much fat as nicely plump with a friendly round face, and her behavior seemed quite well bred—at least for a door-to-door vendor. Yukari was taken in enough by her engaging demeanor to ask what carrot wine was, speaking herself in a friendly tone of voice.

"A young lady like yourself wouldn't know, of course," said the middle-aged woman, and she explained that what she had for sale wasn't made of even the very best Japanese produce but ginseng directly imported from the home of carrot wine, Korea. It was a medicinal drink, a wine particularly effective for renewing that sapped vitality, good for one's health in general, and very palatable and pleasant to the taste.

"Could I borrow a tumbler or glass?" she asked, taking a beer bottle out of one of her baskets. The bottle was two-thirds full, and a long, black, hairy root was floating about in it like a specimen pickled in alcohol. Yukari hesitated, but the women said:

"It's more a medicine than a wine. Perhaps I could have two glasses since I feel a little like partaking myself."

So Yukari went off to the kitchen to get the glasses, and when she got back the woman was sitting on the wooden step that leads up from the entrance, mopping the sweat off her face. Yukari sat there as well, and they both took half a glass of the wine. The clear liquid seemed fairly potent, with a raw, bitter reek to it. Yukari drank hers up in one go and felt slightly giddy. When she had recovered, she looked at the woman and noticed that she still had a third of hers left, which she was drinking very slowly, and that she was smiling at her. The smile continued, and she said:

"Don't you like the taste of it, missus?"

"Not much."

"That's because it's a medicine," the woman continued, smiling even more. "Drink that amount every day and you'll lose that nasty chill around your hips. It's a good thing to get your husband to drink as well, you know."

Quite naturally the talk became very frank from this point on, even obscene; Yukari didn't know what to do except listen and make brief, appropriate comments when required. Finally it came out that the carrot wine sold in department stores was Japanese-made, and although it might perhaps contain real Korean ginseng it was twice the price of this, and she urged her to buy a bottle.

Yukari dithered about, wondering if she should buy or not. In particular she didn't want to make a fool of herself by accepting the starting price, but she wasn't sure what offer to make herself as an opening bid. She continued wondering what to do, also wondering if her indecisiveness wasn't one effect of drinking the wine, but this minor business discussion was brought to an end by the return of Utako and Tsuru.

"Home at last."

"It's so hot today."

"Look, the door's open."

"Perhaps there's a visitor?"

This loud conversation announced their return some yards away, but when Granny came in at last through the front doorway she was so astonished by what she saw she dropped her silver-gray handbag. This was an old one of Yukari's of French make which she'd finally cajoled her into letting her have. Despite the importance she attached to the bag, she made no attempt to pick it up.

"Otoyo!" she cried, at which the vendor of carrot wine shouted out "Utako!" in a husky voice and staggered to her feet, and the two of them embraced before the dumbfounded Yukari and Tsuru. While this embracing was going on the two kept up a noisy, disconnected exchange, from which it was possible to work out firstly that they'd been fellow inmates of the Tochigi Women's Prison, and secondly that this was the very person Granny had assisted in the "jailbreak."

As Otoyo apologized sincerely for being involved in the vulgar trade of hawking carrot wine, Utako replied affably:

"That's all right. I know how crazy you are about men."

Otoyo was embarrassed by this remark and made a playful gesture as though about to slap her. Then Utako said:

"I'm going back tomorrow, you know. . ."

So overcome was she by emotion she could say no more and burst into tears, only managing to blurt out "to Tochigi" through her sobs. Otoyo suddenly became very tense and serious, and said:

"Well, what did they get you for this time?"

Otoyo's swift leap to the wrong conclusion made Utako screw up her face and weep much more, but now it was with mirth. When she'd finally stopped laughing she explained why she was going, and Otoyo seemed really surprised.

"You certainly have some funny ideas," she said.

"Well, I feel sorry for them with no proper grub to eat," said Granny apologetically, staring glumly at the ground.

"They'll all be overjoyed, anyway. It's the really bad time now. . ."

This hurried effort to add something positive to her previous remark had its effect on Granny, for she perked up and picked up her handbag.

"Anyway, Otoyo, let's all go inside," she said grandly.

"Yes, of course," Tsuru chimed in immediately. "We can't just stand about in the entrance talking."

Yukari was a little behindhand in her own invitation since she was puzzling over how she should behave toward this new guest whom she'd already met in a different capacity; so she stood about vaguely, failing to get a word in edgeways.

Otoyo went off toward the guest room, adopting a humble posture as she went and leaving her two baskets of bottles discreetly in a corner of the hall. Granny kept telling her not to be so formal and make herself at home, and Otoyo just as repeatedly praised the house. From then on Tsuru and Yukari found themselves continually employed in a kind of relay service, bringing in lemonade, melon, tea, *petites gaufres*, green tea, sweet cakes, wafers, coffee, waffles, dark tea, crackers, grapes, pears, Coca-Cola . . . just about everything we had in the house. Granny did leave a certain amount of what she was offered, but Otoyo ate up everything with great scrupulousness.

The combined knowledge gained as they went back and forth picking up snatches of the conversation was that Otoyo had been released a few years after her attempted escape and left prison well before Utako. Since then they'd never met. They had both firmly promised to write to each other, but while they were still not quite getting around to it Utako herself returned to the outside world. The younger woman, who had two previous convictions for theft (Yukari had overheard this), liked writing about as much as she liked hairy caterpillars (Tsuru had overheard this interesting phrase). The thing that Yukari and Tsuru most wanted to hear, namely whether she'd met up with the man she'd loved well enough to break out of prison for, must have been discussed when neither of them unfortunately was in the room. However, while the green tea and sweet cakes and wafers were being served, Tsuru heard that she was living alone in an apartment, which Yukari judged to mean she'd broken off with that man, although Tsuru was of a different opinion, saying she was quite convinced he was now doing a stretch in Abashiri (the notorious prison up north) and she was looking after their little home until he returned. Thus these two women of two quite different generations were absorbed for some hours in the strenuous exercise of their imaginations and in whispered conversations.

At six o'clock, when the television switched to children's programs, they started worrying whether they ought to give her dinner. There was the fact that she wasn't a proper guest but only a door-to-door vendor, and then she was, after all, an ex-convict (as, after all, was Granny), and since she'd eaten so much already she must surely be full; so they hesitated until Granny appeared and said her guest wouldn't be leaving for a while so would they order sushi for two, and they also wanted some saké to go with it (although she wasn't going to touch a drop herself).

Otoyo was apparently delighted with that gold-leaf saké I'd once received from a local politician, and asked for another bottle of it. Porcelain flasks for holding warm saké are usually fairly small, but the ones we have at home are quite large, with the result that she managed to drink very nearly two pints of the stuff. So the woman with two previous convictions grew very gay on the saké, sometimes producing loud cries for which she was scolded by Granny. However, by the time she left, around nine o'clock, although somewhat flushed about the eyes, she was sufficiently in control of herself to make a very respectable statement of thanks, and to offer a bottle of carrot wine as a humble token of her respect. Her posture and general demeanor as she offered this eccentric gift were, indeed, fairly impressive, much like what one might expect of a lady of quite distinguished family. Unhappily this impression was quickly dispelled, for as she went out the front door, a heavy basket in each hand, she looked about her and offered this strange advice:

"This house could do with a good burglar alarm," and she grinned at Utako, ducking her head apologetically and going on her way.

"Didn't she say something about an alarm?" said Yukari suspiciously.

"Seems she's still at the old game," said Granny bluntly, and she lightly crooked her index finger. Otoyo did, in fact, go from house to house selling carrot wine, but this was a front for another activity, for if she found a house where no one was in she would revert to her other trade of burglary. Since carrot wine was her trademark, she was widely known among the fraternity as "Carrot Otoyo."

"Well!" said Yukari.

"A nice-looking person like that!" sighed Tsuru.

"We'd better get a burglar alarm, quick, or we may be in trouble," said Yukari in some panic, but Granny replied that although Carrot Otoyo may have "cased the joint" it was unlikely she'd actually "bust" a house in which a person to whom she owed so much was being cared for. Granny said this as if it were some absolute guarantee of immunity, and her comment probably did make perfectly good sense.

Granny thanked Yukari repeatedly, saying she'd had a really good time, although the one thing she now bitterly regretted was forgetting to ask Otoyo for her address.

"I bet she's kicking herself about it now, too," she said; but when Yukari and Tsuru were alone together they decided Otoyo had probably done it on purpose, since she might have been worried they would inform on her.

I got home around ten o'clock and found some of the account Yukari gave me fairly amusing (Granny and Tsuru, since they had to get up early next morning to prepare the food Granny was taking with her, were both just about to go to bed). However, to tell the truth, the part I was amused by was what took place in the hallway only, for when I heard that a woman with two previous convictions who was still an active criminal had been shown into my guest room and plied with food and drink, I couldn't help feeling that the very sanctity of my home (perhaps an odd way of putting it but I felt something close to that) had been defiled by this intruder. Yukari must have read this from my response for she said:

"Honestly, I had real doubts about whether a person like that should be allowed in here. Still. . ."

"Yes, but meeting the woman who'd done the jailbreak, right on her own doorstep, she could hardly have turned her away with a simple hello and goodbye. Obviously they must have had a lot to talk about. It would have looked funny if they'd gone off to a cafe. . . Anyway, it's all over and done with now."

"I don't think she'll come again," said Yukari, but with no great conviction in her voice.

I made some sort of reply to that, although I was rather feeling I'd like to meet her myself if she was as sexy as Yukari seemed to think.

"I decided the guest room would be best," said Yukari, defending her conduct again. "If it had been the living room, it would have been like treating her as one of the family. That wouldn't have been very nice, would it?"

I nodded again, wondering aloud if this might not be a good opportunity to have a burglar alarm installed at last; and then I was overcome by curiosity and had Yukari bring me the bottle of carrot wine. I had two glasses of it and, although the taste wasn't up to much, its efficacy in that area of vitality which Otoyo had mentioned was really quite remarkable.

Yukari getting out of bed must have woken me up, and as I half opened my eyes I heard her giggling and saw her white, naked body come into the room. The dim light from the corridor was suddenly wiped out as the door shut behind her, and the darkness closed in again. Thus I spoke to her in the dark.

"Were you wandering about naked?"

"Well, I'm so hot."

223

"That's because you were being so athletic a little while ago."

"You mustn't say that. You mustn't say it ever again."

She was, of course, not bothered at all but just being coy, although there seemed to be an additional huskiness in her voice when she got into bed beside me.

"I was outside in the corridor and Granny saw me."

"Did she?"

"Came out of the bathroom and she was right there. Awful thing to happen. Still... Stop that, please, it tickles."

But the thought of Yukari creeping downstairs naked and being seen by her grandmother had stimulated my imagination, so I continued, although that didn't stop Yukari talking.

"When I tried to rush past her..."

I chuckled.

"What did she say?" I asked, and snickered again at her reply.

"She screwed up her nose and said, 'You smell of man all over.' She's really dirty-minded is our Granny."

I allowed my fingertips and palms to wander over her smooth skin, slowly guiding them toward the lower regions.

"Let's intensify that odor, then," I whispered, placing my lips against the softness of her ear.

The next morning I looked at my bedside clock by the light filtering in through the curtains, and realized it must be about time to start getting up. Normally Tsuru would come upstairs to call me, but I imagined she'd be so occupied with the preparations for Granny's trip she would probably forget. I could hear the voices of the two old women downstairs, but couldn't make out what they were saying.

Although it was still only June, the bedroom was sultry with the heat of morning. As if gazing on something far off, I looked at Yukari lying with her shoulders and back exposed and saw she was soaked in sweat. I couldn't see her face for it was turned away from me. I turned on the air conditioning. As the air grew cool I could sense I was physically in particularly good shape this morning, with a pleasant lightness about my waist and thighs. I must have slept like a log last night, and I started grinning as I decided it must have been the result of performing three times. However, the grin was suddenly wiped off my face before it had time to cover more than half of it, for I heard the voice of Yukari, still half-sunken in sleep and presumably pleased with the new coolness in the room, quietly saying:

"Um, that's lovely!"

It wasn't those words that wiped out the smile, only that the husky voice had suddenly taken me back to the night before and made me remember all that had happened in one instant recall.

Before we had married, when we made love in Yukari's apartment we'd both gone naked to the bathroom, either after we'd finished or between one bout and the next, and had thought little about it. I would always go without saying anything and then, when I'd come back, Yukari would tell me not to look and make me close my eyes and then go. Once we were married, however, we could no longer do that. We had Tsuru to think about, and also the bathroom and toilet were now much further off. Another reason may have been that Yukari had ceased to be my mistress and was now my wife, although the motives at work here are extremely involved and it's never easy to say anything precise about them. However, last night Yukari had wandered out of our bedroom stark-naked, met Granny, had a blatantly obscene conversation, and then a good laugh with me about it. I felt ashamed of the whole incident and was assailed by the thought that, no matter how much I might not want to admit it, this was just like living in a whorehouse. Wouldn't a tart who had no customer that night use exactly those words to another woman who'd just left hers if she happened to meet her like that? And wouldn't the woman who "smelled of man all over" feel proud of the powerful odor she spread about her? As I lay there in the cool I found myself blushing, and told myself again it was like living in a brothel.

Yukari muttered something sublinguistic, and then asked me in a very clear voice if I was getting up. I said I was just thinking about it, and Yukari turned over toward me and half opened her eyes. In the inadequate morning light I couldn't see all that clearly, but I got the impression that the look on her face was of a woman who was totally satisfied with the events of last night. She closed her eyes again. As I looked at her pale, sleeping face in the half-light I felt things just couldn't go on like this, and unless we drove Granny out of the house as soon as possible our home life would be destroyed.

I went downstairs to the living room and ate two of the balls of *inari zushi* that were arranged on a large plate there, decided not to try the rice balls with beach clover and, with a skewer of grilled chicken in my hand (these were the three kinds of food she was taking to Tochigi), urged Granny to spend the night in some suitable hostelry near the prison; it seemed a pity to go all that way and return the same day when by coming back tomorrow she'd have all that much longer to spare for her friends. Granny bowed in placid agreement and then began a long rigmarole of thanks, as if I were forking out for some health trip to a hot spring resort. Tsuru also gave support from the sidelines, saying what an excellent idea it was, although the idea as far as I was concerned was simply to have her out of the house tonight so I could discuss with Yukari what we were going to do about her (information that would then be passed on to Tsuru). Fortunately I had no engagements for that evening.

I went upstairs again to change, and the noise I made woke Yukari so I opened the curtains. Tsuru shouted from the stairs (presumably also with the aim of waking Yukari) that the company car had come. While I was knotting my tie with my back to my wife I said we would discuss matters this evening, and that I thought Granny might spend one night away and I had given her the money for it, and I wanted Yukari to tell her to do so as well, and that she would see her off from the station, I supposed. No matter what I said, Yukari replied with the same brisk, cheerful word of assent. In reply to my final remark she said she would get up, which she did, putting on her dress and giving a little yawn of contentment plus a great big look at me as she went by.

"Otoyo's carrot wine certainly seems to work okay."

I nodded silently in response to these sweet nothings, for I was thinking we really had got to do something about the problem of Granny Utako, and quick.

As luck would have it, however, I wasn't able to return home early that evening. Our president and managing director had invited out two leading stockbrokers that night, but the president had suddenly gone into hospital with pains in his stomach, and our managing director said he didn't want to do it alone and would I mind putting in an appearance. There was no way I could decline, so I promptly decided to go over the Granny question the next morning and accepted his invitation. He nodded his thanks and said there was nothing in particular on the agenda this evening, the get-together being purely for sociable reasons, so as not to let our relationship with these two cool off. One of the two guests, he said, had been to the same high school as me, having been my senior there, and the other had enjoyed the services of my former wife's father as go-between when he married just after entering the Ministry of Finance. I was struck by the weird amount of out-of-the-way information he seemed to have at his disposal.

His out-of-the-way information turned out to be quite correct. Such personal connections always provide an easy opening for some appropriate chatter, and the party had started with a real swing and was going very smoothly when I was interrupted by being told there was a phone call for me, although the person at the other end of the line wouldn't give his name no matter how many times he was asked. The maid showed me to the telephone, then quietly and promptly departed. I had a good look up and down the empty corridor and addressed this unknown caller.

It was Murata. I immediately expressed my thanks for Granny's box, but he paid no attention to that, keeping up instead a stream of apologies for having called me to the phone (the very persistence of this apology made me realize he was drunk), before explaining that he'd managed to drag the information as to my whereabouts from the managing director's secretary.

"Mr. Mabuchi, the fact is, just now, I called in at your home, just a casual call, you know, just meaning to drop in for a moment..."

"Hah."

"Well, I did. And what I want to know is, was that at your instigation?"

"Was what at my what?"

"Didn't you tell her to tell me that if I came is what I'm wondering."

"Look, Mr. Murata, I can't quite... Are you still there?"

"Yes, still here."

"What on earth has happened? What's all this about my instigation? You sound as if you're trying to pick a fight with me. I must say I find it difficult to believe it's really you speaking."

On hearing this Murata made a considerable, if not totally successful, attempt to restrain his excitement and explain the situation to me, but it was difficult to take in since although in certain parts he was ludicrously painstaking he also tended to jump about erratically at others. He claimed, for example, that although he'd realized Tsuru was alone in the house he thought it very odd she'd shown him straight into the guest room. Surely she hadn't been told to behave like that when she was all alone looking after the house. I thought it was a bit funny myself, but it did cross my mind Tsuru might have a different attitude toward the guest room after yesterday's visit by Carrot Otoyo, and once an idea of this kind has occurred it is very difficult to get rid of it when there is no means of investigating its validity. Anyway, while Murata was sitting in the guest room drinking tea and talking about this and that with Tsuru, she suddenly told him—to his considerable surprise— not to come to this house again. My immediate reaction was to think something as eccentric as that simply couldn't have happened, for Tsuru would never say anything so unlike herself; yet on second thoughts the whole thing didn't seem all that unlikely. I felt confused and so I asked him to confirm what he'd just said.

"Mr. Murata, did Tsuru really speak to you in such impolite terms?"

"Yes, she did. I don't remember exactly what she said but that's what she said."

"In that case, assuming it *is* the case, I can only offer my apologies for my servant's rudeness."

Murata gave a short, low laugh, presumably at the qualified nature of my apology and its bureaucratic tone. I, on the other hand, was very conscious of that laugh as I went on:

"Once I have confirmed this affair with Tsuru I will make further amends."

"No, no, there's no need to ask her about it, please," he said a little hurriedly.

"Why not? That would seem to imply there's something in your version that doesn't square with the facts."

"No, no. The only thing I was concerned about was whether what she said reflected your own sentiments. That was what I wanted to hear from your own lips. Now I shall feel free to continue to trouble you with my presence from time to time. The fact is—though I'm a bit ashamed to admit it, which is why I've kept quiet about it up to now— your Mrs. Nabeshima is the exact image, in the way she looks and talks, of my dead mother."

"Well, really, I didn't know that..."

"Of course, my mother was nothing like as genteel as Mrs. Nabeshima."

"Oh, come, surely..."

"That's why, you know, I sometimes feel I want to see her, and so you'll appreciate my saying I'd prefer to drop the whole matter now. If Tsuru hears I've complained about her she'll really turn against me, making it very difficult for me when I visit you next time."

"Of course. I imagine you must have found Tsuru's hysteria quite terrifying this time."

Having said that, I found I wasn't really happy with what I'd implied, so I continued:

"But why should Tsuru have so forgotten her place as to talk like that?..."

This ruminating expression of dissatisfaction seemed to have some effect on Murata.

"Could be hysteria, of course. Might also be loyalty..."

"Loyalty?"

He hesitated a little, it seemed, then spoke in the voice of a plain man laying his cards on the table:

"Yes. I think it may be because I've never said beforehand quite plainly that my interest is in Mrs. Nabeshima. This has most likely been the cause of some misunderstanding. At least I get the impression I'm now the object of some suspicion. You know, about me and Yukari."

I said nothing. Naturally there was the question of not knowing quite what I should say, but the unexpected wave of intense displeasure I'd felt pass through me was inhibiting as well. Murata seemed unnerved by my silence and shouted:

"Hello. Are you still there?"

"Yes."

"I'd better make it quite clear that there is absolutely nothing between us, nor has there ever been."

"Ah."

I myself thought that was a stupid reply. I regretted it and was searching for something smarter and wittier to say, which only spurred him on to more fervent denials.

"Mr. Mabuchi, I absolutely swear..."

Inside I was telling myself it didn't matter a damn to me anyway, although I didn't, in fact, think so at all, and I can only assume I was lying to myself. At this point Murata changed his tone to one of easy, relaxed humor.

"Well, of course, I admit, a pretty long time ago, I did sort of try something on—nothing much, mind—and got very smartly rebuffed for my pains."

He laughed. Then so did I:

"Happens all the time, I suppose. We should both know."

This produced another mutual burst of laughter.

"Very neatly put, I must say," he said. "Well, that is a great weight off my mind, hearing you respond in that way. . ."

He added an even more cheerful expression of his best wishes and soon rang off.

Two maids passed by. I put the receiver down slowly, and then, aware that I should hurry back to my guests, I stared at the polished boards at the far end of the corridor and the dull wall above them. I was trying to work out what that had all been about. I found it very hard to believe Tsuru had spoken to him in the way he claimed she had, or even that Utako looked exactly like his dead mother. It would be easy to assume it was just the ramblings of a drunkard, but this still left the problem of why he had bothered to telephone anyway. It surely couldn't be he was trying to make some devious insinuation about Yukari? What most bothered me was the thought of some relationship between Murata and Yukari in the past (though I was quite prepared to believe there was nothing going on now). This worry wouldn't go away, making me depressed enough to recall a few things I'd never fully understood, such as all those electrical goods Yukari had in her apartment which she'd refused to bring with her on some pretext or another. As I went on staring at the floorboards and the wall I began to wonder about my own response, for if I'd vowed so sincerely to myself never to question her past and could still be reduced to this depth of gloom, surely it meant that I didn't mind whom she had been intimate with, providing it wasn't Murata? This reflection must have calmed me down a little, making me decide these things weren't important enough to be worth bothering about anyway, and I began to feel my depression was lifting at last.

Three geisha passed along the corridor, bowing to me, and I thought

I'd seen the face of the old one before. I couldn't think where it was, and as they went away I let out a surprisingly deep sigh, so that one of the younger women turned back and looked at me with a mystified expression.

I thought I'd better try to clear up the situation by ringing home, but nobody answered—the phone just went on ringing for ages—and I was still wondering why neither Yukari nor Tsuru were in when I went back to the party.

We went on from the restaurant to a drinking place, and after a while the stockbroker whose wedding had been arranged by my former father-in-law left us, but the other one said he would stay a little longer. Our managing director left me to entertain him and pushed off himself, and my high school senior said we should take some of the girls with us and have a late-night meal somewhere, with the result that it was near-ly three before I finally got home.

I turned my key quietly in the lock, but as I entered out came a sleepy-looking Tsuru to greet me. She was wearing a *yukata* instead of a nightdress, and I can remember vaguely noticing that the rather dramatic pattern of indigo and lavender on a white background was very different from the modest pin-stripe she'd favored up to now.

"Sorry. Have you been waiting up for me?"

"No, sir. I've been lying down having a little snooze," she said rather shamefacedly, and then related the day's events. Just as she was going out Yukari had said she would take care of dinner that evening, giving her some money and telling her to go and see a movie and have a pork cutlet or something afterward. (According to her own confession, Tsuru was as crazy about pork cutlets as *yakuza* films.) Tsuru left the house quite late and didn't get back until ten o'clock or so when, to her sur-prise, she found Granny was also back and was drinking tea with Yukari, who was gently upbraiding her for going to the trouble of bringing more of those dried gourd shavings as a present for us all.

Granny said she thought it would be very wasteful to spend a night away when there was a perfectly good train back, and it would be much better to use the money to buy something nice for young Shin, so she decided to return the same day. Just before she got on the train she sent a telegram from the station giving her time of arrival in Tokyo, which Yukari received since she'd got back almost immediately after

Tsuru had gone out; and so, leaving a letter for me explaining the situation, she went off to the station.

"I see. I must have rung up while she was still out. Is Granny okay?"

"Yes. Apparently she did look rather tired when she got off the train, however."

"Did the food and the presents go down well?"

"Very well. She said the grilled chicken vanished almost at once."

"I suppose they don't get enough animal protein."

It was in the comfort of the guest room that I received this information, not sitting in the shadow of the handless clock as usual. No doubt my real motive for going in there and making Tsuru sit down was that I wanted to hear what had happened between her and Murata, and before I'd brought the matter up myself she mentioned it.

"Then Mr. Murata paid a visit this afternoon. . ."

I gave a low, fairly drunken laugh.

"I know. I heard about it. He telephoned me. Now, what is all this about forbidding him entrance?"

I realized she didn't seem to grasp what I was saying, and this made me feel sorry for her. It must have been a very exhausting day for her with grilled chicken and *inari zushi* and beach clover and a pork cutlet and a *yakuza* movie, and now she must be sleepy and her mind could hardly be ticking over very well, so I felt I just couldn't be hard on her and tried to relate the contents of Murata's telephone call in as calm and cheerful a way as possible. It didn't go very well at first, partly because I was a bit drunk and my narrative tended to lack form and consistency, and also because of the devious way of speaking I tend to adopt when trying to be careful of my servant's feelings. She still looked as vague and uncomprehending as ever; but then suddenly she seemed to catch on and her face assumed that tart expression she always had when she'd just eaten something very bitter, and she began to rebuke and revile Murata with cries of "I like his impudence" and "A pack of lies."

I thought this very odd, because I'd been rather concerned she might burst into tears; but then I also remembered I had only ever seen her cry on two occasions. The first was when I was at junior high school and she'd wept for reasons I have never understood to this day; and the second was on the eve of my first marriage when she came back from the hairdresser and I teased her a bit too much about her new hairstyle. However, I also remembered that on both those occasions she had assumed this very same expression before the final outpour, and I suddenly became very nervous indeed.

"It's all right, honestly, it's all right. It would be a relief to me if the man never came here again, believe you me."

As I consoled her in this manner, what had actually happened became clear. Tsuru had never told him not to come here again. All that had in fact taken place was, after talking about perfectly ordinary things, he'd asked her what her salary was. She'd told him and then he'd said he would double it if she'd come and work for him. At first she had thought he was only joking and she hadn't said anything definite, but once she noticed how serious he looked she said quite plainly she intended to remain in this house for the rest of her life, making it perfectly clear she was refusing him, although he still went on and on about it. After a number of these refusals she'd finally said she had things to do and she must ask him to leave, if he would be so kind. She did not think she'd spoken in a particularly stiff manner, but Murata had plainly been displeased and went away in something of a huff.

"I suppose he felt he'd been insulted and wanted to let me know. Probably some careless misunderstanding on his part," I said and smiled.

Part of my reason for smiling was the satisfied feeling that I was employing a maid worth double what I was paying her.

"Still, I can't say I admire his behavior, coming into my house when I'm not in and trying to recruit my own maid," I said happily—feeling, indeed, very happy about it.

Tsuru then went on to give a painstakingly detailed report on her reasons for showing him into the guest room, which was surely a strange thing to do when all the household were out, she admitted, but he'd said he would like a cup of tea and it would have looked odd if she'd served him in the hall.

This produced yet another good-humored response from me.

"I thought it must have been something like that. Still, why shouldn't he be treated on the same level as somebody selling carrot wine? No reason at all," I said and, after this cheerful outburst, went on: "The

233

man does seem to be a bit thick, he really does, going on about some relationship between himself and Yukari which I'm supposed to suspect him of and saying there'd never been one. That's what he said."

I would have been wiser to keep my mouth shut about that, although the drink was probably to blame for this relaxation of my normal self-control; it may also have been an indication of the degree to which I'd always worried about Yukari's past.

Tsuru, however, frowned slightly and only said that the man was certainly very impudent, and so on. I maintained the same satisfied smile, but felt it would be a good idea to leave this question as soon as possible; so I selected another.

"I wonder why Granny came back like that? She should have stayed overnight. If she wants to give young Shin some kind of treat we could always find the money for that."

"Yes, sir, but with people in a place like that, perhaps they wouldn't be all that pleased once the food had gone."

"You mean once her box was empty she was no longer welcome?"

"Yes."

She smiled in a slightly dazed way. I felt there was something in her eyes that expressed a certain contempt for my inability to understand something so simple, although it wasn't difficult to persuade myself her eyes were like that, not because she was scornful of me, but merely because she was tired.

Anyway, I said indifferently:

"Well, I suppose that's probably the way it would be at a place like that. Not that I've ever been to one."

"Neither have I, sir, you know." And we both laughed quietly, but with an odd sense of melancholy, as if we regretted the fact that both were condemned to arguing about it with no real experience to go by.

There was a sound of footsteps on the stairs as someone descended. It was Yukari, of course. My first worry was that she might be stark-naked, since I didn't want her to be seen in that state by the maid, so I quickly called out her name. She replied from halfway down the stairs, and shortly entered the room wearing a semitransparent negligee through which her brief underwear could be seen.

"Welcome back."

"Thanks. Just been talking to Tsuru, and it seems Murata's been trying to seduce her into working for him at double her present salary."

"Really, 'trying to seduce' me," said Tsuru, and the two women laughed.

"Well, I call that a form of attempted seduction."

"Wouldn't it be awful if Tsuru left," said Yukari.

"Don't worry. She refused. Naturally. Unfortunately she also told him to go away, which annoyed him intensely, so he phoned me in high dudgeon."

"Really? Still, thank goodness it's all right."

"Anyway, that's what we've been talking about."

"What time is it?" asked Yukari.

"Nearly four I should think. Going to feel awfully tired tomorrow morning," I replied. "By the way, Murata said he tried to seduce you once in the past but got turned down flat," I added in a jokey, jovial voice.

"Did he? No idea. Happened so many times I just can't remember."

She gave a brilliant, spectacular laugh. I followed suit and so did Tsuru. What Yukari had said sounded perfectly natural to me; it also sounded like a blatant subterfuge as well.

14

The next morning I thought I'd try to make up some of my lost sleep in the company car on the way to the office. I loosened my tie, undid the top button of my shirt, and immediately fell into a slumber, one disturbed by a dream, or rather a fragment of a dream. I was walking along a narrow, dim-lit corridor when the shadowy figure of a man blocked my way. The man stared up at me, and teasingly asked me if I knew him. I was convinced he was my son, but couldn't speak and, as I strained to do so, I woke up.

The car was gliding smoothly along. I looked at the outside world in the rain and wondered why I should have had a dream like that, seeing I had no child; and I was seized all of a sudden by the thought that the small man wasn't my son but perhaps Murata. This interpretation seemed to make sense as it provided a link with the events of last night, although it wasn't particularly pleasant to realize how much a creep like that could bother me. I was making a gloomy, grim-faced attempt to devise some slightly different interpretation when again, just as suddenly, I experienced an intense feeling of remorse at the thought of my absolute foolishness in telling Tsuru about Murata and Yukari. It meant I'd revealed to my maid that I suspected my wife with another man. Despite the fact I could claim I was drunk at the time, I'd said things I shouldn't have done and she now had excellent material for making a fool of me if she wanted. This had not only seriously weakened my own position as her master, but made Yukari's as the lady of the house very difficult as well. The additional fact that I had then told Yukari, in front of Tsuru, Murata's story about making a pass at her and being rebuffed meant that I looked even worse. Assuming that Tsuru wasn't actually thinking in such critical terms about me at the moment, it could only be a matter of time before she started to do so. I looked at the lines of cars glistening in the rain and the men and women carrying umbrellas hastening over the pedestrian crossing, and wondered again why I'd been such a fool as to open my mouth like that, a regret that added to the feeling of heaviness created by my hangover.

"We'll be there quite soon, sir," the driver said discreetly.

"Thanks. I've had quite a good sleep."

I did up my top button and adjusted my tie.

"Have you heard anything about the president's illness?"

The directors' chauffeurs gossiped to each other while reading their weeklies or dusting down their cars, and if you pooled the various bits of casual chatter you picked up from them it provided a very accurate account of what was going on. I assumed the other directors probably did the same as me, which was to hand out "tips" occasionally in order to obtain such information.

"It doesn't seem anything much, sir. They say he should be able to leave the hospital in two or three days."

"In that case I'd better get my visit in quick."

The driver only nodded in reply. He was well trained and, anyway, we were just arriving in front of the company building.

That day, however, I was too busy to pay any visit to the hospital and had to put it off to the next. The weather was depressing, with continuous rain, and I seemed to have double the usual amount of work, on top of which I was suffering from lack of sleep and a hangover. I didn't get home until after nine that evening, hardly said a word to anyone, but simply had my bath and went straight to bed. As I was about to drop off Yukari came into the room exactly like some figure entering a dream.

"Tsuru wants to have one day off a week," she said, obviously meaning to discuss the matter with me, but I was so dog-tired I've no real idea what I replied. I feel I said something like, "All right, that'll be better than having her clear off altogether," although according to Yukari I only muttered "Tomorrow morning."

Anyway, we returned to our normal way of life, or at least to something that fairly closely resembled it. Ever since the president had been taken ill I'd been so busy I'd not even had time to read a book, and I even thought of using one of those tapes for listening to in the car, although I soon dropped that idea since it seemed too much like the way some elderly person would behave. Granny still did her flower arrangements, but she complained the only flowers you seemed

able to get hold of nowadays were Western ones like gladioli and ger-
bera. Yukari went twice to do some modeling work, but one of these
sessions was a sudden call that clashed with Tsuru's day off, leaving
Granny to look after the house; for some unknown reason she took
it into her head to work away all day and was apparently exhausted
by the end of it. Tsuru, equally exhausted by her day off, arrived home
late that evening and, presumably feeling apologetic for the state
Granny was in, asked if she might have her day off on Sundays from
now on.

On the Saturday toward the end of July when the president at last
turned up at the office, I finally managed to get home in time for dinner, and yet dinner was by no means ready and the three women were
all in a considerable state of excitement about something. Tsuru had
made the remarkably rare mistake of putting the wrong amount of water
in with the rice and had been obliged to start all over again. While Yukari
and Tsuru were waiting for the rice they were both sitting with Granny, who had an ominous-looking bandage on her left hand. They were
hearing the story all over again, for it seemed Granny had been the
victim of an armed robbery.

That afternoon, having noticed in the newspaper that a *yakuza* film
was on, she'd gone to the movies. She'd asked both Yukari and Tsuru
if they would like to come along, but her granddaughter showed little
inclination since the weather was so hot, and the maid declined because
she was the maid and it was her day off tomorrow and she really wanted
to get all the laundry done today. So Granny had to go by herself.

Despite its being Saturday afternoon there were only a few customers
in the cinema, but it had been just the same on the three occasions
she went with Tsuru before so she wasn't particularly bothered. She
bought some chewing gum at the kiosk, then chose a seat right in the
middle of the hall and, since the air conditioning was working so nicely, she settled down to enjoy a film all about Tokyo in the late 1920s,
a period when she herself had been twenty years old.

"It kept reminding me of so many things of that time; so nice to
remember the good old days."

Of course the kind of research the director had done into the period
would have been pretty perfunctory, and the film was probably full of
flagrant errors. Presumably the reason why these things didn't seem

238

to bother Granny was that her own image of Tokyo was a confused mixture of the present-day city and of how it had been fifty years ago. The genuine shock she'd received on returning here after thirteen years' absence, dumbfounded by the changes that had taken place, had perhaps produced a mental state no less confused than this hodgepodge of images from various decades of the past half-century which is the standard world of the *yakuza* movie. Consequently, when she saw a house in which the refrigerator was a genuine old-style ice box with blocks of ice in it, and yet none of the automobiles passing by had running boards, she wasn't disturbed, any more than when she noticed the large Coca-Cola sign that served as a background to the secret tryst of the two lovers, dressed in proper period style. But as the film worked toward its climax on this bogus summer night, Granny had an unbearable desire to go to the toilet, perhaps brought on by the coldness of the artificially cooled air. Our young hero, the lone, wandering stranger, had finally found he could no longer endure any more indignities and was now entering the enemy's stronghold; while the good *yakuza* boss's daughter (in love with him, of course) heard of his resolve against the background of a sky in which, far off, fireworks were exploding. The last tragic, grim, pathetic, remorseful rumpus was about to begin, and naturally Granny didn't want to miss it. She was also conscious of the sign that asked patrons only to use the cinema toilets during the intervals if possible, since lately it had become dangerous to do so at other times. Should such a visit be unavoidable, one was requested not to go unaccompanied. However, she certainly couldn't wait right to the end, and if she went off now and hurried back she should be in time for the real climax. She told herself there couldn't be all that many criminals in the world, so she set off through the dark almost at a trot.

Once through the door she noticed there was no one in the kiosk or the corridor. She completed her business, dabbled her fingers under the tap a little (with her handbag dangling from her wrist), and didn't particularly notice that whoever had been in the compartment next to hers suddenly opened the door and came out. However, this person then stood right behind her, pressed something hard into her back, and hissed at her to hand over the handbag. Strangely enough she didn't realize the thing sticking into her back was a pistol, nor was she really aware that the character standing behind her was holding her up. She just felt something very peculiar was going on. Her response was to scream out something and turn around to face the young man, who looked, she said, like an ugly version of Kaizuka.

The young man became even more flustered than she was, sticking the hard object into her stomach and telling her to shut up or else, his face contorted as he gave this order, and at last Granny realized she was being mugged. She was so terrified now she let out a cry (not so much a cry for help as a purely hysterical scream), and was herself astonished by the great noise she made. The robber hissed at her again, then started beating her heavily on the left hand with the black object he'd been pressing into her stomach, presumably in an attempt to get hold of the handbag. She dropped the silver-gray bag on the floor. She also thrust away with her right hand (all in a flash so she wasn't certain about this) the right hand that was beating her, and the black object the man was holding dropped onto the floor as well, where it bounced two or three times, making a brittle, plastic sound, and finally slid to a halt, now assuming the shape of a pistol.

What ought to have happened then, in theory, was she should have become even more afraid on realizing that this was a pistol and she had been threatened with it, discovering, however, it was only a toy and so regaining some kind of composure. However, the pace of events didn't even allow any increase of fear, let alone the subsequent composure, and she just stood there in a daze. It was while she was standing speechless that another man burst into the room.

"You bastard!" he howled, and struck the thief, who was trying to escape, smack in the face with his fist, which sent him flying over backward. The youth, dressed in a grimy sweat shirt and cotton trousers, was now being kicked by a wrinkled but powerful-looking man in his fifties. He had his hands over his face, his knees drawn up to protect his belly and groin, and was squirming desperately, howling and groaning. The older man, in short-sleeved open-neck shirt and gray trousers, went on kicking the fingers, hands, and shins of the thief, sweating profusely as he did so. He bawled out "Thief! Thief!" and Granny Utako joined in the chorus as well, squealing "Thief, thief" in her shrill voice, although she was trembling so much she could hardly stand. Suddenly the small ladies' toilet was full of men, so many she was surprised there

240

had been such a large audience for the movie; and she was pushed right over by the window. She still managed to give one more cry of "Thief" before somebody told her it was all right because the thief had now been caught. As the men gradually withdrew she noticed her handbag lying on the floor, where it had taken a dreadful battering from their shoes and sandals.

"Ah, you're the injured party, are you, lady?" said a man with a black jacket draped over his shoulders despite the heat, who was standing immediately outside the toilet. She could tell straight away by the look of him and his clothes he must be a detective, and also by the fact that he had one of a pair of handcuffs attached to his left wrist, the other being fastened, at the end of its short chain, to the wrist of the young man, who was leaning against the wall with his face turned upward to stop the blood that had poured from his nose and covered half his face.

"Don't mind just giving me a little of your time, do you, lady?" said the detective. Granny was still trembling and feeling very unsteady on her legs, and she tried to pick up her handbag but couldn't make it. The girl from the kiosk picked it up for her.

She was taken to the cinema office. Three or four people were hanging about outside the open door and peering in. They all looked remarkably like the thief, and were about the same age too. As she went into the room the man in his fifties wearing the open-neck shirt was modestly but firmly declining a chair the detective was offering him. Granny thanked him for his help, but the man with grizzled hair and a long, thin face just as modestly disclaimed these expressions of gratitude. He was standing in front of a series of posters, which were neatly lined up apparently according to their degree of discoloration.

"Still, I'm glad to see you're all safe and sound," he added in a crisp, clear voice. His attitude was quite different from the courageousness, or even brutality, of his previous behavior, being simple and friendly, and she wondered what kind of employment a man with two such different sides to his character might have.

She thanked him again for rescuing her from such a perilous situation, choosing her words carefully and bowing her head respectfully, which produced more powerful disclaimers, and then he leaned toward her and said:

"I was just wandering about, thinking I might drop in and see a film

241

for a bit, and I heard someone screaming. After that I just seemed to let myself go. . ."

"Really, I can only thank you again for. . ."

"There's lots of wicked people about nowadays. I mean, hanging around for someone in a place like that. I ask you. Still, I reckon he'll have a good think before trying it on again, after taking a thrashing like that," the man said, jerking his jaw in the criminal's direction. The latter was standing next to the detective, who was seated at a heavily scarred table with a pencil in his hand. Someone had stuck pieces of toilet paper up the young man's nostrils to stop the bleeding, but occasionally he let out a low whimper and each time the detective bawled at him. On the table were an ashtray, a sports paper, a bowl of fried rice, and the toy pistol.

Granny was urged to sit down by the man in the open-neck shirt and by the cinema manager. The detective, who remained at some distance, occasionally displaying his black notebook for a moment, then questioned both of them. Her rescuer turned out to be the caretaker of a block of apartments, and she was surprised to hear that he wasn't in his fifties but already past sixty. The detective took down the main points of their evidence in his notebook, then thanked the caretaker (whose name was Yoshiji Hirayama) in an indifferent voice and said he would probably receive a police award for this.

Eventually the witnesses left the temporary investigation room. Granny asked him if he wouldn't mind writing his name and address down on something for her, but instead he produced a visiting card. Granny showed it to me.

"There were two films and I didn't even manage to see the whole of one of them. And that handbag's no good at all now," she complained.

"It doesn't matter," said Yukari. "I'll give you another one next time."

In addition to this consolation, Tsuru said from the kitchen that the important thing was she'd suffered no real injury, while I was foolish enough to chime in with the remark that she had nerves of steel, hurriedly changing the subject as I realized things could move in an unfortunate direction.

"Well, I think I ought to have a department store send Mr. Hirayama a bottle of whisky. Perhaps saké might be better, since he's over sixty?"

That was my suggestion, but Granny sat up very straight and rejected it.

"Eisuke, I think in this case I really must pay a visit myself and offer my thanks in person. Perhaps even tomorrow. He is, after all, someone who saved my life. It's a matter of duty, and I feel I can do no less..."

This was said in a low voice, full of feeling, so naturally I didn't hesitate to give my assent.

The next day was Sunday. Tsuru prepared a light meal, a combined breakfast and lunch for four, ate one of the portions herself, washed up quickly, changed into her Sunday best, and then went out (or so I heard). There was nothing Granny could do but have her meal all by herself, though a little later than usual, in the living room. Then, feeling somehow it would be bad if she didn't, she washed up her own things as well. Just before noon Yukari and I came downstairs and heard what had happened from Granny, who was all dressed up in a dark blue gauze kimono. I merely wondered how even so feudalistic a servant as Tsuru could gradually change, but Yukari was quite offended by this behavior, saying in a slightly coarse voice she had no need to dash off like that as if she were scared we were going to make her work on her day off. Granny said she probably had an appointment at the hairdresser since she hadn't asked her to do her hair; and then she changed the subject and asked if she could have a handbag to go with her kimono. Yukari produced a rather fancy one and told her to be very careful with it, but Granny only nodded as though she wasn't really paying attention.

Professor Nonomiya turned up about an hour after Granny had left. I'd been watching television and reading the newspaper and was just about to go upstairs to look through some of my business papers, when the bell rang in a slightly importunate way. I went to see who it was and there was the professor in a half-sleeved shirt with tie neatly knotted and his suit jacket over his arm, standing with a stern expression on his face.

"Eisuke, truly a dreadful thing has happened!"

The truth is I had not been particularly impressed by the attack on Granny, since the only damage done was to that handbag. The injury to her hand was about as serious as an insect bite, and that elaborate bandage had been simply an expression of the desire of all three women to show off (as witness the fact she hadn't had it on when she went out today). I'd consequently made light of the whole business, and merely advised her to use cinema toilets only during the interval. But, on hearing the professor's words, I came to the erroneous conclusion that Yukari must have telephoned him about the incident yesterday and he'd dashed over today to see how she was. It seemed that he, at least, had been deeply affected by the news.

"Yes, a dreadful thing," I said, "Granny's armed robbery. Yukari," I called out, "your father's here."

Before she'd replied, however, the professor let out a cry, his face contorted as he said, with a long, terrible moan:

"Oh no, not again."

On this occasion I did manage to make the right reply immediately.

"No, no, you've got it wrong. She was the one who was robbed. Still, you needn't worry, because it was only an attempt and didn't come off, so no harm was done."

"Ah, she was the one. I see. It happened to her. Well, thank heaven for that, at least. Every cloud has a silver lining. I must say, Eisuke, your remark was rather abrupt, you know, like an arrow from the blue."

He took off his shoes while saying this, showing no interest except in the fact that she'd been the robbed and not the robber, and apparently quite indifferent to whether she'd had anything stolen or not. Yukari then appeared, and as I listened to her chatterbox account of the attempted theft I was struck by that phrase of his about every cloud having a silver lining, since it was just the way Oguri talked.

The professor knelt down in the living room, ignoring my plea that he should make himself at home and sit more comfortably. Instead, he placed his hands formally on his thighs and apologized for all the trouble he was causing me, bowing humbly at the same time.

"I am unable to apologize deeply enough. I have sometimes discussed this question with Kyoko, but the trouble is Mother does seem to find it very difficult to live on her own, always wanting people about her, apparently unable to grasp that the essence of modern city life is solitude and loneliness. We have the example of Poe's short story 'The Man of the Crowd,' and it is only one short step from that to Riesman's *The Lonely Crowd*. However, our contemporary citizens still seem, generally speaking, unable to comprehend their condition and so, as individuals, they attempt to ameliorate it. Not just them, of course, but all of us: myself, anybody. In Mother's case, naturally, she is old and can do little about it so one is inclined to sympathize, but I also feel she has always tended to be like that anyway. As far as her crime itself is concerned, although admitting economic and other factors, I feel in terms of depth psychology one has to accept that the loneliness of the life she led after Kyoko married must have had a great deal to do with it. Naturally a person of that kind, having spent a dozen years and more in a large, closely knit community, will only have had that tendency deepened."

"She went to Tochigi only the other day. She was as excited as if she'd been going home," said Yukari, pouring the tea.

"Yes, I heard about that," the professor nodded. "I can't say I was surprised. Bound to happen, I thought. A proper critical apprehension of any situation is continually reinforced by the appearance of such additional facts. However, if we can get down to the actual problem, I must say I don't think it acceptable that she should just go on living here forever. I mean, the real responsibility for her is with me. If one considers the question objectively, that is the sole conclusion one can come to. I have been doing my utmost to work out some solution, and in some haste, but there has been this long-drawn-out trouble at the university, and now I am to take my leave of all that..."

"Oh, you're retiring already?" I asked inadvertently, and this seemed to anger my father-in-law.

"No. It's nearly another ten years before I'm due to retire. I have, in fact, made up my mind to resign."

"Ah-hah."

"Indeed I have already done so, and it is for that reason I must ask you to look after her for a little while longer. I apologize, naturally, for the impertinence of this request."

He bowed again deeply and then, before I'd managed to say a word, slipped quickly into a more relaxed sitting position.

What took me aback on this occasion was the complexity of this "critical apprehension," and I had to admire his ability to combine so many things (the sudden announcement of his resignation, the forced logic that ensured we were still stuck with Granny, the problem of big city loneliness, and Granny's living with us being seen as a mere extension of her crowded prison life) in what was virtually the same breath. So I could only grunt, or gasp, in reply, which probably sounded as if I were accepting his proposal. Yukari, however, in contrast to my dazed self, got straight down to the roots of the matter by inquiring into the manner or process by which he'd arrived at his resignation.

The professor replied only reluctantly to Yukari's persistent questioning, but a synthesis of his various answers led to the conclusion that he had, in fact, resigned only on the spur of an unlucky moment. Five days ago the general faculty meeting at his university had decided temporarily to break off their joint negotiations with the student body, and as all the professors, assistant professors, and lecturers trooped out of the assembly hall they were confronted by noisy throngs of students who tried to prevent their leaving. On this occasion Professor Nonomiya was the very last to leave (he was trying to stay as far away from trouble as possible) when one of the graduate students (who hadn't said a word right up to that moment) appeared in front of him, howled out something, and snatched at his tie. Father-in-law brushed his hand away, or rather, in the attempt to do so, thrust out a hand that came into light contact with the student's jaw. This immediately became an issue of crisis dimensions, and placards were set up and leaflets distributed denouncing Professor Nonomiya's violent behavior. So one more demand was added to the students' list, namely that he should be made to apologize forthwith.

A faculty meeting was convened on Friday, which was two days ago, to discuss this problem, and although Professor Nonomiya argued forcibly that it was rather the graduate student who should be made to apologize to him, nobody was prepared, it seemed, to support his position. The general view was that what he said might be all right in theory but was too idealistic, and was in fact to be condemned as mere formalism since it ignored present realities. What was most awful was that the man who'd appeared to be most in sympathy with him up to this point, a professor of the hawkish faction (my father-in-law belonged to neither the hawks nor the doves, he said, which I assumed meant he didn't like to commit himself to anything that might prevent him saying whatever came into his head), announced that Professor Nonomiya's insistence on wearing a tie at a joint negotiation with the student body was an indication of how totally removed from reality his whole outlook was. This created a general hubbub of agreement, factional distinctions of doves and hawks being waived at least over this question, and even the dean stood up and confessed with some complacency that it was his own habit to remove his tie in the dean's office and keep it in his shirt pocket whenever he went outside on a bargaining mission. This turn of events Professor Nonomiya found particularly vexatious, and he let slip the remark that if this was the faculty's attitude then he had no desire to remain at this university. Normally at such moments one could rely on someone standing up and persuading one not to do anything drastic, but the meeting had been in session from two to seven with no dinner provided (that old professor who was so meticulous about such things happened to be absent on this occasion) and they were all so tired and hungry nobody said anything. So Father-in-law wrote out his resignation there and then.

"Seems a bit of a rash thing to have done, surely?" said Yukari, but the professor didn't look at his daughter, turning instead to me and saying, in words of some feeling:

"I'm afraid a woman can never understand those motives which decide a man's course of action. Kyoko said exactly the same thing, you know: 'You've been working at that university for thirty years and there's no call for you to stop now.' Of course, I don't wish to maintain that I have no regrets. I have them. It would be untruthful to deny it. Still, the truth also is that the present-day conditions of our universities are such as to make them unsuitable places for a pure researcher like myself. For some time now I have been thinking in terms of resignation, strengthening my resolve as it were, and now I find this unexpected stroke has allowed me to accomplish something I've been wanting to do for years. Eisuke, rather than bewailing my lot I am indeed delighted with it."

"Yes, I can see how you might well be."

"When you yourself left MITI, I am sure you were saddened by the experience. But no matter how sad it may be, a man has that straight road he must travel alone."

"No, well, it wasn't all that straight in my case..."

"However, it is a fact that your true motive, no matter how far removed, for declining to go to the Ministry of Defense was that you weren't prepared to sacrifice your anti-militarist beliefs."

"Well, there may have been a little of that, but the whole thing itself was much vaguer and, anyway, I didn't actually leave until some years after that incident."

"I admire your modesty. I respect you for it. But modesty must not be taken too far. Whatever the complexity of the situation may have been, the fact is you stuck to your beliefs, you retained your intellectual and spiritual integrity. . ."

I looked down in confused embarrassment at this eulogy; but at the very moment I realized my father-in-law was only, in effect, praising himself, Yukari said something quite cruel:

"Still, that does seem a bit different from resigning because someone pulled your tie."

Professor Nonomiya shook his head in denial.

"That is because you only observe the phenomenon itself. If you considered the essential nature of what happened you would be able to grasp the similarity."

After this casual dismissal of his daughter's objection, he suddenly launched into a reckless attack on bureaucrats, the bureaucratic nature, the bureaucratic system, in fact bureaucracy in all its aspects, prefacing his remarks by saying he felt justified in making such statements in my presence since I was no longer a bureaucrat myself. As he saw it, one of the greatest evils of contemporary civilization was bureaucracy, something that existed equally in the United States and Soviet Russia, and whose calamitous effect in those areas that the communist and capitalist systems had in common was so huge. A particularly awful example could be seen in Japan, a result of the extent and prolonged endurance of the clan government system whereby feudalistic and bureaucratic elements had fused into one and the same thing, and thus none of those virtues Western European bureaucracy might be said to possess had been transplanted successfully to Japanese soil. Again, in Japan itself the worst form of bureaucracy could be seen in the universities, since it was not that of real bureaucrats but only a poor imitation, a mere confusion in which any basic indoctrination into the mysteries of the trade was lacking, and thus all that existed was an unprincipled mess of rules and precedents and turning a blind eye and cliques where henchmen did their masters' bidding and got looked after in return, where appearances were kept up and faces saved and people cooked up specious reasons for their malpractices ... and other innumerable institutionalized vices. Unquestionably the process by which a discussion of the violent act of a graduate student had been transformed into one concerning the clothing of the teaching staff was a classic example of such university bureaucracy at work.

At this point the argument developed into a critique of the present student struggles within the universities. People maintained it was peculiar that the students should express their opposition to society by taking it out on the university authorities, but he gave it as his opinion that the students were not necessarily wrong in so doing. If one accepted that the greatest evils in contemporary society were its bureaucratic elements, then one could also accept the actions of our youth who had come into contact with bureaucracy in its lowest forms at their universities and were thus, not surprisingly, expressing their rejection of our society by first attacking the target that was closest at hand. Of course, there was always the question of how genuinely conscious they were of what they were doing, indeed if they were conscious of anything at all; and there was the definite possibility that part of their motivation came from being confident they wouldn't be treated all that badly by the universities to which they belonged. However, it would be mistaken merely to understand the problem in such terms, but rather we should feel genuine compassion...

He went on to blame the university authorities, who had made a number of mistakes in their early handling of these disturbances, and yet had merely tried to cover things up or bluff their way out, thereby enclosing the whole business in a thick coat of lies.

"The best thing always is a frank, honest apology. If you behave like that, then the students will understand and let it go. Students are like that."

This highly optimistic remark induced a mild questioning from me, but he remained adamant in his belief, and gave an example to confirm it. Just after the war had ended he'd lost about two hundred answer papers (all those of two classes) for the end-of-term English exam, which he'd wrapped up by mistake with the old newspapers and sold to the wastepaper man. He had even gone to the depot to look for them, but they were nowhere to be found, so in class he confessed the situation to the students, bowed his head, and apologized; and they quite cheerfully accepted the idea of another exam, with not one word said in protest.

Up to that point it was certainly a very improving and moral tale, but from then on it became a little peculiar, for he was so impressed by their behavior that, as a reward, he passed every single one of them.

"You mean even those who turned in a blank paper got their sixty percent?"

"Of course," happily replied my father-in-law, apparently unaware that my remark was meant to be critical.

"Ah-hah," I said.

"It was the logical conclusion of my decision, so naturally I did so."

"That was a bit hard on the students in the other classes," said Yukari, pointing out something that was undoubtedly true.

"Women are always worrying about details," he smiled. "The point I was making is that one should never attempt to lie to one's students. It is quite the wrong attitude, for they loathe that kind of officialism. One can, in fact, reverse the terms of the argument, and say that the very fact our universities do not make use of this aspect of student pyschology indicates their lack of any true political sense."

This seemed to imply that he personally was remarkable for possessing this sense; but I only nodded and said I saw what he meant, and went on:

"However, from the point of view of a former civil servant like myself, the emphasis you place on this quite radical logic would seem to be a form of rejection of society, or at least of the system, even a kind of anarchism..."

"Yes, there is undoubtedly an anarchistic tendency in my argument. In general, people who dislike politics always tend to find their political ideas tinged with anarchism. However, there is a question mark, surely, about such ideas being a rejection of society as such. Should we not rather say that my vision is of a society that is no longer being suffocated at its roots by our present-day system, one from which that pressure has been removed and which has grown healthy again? As an amateur in these matters I have no practical policies to put forward, but in very general terms that is the direction in which my wishes tend."

This wild romanticism produced a vague grunt and nod from me, although I found it quite unacceptable.

"Still, students nowadays are rather different in many ways from what they were two decades ago, I should think," I stated cautiously, but he agreed with that quite readily.

"Yes, they are, and therefore I confess I have no proof that my student policy is totally correct, although I do claim that it is superior to what is now in force. The students have certainly changed. I suppose one can say this is due in part to the considerable increase in their numbers, and yet we must also recognize the background to such change, the phenomenon of the mass society. There we find the reason why our students are so absorbed in these hideous, juvenile cartoons, or comic books as I believe they are called. There has been an unhealthy decline in taste; one might even speak of a total deterioration. Yes, a total deterioration we may call it indeed, although we should also recognize in such changing tastes a certain desire to display a rebelliousness toward the adult world. In that graduate student's hostile attitude toward my tie one can discern a rebelliousness toward society itself—not a denial, which would be a different thing—and a hatred of bourgeois taste. Or it may well be we can see there an expression of his fear that he himself will shortly be in a position where he too is obliged to wear such a tie as a member of that society. At any rate, we are obliged to recognize quite simply that there has indeed been a decline in taste as such."

"Which tie of yours did he grab hold of, Father?" Yukari put in at this point, but the professor shrugged off this irrelevance in his usual style, and went on:

"The way these students dress, their hairstyles, their comic books, the language they use, and various other phenomena all indicate quite clearly a transition toward a popular, mass culture, a mass society. The awful crudeness of line in those cartoons they admire really is. . ."

He held forth for a while on the subject of the comic book from his own specialist position as a critic of the fine arts, and then concluded:

"These two questions, that of the bureaucratic system and the coming of mass society, are the major problems of our day; and yet it is an interesting fact that Marxism seems never to have considered either of them, nor even attempted to consider them."

Since I was worried I mightn't look like much of an intellectual if I didn't make some contribution here, I said:

"Given the extent of the writings of Marx and Engels, it's possible they may have touched on them somewhere, but I must admit I've never come across such a passage in my own reading. Not once."

"That's right. Nor have I," my father-in-law agreed.

"Maybe they didn't exist in Marx's time," I went on, and he agreed with me again.

"Despite that," he said, "the students use Marxist terminology in their struggle against the bureaucratic system, enlivening it with elements from popular culture. You can see the same pathetic, ludicrous behavior in those critics of the official left who insist, regardless of whether they are attacking the bureaucratic system or popular culture, on solving all problems with quotations from their team of Marx-Engels-Lenin-Mao. My own guess—a pure guess, of course—is that the low language Marx was in the habit of employing when he poured vilification and abuse on one of his rival theorists may well have been something he picked up from the popular culture of his own day, such as the music halls or the comic theater, or something like that. . . Still, what is a definite fact is that our present cultural condition is something of very grave concern since it indicates the extremely low standards of contemporary Japan, and I have serious doubts as to whether I shall be able to live by my pen as I intend henceforth. . ."

"Oh, you don't mean to teach at some other university?"

My question had a great effect on my father-in-law, for all his briskness vanished as he answered cheerlessly:

"I don't say there aren't places I have in mind, but still, you know. . . There no longer exists a university anywhere in this country where a genuine scholar, an intellectual of the first order, could be properly at home. I feel that very, very strongly. Consequently I wish to be free of it all, writing just as I please."

"Yes, I see. That probably is the best thing to do. At least for the time being you can take it easy and look around, and then. . ."

"No, I certainly can not. First of all I receive almost no severance money."

"What!" shouted Yukari.

"Why should that be?" I asked, sharing her amazement, and the following remarkable situation became clear.

According to my father-in-law's deliberately calm account (or his deliberate attempt to be calm), he'd made considerable borrowings from the university. One of these had been for the trip to Europe some years ago, and another for Yukari's wedding. Naturally these loans had all been in the form of advances on the money due to him on retirement, and this was something he hadn't taken much into consideration (if he had indeed considered it at all) when he wrote out his resignation. On top of that it seemed he'd chosen a very inconvenient year in which to resign as far as the length of his service was concerned, for if he had stayed another two years the lump sum he'd have received would have been considerably higher. He didn't appear to accept the way this calculation had been made, condemning it violently as one more manifestation of university bureaucracy.

"Yesterday I heard from the chief accountant, who suggested I ought to stay on another two years, but I can hardly withdraw my resignation for that kind of reason."

"Um," I said ambiguously, unlike Yukari who said quite clearly he'd be better off not resigning at all, but she was scolded for this interruption. His rebuke was obviously halfhearted, but there seemed no chance of any retraction, partly I imagined from the motive of vanity because it would look very undignified to go back on his resignation, and also because he really did appear to be sick to death of university life and wanted to get out of it. He even said, as if he owned some important private collection:

"If the worst really comes to the worst I can always manage by selling off my paintings one by one."

After this and other statements of a similar stirring boldness, he asked me to write him a letter of introduction to Oguri since he'd heard the publicity magazines of business enterprises paid well for manuscripts. I began to wonder what all this had been about, although I said I'd certainly write one for him, but the magazine itself was of a very low, indeed vulgar kind, and the amount offered per manuscript page tended to be minimal. I also stressed that, since the articles demanded were always very short, it was unlikely he would earn a sum of any significance at all; but this didn't seem to deter him.

"Don't worry. I can write something short and sweet. No doubt it will go down well and orders will come rolling in from various other quarters."

So I decided the whole thing had been part of a plan to gain access to a beer magazine and secure his first piece of work following his resignation. This insight aroused a complex of feelings in me, but if analyzed I suppose they'd have consisted principally of a sense of the ludicrous and a slightly forlorn sadness.

As soon as he'd left I went upstairs and rang Oguri at his home. I was worried the professor might suddenly turn up at Oguri's office and not be given the reception he was expecting. After some time Oguri answered.

"Sorry. Did I wake you up?" I said.

"No. Just doing a few odd jobs about the place."

He sounded slightly embarrassed, but he responded in a positive, encouraging way to what I had to say about Professor Nonomiya writing for him, even though he only said he'd ask him to submit a piece sometime. When he heard of my father-in-law's expectations of this starting off an avalanche of orders from other sources he was modestly skeptical, saying he only wished he edited a magazine with that sort of prestige.

We next talked about the university riots and I retailed the ideas and information I'd picked up from my father-in-law and Kaizuka, with the result that Oguri asked me where I'd got hold of all that. He then gave me what the minister of education and some undersecretary of something had allegedly stated on the subject.

"Anyway, how are things with you lately?" he asked.

"Work? Or home life?"

"Whichever you like."

"Nothing much at work, although there's been a bit of turmoil at home."

That was a mistake. There's nothing like the word "turmoil" to whet a journalist's curiosity. Oguri was immediately all ears.

"She's pregnant? No? Then other kinds of rumblings?" (By that he was implying divorce, although presumably wishing to avoid the word itself.)

"Then who has done what?" he asked, so I had to reply.

"Yukari's grandmother has come to live with us."

I gave him an account of the innocent aspects of the affair, leaving out the murder and prison sentence.

"You seem to have been saddled with a weird one there. So the two of you aren't hitting it off?"

"No, nothing like that. Can't really talk about it on the phone. Let's leave it till we meet sometime."

While I was evading the issue, something distracted Oguri's attention (some delivery from a shop or maybe the postman) and he suddenly shouted out to someone to hold on a moment. Thus our Sunday afternoon conversation was brought to an end.

Having said my home life was in "turmoil" it seemed no longer to be so. One reason must have been the remarkable uneventfulness of dinner that evening. Neither Granny nor Tsuru had come back, and Yukari and I managed to have a nice, peaceful meal (Yukari's cooking repertoire was certainly limited, but she always cooked large portions and it really tasted not at all bad), making the occasional perfunctory remark about where Granny might have got to; and it dawned on us that this was the very first time we'd ever dined alone in the house. We talked about her father's resignation.

"Well, no doubt it was a bit drastic, but at least he's honest," said Yukari, taking his side.

I pointed out that a man who could produce his family register in that manner, urge me to investigate his affairs to my heart's content, and yet manage to conceal all trace of Granny's crime could hardly be labeled honest, but since I was feeling sorry for him there was no harshness in my comment, and Yukari saw it as the joke I'd perhaps intended it to be.

"That's right. Only goes to show there are all sorts of honesty," she said, delighted with her own remark.

Tsuru came back at nine o'clock, put in a nominal appearance in the living room, and immediately shut herself away in her own room. Presumably she must have seen a particularly powerful *yakuza* movie since she looked rather exhausted. One more thing, although I hadn't really noticed myself, was that she must have been to the hairdresser, as I realized when Yukari later mentioned it to me. Thirty minutes after that Granny came home, slightly tipsy (Tsuru didn't go out to meet her so Yukari had to), and explained that she'd been persuaded to have some of the saké she'd taken with her. Perhaps because we were watching television we didn't particularly notice she'd finally broken her teetotal pledge, and Granny herself was presumably not much bothered about it. In fact we were more interested in her absurd response to the news of the Nonomiya tie incident.

"Well," she said, "trying his best to look smart, as always."

My own feeling was that this could be considered a surprisingly sharp comment on the ridiculous, futile nature of the whole university rumpus, but Yukari smiled and said:

"Father's always been a smart dresser, and Tsuru has become one as well these days. You're pretty smart yourself, Granny."

So it looked as if these peaceful, uneventful days might continue for some time, and this seemed true of life both at home and at the office; I came to forget that mad period when I'd been snowed under with work and also desperate for a quick solution to the Granny problem in the intervals of my office labors. However, this lasted only ten days, and on that tenth day (Yukari had left early that morning because she had a modeling session) the first catastrophe occurred, swiftly and quite unexpectedly.

I got home around eleven in the evening to be met by Tsuru, who told me that both Yukari and Granny had gone to bed early. Then, with a strangely tense expression on her face (to which I didn't, in fact, pay much attention), she pointed ambiguously in the direction of the guest room and said there was something she wanted to discuss. I think the reason I didn't particularly notice the tension in her face was because I was more occupied by the fact that she'd not referred to me as "master" but in her old manner as "Master Eisuke." I thought it a bit odd, but said "All right" and went into the room. There we sat on chairs facing each other, Tsuru beneath my tiny Umehara nude; and I found myself listening to her request that she be allowed to leave my service at the end of the month.

At first I really did believe I was dreaming, but I only had to look at Tsuru, wearing an odd sort of outfit, a sort of compromise between a summer kimono and a Western dress, with that severe expression on her face, to understand that this was no fantasy. Tsuru at least was very real, and there could be no doubting her. So I asked, just to make sure:

"When you say the end of the month, you mean this calendar month, July?"

"Yes," she said.

I told myself I must believe my ears, since I was now being confronted by reality in the form of the nationwide, indeed the worldwide, servant problem. It came as a profound shock, but there was nothing strange about the intensity of this feeling, for if Tsuru were to go it meant the basic premise of my existence, the essential precondition of my everyday life, went with her. The word that came to mind was "rebellion." This was a rebellion, an uprising, my maid had turned against me: such was the thought that assailed me as I sat there, feeling I could neither sit still nor stand up, with a cigarette stuck awkwardly in my mouth, the feeble, faint flame of the match trembling slightly in my hand.

Finally I managed to light it, and tried to find out her reasons, asking if she intended to go back home or become a maid in another house in Tokyo, but the response was negative in both cases. What most struck me was she didn't actually say anything but merely shook her head. Certainly Tsuru could never have been considered talkative, but she'd never replied to a question from me in that way before, or to one from anyone else as far as I knew. However, she didn't look as if she was actually annoyed by my questions, so I tried again, not exactly enjoying myself.

"Well, then what is the reason?" I asked, adding: "It looks as though I'll have to hear the whole story from the beginning."

"Yes, well, the fact is that this time I. . ." She hesitated at that point, then, with a strange, impudent smile, she said: "Master Eisuke, please don't laugh, but I'm going to take over a snack bar."

"A snack bar?"

"Yes."

"You mean the kind of place where they serve hard liquor? Opens in the early evening and gets crowded around midnight? Provides late-night food as well?"

"Yes."

"Rice and pickles? Iced tofu? Pork in ginger?"

"Yes."

"Ever been to one?"

"Yes. Just once. It was early in the evening, though."

"Just starting up, or. . .?"

"It's been going quite a long time. But there have been problems, so. . ."

She looked as if she didn't want to say what the problems had been, so I said:

"Well, there's no need to go into that. When you say you're going to take it over you mean you're going to become the mama of the place?"

"Oh really, the mama, of course not, I mean, how could I, really, it's too. . ."

"But look here, Tsuru. . ."

I tried to explain in as serious, sincere, and low a voice as possible, but inside I was having fits of laughter. This wasn't only at the comicality of the situation but more a tremendous feeling of happy relief. Tsuru actually intended to begin that kind of work, work that involved constantly trying to please numerous customers, with no experience, at her time of life. If she'd been young there might have been . . . but no matter what angle one considered it from it simply couldn't work out. It was impossible. It was bound to fail. Explaining to her and convincing her how rash her plan was would be as easy as twisting a baby's arm.

"Look, Tsuru, there's no doubt that if *you* were to prepare the food that sort of place dishes out it would be the best in the whole country. What they want there is the old-fashioned stuff, home cooking just like mother makes, and you're the kind of authentic mother figure to provide the goods. Young girls nowadays rely on those damn cooking cards or whatever they call them in magazines, and obviously food prepared by looking at one of those just doesn't begin to be in the same class. They're bound to love you. You'll be famous."

Having cleverly flattered her in this way I began to spell out what was wrong with the idea.

"Still, it's not enough in a place like that to provide tasty food. Prob-

258

ably much more important is the way the customers get treated. You probably know that anyway. And, certainly, as far as intelligence is concerned you should have no problems, and there's no trace of your accent left so that's all right. The trouble is you have to be very, very talkative. You've got to like talking your head off. Now, Tsuru, what about that, then? I confess that worries me a bit. I mean, look how angry you made Mr. Murata. And you can't really force yourself to speak if you're not that way inclined, particularly all those cheap little things you're expected to say, you know. I don't see how a serious woman like Tsuru could ever manage that, do you? It's all so light, so frivolous. Of course, if it's a young woman she can get by with being a bit clumsy in the speaking line because she's got all that sexy charm. But honestly, Tsuru, I don't want to be rude, but at your age. . ."

"I know. I'm an old woman. No ordinary man would ever look at me."

I found this sudden remark slightly ambiguous. After all, if you turned it inside out the statement implied that a man who was out of the ordinary could well unearth her latent eroticism. I didn't think too hard about that, in fact, but simply started to have my suspicions. I went on:

"You see, in that business, you have the problem of credit. People buy on tick and you've got to get the money out of them. It's a hell of a business. Any number of people have been ruined by it. Then there's your competitors, who're trying to make sure you go under. Why, recently, even first-class bars in Ginza. . ."

I continued for a while like this, pretending to considerable inside knowledge, and bringing it to a close by saying there was no need at present to go into all the details of the trade. But Tsuru dismissed my warnings just like that, saying she didn't have to worry about such things because she'd have nothing to do with that side of the business at all. Although she would be the actual mama, she'd only be responsible for the bookkeeping, the cooking, and the general overseeing of the place, and wouldn't have to deal with the customers in any way. They would be looked after by a middle-aged woman (who still had some of that sexy charm) and a young, rather plump girl. As far as the customers were concerned, the older woman would appear to be the one in charge, but in fact she'd merely be working under Tsuru's orders.

I was surprised how carefully it had all been worked out, and could only give a slight gasp.

"Mr. Murata really is a most clever gentleman," she said quietly.

I held my breath for quite a while; or at least I thought I was doing so, until at last I said:

"You mean the place belongs to Murata?"

"Yes. I kept on refusing, but he just wouldn't take no for an answer."

Tsuru looked very pleased with herself as she said this, much as I imagine a prize racehorse might look on finally hearing that some famous judge of horseflesh had stated its true worth.

I tried to restrain myself. I wanted to point out that only a month ago she'd said she intended to remain in this house forever, and the spiteful words were right on the tip of my tongue, but I just managed to swallow them back. I also wanted to ask her very pointedly when exactly she'd become so friendly with Murata and how the leopard had been able to change its spots so damn quick, but I held that down too. I did, however, ask her how much she was going to be paid, since I imagined I might hit a weak spot here, but since it transpired she would receive, even counting things like the food and other extras she got here, almost three times what I gave her, this only added to the blackness of my mood.

"That's pretty good money," I said, aware myself of the feebleness of both my reply and my position. I was now full of only the bitterest of feelings at this betrayal by my servant.

As if to excuse her own conduct Tsuru said she was very grateful for the long years she'd spent in my service, but now she really had to think about the future. Presumably I was looking so cross at the time she felt obliged to say something like that; or maybe it was meant to be some reproach, for I must admit I'd never given Tsuru's future a single thought. So eventually I had to say I understood, which only seemed to encourage her to continue in the same vein.

"There's unemployment insurance as well. . ."

"Um."

"I'm sorry I shan't be able to look after you any more, Master Eisuke, but, well. . ."

"Which means I won't be able to eat sesame tofu ever again, I suppose."

In order to achieve a change of attitude on my own part here I'd meant to sound jovial, but somehow it came out surprisingly gloomy and heartfelt. The fact is sesame tofu had long been one of Tsuru's specialities as well as a great favorite of mine.

"Yes, but I'm thinking of making it at my new place, so you could always come and have some there."

This reply annoyed me. At first I meant merely to point out I wasn't so obsessed with sesame tofu as to be prepared to go all the way to some dodgy snack bar to eat it, but instead a number of emotions seemed to be pressing inside me for expression and I suddenly lost my self-control. They say hell hath no fury like a man deprived of his food, and the complaints I now let loose seemed to be a prime example of that. My first complaint was that when she'd encouraged me to marry Yukari she'd said she would take care of all the cooking and household chores and so I needn't worry about a thing. Since that had undoubtedly spurred me into marriage, how could she now be so irresponsible as to go back on her promise? My second point was that her own wishes had been at least half responsible for Granny being here in this house, and now she was simply pushing the whole burden of looking after the old lady onto us two. Did she really think that was fair?

I admit there was a certain amount of prejudiced thinking in both complaints, but I also felt the very fact that I'd uttered them must mean they made pretty good sense, and as I listened to the sound of my own voice my powers of self-control grew gradually weaker and weaker. It ended up with me pleading with her, in a voice of such seriousness it sounded as if I might shortly be reduced to tears, to stay on in this house and I would raise her salary to the level that Murata was offering. But this assault on her emotions had no effect.

"It's very kind of you to say so," she replied promptly, and merely bowed. It needed no great intelligence to work out this would be followed by a statement of how happy my words had made her, but unfortunately. . .

I felt a flush of shame come to my face as I observed her slightly affected bow. It was like the return of a sense of drunkenness after you thought you'd recovered, and now it was much heavier, much more painful and depressing.

Then Tsuru raised her head and, looking me straight in the eye (I was still suffering pangs of humiliation), started to say something. At first I couldn't take in what it was at all, and then I grasped that she was explaining why my criticism of her for breaking her promises was unjustified. She argued, at tedious length, that she could certainly not be accused of irresponsibility, for her conduct only showed just how responsibly she'd taken her part in encouraging my marriage and how much she'd done to preserve it.

Since calm, logical argument was not her strong point it was difficult to work out from her elusive, volatile reasonings what she thought she was getting at, but it seems she'd guessed at some point that there was a previous relationship between Yukari and Murata, saw her suspicions grow into something like certainty, and felt her own position, as someone who'd urged this marriage on her master, could well be in jeopardy if she didn't intervene and prevent such a man, or at least a man under such a suspicion, from visiting the house; so she'd gone to see him and told him to stay away. Before going, she'd known she would inevitably clash with Murata since he was that sort of man, and there would be bad blood between them, if only because he was bound to misunderstand her motives. However, a bond had been created between them in this way, and he'd asked her to take charge of one of his establishments. Presumably this happened quite on the spur of the moment with Murata, who'd been having trouble with the people working at his snack bar, and it must suddenly have crossed his mind that a woman as loyal as this was just the kind of person to put in charge of the place.

Much of the above is guesswork on my part. One thing Tsuru did actually say was:

"Luckily, he did understand my motives, and I suppose that helped me decide how I should behave from then on, so I can only say I'm really grateful I went to see him the way I did."

This display of smug self-satisfaction only made me smile bitterly to myself.

"I see. So your first motive was only to be of service to me. What a wonderful surprise the outcome must have been."

My own very slight awareness of the personal, selfish motives that swayed me was amply compensated by an appreciation of the farcical side of Tsuru's excuses. There was something splendidly ironic about a maid's professed loyalty to her master resulting in her pushing off elsewhere, and I need hardly say that the way she'd read the relationship between Yukari and Murata wasn't exactly to my liking.

I was now, in fact, feeling confused by the situation, and in an attempt to regain control of things, I started to talk about another drawback to her new situation as if I'd only just thought of it.

"There is one point, of course. I don't suppose you're going to find it all that easy to get somewhere to live..."

I said this in a deliberate, easily comprehensible way. Naturally I was hoping to put some pressure on her by this new approach. But Tsuru again replied quite readily, as if speaking about something that should be clear to anyone.

"Yes, I shall use some of my retirement allowance for that..."

She had the whole thing worked out, a sum based on her present salary plus the value of the food she received, multiplied by the number of years she'd been in service. She spoke in a very cool way as though just asking someone to pay off an obvious debt they owed. I sighed as I realized that Murata must have masterminded this, and also reflected that in an age like ours when servants were so scarce perhaps it was only to be expected that large sums should be handed over to maids on retirement. When my father, grandfather, or great-grandfather had been in a position of this kind, they'd handled it easily by just giving the maid a decent walking-out kimono and that was the end of it; we were living in a really bad age when it came to a maid taking her leave of you. The despair I felt at that moment consisted of two contradictory elements: firstly a feeling of how pathetic it was that so close a relationship with Tsuru over all those decades could be calculated and transposed into this niggardly amount of cash, and secondly a sharp anxiety about how I could possibly lay my hands on such a huge sum of money before the end of the month.

Perhaps because unconsciously I was trying to put off the payment of this retirement sum, I launched into a different subject.

"Still, before we get down to the details of your retirement money, there is the question of your successor. Do you yourself have anyone in mind?" I said, thereby making a mild attempt at a counterattack, hoping to take advantage of the fact that my adversary was bound to quail at the thought that no replacement could possibly exist. "I

263

think we're going to have great trouble finding a substitute. The custom has always been in these matters, since way back indeed, to give a month's notice. This particularly applies at a time like this when servants are so hard to come by. Anyway, can't you wait a little longer? Let's say at least until the end of August. Of course the best thing would be if you were to wait until the new maid has actually arrived."

On hearing this request Tsuru lost her temper. Probably some criticism implied in my words had annoyed her. Anyway, she suddenly looked very worn and tired, and her expression suggested she was highly displeased.

"Master Eisuke, I strongly recommend that you do not refer to the next person who comes here as 'the maid.' You would also do well to advise Mrs. Mabuchi and Mrs. Nabeshima to do likewise."

She said this in very sharp, clipped tones, and I hurriedly replied that of course I'd do that, of course, attempting to let the matter pass. But Tsuru kept on remorselessly, letting loose all the rancor pent up over the years, in a voice that may sometimes have grown husky and hesitant but with a real eloquence too.

"It is quite natural that you, Master Eisuke, should refer to me as 'the maid,' although I must say I felt it was perhaps slightly out of place when your former wife used to do so... Don't you agree? I had hoped she would refer to me as 'the lady help,' as is normal nowadays. In Mrs. Nabeshima's case she is, of course, very old, and has also spent such a long time in that sort of place, so I suppose it can't be helped; but frankly I found it very upsetting when she referred to me in places like the vegetable shop as 'our maid.' Yukari's references to me as 'our help' always seemed to me a little too abbreviated, too curt..."

I was impressed here by the way the servant problem had now turned into this linguistic issue.

"Yes, I see. I understand how you feel. I understand very well," I said, and then gave her a brief lecture on the use of honorifics, explaining, for example, that to call her "Lady Help" (or even "Our Lady Help") would surely be a bizarre form of address, being so polite as to be positively misleading. As I saw it, both Yukari and Granny were in fact struggling with problems in the use of such honorifics that had become increasingly acute during the course of this century, and they shouldn't be held personally to blame. It was a national, not a private, issue. Unfortunately only rather dim-witted people went into the Ministry of Education, and they did seem quite incapable of handling it.

I had thus sidetracked the whole issue and ended up at this distant remove, but at least Tsuru seemed to be taken in by it and nodded positively in what seemed to be agreement.

However, considering the difficulty I'd had extricating myself by such emergency means from the problems aroused by her aversion to the word "maid," I was able to gauge how much she must dislike the work itself, particularly as she seemed to consider the post of snack bar woman one to be held with pride. Obviously it would be quite impossible to keep her here. I felt a profound despair and, half as a consequence of my despair and half out of simple disbelief, I said, as if talking to myself:

"Still, working for someone like Murata. After disliking him so much, too."

Tsuru said nothing, so I went on:

"Just can't understand it at all."

This time she did reply, and the reply hurt me.

"Yes. You see, he looks after me, like a parent almost. Nobody has ever cared about me like that before," she said in a strangely feminine, tender voice.

This was obviously a criticism aimed at me as someone who'd simply made use of her as a mere convenience, had never once considered what would happen to her when she retired, but had just thought vaguely that when she could no longer work as a maid she'd go back home to the country. I admit I was shaken. All I could do was groan in assent, and then say:

"I suppose, if you consider your future, maybe you are doing the right thing, in fact."

"Yes, I think so," she replied, turning her face a fraction to one side and placing her fingers against her cheek. It was exactly the pose my former wife had assumed when she was giving herself airs about something.

"Tsuru, that's the first time I've ever seen you do that. It makes you look really quite seductive."

I said this on purpose in an attempt to end the discussion on a pleasant note by mildly teasing her (regardless of what the pose was actually like), and as she glared back at me in mock outrage there was certainly a kind of feminine charm about her. Still remembering my former wife I said:

"I think I need a little time to work out the question of your retirement money, Tsuru. I'd better find out what the situation is now about these things. I'll get in touch with my brother back home. I've also an acquaintance in the Labor Ministry I can talk to."

The maid turned to face me again and bowed humbly.

"So you'll be with us to the end of the month, is it? Well, you've served me a long time, and I can only offer my thanks for that."

"Yes. It's the seventeenth today, so just a fortnight more," she said cheerfully.

"The seventeenth, is it? So that's why Granny's sound asleep."

I nodded and stood up.

"I think I'll take a bath," I said, but Tsuru didn't reply to that.

Instead she lowered her voice as if she were telling me some deep secret and said:

"She wasn't dressed in mourning when she went out today because . . . she went to the races!"

15

August and September of that year were probably the most awful two months I've ever experienced. What made it all the worse was that the cause of this misery was the silly, trifling fact that the maid had left us. It kept occurring to me that, if I did have to suffer, I would have been much better off with some high-powered problem, such as the existence of God, or the various merits and demerits of the capitalist and communist systems.

From the middle of July to the end of that month I tried everything in my quest for another maid, putting advertisements in three different newspapers, but when the appointed day came I still hadn't found one, and so on the first of August, on a hot, sultry morning, Tsuru departed. Thus began a maidless way of life, something I'd never experienced before (if one discounts the three years spent in lodgings while I was attending high school), although it would be truer perhaps to say the maid's role had now been passed over to Yukari and Granny.

This doesn't mean that during those two months the tiny maid's room was empty all the time. Early in August, through the good offices of an old man in our administration section, an old lady, a distant relation of his, turned up to do the work. She was supposed to be the same age as Tsuru, but in fact looked considerably more ancient than Granny Utako, and despite her always saying how fit and healthy she was she just couldn't manage things. The heat probably had something to do with it, for she was constantly neglecting her duties to have a little lie-down, so after three days we were obliged to send her home.

Then at the end of August my elder brother arranged for a young girl to come up from the country. Apparently she wanted to go to high school, and one of the conditions of her employment was she should have Sunday off as well. This meant she wouldn't be able to prepare the evening meal because she'd be at school, and on Sunday she wouldn't work anyway, so it was exactly as if we were having a high school student to lodge in the house; even so, I didn't demur or offer one word of complaint but hired her. However, the very evening after she'd registered at her new high school, Granny Utako said she thought the child was pregnant. Neither Yukari nor I were prepared to go along with that, since we thought it was simply out of the question, but Granny was so positively convinced we felt we'd better just ask to make sure, and the girl admitted quite openly that she was four months gone. I immediately rang up my brother to get his consent, and then packed her off home.

After that we found we were getting no response at all from the other places we'd tried, and any new attempts we made were met in the same way, either by being politely told it was doubtful such things as maids existed any more, or by large hints that meant much the same. So we gave up the idea of having our own maid and applied to an agency to find us a part-time domestic. The first one who came certainly worked very hard, but on the first day Yukari saw her taking a bottle of whisky home with her. We decided to overlook that, but on the second day Yukari saw her opening Granny's purse, and since there was no way of knowing what atrocity she might commit if allowed to continue like this, we dismissed her. The next one was almost a total imbecile, and she put so much salt in the food it tasted as though it were about to take off, but we felt we could put up with that. The real problem was she simply had no idea of hygiene or cleanliness, so she had to go as well in just five days. What complicated matters was when Yukari rang the agency about this. Perhaps because she didn't explain things very well, the conversation ended up at complete cross-purposes, and the boss of the outfit finally became so incensed that Yukari was told they'd never send anybody to our house again. We tried a few other agencies but they all gave the same disheartening reply, to the effect that there didn't seem much hope at the moment, but if we were prepared to hang on for a while they might, at some time in the future, possibly be able to send somebody. So, in mid-September, we settled down to a way of life in which there was no domestic help in any form.

Of course it's questionable whether during the month and a half up to then we could have been said to have had "help" anyway. Of the four, the one with the kleptomaniac tendency had been (if one ignored that large failing) miles better than the others, although even she, in terms of efficiency and capability, could never have been compared to Tsuru. Both Yukari and Granny, who'd seen her at work, said so, and I was all too ready to agree with them. As for the high school student and the other two, they'd been a hindrance rather than anything else.

Still, now that we had nobody, the work obviously had to be done by Yukari, Granny, and me, although it may sound exaggerated to include myself among the workers, the things I had to do seeming perhaps so minimal as to make it comic to claim they were work at all. For example, I had to polish my own shoes once Tsuru had gone, since it had been no good getting any of those domestics or Yukari to do it, as none of them could manage anything like a decent shine. Another, lesser matter was that of my clothes after they came back from the cleaners, for now they'd be hung up in my wardrobe or placed in my chest of drawers with the laundry tags still on them, and I had to tear the things off before wearing them. I found little details like that particularly trying, and would long for the days when Tsuru had been here. Another trying thing was that, after Granny and Yukari had taken over the cooking, no matter which one of them was doing it, either while the cooking was in progress or just when the meal was ready something was invariably found to be missing, seasoning or whatever. When one of those incompetent domestics had been around they could always be sent to the shops to get it, but now I was the one who had to go. In one extreme case (when Yukari was doing pork cutlets fried in batter), not only did I have to go off to buy bread crumbs before the cooking began, but when all three of us were seated at the table about to start I had to go back to the very same shop to get some sauce.

At first Granny had been extremely reluctant to make me run off on such errands, apologizing at irritating length whenever she did so, but by the second half of August she seemed to think nothing of it. I can remember one day when Granny was in charge of the cooking and the menu was plain fried chicken with cold tofu, she came out to the entrance hall to greet me when I returned home (a very rare occurrence, indeed something that had never once happened since Tsuru had left), but only to tell me to dash off to the shop to get some ginger she'd forgotten to buy.

Granny undertook the cooking, at the most, twice a week. When she really felt like doing it she could dish up some pretty fancy stuff, but when she wasn't in the mood she was slapdash, and it was little wonder to me her marriage hadn't gone very well and her husband had been driven to drink and other consolations. For example, she produced some very odd combinations, such as cabbage rolls and seaweed rolls in the same meal (though perhaps her desire to use up all those dried gourd shavings she'd brought back from Tochigi as filling for the rolls was a mitigating circumstance here). Also she once served up a meal consisting solely of thin noodles and hashed cucumber, and although the noodles had been craftily boiled up with bits of sea bream and the quality was first class, it certainly was nothing like a meal for a grown man, or woman, and Yukari and I were obliged to warm up some instant food almost immediately afterward.

The same criticism could not be made of Yukari's cuisine, but she was in the habit of serving yesterday's dinner leftovers for today's breakfast, and she tended to produce regularly the same evening meal on the same day of the week with boring monotony. Obviously I wasn't happy about this, but both Granny and Yukari seemed to be allergic to cooking, and on those evenings when I wasn't there they nearly always ordered food in from outside. Whenever I saw the empty bowls from the noodle shop or the Chinese restaurant—or, on special occasions, the two boxes from the eel restaurant—in a corner of the kitchen, I felt I could almost hold in my hands, as it were, their attitude toward the food question. Nowadays, quite unlike the past, every morning when I left for work I never had to point out to anyone I might be late that night since I was invariably asked if I'd be back for dinner or not, and there was unconcealed rejoicing when I said I wouldn't. There would be the same happy response whenever I rang up from the office to say I'd not be needing dinner, and although I could put up with the unhappy feelings this obviously aroused in me, I found it extremely irritating to keep on having to do this whenever there was a chance I might be late.

Besides the cooking, of course, there was plenty to do about the house, such as cleaning and washing, and then the shopping, plus a host of minor things, and whenever I reflected that Tsuru had been able to do the whole lot by herself with apparent ease I was struck again with admiration. Up to this time Granny and Yukari had been under the impression they'd helped Tsuru out a great deal with the cleaning, but now that they had to do it all themselves they hardly seemed to know where to start. When they did start it took a tremendous amount of time, no doubt because they never seemed able to work out in what order they should do things. On such occasions Yukari would complain that the house was too big and just impossible to clean, and then immediately say how nice and easy cooking would be if only the kitchen were twice the size, and she even drew up a plan of the projected new kitchen on the back of one of those advertising handouts that come with the newspaper. She didn't seem to mind the area of the house increasing in that case.

At the end of August the vacuum cleaner broke down so we had to buy a new one, and then in the middle of September we bought a clothes drier. Yukari had been complaining for some time it was such a terrible nuisance having to keep hanging the things out. I'd managed to get a vacuum cleaner from the company at a discount, but the only good electric clothes driers were made in America, according to some magazine, so we had to buy one of those, and the drain on my pocket was considerable. I was worried a demand might be made for an electric dishwasher, so I got in first and explained with great persuasiveness that all dishwashers, from those made by my company right up to the latest American models, were totally useless. I can give no detailed figures as we weren't keeping any accounts, but our living expenses had rocketed after Tsuru left, and at the end of each month I found my face growing longer and longer. One reason was the uneconomical way we were buying foodstuffs; another was the quantity of clothes sent out to the laundry; and the amount of money being spent on meals ordered from restaurants was simply ridiculous.

So I told Yukari from time to time she really ought to be a bit more careful, and each time I did this she would sulk. What she said in reply, of course, was always preposterous, such as she never expected to be told off like that when she and Granny were wearing their fingers to the bone, or that my brother back home wouldn't find a maid for us because he'd probably taken a dislike to her, or that if only we had a maid she could do more modeling and make more money, or that she thought I'd get a much bigger salary when I became a director but it was hardly any raise at all; a mass of irrelevancies each time. What it meant was that Yukari's housekeeping talents made it impossible to hope for any economies for the time being, and Granny was even more incompetent than she was.

Granny was, in fact, of very little help. She was clumsy at any kind of cleaning, for though she wasn't particularly lazy, being willing enough to do her bit since she was in the position of being looked after, all that happened was a considerable output of psychological energy with no corresponding beneficial results. I confess her sheer incompetence often surprised me, and Yukari was always complaining about it, saying she must have had a really tough time in prison, and wondering how the guests could have survived in a boardinghouse run by her. I was able to gather how much mental strain this futile expenditure of effort upon household work was causing her by the fact that she'd suddenly stopped doing her regular flower arrangements, and on those rare occasions when she did decide to do some the house would be full of identical displays of the same flower. I was made particularly aware of how extreme, even neurotic, the arranging impulse had become in her when I returned home one evening in late August to find there were sunflowers in every nook and cranny of the house, a display, however, that turned out to be her last as an artistic achievement and her grandest in both style and scale. Granny herself seemed pretty pleased with it, assuring me it had a tasteful effect all over and apparently expecting me to agree with her, but the only effect I perceived was that, with large yellow flowers blooming in the living room, in her own room next door, in my study upstairs, and in the guest room too, it was as if someone were holding an exhibition of Van Gogh prints throughout the house. It was the arrangement of one of these yellow summer flowers under the unmoving, handless clock in the hall that made the deepest impression on me, a symbolic statement of the fact that order in this household had been seriously disturbed.

Next morning, just before I left for work, I looked at the sunflower fringed by iris leaves in its square, flat bowl, and was suddenly visited by the feeling that I'd made a discovery of some kind, although it hadn't yet reached the stage where I could apprehend it clearly and say what it was. I then forgot about it in the way one absentmindedly leaves something behind. But that night, as I was lying next to Yukari with my hands cupped over her small breasts, that morning's vague *aperçu* returned with a sudden burst of surprise, or perhaps it was even some earlier insight which then took on a positive, real shape in my mind. It was a suspicion that the main reason Granny had wanted to live with us was because we had an efficient, useful maid. This, I had to admit, was probably true; at least it was an idea I couldn't just dismiss out of hand. As I arrived at this judgment I found myself smiling wryly, yet also tolerantly, at my own failure to grasp this fact much earlier; and then returned to the activity my thoughts had interrupted. As I fondled my wife's body she shuddered and moaned.

I decided I was justified in smiling so cynically at my own insight. Here we had an old woman, just out of prison, who came across a happy home and decided she wanted to share that happiness. What it had to offer her, however, was not any happiness her granddaughter's love might provide, nor any joy that the sight of her splendid husband, so lavish in his affectionate dealings with his bride, might bestow. Instead what she'd understood, even if only vaguely, was that here was a well-trained maid who would do things for her. Happiness, for Granny, was a maid; that was an insight deserving something more than just a wry smile, however, since it was downright funny. So as I lay there in the darkness listening to Yukari's gentle breathing as she slept beside me, this time I gave a broad and cheerful smile. But now one more serious doubt rose slowly to the surface of my mind, a sadder one of real significance. Might it not be that Yukari too had married me because I had a maid?

I gulped hard and held my breath for a long time, much like a child who's trying to see how long he can do it for. The idea that Yukari didn't love me now and never had was horrifying. I tried to deny my own doubts, but when I considered how much Yukari disliked housework then, even if one didn't make that her whole motive in marrying me, it was certainly conceivable it had been some part of it. How much, of course, was the question. Would it be a quarter, a third, perhaps even half? I hurriedly decided to try no higher ratio. However, even if one fixed the ratio at a quarter, or less than that, it still implied a family, a household, had been created because a maid existed; two people had come together because of a servant one of them had in his employment, and this showed not just a contemptuous attitude toward the concept of the home and the institution of marriage, but was a deliberate, malicious insult aimed at them both. What was even worse was that the more I thought about this the more real it seemed, and so the more likely to be true. I finally let out my breath and attempted to contain the feelings of displeasure my thoughts had aroused.

Yukari opened her eyes and placed her hot leg across my body. I pushed it away. She whispered in her husky, low, sexy voice:

"Ooh, you'll have to drink some of Otoyo's wine."

I gave a short laugh in response, but did nothing else. She seemed to reconcile herself easily enough to that and started talking in a quite different tone.

"I wonder if Granny's having an affair?"

This made me really laugh, because Yukari had sounded so serious.

"With the caretaker?"

"Um."

"Name of Hirayama?"

"That's right."

"But you said the same thing before once, didn't you? Teased her right to her face about her 'lover,' as you called him."

Since the day he'd saved her in the cinema, they'd been to the races together (on July 17) and he'd been once to our house when I was out. Yukari often teased her about it, in fact, but I had assumed from the way she responded to her granddaughter's jests that they were "just good friends." I admit there was something improper in going out with another man on the day supposedly set aside for commemorating her husband's death, particularly just to gamble on horses, but I wasn't in any position to be straitlaced about it; and anyway on the next day (or perhaps the one after that) it seems she did visit the cemetery, even though she wasn't dressed in mourning. Then on August 17 (still not wearing mourning) she'd gone out in a somewhat melancholy mood, and I was pretty sure she must have gone to the cemetery on that day too.

I mentioned all this to Yukari, but she became quite annoyed by the fact that I hadn't agreed with her.

"I'm not talking about anything like that. I mean it's a real love affair."

She went on to explain that quite recently Granny had taken to going out much more frequently than before, and she was always asking if the mail had come yet, or wondering why nobody ever seemed to telephone, and the way she fretted about these things was exactly the way it was with a woman in love. As far as Yukari knew, the caretaker had sent her one postcard and telephoned two or three times, while Granny had rung him up once from home.

"I see. Is he married, this old man?"

Yukari was unable to give any precise answer. Granny hadn't actually said anything on that point, but since she never mentioned his having a wife it seemed pretty certain he must be a widower.

"Still, you can't do a job like that all by yourself. Just about impossible, I would've thought. Not a caretaker in a block of apartments," I said, although my principal interest was not in that question at all, but rather in the remark I made very casually after it.

"Were you always waiting for me to telephone you?"

"Of course I was. What do you expect?" she answered straight away, which filled me with considerable delight. But she went on to say she still did, and that only made me think of how she must wait each day longing for me to ring up and say I wouldn't be home for dinner. I began to question the romantic implications of the first statement and the joy I'd experienced on assuming it must mean she'd married me because she loved me, and not because I had a maid. Even so, there was still enough happiness remaining, and I laughed and said I wondered, and went back to the original subject.

"I don't really think I'm with you when you talk about a love affair. They're just friends, you know; just hobnobbing with each other."

"Hobnobbing?"

I explained the innocent meaning of the word, while Yukari kept up a meaningless prodding of my ribs as I did so.

"Well, I wonder. I don't think it's like that anyway."

"Oh," I said.

"Don't you think Granny's become a bit sort of erotic recently?"

"Not really. . . I mean, how should I know? Besides, people tend to look younger even in just platonic affairs. It's only natural."

"Well, I simply feel it's not like that, that's all. I'm convinced it's not."

"Um," I said, and then whispered, as if I'd been bowled over by the power of her argument:

"Smelling of man all over, is she?"

275

"For heaven's sake, do you have to be so obscene?"

"But you started it. After all, at that age. The man himself is over sixty."

"I've got a fine lookout, then, if a man can't be expected to be up to it still when he's past sixty," Yukari replied, and as I nodded wisely in acknowledgment I decided I'd have to drink lots of carrot wine to show her that I, at least, would still be right up to the mark.

One reason I remained uncertain about Yukari's motives in marrying me was because of what Tsuru had said before she left. Since the business about her retirement money dragged on a while, Tsuru finally became very ill-tempered and, having jumped to the quite unfounded conclusion it was Yukari's fault that the amount had been reduced to some degree, she was in just the mood, presumably, for a long recital of unpleasant home truths. However, she was still in my home, so there was some inevitable restraint as to what truths could or could not be said in this context, and since she was obviously not out to annoy me as it might mean receiving no retirement money at all, but only wanted to get certain things off her chest, she could say nothing really awful. So she restricted herself to various hints and insinuations that could have been oblique references to Yukari's premarital life. This took the form of pouring tiny drops of poison into my ear so they would gradually accumulate into something deadly, a criminal method one often comes across in detective fiction. My response at the time had been to feign obtuseness in the hope it might discourage her from saying any more, but now that she was gone the poison began to circulate and have its effect, and I endured the pangs it caused in solitude. Naturally I mentioned none of this to Yukari, nor did I ask her anything that might have been related to these allegations in any way. I felt that as long as her present behavior was above suspicion there was no point in asking anything.

I must admit there was an immediate decline in the effectiveness of her poison for a rather funny reason. This was something that occurred on August 1, our first dinner together without a maid, when both Granny and Yukari produced a whole series of insults about Tsuru as if some hatred stored up for ages had at last been let loose. The violence of this was such that I began to wonder just what the two of them would say about me in my absence, or indeed what they had already said when the three of them had discussed me over dinner. It was such a total contrast to the night before, when the four of us had gone to a Chinese restaurant for Tsuru's farewell party and Granny and Yukari had vied with each other in their unctuous flattery of her, that all I could feel was complete astonishment. I could do little else in fact but sit in a daze listening to it all, since neither of them would allow me a word in edgeways, and yet the interesting thing was the remark of Yukari's that had started the whole slanging match off. What it boiled down to was that, despite her cheerful assurances to the contrary, Tsuru had never finally taught her the secrets of her three grand specialities (all three great favorites of mine), the proper preparation of sesame tofu, Koya tofu, and oxtail stew, but had just kept fobbing her off with some silly reason or other, on purpose of course, until the day she left.

The more spiteful their attacks on Tsuru's dog-in-the-manger attitude became, the more my dislike and contempt for women grew, and that proved a kind of salvation for me. While Yukari and Granny raged I found I was beginning to smile, and I went on smiling for some time. I decided whatever that intimate of Murata's, that maid, might have said or implied was just as ludicrous as these insinuations I was listening to now, and therefore (I confess to a certain logical leap at this point) there was no good reason why I shouldn't ignore them completely. So I did that; or at least I tried my best to do that.

Thus the two long, trying months slid slowly by: August hot and parched like the brown stamens of the yellow sunflowers, and then September with its soft dusks in which the blurred Michaelmas daisies bloomed, its days blue with gentian and white with cosmos (but none of these flowers were arranged in our rooms). In the latter half of September Yukari told her modeling agency she was prepared to do any jobs they had for her, no matter how poorly paid, showing, I thought, how anxious she was to escape the housework. Now the kitchen was only decently tidy on about one day a week and the corridor always seemed to be dusty, although Granny Utako must bear some of the responsibility for that. In fact Granny had taken over all the polishing and dusting, or so she claimed, but she didn't seem to put much effort into it. Since she had this lover she spent a great deal of her time out, and often three or four days would pass with nothing being done at all. The cleaning of my study and the bathroom became my job, so every Sunday morning I had to sweat away scrubbing out the bath and polishing the tiles, envious of my fellow directors enjoying themselves out there on the golf course, although up to that moment I'd never had the slightest interest in playing golf. I felt genuinely jealous of what I assumed was their happiness, yet happiness for me was still one thing, and one thing only: having a good, efficient, loyal maid.

One day early in October I returned home at seven o'clock to find a message from Yukari waiting for me.

> Just heard some retakes have to be done so going out. Sorry and all that. The staff said dresses hadn't been ironed properly at back so creases showing in front too and no good. I've cut up a few things and you'll find them on top shelf of fridge, so make yourself some fried rice. Granny's out on a date. Bye now.

Bye now, indeed, I thought, cooking the fried rice, but that alone seemed sadly inadequate so I warmed up a can of soup as well. When I'd finished, I managed to get one good laugh out of a cartoon in the evening paper, but couldn't find anything worth watching on TV as I flicked through the channels. Since I didn't feel like going upstairs immediately after dinner to get on with reading my business papers, I took a cushion out into the hall and set about polishing some shoes as a way of helping my digestion. I had prepared rather a lot of fried rice and eaten up every scrap of it.

I'd just got to the right shoe of the second pair when it struck me that this was just the right sort of work for slaves. I grimaced at the thought with half my face and told myself I'd be better off not thinking in such terms, but even by the time I was on the left shoe the idea hadn't gone away, and persisted right through to the third pair as well, seeming particularly relevant at the point where I was scraping ingrained chewing gum off the sole of one of them. So finally I stopped, and was aware that I was gradually becoming absorbed in reflections on the nature of slavery.

The first question I considered was to what extent a maid was a kind of slave. Even if she wasn't an actual slave, she was still obliged to do only work of the dreariest, dirtiest, most boring kind, such as polishing shoes, cooking fried rice, scrubbing bathroom tiles. Now, I admit this was a pretty wild sort of opinion to have, as well as being remarkably commonplace and obvious too; but when I considered how nobody ever actually *said* anything like that, and you never saw it written in the columns of the newspapers, I began to wonder why. Was it because it was so very obvious, or because the statement was too crude and simpleminded; or wasn't it rather because it might cause offense and so everyone kept a respectful distance from it? I began to think the last answer was the correct one. People were actually afraid to look the idea in the face. Having come to this conclusion I had the feeling I'd discovered some major truth, although I didn't experience any of the joy the discoverer is said to feel, but rather the exact opposite, a sense of gloom at the realization that for years I'd been maltreating one of these slaves and was now for the first time doing slavework myself.

Having decided I was performing the tasks appropriate to a slave, inevitably this meant I would get involved in the question of whether Yukari was a slave as well; but since I felt it would be tiresome to have to establish distinctions between maid and wife at this point in my argument, I decided to leave that question for a moment and concentrate my scrutiny on the proposition that maid equals slave. My first conclusion that nobody wanted to become a maid because maid did equal slave, or at least because maids performed slavish tasks, found complete confirmation in my own experience of the past two months. However, the thought that immediately followed this one was of much greater moment and so unexpected I was genuinely flabbergasted by it. The new proposition came in the form of a large question mark, a powerful suspicion that what had been built upon the system of slavery we called "service" was none other than the bourgeois household itself.

At first I rejected the idea out of hand. It seemed to me a terrifying sacrilege to maintain that the cornerstone of our healthy, solid, civil society was in fact slave labor, and I personally found the idea unbearable. However, when I considered the case of the Hanseatic League—a classic example, surely, of the solid, comfortable way of life a bourgeois society, a society of good citizens, can achieve—it seemed to me I was obliged to think in that way. If maidservants had not existed (and if they hadn't existed then menservants hadn't either), the home of, say, a banker in Amsterdam or Hamburg would have had its corridors always grimy and clammy with dust and the kitchen would have had lots of vegetables rotting among the tea leaves (Indian tea leaves, of course), and the banker himself would most likely, indeed certainly, have had to clean his own shoes. Whether he would have had to prepare his own fried rice or not was a point on which I had considerable doubts, but presumably it would have been something similar, only in Western style. Anyway, one could surely assume he'd have found himself eating the remains of last night's oxtail stew for breakfast. At this point I suddenly found I had a great desire to taste Tsuru's cooking again, so actively had my imagination been working, and as I brooded on this a further proposition came into my head, namely a fundamental suspicion as to whether the whole fabric of society as we knew it might not be based on slave labor as well.

This was a dangerous way of thinking, since it contradicted the vague image of society as something bright and cheerful that I'd previously had—the result, of course, of no real thought on the matter, so it was a conventional picture rather than a set of ideas worked out for myself and believed in. In what can only have been an attempt to avoid the awkward conclusions this could lead to, I took up my shoe polishing again. However, I stopped after two or three rubs with the cloth, for my thought had progressed to the stage of wondering about the moral implications of imposing various household tasks of this dirty, boring, meaningless kind upon others. Wasn't a citizen who acted thus and yet rejoiced in, indeed flaunted, what he was doing as demonstrating the virtues of cleanliness, decency, and thrift behaving in an immoral, or anti-moral, or perhaps just amoral, way? Naturally the picture of the citizen now imposing itself upon me was a sad, even inhuman one, particularly as I was such a citizen myself; but my real problem was that, no matter how much I puzzled over the question, I couldn't help feeling this was indeed the true face of your ordinary, respectable member of society.

Once I'd adopted this altered viewpoint I came to see the old American South, which had achieved so palmy a state by using Negro slaves like domestic animals, as the very pattern of all civil societies, or at least as a true if tasteless parody of their essential nature. Of course, the fundamental form of the civic state had been created in ancient

Greece, where of the total population only half (or was it a third, or less than a quarter?) were actual citizens while the rest were slaves—political, proprietary, and all other rights being held by citizens only. All subsequent civic states had been determined by these Greek city-states, and thus the citizen as he'd always existed had been essentially a force for conservative feudalism, just as my great-grandfather, in his struggle against his feudalistic enemies, had been remarkably feudalistic himself.

I recalled the house in which I'd grown up, with its numerous maids (even two menservants), and how people had said there'd been many more in the good old days, and a composite figure of the typical bourgeois citizen appeared before me, consisting of that rugged, determined businessman, the battler for civil liberties who refused to take one step backward in his struggle against the samurai class, plus an ancient Greek trader with a fondness for philosophy, and a really vicious landowner from the Deep South. The homemade version of world history created in this haphazard way made me feel very queer. It gave no sensation of having stumbled on some intellectual discovery but more of having fallen into a nightmare. Of course I knew well enough that this historical image I'd created was crude and juvenile, but there was a part of me that didn't feel this affected the truth of that conception, for I was bound to produce crude, juvenile thoughts, given the length of time since I'd thought in basic terms about anything.

The odd thing, however, was that although I'd arrived at a point where I could only condemn the immorality of the citizen who made use of a maid, when Yukari came home my ideas were instantly turned upside down and I again found myself fervently desiring one.

I heard her high heels coming up the short pebble path from the front gate to the door, and as soon as the sound stopped I called out if that was her and opened the door before she'd rung the bell. Her face was flushed from walking quickly through the night streets. She asked me first if I'd managed my dinner, adding that the others had asked her to go dancing with them but she'd refused. She then noticed what I'd been up to.

"It's like a shoe shop," she laughed, and sat down beside me. I shifted slightly, offering her half the cushion, so she sat down there and started polishing although she'd had no dinner yet. Thus we sat together brushing off the dirt, wiping with the cleaner, putting on the shoe cream (and I admit there was a certain satisfaction, even happiness, to be gained from the situation), and sometimes discussing the perennial question of how we could manage to hire a maid. Eventually I got tired of a conversation that could never get anywhere and said:

"You know, I was just thinking how a maid's exactly like a slave."

"You sound like Dad," she said, airily dismissing the idea.

Just at that moment Granny came back. She slid open the already partially open door with great zest and bustled in, standing there in the hall looking very lively.

"Well, well, the two of them sitting nice and snug together. No need to cuddle up tight in a place like this when you could be upstairs, you know."

"Still, we don't want to be too friendly upstairs, do we?—or we might start disturbing the people below."

I appreciated that Yukari had been enticed into this remark by Granny's comment, but I couldn't see the need to outdo her in vulgarity. This convinced me that our house had indeed been turned into a brothel, and since I was apprehensive of what might happen if "the people below" began some discussion of the nature of the "disturbance" I hastily tried to change the subject, although in my haste I didn't manage to do so.

"Just back from your date, are you, Granny?"

"Not sure you could call it a date," she said with a trace of embarrassment. "We didn't do anything special today; just talked."

This seemed to be a direct admission that on other days they did indeed do "something special," and a big, broad smile appeared on her face as if she were remembering whatever that was. For a moment her eyes shone in an unquestionably erotic manner, giving me one more image to add to the others in my private nightmare.

16

The coffee shop was almost full. The customers were all men, apparently members of a demonstration that had been dispersed, and now waiting for some fresh disturbance to start up, reading newspapers or weeklies, or dropping off to sleep, with the occasional ones talking, either about the area tonight's riot was expected to occur in, or of what had happened a week ago. On that occasion it seemed the students had been out in force and the riot police had been able to do little but retreat, so this evening a more interesting show was expected and a crowd of idle spectators was gathering.

I was displaying a very decorative handkerchief, since this was the sign by which I hoped to be recognized, but I'd walked all around the coffee shop and still nobody had addressed me or made as if to stand up. I certainly hadn't come here to watch the riot, but because there was a possibility of hiring a maid. I had, in fact, completely given up the idea, when I heard from a woman who worked in the editorial section of a fashion magazine that there was a young girl living in the country not far from Tokyo who was looking for that kind of post, and I'd arranged to meet her father here. Yesterday he'd got in touch with me at the office, saying he was up in Tokyo on business, so we'd chosen this place because it was near the station. Immediately after I'd put the receiver down I'd heard it rumored that the students were expected to choose that very area for a roughhouse the following evening.

I found an empty chair, sat down, and ordered a cup of coffee, when I noticed a young hippie type sitting next door who began smiling at me.

"Don't you know me, Brother-in-law?" he said.

His remark told me at once who he was, and I ought to have known from his face since he did look like Yukari. It was her brother, Shin'ichi, the hippie-style student at the Christian college.

"Come to watch the violence?" he asked, and since I didn't reply he added in a cocky voice: "It can be dangerous for amateurs."

"Don't be absurd. I'm just meeting someone. You're the one who wants to be careful, anyway. How's your arm?"

"It's okay. I'm just watching this time. One of the crowd," he replied, ignoring my question about his arm and telling me about tonight's projected troubles instead. According to him, as he leaned toward me and whispered these great secrets, the main student force was assembling in a park near the neighboring station. At six o'clock they would advance along the railway line and force their way into the station. At the same time another group, assembled in front of the station, would charge in and join forces with the main group. This joint force would intercept and stop a freight train carrying U.S. Army weapons and ammunition, and if things went well they would seize the weapons themselves . . . and so begin an armed uprising.

I listened to all this with a slight grin playing about my lips, but inside I couldn't prevent various shudders of alarm, and I began to suspect that Yukari's brother, seeing how well informed he appeared to be, was perhaps one of the ringleaders. Still, he was only very lightly equipped in a thin sweater, although it was conceivable this was his way of duping the authorities as to his true identity.

The bearded youth looked at his watch and started to stand up.

"Well," he said, "you wouldn't want your wife's brother spoiling your date, I suppose."

This cool wisecrack caught me a little by surprise, so I blurted out it wasn't a date—I'd just come here about the maid. I was struck myself by the crude, fatuous nature of my response, so I changed the subject and asked after his father.

He stood there with his bill in his hand and said:

"He's going to some sort of meeting this evening, all dressed up in his turtleneck sweater too. He's trying hard to look young these days."

"Seems to be writing quite a bit, in newspapers and things," I said, trying to keep the gossip going about the ex-professor, but my brother-in-law wasn't prepared to keep me company and left in a hurry.

It was well past the appointed time of five o'clock and still the man I was supposed to be meeting hadn't turned up, so I started looking anxiously toward the door. How much of that tale Shin'ichi had given me was true I didn't know; it sounded both true and false at the same time. Whichever it was it was still unpleasantly disturbing, but I didn't

284

feel like just pushing off and abandoning this chance of getting a maid. So I pulled my handkerchief a little further out of my breast pocket.

People were still to-ing and fro-ing about me, some just going to the door and gazing outside, wondering when it would all start. One even seemed to give up and left, saying he was going to play pinball. Then a crowd came in and some of them had no seats so they had to stand. Two giggling girls entered, and ordered only cake with no tea or coffee to drink. A young man with three others kept up a constant stream of complaint about some noodle shop they must have just left. It had grown dark outside; a depth had come into the sky which varied between blue and navy blue.

I looked at my watch and sighed. It was half past five. I realized the whole thing had probably been too good to be true from the start, and then anger rose in me again as I wondered why I had to go through all this misery just because of the servant problem. I got up and went to the telephone to ring home, partly as a method of killing time, probably also because I didn't like the thought of having to go home and disappoint Yukari without giving her some sort of warning, and maybe because I wanted someone to share my grief over the fact that once more our situation as regards finding a maid had become desperate. Yukari, however, said quite calmly that the man in question had already telephoned to say he'd heard this area was likely to be dangerous tonight and had decided not to go.

"Apparently he rang your coffee shop but they said they were much too busy to bother about something like that. Nice of them, I must say. How is it there, anyway?"

"Nothing at the moment, as far as I can see. Still, what does he mean to do?"

"He said he's going back home tonight but he'll ring you again later about it and sends you his regards. He sounds very polite and proper. I should think his daughter would probably be fine."

I didn't want to believe there was no reason to place any trust in that sort of optimism, so I said:

"Yes, that's the impression I got when he rang yesterday."

I was trying to keep her hopes alive, but she replied in a very anxious voice:

"Granny's not back yet, you know."

"Where's she gone, then?"

"Another date, I expect. Got all dressed up and went out after lunch. And she's borrowed a handbag again, too."

"Ah well, she'll be back soon," I said lightheartedly.

"Suppose so," she agreed, adding that we were having a pot stew tonight so would I like some saké to go with it. We both assumed that within less than an hour we'd be sitting down to a hot meal, poking about with our chopsticks at the good things in the pot.

When I rang off I realized I'd forgotten to tell her about Shin'ichi, and then I looked toward the door where someone dressed all in black and wearing a helmet had just come in. He had a camera slung from each shoulder and a canvas bag hanging from his waist, and when a waiter told him to take off his helmet he did so obediently.

"Kaizuka," I called out, and the photographer stopped for a moment. Then a slow smile spread over his face. He came up to me.

"How's your wife?" he asked as greeting. I particularly noticed his white armband, which had the English word PRESS stuck clumsily on it in red letters cut crudely out of cloth. I assumed he must have made it himself.

"She's fine, thank you."

"And Granny?"

"She's even finer."

On hearing this he smiled happily, showing his remarkable white teeth, and then walked back with me toward the table I'd just vacated.

"Thank goodness for that. I was a bit worried about her. After all, it must be..."

He seemed unable to find the right words for whatever it had to be, but at that moment I spied two vacant seats nearby and we sat down in those. Kaizuka ordered a Coke and a sandwich, and I retrieved my bill and asked for another cup of coffee to keep him company.

He placed his ominous-looking helmet on the table, which ensured we talked first about the trouble due to take place that night. Kaizuka had come to cover the riot for one of the weeklies, so naturally he was well up on everything and told me a number of things he'd heard from other photographers and also from the students. Since he spoke quietly and objectively I felt I could believe what he said, and I was struck by his grown-up refusal to make snap judgments about the various ques-

286

tions at issue. His way of qualifying his statements provided a complete contrast to my brother-in-law, although there could only have been two or three years' difference in their ages. When I asked him how true Shin'ichi's information was, he said it was only rumor, with probably nothing in it.

"It would certainly be interesting if it were true," he smiled, and that in itself seemed to demonstrate the sensible moderation of his views. My liking for Kaizuka conditioned my attitude toward Shin'ichi, although that still remained ambiguous since he could have told me all that rubbish merely as an irresponsible camp follower, or deliberately lied to me because he really was one of the leaders of the projected riot. Whichever it was, I saw Shin'ichi as a member of a different, alien generation, and Kaizuka as one of those rare exceptions that still existed in the same age group.

We talked next about the people who had turned out just to watch. I pointed out that I had come to meet the father of a maid, and Kaizuka himself was here on business, yet we were obviously special cases. As I looked around the place I said:

"There seem to be an awful lot of people with nothing to do."

Kaizuka smiled: "The students like to draw big crowds. Guerrilla warfare would be impossible without them. Naturally they cause the police big problems, and I think they mean to start getting tough from tonight and have some kind of crackdown. Still, there are three main types of observer..."

"Ah."

"Type number one is the kind who behaves exactly like a student. He joins in and throws stones. Some of them are even more violent than the students themselves. The second type don't actually throw stones, but play some part in the action by covering up for the students when they run away. The third type keep well out of it and just watch from a distance..."

"Genuine spectators?"

"That's right."

"What about the first group, the radical ones? Do they have any special characteristics? I mean their age, their work?"

"Well," said Kaizuka, cocking his head as he ate his sandwich. "Most of them are men in their thirties. All kinds of trades and professions.

Some are office workers; some laborers. More than that I don't really know."

"Drunks?"

"A few. Some even drink while they watch."

"Getting rid of their frustrations, I suppose."

"Yes; it keeps building up inside them: a hatred of city life. An obsessive kind of resentment you could even call it." He then launched into a scathing criticism of contemporary city life, arguing with a passion quite different to the sensible, moderate way he'd been talking only a minute ago. I felt completely bewildered; I was simply relegated to the position of listener and said not a word in opposition, just nodding my head occasionally and smoking. I could only assume that even a strong-minded, sensible young man like this was bound to get somewhat worked up at the prospect of going off into the thick of a riot to take photographs.

Kaizuka went on and on about what seemed to be some homemade theory of his which he referred to as "city death." Cities in ancient times, he said, had been alive. Cities in medieval, even in recent, times had been alive. But the contemporary city had died.

"There's no nature left in them, or virtually none. Pericles's Athens, Leonardo da Vinci's Florence, Sen no Rikyu's Sakai, even the old Edo; things weren't like that then. All the trees dying, no water flowing; even the birds have stopped coming. It's like a landscape from hell. You know, it's very interesting the way there's never any nature in pictures of hell. The mountains aren't covered with trees but great needles, the rivers flow with blood instead of water. That blood is the black filth we've got in our rivers here; the TV aerials sticking up everywhere are just like the needles on those mountains. Recently even the colors of the flowers have faded, like the hydrangeas nowadays. All the evils of capitalism accumulate in the cities, creating this complete waste and ugliness. Industrial society is responsible for the way the cities have died."

"I see. City death," I said. I was interested in the way he idealized city life in the past, for that seemed the basic assumption behind what he was saying. I would also have liked to ask him if he was only referring to Japanese cities, despite his claim to be talking about the city in general, and to remind him that cities in Europe and the United States still had magnificent parks; but the young photographer didn't really give me a chance to say anything.

"Look, they say people come to the city to die. Why, it's just like an elephants' graveyard. Still, before that can happen, the city has to be dead itself, a place of death, which it is. I reckon human relations are moving in the same direction, too."

He went on to criticize the loneliness of dwellers in cities. They were no longer treated as human beings but as mere units, nameless existences that just heaved and pushed each other about like bees in a hive or ants in a nest. Thus our dead citizens in our dead cities had lost all sense of being in one place, but simply drifted like vagrants, like floating grass without roots. Obviously this was true of the people who flowed into the city from the countryside, but it was equally the case with someone whose family had lived in a city for umpteen generations, for the city was not the one in which his ancestors had lived but had been completely transformed. It wasn't even anything like the place his father had grown up in, and so the idea of home, of this being one's native place, the place where one had roots, just could never be experienced. In the same way all the towns throughout the country were losing their individual characters, becoming mere replicas of each other, one enormous, giant graveyard.

"I reckon we ought to burn up all these filthy towns and go back to village life. The only function our contemporary cities seem to have is as places where the urban guerrilla can really let himself go."

Kaizuka rejoiced in his own joke, laughing happily. I went along with him in the sense that I smiled, but I stayed quiet, not so much because I actually disagreed with these wild statements of his, but because I was skeptical of the assumptions behind them. I didn't particularly mind his attacking city life, but I had reservations about the implied eulogy of life in the country. I suspected this young man had no real knowledge of provincial life, and I began to reflect how things would be if Yukari, Granny, and myself were now living in that small town back home where every detail of our lives would be known: from how much Tsuru had squeezed out of me in retirement money, to what sorts of comings and goings Yukari had enjoyed with men before our marriage and, most of all, how Granny was a murderess who'd now gone crazy over some man. The whole town would know everything, and any reputation I might have had would be completely gone. I'd no particular wish to contradict his belief that city life was a form of hell, but provincial life provided other forms of hell which had a much greater vividness and clarity for me, and were more oppressively painful.

Kaizuka noticed I wasn't saying anything, so he resumed his usual calm expression.

"That's how it's seemed to me lately," he said, pouring the remainder of the Coke into his glass.

"Well, yes, a very interesting view of things, I admit, although there are a few points I have my doubts about. Of course, I accept what you said about the urban guerrilla without reservations."

That final remark seemed to please him and he asked me politely to proceed.

"Do you know the country at all?" I said.

"Yes, I do. But, you know, I'm not making any total affirmation of the virtues of provincial life."

"Okay. Still, you say you know about country life. Ever lived there?"

"No, I've only been there to take photographs. I have lived for a week or so in farmers' houses occasionally, and I suppose if you put all that together it would come to. . ."

At that moment a distant hubbub could be heard outside, not the noise of one or two people but more like a great host suffering on a dark blue evening in hell, screaming together in unison. Someone outside gave a sharp cry and then, nearby, a metallic shower appeared suddenly to have started to fall, as the steel shutters of the coffee shop were half lowered. Everyone stood up. A waiter got on a box or something near the entrance and repeated in a very relaxed voice (totally inappropriate to the situation and the words he was using):

"For your safety the shop will now close. For your safety the shop. . ."

Kaizuka put on his helmet, fastened the brown strap under his chin, then snatched up his bill, knocking over the Coke bottle which rolled diagonally across the table and fell off.

"I'll pay," I said. "You hurry along."

He bowed and thanked me, then dashed away.

Finally I too went outside, stooping under the shutters. How quickly this transformation had taken place I didn't know, but now there wasn't a single vehicle on the street, and both the roadway and the sidewalks were filled with a great mob of people hurrying in disorderly fashion toward the station. I could see no students or policemen, but only this mass of ordinary citizens, mostly men of course, yet with the occasional woman among them. Some were running, some trotting, some just walking. One of them was whistling a song. Somebody, separated from his girl, called out her name, and someone else replied in a high, false, feminine voice, which caused great bursts of raucous male laughter. A middle-aged woman who was wandering hesitantly about came up to me and said she wanted to get home and wondered what kind of transport she should try to take. I said I'd no idea, and then a young man in a pink shirt took over and explained in some detail that the trains, buses, and subways weren't moving, and taxis wouldn't come into this area so she'd have to walk quite a long way. The woman thanked him but said she would go to the station anyway just to make sure, when suddenly there was a muted roar and the crowds were being slowly pushed back in our direction. Low down in the sky ahead of me and slightly to the right there was a brief flash of light. The young man who'd explained the transport situation told me it was a searchlight.

I walked in the opposite direction for a good hour and managed to pick up a taxi; and after a roundabout journey I finally got home to find Yukari worn out with waiting for me. She said she'd got the dinner ready ages ago and had spent the time since eating biscuits, drinking milk, and watching TV. At first I paid little attention to her various complaints, but I was genuinely startled when she said she was bound to be worried when nobody phoned her, neither I nor Granny. I realized there must be something wrong if Granny wasn't back and hadn't been in touch either. I started worrying that perhaps she'd been taken ill suddenly, which was quite possible considering her age, and even began to imagine she might in turn have been the victim of some vicious attack by this man of hers. I didn't like to think she'd committed another murder, since she could hardly do things like that all the time; but the thought also encouraged the opposite idea, that maybe it really could become a habit. Still, on reflection, she wasn't a child and she had somebody with her, and that was a source of reassurance for both of us. After taking a bath, I had my dinner with Yukari while watching a television report on the rioting students. I had a powerful appetite so the saké tasted particularly good, and I also felt that Yukari's

291

cooking had got much better recently. Since I'd been close to the scene of the wildness now going on before our eyes, Yukari asked me a lot of questions and became quite angry because I didn't seem to have seen anything at all.

We'd started late and I'd also been drinking slowly with the meal, so it wasn't surprising that dinner came to an end well after it normally would have done. We talked about the business of the maid and about Shin'ichi and Kaizuka, but hardly at all about the student riot. We also joked about Granny, imagining the number of love affairs she'd have if we put her into one of those luxurious old folk's homes that had become fashionable lately; and while we were talking we would occasionally express anxiety about her being so late. Yukari got up once and rang her parents' house. Her mother apologized profusely for all the trouble Granny was causing, and said she'd just heard from Shin'ichi that he was playing mah jong at a friend's house, although Papa had gone to some publisher's meeting and wasn't back yet and hadn't telephoned either, so she was anxious about him. This made Yukari grumble about her mother, saying it was strange she seemed to be no more worried about Granny than she was about Father, as if she'd passed over the entire responsibility for her to us. I must say I was starting to get into the same way of thinking myself, feeling if anything happened to Granny it would be half my responsibility, although this stirred me to no form of action. Once the meal was over I used a cushion as a pillow and had a snooze on the tatami, despite the fact that Yukari kept on at me to go upstairs and have a proper lie-down. Admittedly I did find the noise of the TV annoying, and then there was a phone call from Yukari's mother which irritated me as well.

Apparently Yukari shook me a number of times before I woke up.

"Look, it's half past eleven," she said in a very grave voice, at exactly which point a taxi pulled up outside the house. I got up, and Yukari half rose; then the doorbell rang. We both rushed to the door, almost fighting as to who should get there first, to find Granny, dressed in that Oshima kimono and Shoso-in sash, with a weirdly tense look on her face; while at her side stood Kaizuka, who'd brought her home. Both had bloodshot eyes with black rings about them; both of their faces were streaked with some kind of gray dust or powder. In Kaizuka's case this resulted in a rather intrepid look, but Granny was simply wretched, particularly pathetic as that brown penciled part of her eyebrows had disappeared again and only the bushy black halves remained.

We both groaned out something, breathing in, as it were, the heavy atmosphere of that scene of violence from which the two had clearly just returned. There was no need for Granny to explain from what perilous part of town she had come.

Granny was standing about vaguely as if she'd no idea what to do next, but the young photographer wearing the American helmet began talking excitedly at some speed.

"Met completely by accident. She'd been separated from the man she was with. Granny will tell you all about it. There's a taxi waiting so I'll have to. . ."

Granny kept bowing to him humbly and offering her thanks, and we kept expressing our gratitude as well, urging him to come in at least for a moment, so there was quite a hubbub going on to prevent his departure. He kept saying he had his films to develop and print, but then he suddenly remembered something.

"By the way, please don't be angry with her. I'm asking you this personally. Please don't scold Granny," he said, addressing his remarks principally to Yukari, who, of course, said immediately that she wouldn't, although this didn't stop him insisting on the same thing a number of times; then, after telling Granny it should be all right, he tried once more to take his leave. We stopped him again, saying we could always phone for a car for him, so he needn't worry on that score. I went outside to pay off the taxi, and incur the driver's complaints that there wouldn't be any customers at this time of night.

Yukari was, indeed, very nice to her grandmother, perhaps because Kaizuka had put in a few good words for her. As Granny sat gloomily in a corner of the living room, she asked her if she'd like some tea, or perhaps she'd prefer a bath, showing a concern and desire to comfort her. But Granny went on sitting there with a look on her face as if she knew she was about to catch it, saying nothing and just shaking her head. It took the combined efforts of Kaizuka and myself in urging the bath on her before she finally agreed to the idea. She stood up to go, but then immediately knelt down again as if changing her mind, and began apologizing in a tearful voice.

"Yukari, I'm so sorry. I just don't know what to say."

"What's the matter?"

"I've gone and lost that brocade handbag of yours."

"Oh no! Why, that was really. . ."

"Expensive, I suppose," Granny said in a woeful voice.

Yukari remained pointedly quiet for a while, staring at the wall, but finally, in a voice of forced cheerfulness, she said:

"Oh well. Never mind. Can't be helped, I suppose. Just you hurry up and have your bath."

Granny looked wonderfully relieved at this display of generosity, and showed her appreciation of the serious nature of what she'd done by mumbling that it was the second time she'd done it and she didn't know what to say, bowing her head again as she didn't say it. This produced more assurances from Yukari that it was all right and never mind because it was all right.

"Perhaps I'd better go again tomorrow and have another look," Granny added, not, I assumed, because she had any hope of finding it, but because she was so overjoyed at the magnanimity shown her that, in a spirit of courteous gratitude, she wanted to cheer Yukari up. This did, indeed, have some effect, for a faint glimmer of hope seemed to rise in Yukari's breast.

"Might be a good idea," she agreed, but Kaizuka, who'd unstrapped the canvas bag around his waist, immediately poured cold water over that idea.

"Complete waste of time, Granny, after a riot like that. Even if you did find the handbag it wouldn't be any use to anybody now."

Granny became quite crestfallen again, so I urged her once more to take her bath, and she obeyed me quite meekly like a small child. As we watched her totter dejectedly out of the room the three of us looked at each other with head-shaking smiles.

"Beer or whisky?" I said to Kaizuka, who hesitated a bit and then said:

"I suppose you wouldn't have any food? The fact is. . ."

But before he could finish his sentence Yukari had indicated that food was available, and she nipped out smartly to the kitchen with a brisk strut quite different from the way she usually wandered about, which gave a powerful impression of the businesslike, efficient young wife who had complete control of whatever went on in this house. I confess I felt rather proud of her, experiencing a glow of happiness at the thought that she'd probably be able to handle our next maid with some skill if she continued to make progress like this. My optimism was perhaps a reaction to what I'd felt on coming back into the house after paying off the taxi driver, having been appalled by the filthiness of the entrance hall, and particularly the kitchen, and worrying how this might look to an outsider.

Kaizuka switched on the television and flicked through all the channels with one twist of his hand.

"Not on anywhere," he said.

I thanked him yet again for what he'd done, and then, as I poured out some tea for him, I asked what on earth she'd been up to. He hesitated very obviously before replying.

"I don't really think I want to say what she was doing. Still, you remember we were talking in the coffee shop about how the spectators at those things could be divided into three groups?"

"Yes," I said, and finished pouring his tea. He drank it down slowly.

"Ah, that's great. Could I have another? Perhaps you could fill it right up this time. Anyway, she was behaving like someone in the first group."

"The first group."

"That's right."

I was taken aback, and then, after a moment, I found myself almost howling my reply, since I'd at last got a picture in my mind of her doing it.

"You really mean she was. . . ?"

Kaizuka nodded. "That's right. She was throwing rocks at the riot police."

"Gosh."

"Naturally they all missed. Or perhaps one of them might have hit one of the shields. Hard to say in that kind of confusion. She could conceivably have grazed a helmet with one."

"Oh no," I groaned (or perhaps moaned would be the right word, for I'd sustained a considerable shock). I thought the worst group she could have been in would have been the second one. Students may have been in the habit of fighting the police for a long time now, and you could explain away even quite nasty bits of violence by saying they'd become a normal occurrence; but for an old lady in her sixties to throw rocks at the police was surely a rarity, and the whole business became particularly serious when the old lady was a member of one's own household.

I went on groaning, and Kaizuka seemed to interpret this as meaning that I didn't believe him, so he gave a detailed account of what had happened. After he'd left me he'd got into the station without any trouble, but a short while later there were so many stones flying in all directions that he was stuck on one of the platforms for ages, quite unable to move. When he finally managed to get outside it was nine thirty and the riot police were by then gradually driving the students back. He had to make his way over several tracks and the intervening platforms. On the tracks behind him some of the sleepers were burning here and there, and far off a black line of freight cars had been stopped and what seemed to be station staff were running this way and that. He then stepped over a fence that had been broken down, and climbed up a small rise from which he took a number of shots, using his telescopic lens, of the railway overpass to his left. There were two vehicles on the overpass, apparently police cars, which had been overturned and set on fire. There was not one policeman near the cars, or any sign of a watching crowd. A lot of stones were scattered about, plus a couple of what looked like bamboo lances which must have been dropped or discarded. Some fifty yards away, standing about under the eaves of a building, he at last noticed a dozen or so spectators quietly watching the flames envelop the two cars.

The main battle seemed to be going on somewhere away to the right, where the riot police, using a number of vehicles with flashing searchlights as their base, were gradually bearing down on the students. A variety of sounds were coming from that vicinity, a distant tumult like the breathing of some giant, ascending into the night sky. The road below the small knoll on which he was crouching was covered with pebbles and gravel from the railway tracks, and he realized the fighting must have been going on here only a short while ago.

Clutching his two cameras carefully to his chest, Kaizuka leaped down onto the road, avoiding the small stones and bits of gravel, ran across the tracks again, and entered a narrow, brightly lit side street which was strangely deserted. Not a soul was in sight, only a few stray dogs burrowing among the garbage in plastic bins in front of a shuttered store. As he passed, the dogs didn't even bark. After walking a while along the same deserted street, suddenly, straight ahead of him, five or six riot policemen dressed in heavy protective clothing came running ferociously in his direction. His immediate reaction was to be scared they'd mistake him for a student and half beat him to death, so in a panic he hid behind a standing signboard propped against the front of one of the shops. With his back glued against the wall he saw the policemen rush by right in front of him, gasping and panting for breath. The dogs he'd just passed began barking in chorus, and went on barking.

He'd more or less worked out where he was when he turned a corner and was astonished to see great crowds of people standing about as if it were some day of celebration. The crowd was much larger than any gathering of bystanders he'd seen at riots up to now, and also seemed to be made up of more ordinary citizens than before. He saw a middle-aged lady in a kimono who looked as if she ought to be carrying a lapdog, an old man in a raincoat with a dirty slouch hat pulled down over his eyes, a drunk who looked like an office worker and someone sober who also looked like an office worker, a cook dressed in white clothes liberally stained with soy sauce and clattering along in high clogs, a young man in jeans and a dark blue *happi* coat, a young girl apparently out with someone although it wasn't clear who, a man wearing kimono and wooden-soled sandals, a man wearing a suit and a tie, and a man wearing a suit and no tie; in fact all sorts and conditions of men, and it was through this excited, buoyant throng that he made his way. One of them had a sweetish smell about him, and Kaizuka thought it might be chewing gum, though he may have mistaken the odor of tear gas.

These were observers of the third kind, but once he'd gone a little further he noticed there were no more women and a bitterness stirring in the air irritated his eyes and nostrils. Now he had reached members of group two, who were jeering and shouting abuse at the police.

Somebody shouted out the words "eye lotion" twice, but whether because he was offering it to someone or wanted it himself wasn't clear. As Kaizuka tried to break through the human wall, he noticed a middle-aged man wearing a beret and a youth who was covered in blood, crouching down and groaning, and the older man was gently embracing the youth in a way that suggested he had sexual designs upon him.

Two white helmets had been placed beside them, looking like cheap saucepans in the little home they had just set up. Kaizuka crouched down himself and took a shot of this, using a wide-angle lens, but the flash alerted the man in the beret to what was going on and he bawled at him, so he moved away.

Quite shortly he was at the battlefield proper. The road immediately to one side of him looked much wider than its usual size since there were no vehicles passing, and also much brighter than it would have been at this time of night because of the searchlights. Diagonally away to the right the actual square looked quite small. With the beams of the searchlights behind them the line of duralumin shields was a dull gray, edging forward and back, then surging forward suddenly with savage cries but just as quickly retiring. The students, hurling handfuls of pebbles and gravel, also advanced toward these shields and then retired, advancing again and then once more retiring. The distance between them at its fullest extent must have been around thirty yards. Pebbles and grit kept rattling against the metal shields, and at various places all around, often surprisingly high up, glass would be shattered. Sometimes just one pane would break, sometimes a number all together. Red, green, and yellow, the traffic lights kept up their orderly, precise, and quite meaningless signaling. Kaizuka crawled out into the road and took pictures of the irregular ranks of students. He shot faces covered with dark, soaked towels; he shot banners waving under the neon lights which stained them in variegated colors.

Then he turned his camera on the bystanders watching from positions along the sidewalk. They were keeping well back against the walls of the buildings, hiding in the slight shadow the eaves provided, sometimes picking up fragments of stone that had fallen near them and creeping out nervously to the edge of the road to hand them over to the students, or even impulsively throwing the odd one themselves. There was an office worker with both hands full of jagged stones handing them over to a masked youth, an artisan raising his knee into the air as he hurled stones with tremendous energy, howling something at the top of his voice, and a man who looked like a painter or a poet or perhaps a copywriter gathering up pebbles that had fallen on the asphalt road and filling his pockets till they bulged. Kaizuka took photographs of all these, completely absorbed in his work, for he'd decided he would make the theme of tonight's riot the ordinary man in the street. Then he was astonished to see what appeared to be a woman dressed in kimono who picked up one stone, threw it, then picked up another and threw that too. At first he thought, since there were a number of homosexual bars in the area, it was some sort of transvestite male prostitute. But there was something unpracticed and clumsy about the way she threw, and when she stood up straight, using the windup technique of a baseball pitcher, he realized she wasn't tall enough for a male prostitute. Also her kimono was too restrained in taste. He couldn't be sure either way, but decided to photograph him or her all the same. Male prostitute or no male prostitute—indeed all the better if it were an actual woman—the subeditor of his weekly would absolutely jump at a picture like that. So first he went into the road and took one with his telescopic lens, then moved nearer and used the wide-angle lens this time. As he edged closer, with one eye warily open for the riot police's gas shells, he realized in a flash that this was Yukari's grandmother, Granny Utako. The old woman was howling something as she went on throwing.

At this point in the story I asked excitedly:

"Do you still mean to sell that photograph to your weekly?"

"Yes, certainly. Of course, I can't be certain until I've developed it."

"Could you let me have it? If that's possible."

"Let you have it?"

"I'd be very grateful if you would."

"I can show you it first," he said, which amounted to a refusal, though he smiled and added, "Don't worry, Mr. Mabuchi. There'll be no invasion of anyone's privacy, I assure you. It wouldn't be used if there were any chance of that. Of course, if it was someone I didn't know. . ."

I thanked him loudly for this assurance and breathed a deep sigh of relief. Then Yukari appeared, bearing a tray.

"I don't know what would have happened if you hadn't turned up," she said. "I thought she must have had an accident."

The tray contained a bowl of rice, some corned beef with butter-fried cabbage, and miso soup in which she'd used the leftovers from our dinner, plus some fresh pickles. She even provided a damp towel. Kaizuka wiped his hands and face and then got down to eating with a voracious appetite.

"Look, I'm sorry," said Yukari, "but could you eat just a little more slowly? I'm cooking some fresh rice and it won't be ready for a bit."

Kaizuka responded by continuing his story as he ate.

Once he'd worked out that the woman throwing the stones was Granny Utako, he called out her name in surprise, at which moment a gas shell, probably aimed just short of Granny or even at himself, fell near the two of them, and he found himself enveloped in yellow smoke. He coughed, sneezed, and with tears starting in his eyes he caught hold of the old woman, who was in a much worse state than he. Granny Utako was coughing away but she kept up a solid resistance, waving both arms and striking at him. He pulled her a few paces away into the shadow of a building.

"It's me. It's me, Kaizuka," he shouted, but she still went on squirming and stamping her feet. Then she suddenly grew quiet and, as if she'd awakened from a dream in the midst of this dusty conflict, she muttered:

"I thought it was a cop."

Shouting excitedly and repeatedly that he was no cop, Kaizuka dragged her off into a side street.

"Time to go home," he said. "I'll take you."

Granny gave a large nod in agreement. Kaizuka then clawed a way for both of them through the crowd. He didn't pause to reflect whether he'd got enough photos or not until some time later, but it did seem what he had should suffice, in terms both of quantity and variety. Granny said nothing but just trudged on behind him, so he turned around and urged her on, still assuring her he would see her home since she couldn't possibly manage it by herself and it would be crazy for her to try.

They hurried along a brightly lit street and then a dimly lit one. They passed over a pedestrian bridge where the light and shade fell in broad stripes, and they wandered right to the end of a dark blind alley which they'd entered to avoid the riot police. When they finally emerged from it they found a faucet at the back of a house on the corner, and here they washed their hands and faces and drank some of the rusty-smelling water. Then, beneath a roadside tree, Kaizuka got the eye lotion out of the bag at his waist, and they applied it to their eyes.

"You must have got quite a lot of policemen with your stones, Granny," he said by way of compliment, and the old woman chuckled gleefully. "You're in good shape, Granny. You looked pretty fit back there, too."

"That's because I had a really good sleep," she said, a reply that he couldn't make any sense of at all.

However, just as they were getting near a main road where he thought they'd be able to pick up a taxi, Granny suddenly stopped dead, although she'd been walking well enough up until then. Kaizuka asked if her feet were hurting, or her eyes, but that wasn't the problem at all. She said she'd dropped her handbag back there at the scene of the riot. He laughed at first, telling her she'd simply have to think of it as lost, but although she nodded in reply she still made no attempt to move.

"Was there a lot of money in it?" he asked, but after she'd felt at the top of her sash and made sure her purse was still there she shook her head.

"Was there something else of value in it, then?"

"No," she said quite clearly, but added, "Mr. Kaizuka, I really am very sorry, but I'll just have to go back and get it. It's not all that far."

She started walking back. He asked her what it could possibly be that made it so important, and she at last said shamefacedly it was something she'd borrowed. When he finally learned it belonged to Yukari he gave a rather contrived laugh and said:

"Come on, she's not going to be bothered about something like that. I'll apologize for you. After all, Mr. Mabuchi can always buy her another one."

But Granny Utako still wouldn't agree. The handbag was made of Saga brocade and must have cost an awful lot of money, besides which she'd already ruined one of Yukari's handbags and if it happened again she just wouldn't be able to look her in the face. So Kaizuka changed his mind, telling her he would go to look for it and she should stay right here under this dentist's sign and wait for him to come back; but as Granny said she was frightened and insisted on going with him, there was nothing for it but to go back together.

The battleground had now shifted well away to the left of where it had been, and there were only a few scattered members of the third group of bystanders in that spot where Granny had fought so courageously. The two of them searched all over the ground, in particular the area around the pedestrian crossing, even going over to the other side of the road once, but all they discovered among the broken bits of stone and gravel were magazines folded in half and hand towels. They never managed to find the brocade handbag.

"Come on, let's go," said Kaizuka, and Granny reluctantly gave in to his persuasion, but just as they were crossing the pedestrian bridge for the third time she said she now felt she already didn't have the handbag by the time she'd got to the place where they'd just been searching.

"All right, then, where were you before that? Where were you when you're last sure you had it in your hand," he said coaxingly.

Granny looked up into the moonless, starless, murky sky as if she were gazing at some map of the area, but, although she mentioned a few place names, she had only a very dim recollection of where she'd been before meeting Kaizuka, and certainly no precise idea of the route she'd taken; she was even less clear about when she'd been holding the handbag and when not. The one thing she was positive about was that she had been holding Yukari's handbag when she left the hotel just after it had grown dark. On hearing this Kaizuka wondered what she'd gone to a hotel for, but he didn't ask her why, and indeed he had no time to since she suddenly gave a loud scream and clung to him, and so he found himself holding her surprisingly soft body. A man with three companions crossing the bridge at the time laughed. Below the bridge sudden swarms of cars with red taillights had begun passing along the road again, presumably because the traffic blockade on this stretch had just been lifted.

Granny started to call out the name Hirayama repeatedly, and when he asked her who this was she didn't reply directly but only said, in a disjointed way:

"It was that gumshoe, you see . . . suddenly came up behind him . . . just like that . . . then pinched him. . . ."

At that moment Kaizuka suddenly understood. Hirayama was Granny's lover; she had been sleeping with him in a hotel in that area; he had thrown stones at the riot police, and a plainclothes detective had arrested him. "Gumshoe" meant a plainclothes policeman and "pinch" meant to arrest, both being words she'd picked up in prison.

As they stood on the dark, narrow bridge with scraps of paper all about them, the young man was worried she might begin to cry. Nevertheless, he asked her if Hirayama was the man she'd been with, if the plainclothes policeman had been mingling with the crowd, and if Hirayama had been handcuffed. Granny replied with a bitter expression on her face, yet in a clear voice with no trace of tearfulness, that what he said was so.

Kaizuka was lost in admiration for a while at the thought that what he'd been witnessing was Granny's retaliation, her struggle for vengeance; but then a doubt arose in his mind as to whether she was trying to strike back only because her lover had been taken from her. He was unable to restrain the romantic suspicion that some other kind of hatred was involved, some deeper wrath and rancor, some more living need for revenge which had driven this aged woman to make her precise imitation of the baseball pitchers she'd seen on TV, performing her impeccable windup before throwing each stone, and then going through the same performance time and time again. As each jagged rock cut momentarily through the night sky it was aimed, not only to clatter firmly against the metal shields of the men in uniform who wore another steel uniform underneath, but more essentially at a distant, abstract, and deeper darkness, flying far off with greater violence to strike, and strike viciously, against the system, call it the state, call it society, that had put her into prison all those long years ago. All capitalist states, indeed all those states as well that claimed to be socialist and yet were so in name alone, maintained their crumbling regimes only by the use of armies and prisons. It was by these two systems, by these two forms of black intimidation of the public, that the people were silenced, forbidden to rise up, and finally deprived of the will to do so. The pebbles and gravel the students had collected on the railway tracks, then carried in their pockets mixed up with scraps of tobacco and bread, with the thin red husks of peanuts and all that fluffy dust which tends to accumulate in people's pockets—these objects were finally thrown, not by any student's hand, but by an old granny, an ex-jailbird, a previous offender, and thrown at what was, indeed, a kind of army. Here, surely, was a true image of what revolution was all about. Could there be a finer symbolic act of rebellion than this?

Kaizuka had put his bowl and chopsticks down when he reached the climax of his oration, his cheeks flushing while he talked as if the day of true revolution, of the genuine socialist state, must dawn sooner or later, and as if the revolutionary government would inevitably be on the side of crime. My own reaction, which I kept cynically to myself, was that when that time came they'd put up a bronze statue of the rock-throwing Utako in the station square, and there she would watch eternally over the mammoth food center, the two banks, the little shoemaker's, the cheap hire-purchase department store, the coffee shops and restaurants, the shop selling film star photographs, the camera store, the vegetable and fruit shop, and the place that sold ten thousand Chinese bean-jam buns a day. Perhaps the statue wouldn't be in the rock-throwing posture, however, but show us Granny with a razor in her hand.

Kaizuka had probably noted with some anxiety that I remained silent, so he said, half apologetically:

"Well, that's how it seemed to me then. I've just given a pretty long-winded, diluted account of a feeling that just came to me at that moment."

He smiled as he said this and his expression had some of the bland serenity of the toy emperor and empress in the Dolls Festival. I rather liked that, and certainly felt well disposed toward him personally, but I still said nothing. I was, in fact, thinking about things, not the cynical joke about their putting a statue of Granny in the station square, but the much deeper question of whether prisons would really disappear if an ideal socialist state was created. Here the formal discriminations of the former civil servant came rumbling into action: *videlicet*, a utopia was an impossibility, or, rather, theft, fraud, arson, and murder could only continue to be committed in that imaginary country as they always had been, and Granny Utako would cut up her husband with a razor there, would be put in prison, and would assist the jailbreaker by thumping on a toilet door. The fact that the so-called socialist countries of the present day allowed no mention of crime in their newspapers but kept their populaces under duress with the menace of distant penal colonies would, I knew, be seen by Kaizuka as no demonstration of some inadequacy in his ideal but rather as showing that such countries were merely a crude caricature of his utopia. For my part I felt this attempt to argue that Granny's behavior was symbolic of the revolution simply endowed it with a grand meaning it couldn't possibly have, a completely hollow piece of sophistry. It was, of course, arguable that revolutionaries and criminals were both enemies of the system, and that both were in confrontation with the peaceful everyday life that the ordinary citizen led. But it did seem to me that to decide, on those grounds alone, their separate ways of going against the establishment were, in effect, one and the same was extremely rash and simpleminded, indeed juvenile, a bypassing of the problem which told one nothing. In fact I did even entertain the rather spiteful notion that the reason why young people sympathetic to the revolution liked to link revolutionaries and criminals was that they lamented their own lack of savagery, and so this was a kind of tune they whistled, not just to keep their spirits up, but as a spur to prod their feeble selves into positive action. Even so, while I was listening to Kaizuka's impassioned statements I allowed no wry little grimace to appear on my lips nor did I offer one word of opposition, which was merely my way of expressing gratitude to the young man for having brought Granny back.

"She was really that worried, was she? As if a handbag could really matter! The main thing is she managed to get home safely. Of course, that handbag was certainly expensive. If you bought it in a shop, that is. Luckily I was able to buy it direct from the makers, and only paid half price, I think. Might have been only a third."

Clearly my wife had been occupied with a very different problem from ours for quite a long time. Then she started to show concern about something else.

"I wonder what happened to him? That Mr. Hirayama?"

"Detained in custody," I replied.

"That's right," said Kaizuka, putting out his bowl for more.

"Will he be given the third degree?"

"Of course not."

"Should be all right."

"Hope so, anyway," said Yukari, putting the bowl on the tray and going out to the kitchen, returning with a slightly smaller amount of hot rice in it, and also with Granny, now fresh from the bath and wearing an everyday kimono. Her eyes were still slightly sunken, but the color and life had come back into her cheeks, and her damp hair was shining. She was quite a different Granny to the one who'd been in the room only a short while ago.

305

Yukari made a joke about her picturesque appearance, but Granny, on seeing Kaizuka's meal, said playfully she could do with some of that as well. Yukari expressed histrionic surprise at this, but it didn't bother Granny since she said she'd only had a measly little bit of sushi all day. She criticized her evening meal (whether provided by Hirayama or herself she didn't say) in a cheerful parody of that weary contempt for such things affected by a lady of class. This made us all laugh, and the whole atmosphere of the room was suddenly relaxed.

Yukari went into the kitchen and started frying something. Kaizuka was worrying about getting a car, so I let him phone and they said it would be right over. Finally Granny's late supper was all ready on the table.

"We've heard some stirring tales tonight," I said, and went through the motions of a pitcher winding up, which made Granny embarrassed and she wouldn't pick up her chopsticks. She reminded me of a little girl who's been teased for behaving like a tomboy as I smiled and begged her pardon, while she kept her face turned to one side and sulked. It was then I noticed that, although she hadn't put on lipstick, she'd penciled in her eyebrows again.

Yukari turned on the television, but there was still nothing about tonight's riot. One channel had a number of variety artists playing the fool with neither artistry nor variety. On another channel there was a Western movie, and the other two were showing war films. The images they provided, of battle, of adventure, and of witless mirth, seemed as distant to me as Granny's heroic exploits. Yukari switched the TV off and then Kaizuka, probably in an effort to help Granny out of her embarrassment, talked about what had happened to him after he'd left me until the time when he'd managed to get out of the station. While we were listening to this, Granny at last started eating.

Kaizuka found it very easy to actually get inside the station. Along with the rest of the mob of bystanders he followed the student column as they went in. However, this freedom only lasted half an hour, during which he managed to get a lot of photographs, but then the riot police launched a counterattack and rocks started flying about all over the place. As there was no letup, all he could do was take refuge in the deputy stationmaster's office in the middle of the platform.

When he opened the door there was no one there, but just a number of borrowed mattresses and quilts spread on the floor. Obviously the station staff had intended to spend the night here and had rented them for the occasion. Kaizuka stood hesitating near the door, but then one of the quilts started moving and a station official poked his head out. When he saw Kaizuka, however, he yelled that they'd come, and burrowed beneath the quilt again. He must have assumed the helmeted young man was a student. After a while, though, four of the staff emerged slowly from their hiding places, and asked him how the situation was.

While he was talking to them the distant noise of breaking glass could be heard coming nearer. A number of men carrying sticks or bamboo spears or mops were smashing the glass timetables hanging from the low platform roofs. They were also obliterating the name of the station and other signs in the same perfunctory manner with one sweep of the stick. There was a youth wearing a light blue shirt among them. There was also a middle-aged man with a beret, who was so small he had to leap vigorously into the air each time he thrashed at a sign with his stick. A man in a white coat who looked as if he was a chemist was patently drunk; unlike the others, he laughed and swore loudly as he worked. Finally came a man wearing a red sweater who ran close by where Kaizuka was standing and methodically smashed two of the office windows with a placard advertising a pinball parlor. Only Kaizuka saw this since all the station staff had burrowed deep down under their quilts again.

Granny Utako shook her head as she listened and said how wasteful it was and sighed; even Kaizuka was critical:

"I understand them wanting to let out all the feelings they've got bottled up in there, but I must say it was a bit dangerous. Someone could have been hurt."

Yukari was also very hard on these people, and naturally I didn't have a good word to say for them, only a number of bad ones. There seemed to be some kind of unspoken agreement between the four of us that no one should mention the wastefulness and danger of breaking glass in public streets.

This may have had something to do with what I did next. I was well aware that if I let the opportunity slip now it would become very difficult to talk about the matter later on, so I gave Granny a little sermon on tonight's doings. I began as soon as Granny had put away her late supper and was drinking her tea, prefacing my remarks with the statement that although I myself didn't believe in throwing rocks at policemen under any circumstances, I had no intention of attacking someone else who did, at least insofar as the ethical implications of the matter were concerned, and yet:

"And yet, Granny, you must realize you're still officially only out on parole. If you don't behave yourself for a little while longer you could get into serious trouble. I'm not talking here about questions of good and bad, but simply of what's in your own interest. You'll do yourself no good at all like that. On top of that you're an old person now and you'd be better off not doing such dangerous things. I'd be very glad if you'd stay right away from such places in future. And the police are bound to start taking tougher measures. Since they're public servants you may get the impression they keep falling back all the time, but when the time comes they'll take positive steps, you can be sure of that, and pretty dreadful they'll be. Today, thanks to Mr. Kaizuka, it all passed off safely and you're all right, and I'm very glad; but it won't be so simple next time. Something awful will happen. They'll drag you away; they'll have you locked up. . . ."

I was, quite honestly, about to tell her that if she intended to do this sort of thing again she wouldn't be able to go on living with us, but I was interrupted at that point for the odd reason that Granny quite suddenly let out a little shriek like a whistle and exclaimed, with tears glistening in her eyes:

"Oh, I wonder what's happened to poor Hirayama? . . ."

"Well, they'll have him locked up, I suppose," said Kaizuka, no doubt quite automatically, and this only encouraged her misery, for she sat there, still upright, but now she was sobbing, looking up at the ceiling light with her eyes firmly closed and yet with tears pouring down, and saying what a poor man he was, and how, oh how, Mr. Kaizuka, could they do a cruel thing like that? It seemed the plainclothes policeman had pinned both of Hirayama's arms from behind, used some judo trick to hurl him to the ground, and then started to put the boot in mercilessly.

"I begged him, I pleaded with him, to stop, but he just wouldn't," she went on. "Dirty, mean coward, he was; a real bad lot."

She spat out this final criticism, and I'm mystified now why the thought never crossed my mind that this treatment was almost identical to what Hirayama had dished out himself to the thief in the cinema. Perhaps it only indicates that the principle of political crimes and ordinary crimes being quite different was something my unconscious mind, at least, accepted. It may also be that, again unconsciously, I was trying to forgive the fact that a member of my household had once more committed a crime. However, Granny herself now seemed inclined to challenge this stereotyped, one might almost say classical, method I had of classifying crime.

"Eisuke, I promise I won't do it again. I don't like to cause you both such anxiety, and I like even less the thought of what they might do to me. Still, it's good to see them getting some of their own medicine. Prisons and law courts are just there to keep them all in business. If we could pay them back for it, then we'd feel all clean inside again."

My first response was this at least bypassed the intractable problem of whether there was any point in considering all crimes under a common heading as forms of antisocial behavior. For Granny Utako, taking part in an anti-establishment riot was a pure expedient, something she'd simply *done* (much like killing her husband), with no evil intention behind it. However, there was just one thing I had to ask her.

"When you say 'we' that means, does it, that Mr. Hirayama has a criminal record as well?"

Granny opened her eyes wide and stared at me. She seemed to be completely horrified, as if she would dearly have loved to put a lid on her mouth, but she soon accepted the inevitable and nodded. She looked so upset it was obvious to me how bitterly she regretted this careless betrayal of her man, and I found that painful, even touching. The impression of wretchedness was confirmed by the weird way she now chose to praise her paramour.

"Yes. Twice. For fraud. He's got a good head on his shoulders."

Yukari gave a loud cry of surprise and Kaizuka gasped. I was feeling very pleased with myself, aware that all three of them were impressed by my deductive powers, so I was able to make a generous apology for having been intrusive.

"What were you doing at the time, Granny?" asked Yukari, but her grandmother didn't seem to grasp the question so she added, "When he was being thrown down and kicked like that."

"Well," said Granny, thinking a little. "I didn't do anything really. Couldn't say anything, but just stood there. . ."

"Not surprising," said Kaizuka, obviously wanting to take her part. "In a situation like that, after all. . ."

"Bound to, I suppose," said Yukari. "I see what you mean."

She gave a large nod after this, and then said, as if to herself:

"I expect I'd be just the same . . . if they arrested Eisuke. Bet I wouldn't be able to move a. . ."

"Come off it," I said, hastening to put an end to these imaginings although they'd made me peculiarly happy as well. The middle-aged man was moved, need I add, by the fact that Yukari had spoken about him, not as her husband, but rather as her lover. I was so elated I made a slightly facetious jest.

"Still, I'm not likely to do anything dangerous in that line. Kaizuka's much more your man in that respect."

"In that case Mayo would. . ." Yukari started to say, but Kaizuka disclaimed any relationship with Mayo nowadays, and then Granny burst out crying bitterly again and we all looked at each other; but, regardless of our confusion and discomfort, Granny went on weeping.

"I expect they'll release him tomorrow," said Yukari.

"He'll be all right. The police wouldn't dare let anything happen to him," said Kaizuka.

"How about a nightcap? Probably a sedative will do you good," I said.

But none of the consolation we gave her caused any response other than the constant shaking of her head.

"It's just," she said, whispering a remark into the silence, which intensified the powerful effect it produced on us, "it makes me so sad when I think of him all locked up like that."

My immediate response was to feel this could well have a harmful effect on Kaizuka's education. I admit that it was a pretty peculiar thing to start worrying about when it would have made better sense to concentrate on how much a slur this could be on the respectability of the house of Mabuchi. But Kaizuka already knew all the sordid details: he knew Granny was a convicted murderess, that despite her age she was running around with a man with two convictions for fraud, that she'd gone with this same man to a love hotel; so it was a bit late in the day to start worrying about the respectability of our house. Indeed it would have been quite ludicrous to have done so.

No, what I mean by my concern about Kaizuka's education is this. If, for a moment, we ignore the unusual background to the case, the city riots, and think more in terms of the actual situation, here we had Kaizuka in a peaceful, happy home, and yet here we also had the old granny of the place head over heels about a man and desperate to get him back. This wasn't, as I saw it, something one ought to expose a young man to in such a respectable milieu. The worst thing was that it went quite against the accepted idea of human beings increasing in wisdom as they grew older; it stood the idea on its head indeed. On top of that (and I know there may be some slight contradiction in my insisting on this point as well), here was Granny, who may have wept a little on account of the tear gas but never once for her lover, eventually forgetting her fear of being scolded by her granddaughter over the lost handbag, and then, when her tummy was nice and full, finally deciding she could now indulge in some fond tears for him. As I saw it this harmed the idea of the integrity of the emotional life, and was something to be avoided if one were thinking in educational terms. Of course, one could always alter the terms of the argument and point out that my concern about the young man's education was simply an index of the goodwill I felt toward him.

However, things now took a peculiar turn, as if in total indifference to my ruminations on the matter. First Kaizuka folded his arms in a thoughtful pose, and produced the following remarkable statement as the outcome of his meditation:

"I could always get in touch with the neo-Marxist boys. Maybe I could ask them to get him back for us. Trouble is, it'd probably be pretty difficult blasting a hole through the lockup wall."

"What a terrific idea!" said Yukari, egging him on in irresponsible fashion. I personally reacted with strong misgiving, but of course it was simply a piece of nonsense, and the two of them were no different from Shin'ichi.

Then Granny turned her gray head in my direction, called out my name gently, and said:

"Isn't there anything you could do for him? Oh, please do. It will be the only time I shall ever ask."

I made a fairly positive response to that plea before I'd given the matter proper thought, and then Kaizuka added his bit of encouragement.

"That's a good idea. If you put in a word, the Metropolitan Police should be a cinch."

His view of things was so amazing I couldn't say a word. There was something I could only see as a total lack of integrity about his attitude, something unchaste, almost obscene in fact, as if some left-wing extremist were to join in various underhand intrigues with the leader of the conservative party. I need hardly say that the extreme left seemed to include at this moment not only Kaizuka but Granny as well. Still, I should also add that my ideas of order had been confused by the statements these two had made. I don't mean I'd grown contemptuous of either of them; rather the opposite in fact. In Granny's case, I felt a kind of mystified awe at the intensity of her obsession with the apartment caretaker and, in Kaizuka's case, an admiration for the concern he showed in this desire to undertake rescue operations for Granny's lover.

I closed my eyes and said nothing, while Granny Utako kept on attempting to win me over with her tearful pleas, aided by Yukari with her constant demands that I should get down to it first thing tomorrow, and abetted by Kaizuka, who prefaced his own comments by saying it might seem a bit odd that he should interfere in this business, but. . .

The whole situation was very reminiscent of occasions when I'd been lobbied as a civil servant, the only difference being that, whereas then I'd been able to get away with giving ambiguous answers in a precise tone of voice, in this case such behavior would be unacceptable. While still contemplating the matter I opened my eyes again, and there was Granny, off her cushion and onto the bare tatami, bowing her head before me and keeping it right down.

"Look here, Granny, you don't have to do that," I said. Having made her desist from this supplicatory posture I got Yukari to bring me a pencil and paper and asked for Hirayama's address, his full name, and other details. After due consideration I announced that, in my judgment, something could probably be done about it, whereupon Granny ceased her crying and returned to her cushion. I then proceeded with my questioning.

"Now, what family does he have?" I asked casually, but I realized this had made Yukari go all tense and Kaizuka shift about awkwardly. Obviously they were worried lest mention be made of Hirayama's wife. Granny answered immediately with no show of concern, however.

"He has one girl. Well, not really a girl, seeing as she's thirty-seven or -eight, I think."

"I see. So does this mean he has no wife?"

"Yes. They separated a long time ago. His daughter got divorced too, and came back to live with him. She's a good girl, he says, and looks after him properly."

"That's why he's able to go out so much, then," said Yukari, adding in a cheerful voice that we'd better telephone her, although the cheerfulness was, presumably, not at the prospect of breaking bad news to this daughter, but from the sense of relief at finding out her grandmother's lover was single.

After this Granny and Yukari spent some time debating the pros and cons of phoning Hirayama's daughter. Granny said she simply wouldn't know how to explain the situation, just wouldn't know what to say, and it would probably make his daughter feel more worried if she actually did know what had happened to her father, and anyway it was late now so it would be better to leave it till tomorrow. She was apparently determined to put the problem off for a while, so finally Yukari said she would do it for her, to which Granny was agreeing with considerable reluctance when Kaizuka's car at last turned up, and we all rose.

In the hallway we repeated our protestations of thanks, and Kaizuka used this to good effect by reminding me of the Hirayama business, bowing so politely there was nothing for it but to say as vaguely as possible that I'd see what could be done, although this left no doubt in anyone's mind that I'd firmly taken the matter upon my own shoulders. Granny's face was wreathed in smiles as she heard this, and she made a standing gesture of supplication, hands held together in prayer. Yukari told her that her persistence seemed to have paid off this time.

While Yukari was telephoning Hirayama's daughter ("I'm afraid my grandmother's completely worn out and has gone to bed, so. . .") I went upstairs to look for the visiting card of a man in the Metropolitan Police

Office whom I'd only met on two occasions. Luckily the card had been neatly filed away (not a question of luck, of course) in a box in my desk drawer, and on the back of the card his home number was written in my hand. I noticed that I had, in fact, another ten cards from people who worked for the Metropolitan Police, but he seemed to be making his way up the ladder the fastest of the lot, and so would probably have the most influence.

As I went downstairs with this card, Yukari had just finished telephoning.

"She moaned like hell," she said to me in a low voice, and then in a much louder one, "Sends you her best wishes, Granny. So you can put your mind at rest about that and go to bed now. I'm going to have a bath. We'll leave the kitchen things till the morning."

I tried telephoning my contact at the Metropolitan Police but, as I'd feared, he hadn't got home yet, so I asked to have him ring me on a matter of some urgency either tonight or tomorrow. I'd heard he was bound to become the next chief commissioner after the next (or was it the one after that?), but all I could hear in his house was the sad howling of the dog and his wife telling it to keep quiet.

I'd just sat down in the living room to read the evening paper when the phone rang. I felt this was surely a bit too quick, and when I answered it a fairly drunken voice replied against a noisy background of some sort of mood music.

"Ah. Eisuke. It's me. Nonomiya."

"Oh, good evening."

"Ah, yes; good evening. Er . . . is Yukari there?"

"She's in the bath at the moment."

"Yes, always spent a long time in the bath, even as a child. Something to do with admiring herself, I should think, eh? Come to think of it, I've always just been in and out myself, just a bird bath for me. Anyway, would you ask her something for me? I'm pretty certain that a photographer called Kaizuka is an acquaintance of hers. . ."

"No need to ask. He was here just a little while ago."

"Ah, what a pity I missed him."

"What's up with Kaizuka, anyway?" I asked impatiently, and he explained that, because some ancient art critic had suddenly been taken ill, he'd been just as suddenly appointed a member of a committee for some large magazine to select the winner of their photography prize. The winner had been decided this evening, and it was Kaizuka.

"That's a marvelous piece of news," I said. "Thank you for telling us."

"The photos are all of barricades and bamboo spears, that sort of thing; but they have a considerable artistic aura, quite distinct from the ideology behind them. I pushed for them very hard, as did another of the judges who happens to be a very important photography critic as well as the chairman of the committee, and it was our combined efforts that ensured Kaizuka would be chosen. I myself was struck by the fact that they were more 'picturesque' than 'photogenic.' " (He used the two English words, although "misused" is probably the word since he was saying the photos were more like paintings than photographs.) "Then there was a knack with the 'trimming' " (English again) "which I thought remarkably good, the way he varied the feel of the sensitized paper with different photographs. What I also found interesting was the consciousness that runs through them of placing violence in the center of the lives of ordinary people, or making a contrastive use of the two things. Could have been merely accidental, of course. I think the word I am looking for here is 'cinematographic.' " (Again he used the English term, then gave the Japanese equivalent for my benefit.) "I thought I'd heard the name Kaizuka somewhere, but couldn't for the life of me remember where or when. Then, just after I'd been here a little while, I noticed one of the hostesses wearing a dress much like one Yukari had worn sometime, and I recalled it was a name I'd heard from her lips. So, there, I was quite right. Memory's still ticking over nicely, as you can see. Didn't realize he was a fashion photographer, though."

I explained that he wasn't one in fact but specialized in news photos, and I recounted the events of the evening that had led to his being here (though I left out the details of Granny's love affair). At first my father-in-law seemed quite shaken by all this, but eventually he began to laugh in jovial fashion.

"Still, I can understand her wanting to throw stones. No real problem in understanding a feeling like that," he said with some insouciance, partly the result of drink, no doubt, but also because his ideas would have changed with his change of profession. Now that he'd ceased to be a university professor and was an "independent critic,

315

subservient to no one," he'd discarded his white collar and tie for a turtleneck sweater and, in the same way, I assumed, his ideas would have taken on a marked anti-establishment coloring. Once he'd committed himself to living by journalism, he was obliged to pander to the prejudices of his readers, for they were the ones who called the tune now.

He explained the car that was supposed to be taking him home hadn't turned up yet, which was why he'd been obliged to hang about in a bar as late as this, waxing indignant on the subject for some time, and finally saying:

"Why don't you two come to the prizegiving? Mother had better come along as well. After all, it's in honor of a man she's indebted to. I'll have them send you an invitation."

I agreed to this peculiar proposition, and then Yukari opened the bathroom door, poked out the upper half of her naked body, and asked who it was and what it was all about. I put my palm over the receiver and gave her a summary, and my wife, the steam rising from her body, said:

"Terrific. That's marvelous. There you are, I bet you they're the ones in the biscuit tins. You'll see."

Then she gave a large smirk and added:

"And tell him he'd better phone home quick or Mother will really get cross with him."

17

After I'd signed my name at the reception desk and was just having a blue rosette pinned onto the front of my jacket, a respectable-looking lady of about thirty-five or -six came in. She had a large, imposing figure, and the color of her *haori* jacket (a brown which was prevented from being too oppressive by the restrained, grayish blue, traditional patterning on it) emphasized the voluptuous pallor of her face. I assumed she was some middle-class wife. She had a black bag in one hand, and in the other held a comparatively large bundle (probably some shopping she'd done on the way) which looked quite heavy. She put this bundle on the reception desk and said:

"Is this the meeting for Mr. Kaizuka?" but before the girl could reply she had noticed the sign to her right, which she read aloud in a small voice:

"The *Ginga* Photographic Prize."

She smiled at the three receptionists, and also at me. There was something slightly vulgar about that smile, but it didn't detract from the very refined, indeed genteel, impression she made. I imagined it must be the first time the lady had been to an assembly of this kind, and perhaps she was just a little overexcited.

As she picked up the writing brush to sign her name, holding it vertically with her arm above the table in the proper style, I felt this was going to be a minor disaster for me. The visitors' book in which everyone signed his name was made of thick, traditional paper, lined so that only four names could be written in large characters on each page. I had just written my own name and made a nasty mess of it, being in no way adept at brush writing. My name has four characters. I'd managed the first, easy one all right, but the second, more complex one had ended up more or less as an illegible black blob, and because of the nervousness this failure had aroused in me I'd written the next too far down the page, and thus the final one had to be squeezed in, producing an eccentric sideways extension. I calculated (by intuition, of course) that this kind of lady probably practiced her calligraphy each day, and I feared the flowing elegance with which she wrote would highlight the clumsy incompetence of my own effort.

My apprehensions turned out to be groundless. She had written her name (Toyoko Hagiwara—four characters, like mine) very large, but in a perfectly illiterate scrawl, although she seemed quite unashamed of the crudity of her effort, replacing the brush with a look of satisfaction. This gave so powerful a sense of artless innocence that the very awfulness of her writing took on a form of dignity, seeming to represent an aristocratic indifference to skill or lack of it in handwriting, and thus making my own small-minded nervousness over the question appear an example of what bad taste essentially was.

While I was reflecting in this manner she addressed me:

"Excuse me. Are you Mr. Mabuchi?"

"Yes."

"Oh, just as I had thought. My name is Hagiwara, and the other day I happened to visit your house in your absence and I really feel I must thank you for the hospitality afforded me on that occasion."

"Oh, yes, I'm. . ."

"I'm an old acquaintance of Utako's . . . from Tochigi days. . ."

Luckily at that point the girl from reception approached with a blue rosette and asked to be allowed to pin it on her. If she hadn't I'm convinced I would have called out the name by which I knew her. This was Carrot Otoyo, the lady burglar, standing in the corridor outside a reception room in a central Tokyo hotel, quite calmly and confidently, a lady in her mid-thirties with light, restrained, and yet very attractive makeup, modest and refined in appearance (but also, if one looked closely, with a touch of insolence about her). I found myself glancing toward the bundle she'd left on the desk (the cloth wrapping was of cheap cotton ill-suited to the kimono and *haori* she was wearing), and began to wonder if it mightn't contain the ransackings from some unattended house on which she'd casually performed a job on the way here. However, my expression reflected nothing of such suspicions.

318

"Oh, are you really? Well, well, I must say this is a very pleasant surprise, particularly after all you've done for Granny."

I automatically slipped my hand toward my inside pocket, but reflected it might be unwise to hand over a visiting card to a person of this kind, so I adjusted the handkerchief in my breast pocket instead.

"Incidentally, what brings you to today's gathering?" I asked.

Just then a man in his fifties wearing a cravat and dark glasses came in. It was still some time before the award presentation was due to begin and few people had come as yet, but the arrival of this very photographer-like person provided us with the motive to move away from the reception desk.

Carrot Otoyo answered my question as she was entrusting her parcel of whatever to the cloakroom attendant. What brought her here today was a very simple reason, namely that she and Kaizuka lived in the same apartment house, a wooden building with four up and four down, and they happened to be next-door neighbors. The telegram announcing his prize had arrived while he was out and she'd received it for him. Yesterday, when she took him a bottle of whisky to mark his triumph ("After all, neighbors have to be on good terms with each other, don't they?"), she'd said that his mother would presumably be at the award-giving tomorrow, but he'd replied that neither his mother nor any of his friends would be going. She said that was very bad, and although it didn't matter all that much about his friends he really ought to invite his own mother; but while she was lecturing him in this way it turned out his mother had been in bed with a cold for the past two or three days. If that were the case, she insisted, she would go in her place so she could tell her all about it next time they met, and she'd forced him to ring up the editorial staff of *Ginga* and arrange it. Kaizuka's mother only came once a week or every ten days to clean his room, but Otoyo was on very friendly terms with her.

While Kaizuka was being rebuked for not inviting his mother, he'd felt he must say something in his defense, so he'd let slip the information that Mr. and Mrs. Mabuchi, who were friends of his, would be there, and would also probably bring their grandmother with them, so it wouldn't only be people in the trade. It occurred to her that the Mr. and Mrs. Mabuchi she knew were probably the same people, and that's why, she proudly explained, she'd guessed who I was as soon as she saw my name in that book.

"Yes, I suppose so. Of course. Incidentally, that wine you kindly gave us was really excellent, I thought."

I'd meant this merely as an ordinary compliment, but as she received her tag from the cloakroom girl she said:

"Oh, really, you mustn't say things like that," smiling at me coquettishly, the implication being that what I'd said "like that" was just a tiny bit too crude. That made me grin and she smiled back at me, not looking this time like a respectable lady, but like the mama of some bar. Thus all stiff formality between us had been disposed of, and quite naturally we drifted across to a sofa some distance from both the reception desk and the cloakroom and sat down together.

The first thing we talked about was carrot wine. Otoyo said that since she was going out to this party she thought she might as well combine business with pleasure and so she'd brought some with her, and could let me have some if I liked. I was relieved to hear the bundle wasn't full of stolen goods, and surprised by the enthusiasm she showed for her work; but I had to refuse her offer, explaining I was attending another get-together in a hotel nearby, connected with my work, and I wanted to avoid going there with baggage of any kind.

"Well, you are busy, I must say. Two in one day," said Otoyo, full of admiration, and then she inquired after Yukari. I replied that she'd been cleaning up the house and washing all the accumulated laundry, after which she said she'd be going to the hairdresser, so she would either get here just before it started or probably arrive late. The girl we'd hoped would become our maid had not, in fact, done so, and our servantless life continued. Carrot Otoyo praised Yukari for being so young and pretty, adding that she took after Granny, who was so lovely, and then suggesting that my good wife might take the carrot wine home with her instead. She was certainly very persistent in her desire to sell the stuff, but I didn't want to impose anything on Yukari, who'd be all dressed up for the party, so I responded with little enthusiasm. She took the hint very quickly and asked after Granny Utako to change the subject.

It was rather strange I should have felt like telling her everything that had happened, but probably I'd assumed she would take an unprejudiced view of the matter, and since they'd been prison inmates together I must have judged that Granny herself would hardly have kept it a secret from her, given their relationship of jailbreaker and accessory before and after the fact. Even so, I didn't feel much like talking about her romantic connection with Hirayama so I played down that aspect, simply saying that for some reason or other they'd been together at the time of the riot a fortnight ago, had both thrown stones, and Hirayama had been arrested, although he was due to be released this afternoon and she'd gone to meet him when he came out.

Still, even that brisk account was enough for Otoyo, who immediately worked out what was what. Having heard me out she said:

"Well, no matter how old you get there's always bound to be trouble with the men, I suppose," she said feelingly.

"Oh. Has Kaizuka told you about it, then?" I asked, feeling so stunned by her insight I wrongly assumed some outside source for it. This just meant I'd confirmed what she'd assumed about the relationship between Granny and Hirayama, for Kaizuka hadn't breathed a word to her about the riot.

"It's pretty obvious to me. After all, we did spend enough time together so I know about her."

During her stretch in jail it appeared Granny had shown considerable interest in that aspect of human affairs. Still, Otoyo didn't labor the point.

"Of course she would go to meet him. She has a very good heart, has Utako; very compassionate."

Having nodded her head in contemplation of the mysteries of the human heart she went on, to my considerable surprise:

"Funny I didn't see her there that evening."

"You mean, you were there, too?"

"Yes."

"Throwing stones?"

"Yes."

She looked straight at me, smiling a little shamefacedly. At that moment she didn't look like a respectable wife, or even a barmaid, so much as a little girl a sight too grown-up for her age. I can't say this didn't have its own attractions, but I was too occupied by a larger social issue to ponder the essential nature of a mature woman's charms. What had struck me was that at least three people with criminal records had taken part in the minor rebellion that night (this burglar, the caretaker, and my wife's grandmother), which surely had to imply that others had been present as well. If this tendency were to continue, then we could expect large bands of criminals to rise in opposition to the government and the authorities, a far cry from Kaizuka's symbolic revolution since it would be the real thing actually happening. This thought sent a shudder through me, which was intensified by what Otoyo went on to say.

"Saw quite a lot of con boys about, but thought I must be the only woman. Fancy Utako being there."

I soon grasped that the "con boys" meant those with previous convictions and, although astounded at the accuracy of my own insight, I retained my coolness of expression.

"Not surprising, really," she went on. "Bound to feel bitter about the past."

This was the expected generalization so I paid little attention to it, but the lady burglar took the argument in another direction that I certainly did find odd and unexpected.

"Got to take it out on someone or something. I expect you know the feeling, Mr. Mabuchi."

"What feeling?..."

"Having a grudge against the bosses."

"The bosses?..."

"I heard from Mr. Kaizuka. How you were opposed to the Self-Defense Forces and so you lost your job."

"Now, wait a minute. Now, really, you've got the whole thing wrong. It wasn't like that at all," I said in almost a shriek, which made Otoyo ask me in what way she'd got it wrong; but before I could answer someone called me by name.

My father-in-law had signed his name at the reception desk and was now making his way in our direction. Mr. Nonomiya was wearing a brown sports jacket over a mauve turtleneck sweater and gray slacks, and had a yellow rosette pinned to his lapel, which probably marked him out as one of the selection committee. He looked very different from the depressed figure he'd been at the time of his sudden resigna-

322

tion, full of the health and vitality of a man who was reveling in his new freedom.

I decided to waive all the complex particulars and introduced my father-in-law to Otoyo in a plain, simple manner.

"Ah," he said cheerfully. "You are one of Mother's acquaintances. I'm very pleased to meet you. I heard that she had some other matter to attend to which clashed with this, and would not be able to come."

"And your wife, sir?" she asked.

"Yes, she's been invited to some wedding or other. Well, so you're a neighbor of Kaizuka's? You really should get him to take your portrait, just as you are now. It would be quite charming."

He was obviously in a wonderfully good mood; he went on:

"Well, think I'd better go over and congratulate our prizewinner first of all."

He moved away and we both seemed naturally drawn along after him, so the question of whether I had a grudge against "the bosses" or not and, if I did, whether that grudge would lead to my throwing stones at the police, had to be abandoned.

As I was explaining to my father-in-law that Yukari should be here shortly, a plump, fair-faced man, the magazine's editor, sidled up and greeted him. My father-in-law immediately introduced the editor to us. Then the tall, dark president of the company arrived, and we were introduced to him as well. Both the editor and the president wore red rosettes, but the president's was twice as big. After this round of introductions my father-in-law asked where the man of the hour, the prizewinner, was. The president went off somewhere. The editor was looking all over the now fairly crowded lobby, when Otoyo suddenly cried out that he was over there.

Kaizuka was standing next to a fat pillar that was making some pretense of being marble, talking to a bald-headed man in a dark suit and a bow tie. Rather surprisingly he was not formally dressed but had on his work clothes, a black zippered jacket and black trousers, though he hadn't gone so far as to have his cameras dangling from his shoulders.

We eased our way through the crowd toward the young man, who also had an artificial flower attached to his jacket, and as soon as he saw us he promptly ignored the bald man to whom he'd been talking (or, rather, who'd been talking to him) and walked swiftly in our direction. The man was around sixty, a bit older than my father-in-law I should have said, wearing the yellow rosette of the selection committee, and he was obviously mystified at being discarded in that fashion by Kaizuka. However, he seemed to recover quickly enough and waved his hand at my father-in-law, who waved back.

Kaizuka thanked Otoyo and me for coming, in his usual polite manner, and the editor introduced my father-in-law to him. While they were talking I asked the editor who that bald-headed man was, and he told me he was the distinguished photography critic Takezo Kawashima. As I muttered the obvious response ("Oh, is he?") I found the editor was no longer at my side but had gone to pay his respects to a middle-aged man wearing a sports shirt under his suit. This, apparently, was the novelist Kentaro Horikawa, and he also had the yellow rosette of the selection committee attached to his breast. He was nothing like as good-looking as the photo that appeared in newspaper ads for his books, but nor did he look as cheap and nasty as he'd seemed when I'd once watched him on some television quiz program.

As I stood there I began thinking about Kaizuka's behavior. It was, I suppose, no more ill-mannered than the way the editor had left me to go and talk to someone else. However, Kaizuka was a young photographer who was hoping to make good in that world, and I couldn't get rid of the suspicion that it had been unwise of him to slight an important critic in such a fashion, particularly when the man had gone out of his way to secure the prize for him. Perhaps Kaizuka wasn't aware of that, but, even so, it seemed to me a bad omen of a kind, although still only arousing a vague feeling that there was no knowing what young people nowadays would be getting up to next. This slight unease grew much less as I watched the respectful yet pleasant and easy manner in which he spoke to my father-in-law (as he normally spoke to me, in fact), and finally it disappeared. Mr. Nonomiya was thanking him for having rescued Granny, but in an extraordinarily involved and roundabout way which would have been unintelligible to anyone who didn't know what had happened. Otoyo was standing there with a ladylike expression on her face as if she had no idea what a riot might be.

Kentaro Horikawa was leaning against a wall where he seemed to have been cornered by a very friendly-looking old man who was engaging him in some one-sided talk to which Horikawa made the occasional bored response, but then he suddenly looked in my direction with an intrigued expression in his eye. I was just wondering what was up when I realized the novelist was observing Otoyo, clearly interested in what her occupation or social rank might be. However, some young man, presumably on the editorial staff, approached him and the novelist looked away. As the two of them began talking, the friendly old man was totally ignored as well.

Another young man, one of the *Ginga* photographers I imagined, took five pictures one after the other of Kaizuka talking to Mr. Nonomiya. Then a woman wearing a mini-skirt (*Ginga* editorial staff probably) came up and led Kaizuka away to introduce him to the man in his fifties with the cravat and dark glasses. Kaizuka bowed to him. The *Ginga* photographer took out his light meter and held it at the tip of the other man's nose.

I felt like smoking so I wandered over to where there was an ashtray, when I recognized the profile of a tall man who was standing about doing nothing. It was Oguri. I greeted him.

"Hello," he replied. "I always seem to be meeting you in unexpected places. What on earth are you doing here?"

I gave him a simple account of my presence, avoiding various matters that might have given rise to awkwardness (one of these being Kaizuka's previous relationship with Mayo). In Oguri's case the editor of *Ginga* was a former colleague of days gone by and he was invited every year. He thanked me for introducing him to my father-in-law, whose article had been particularly welcome (or so he said).

"Of course, he's on the selection committee, isn't he? Doing well for himself. If he keeps it up he should have no trouble."

I thought this an optimistic statement to make, but Oguri explained that present-day university students were bored with television, the habit of going to the cinema had now been lost, and since the campus disturbances meant they had all the time in the world on their hands, the sales of books and magazines had picked up wonderfully, so it had become very profitable to be a writer.

"Amazing, really. You can make a living writing about anything now. Unthinkable not all that long ago. The times have indeed changed. Yesterday's perilous gulf becomes today's calm and shallow waters. Or have I got that wrong?"

"Well, near enough," I said, and as I smiled I caught Otoyo's eye and beckoned her over.

"Here we are, Otoyo. Try selling some to him."

I introduced them. Oguri produced his card and said pleasantly:

"So you're in the carrot wine trade. Well, I hope you leave a little room for the selling of beer. Still, as far as providing that kind of energy is concerned, there's nothing like a dark ale with yolk of egg. . ."

The only result of his ensuing brief lecture was he ended up buying a bottle of carrot wine. As I observed this, a mere bystander, I was struck by the skill with which Otoyo seemed capable of talking anyone into buying her wares, and I felt she could surely get by well enough without resorting to her other activity (of which Oguri, naturally, knew nothing). Oguri seemed, in fact, as much taken with her as I was, and he promised her he'd try to get the editor of *Ginga* to buy some as well.

Once again I became aware that Kentaro Horikawa, now talking to some inordinately fat, middle-aged man, was obviously not paying attention to anything being said, but looking toward the reception desk instead. I wondered who it could be this time and saw it was Yukari, who'd just come in wearing a lamé Chinese jacket and purple velvet pantalons.

Yukari joined our threesome for a while but, once the formalities were over, she signaled to me with her eyes, so I bowed to Oguri and Carrot Otoyo and moved a little away from them to hear the latest news about Granny Utako.

"She went out straight after lunch. To the police station. All very cheerful."

"Did you lend her another handbag?"

"Well, I just had to, didn't I? Still, I was a bit careful this time and let her have an old one I've no more use for."

"Good idea. Should have done that right from the start."

While carrying on this conversation I was anxiously wondering whether Hirayama would really pay back the money I'd used to bail him out, and what was going to happen about the fee for the lawyer I'd found him (a man who'd been two grades below me at high school).

The doors of the reception room opened and two of the hotel waiters stood on either side of them, bowing ceremoniously. The plump, fair-faced editor was also standing in that vicinity and called out in a mighty voice that we were about to begin. Everyone started more or less drifting in that direction, like a liquid being reluctantly swallowed into a hole.

Immediately facing the doors at the opposite end of the room was a dais with a narrow aisle leading to it, on either side of which benches had been lined up, enough to seat a hundred people. Chairs had also been placed to the right and left of the dais, facing the audience, although there was only one on the left. Some thirteen or fourteen feet above the dais "The *Ginga* Photographic Prize" was written in large letters, and on the left-hand wall there was another large sheet of paper on which the agenda of today's proceedings appeared, surrounded by a narrow fringe of artificial flowers. I sat between Otoyo and Yukari on a bench two rows from the front to the left. We had a good view from here of the seats to the right of the dais where the members of the selection committee sat, and of the row behind them where the editor and president and other distinguished bodies from the parent publishing company were seated, as well as of the single chair to the left where Kaizuka sat all by himself. Yukari waved her hand at him, and he fluttered his own in response, although he seemed (as one might expect) somewhat overawed by the occasion, and had a tense expression on his face.

"Never thought he'd go all serious like that," said Yukari. I didn't respond with any similar remark and read the agenda instead.

THE ORDER OF TODAY'S PROCEEDINGS
Opening Address
The President's Greetings
Presentation of the Prize
Congratulatory Address on Behalf of the Adjudicators
The Prizewinner's Reply
Closing Address

There were four of these adjudicators already sitting together in the front row of chairs to the right of the dais. Nearest the dais was Takezo Kawashima. Next to him was the man with the cravat and dark glasses, then my father-in-law, and finally a man in a grass-green sports jacket and a red tie. Kentaro Horikawa came in with a bored look on his face and made to sit down in the back row with the distinguished guests, but had something said to him by the president and others and so ended up in his proper place in the front row with the rest of the selection committee and next to the man with the red tie. The editor approached the other microphone, which was placed just a little in front of Kawashima (the main microphone being up on the dais), and muttered a few groaning sounds into it. This made everyone a little quieter, but when he withdrew, apparently satisfied it was in order, the noise and chatter started up again.

"How long will it take?" Otoyo asked.

"Twenty minutes at the most," I said. "The problem is the congratulatory address, but even that should only take about ten minutes."

"Look. What's wrong with Gen?" whispered Yukari. I looked and saw that Kaizuka had got up, walked over to the wall, and now stood there quite still and facing it. There was something oppressive that his black figure, standing there with his back to us, seemed to transmit. It was as if he were painfully pondering some course of action.

"Perhaps he doesn't feel well?" said Yukari.

"No, he's just calming himself down," I said, although I thought she was probably right. Kaizuka, however, then turned around cheerfully, displaying again the flower on his jacket, and went back to his seat with his usual unruffled expression. There was no trace of gloom or depression about him now.

One of the young employees of the publishing company placed a chair on the dais to the left-hand side. The editor now moved forward with a ceremonious formality quite different from his previous style and faced the microphone.

"My apologies for any inconvenient delay. Now that we are all assembled I think we may begin."

He bowed and introduced the publisher's managing director. The man who went up on the dais was about sixty, very thin, and his opening address took quite a long time. The president's greetings were a bit longer still, since he felt called upon to give us information about the sales of his company's publications, and then obliged to offer his thanks to a variety of people in a number of walks of life; but finally the actual prizegiving began. The editor produced a voice many times more dignified than anything he'd yet indulged in and said:

"The presentation of the prize will now take place."

Kaizuka went up onto the dais, and two of the *Ginga* photographers appeared and took up appropriate positions. The president read out the citation; Kaizuka received this, his prize, and the prize money; everybody clapped; and photos were taken all the time. The president descended from the dais. Kaizuka also started to descend but was stopped by an excited and unprepossessing company employee, and so he sat on the chair near the edge of the dais. He sat with all the objects he'd received perched awkwardly on his lap, and looked extremely uncomfortable. I really thought he ought to have tried to relax a bit more.

"And now Mr. Takezo Kawashima, on behalf of our distinguished panel of adjudicators, will deliver the congratulatory address," said the editor.

The bald man stood up with a clatter of his chair, went up onto the dais, walked three paces to the central microphone, and stood in front of it. He bowed as if he'd just been greeted with some powerful burst of applause, and began.

"Er. . ." he said (or started to say), when Kaizuka stood up violently, pointed his outstretched left arm at Kawashima, and shouted something in a very loud voice.

I couldn't catch what he actually said. Since I was sitting in the second row I assume this meant that nobody did, and certainly Kawashima didn't. He just stood rooted to the spot in front of the microphone and looked at Kaizuka in stupefaction. The distinguished photography critic didn't even seem to understand he was the object of Kaizuka's hostility. However, in the deep silence that now reigned over the hall, the succeeding shout was presumably audible and intelligible to all.

"I refuse to be addressed by someone like you. I refuse!" Kaizuka bellowed, although speaking a little more slowly this time.

Now laughter could be heard from a number of places in the audience, although it wasn't clear if this was because the content of Kaizuka's remark was considered funny, or because Kawashima looked so ludicrous standing there in bewilderment. He was still unable to take in what was going on. Probably the people who laughed weren't sure what they were laughing at themselves, merely rejoicing in the fact that this pompous occasion wasn't proceeding at all as planned, in the same way children are filled with glee when somebody just falls over.

My own reaction was not to find this comical, but instead to feel as if I were quietly addressing another person inside myself, telling him that now it had happened and there, I told you so. I felt tense all over, I was holding my breath, and yet all the time I was thinking to myself that I told you so, told you so, told you so.

The two *Ginga* photographers had dashed forward to the front of the dais and were shooting away at very close range. Then two men wearing sports shirts under their suits came forward from where they'd been sitting at the back, leaned against the wall near the dais, and produced pencils and paper. Presumably they were newspaper reporters who wrote for the feature pages.

Kawashima turned away from the microphone and spoke to Kaizuka in a peculiarly relaxed voice:

"But look here, this is a fixed part of the proceedings..."

He seemed to be trying to calm Kaizuka down, but when he'd reached that point he suddenly switched to a totally different tone of voice, one of uncontrollable rage.

"What do you mean by talking to me like that? What do you mean by saying 'someone like you'? It's a ... total breach of manners."

His face had grown completely pale with agitation—the same color, in fact, as Kaizuka's.

"Why shouldn't I talk to someone like you like that? What's so special about you?"

"What do you mean by that? You understand nothing, absolutely nothing. I'm the one who recommended you for this prize. I'm the one who got it for you. Ask anybody and they'll tell you. Anyway, you were a student at my university and you owe me..."

"I have misunderstood nothing!" bellowed Kaizuka, and he began moving purposefully toward him. The critic took two or three steps backward, afraid Kaizuka was going to hit him, and very nearly fell off the dais, only just managing to maintain his balance by flailing both arms about. This was so funny it ought to have made anybody laugh, but only a very few people did, for Kaizuka had leaped forward and taken hold of the microphone.

"Two years ago, Takezo Kawashima ... ah ... ah ... ah..." he began shouting. His voice was being amplified to ridiculous extremes, echoing about the hall like a long peal of thunder. There were also certain points where his voice broke and it wasn't quite clear what he said then; so if one takes that into consideration and also discounts the inordinate lengthening of the endings of certain words to which he'd given excessive emphasis, then his speech went like this:

"Two years ago, Takezo Kawashima, was the faculty, representative, on the board, of trustees, at my university. And what, did he do, then? That is, the question, I want to put, to this gathering. And I, will tell you, what he did, then. He betrayed us. He conspired, with the president, with the chairman, of the board, of trustees, with the director, of the board, of trustees ... and he ... betrayed ... the students! He also betrayed, the conscientious elements, among the ... teaching faculty! Due to his, betrayal, that struggle ended ... in total ... unconditional ... defeat! And so—here, get away, you damn fool!—I absolutely, refuse, to accept, any congratulatory address, from this ... evil man!"

Kaizuka had pushed Kawashima away as he tried to get the microphone back from him (the photographers took a number of shots of this), and a buzzing began all over the hall. I assumed half of this noise indicated disapproval of the young man's behavior, but the other half was a sense of relief at finally understanding what he was protesting about (which didn't mean they necessarily agreed or disagreed with him).

This was further enlivened by a sudden, remarkable, and vigorous clapping that broke out to my immediate left, from Carrot Otoyo, followed instantly by clapping from Yukari to my right. Probably because the palms of their hands had been sweating with the excitement, both these short bursts of applause had a dampish ring to them. Everybody in the row immediately in front of us turned around with one accord, and all the members of the selection committee looked this way as well. The one who showed a particularly enthusiastic interest was Kentaro Horikawa, who stood up and positively goggled at us, looking as if he'd have been prepared to climb up onto his chair to get a decent look if mere standing had been insufficient. Then, to the back and side of me, some considerable distance off, someone else started clapping (I was pretty certain it was Oguri) and this encouraged spasmodic outbursts from a few other places.

Meanwhile, back up on the dais, Kawashima, though still being held off by Kaizuka's left hand, managed to squeeze his face up close to the microphone.

"What happened on that occasion cannot be understood by people outside the university. It was an extremely complex. . ."

"Outside the university? I was a student at the time; right in it. In the faculty of commerce, too, not in any department of photographic art. At least I was lucky enough not to be taught by you. . ."

"This is preposterous. I protest, ladies and gentlemen, at this violent . . . outrage. . . There is no call to confuse photographic and university matters. It is quite wrong. . ."

"What's preposterous about that? I thought you were supposed to be teaching photography there?"

The two of them now seemed to be taking turns to howl into the microphone, the young man with his powerful tenor and the old man with his slightly weaker bass, their voices echoing about the hall; and they looked very like a couple of variety artists singing a duet in remarkably close harmony. This was genuinely funny to watch, and now people were laughing all over the place.

At this point the man in the grass-green jacket and red tie (round about fifty, I thought) stood up energetically and went to the other microphone, so it became quiet again. I'm pretty sure he was a photographer who'd become well known for his studies of beautiful women, and it also seems fair to assume he was under various obligations to Kawashima. Anyway, whatever the reason, it was obvious he was absolutely furious with Kaizuka but was also trying his level best not to show it. So, with his face twitching slightly, he began speaking in a very kind and gentle voice.

"Kaizuka, there's something I want to ask you. Since you have chosen to denounce Mr. Kawashima, who must be to you, as he is to all of us, a true master, a master of our art so removed from you, so above you, as to be in a quite different world; since, I say, you have offered this denunciation of him, why, may I ask, did you submit yourself and materials of yours for this prize? You were surely aware from the very beginning that he would be on the selection committee? That is all I wish to ask you."

The gentle yet fully amplified voice filled the hall, producing one cry of "That's right!" from way at the back somewhere, and the specialist in portraits of lovely ladies nodded in satisfaction.

"I'm not concerned with who may be in whose world. All looks like much the same world to me, much bigger than any of us. Still, what I'm saying is. . ."

". . . very, very peculiar. Exactly."

This interruption was not a quip from the back of the hall but from Kawashima, who had pushed his face in front of the microphone again. Everybody laughed.

"Shut up, you fool. What I'm saying is I don't want to hear someone like that congratulating me on anything. What does it matter if he's on the committee? He's only one of five, isn't he? It didn't bother me there was one of them I happened to dislike. I don't suppose he thinks much of me, either. I just saw his presence as a minor drawback I could put up with, and I submitted my stuff."

"Still, the fact is that I. . ."

"Shut up. You're becoming a real pain. The fact is he recommended me. All right, then. Someone I don't like recommends me. Well, that's a big laugh, that's all. Something I hadn't expected."

"Kaizuka, you still have not answered the main point of my question. Why did you choose to submit work for this particular prize? Will you give me your reasons, please?"

This was, of course, the same man in the grass-green jacket, and since there was a ripple of applause he was encouraged to continue.

"Why did you submit work for this prize when you knew that Mr. Kawashima was on the selection committee? Or was it *because* you knew he was on that committee?"

This was pushing the point pretty hard, particularly as he'd also laid great emphasis on the word "prize," indicating some contempt for the thing itself with its suggestions of bounty hunting.

Kaizuka's face went slightly red, but he replied:

"That's easy enough. It's a useful way of getting people to know my work, and if they look at it they'll start to think. They'll start to think maybe they ought to get up and do something. That's one thing. The next thing is money. That's my second reason. Perhaps I ought to expand on the idea for you . . . sir. I reject the society we live in. I reject this capitalist society. Still, as long as I'm living in a capitalist society then I'm living in it, and I can't reject the commercial magazines, now, can I? Of course I can't. So I sell my photographs to lots of weekly magazines. So I apply for a prize offered by a commercial magazine, and what's the difference? Which means"—he turned around and pointed to the sign in large letters above his head—"that things like this are there to be made use of."

This caused a general muttering in the hall, and I found myself looking toward the president, the managing director, and the editor; but they seemed to have been behaving with some caution since a while before and all three of them sat quite still and expressionless.

"Smart talking, boy," a man's voice cried out from the back, but the words were so drawn out they sounded comical, and everyone laughed, even Kaizuka appearing to smile slightly himself.

At this point the man with the cravat and dark glasses got up, mumbling "Well, well" (which didn't get transmitted by the microphone), and then "The fact of the matter is. . ." (which did). As he began to speak he gestured with his eyes to the man in grass green to withdraw, and then a very accommodating, soft, and friendly voice (unsuited to his dark-spectacled visage) descended over the heads of the audience.

"So you're not prepared to accept any congratulatory address if it's delivered by Mr. Kawashima? Well, I think I understand how you feel. Yes, I understand. Pity, though, because he's a very decent person. Very decent sort, Mr. Kawashima. Can't help thinking myself that the term 'congratulatory address' is a kind of misnomer. Don't want to stretch a point, but it's not really a congratulatory address, more like a simple report from the chairman of the selection committee.

That's just what it is, in fact. A report, no more than that. So why don't we just change the name, and have Mr. Kawashima just say a few words... Would that suit you? Seems a good compromise, and then we could get things rolling again..."

The way he spoke, the way he modulated his voice in particular, was very well done, so nobody laughed at all at the absurdity of the idea he was putting forward, waiting rather with bated breath to see what Kaizuka's response would be. But the youth in the black jacket up there on the dais rejected the idea quite unceremoniously.

"No thanks. I'm not having that. Changing the name from 'congratulatory address' to 'report' is just playing games—an imposture, that's all. A pure swindle. Count me out."

On hearing this Kawashima descended from the dais at high speed with a rough clattering of feet, and stood in front of the other microphone. The man with the cravat hurriedly withdrew two paces. Kawashima glared at Kaizuka and then howled at him:

"How dare you behave like that. Talking like that to one of your superiors. Is this sort of lout likely to become a decent photographer? Who does he think he is? I can't give a prize to a man like that. I refuse. I cancel the prize. I take it back."

"You can't do that, you fool, because I've already got it. Look over there," jeered Kaizuka, jerking his head toward the chair on the dais where he'd put his things when he first stood up. There they lay, all peaceful and quiet, the little pile of the award certificate, and the prize and prize money both wrapped in ceremonial paper and tied with the red and white string used on such auspicious occasions.

This crude response caused a cheerful outburst that filled the hall, a tempest of laughter in which Kawashima's voice was lost. I think the only people who appeared not to be amused were three members of the selection committee (of the other two, my father-in-law gave a wry smile while Kentaro Horikawa laughed quite unrestrainedly, his body shaking as he did so), plus the president, the managing director, and the editor. These latter three, however, certainly showed no sign of any great desire to straighten out the situation. Indeed their expressionless faces showed that cold objectivity of the editorial comment which brings to an end some fierce, no-holds-barred controversy thrashed out in the pages of a magazine over a longish period of time.

It was perfectly clear to me they'd worked out that the greater this rumpus became the more it would be written up in the newspapers, and so the more copies they would sell of next month's edition of *Ginga*.

The laughter died down a little, but Kaizuka was soon in there again, adding in a stage whisper:

"You want to take it back? Shall I give it back to you? Then come and get it, stupid."

This provocative whisper was amplified with a horrible precision by the microphone and boomed about the hall, and this time there was little laughter. Kaizuka had taken the joke much too far, and this had been sensitively reflected in the way people restrained their laughter. Now Kawashima's face was bright red, and he stood there with his whole frame trembling as he repeated "A lout like you, a lout like you..." until he finally managed to explain what would happen to a lout like him.

"You'll never be able to make a living in photography, I'll tell you that. Not a chance of it. You're a disgrace to the world of photography in this country, that's what you are. So get that straight because I, Takezo Kawashima, am telling you."

He gasped for breath as he bellowed his threat, his declaration of war, although how far those present grasped the import of this it would be hard to say. Perhaps few of them understood immediately that what the distinguished photography critic had said before this packed audience really did mean he'd do everything in his power to prevent Kaizuka from making a living out of taking photos. Despite a lack of full understanding, at least everyone seemed to have perceived in an instinctive way that an announcement of major importance had been made, and they all swallowed their breath. Into this powerful silence Kaizuka made his final, tremendous, clinching statement.

"All right, then. You just try it. Do what you like and do your worst. Have yourself a good time and see just what you can do, because whatever it is it's not going to trouble me for very long now, is it? And why? Because, old man, you'll soon be dead, that's why."

In terms of actual age the members of the audience were, on the whole, not young. Kaizuka was probably the youngest person there, representative of a generation conspicuous by its absence. Again, as far as having friends and allies present was concerned, there were few people here who knew Kaizuka well at all, and certainly a far larger number who were acquaintances of Kawashima. Still, the great majority owed loyalty to neither and, perhaps because they'd experienced on hearing these remarks one of those fitful moments of yearning for their lost youth, immediately he'd ended a chorus of clapping, laughter, and encouraging catcalls echoed through the hall and overpowered the murmurs of protest.

Toward the end of this hubbub that lone voice at the back of the hall added its own contribution of "Right on, boy!" or something equally encouraging. Yet it was possible (according to which way one interpreted the matter) to see this, not as a comment on Kaizuka's words, but as a plaudit aimed at my father-in-law, who had just slowly risen to his feet, taken the microphone from Kawashima (who was still standing his ground with face contorted) and, holding it in a light and accustomed way, ascended to the dais dragging the long black cord behind him. He addressed the audience.

"I am Yujiro Nonomiya, art critic and a member of the selection committee. My own private opinion is there is some degree of sense in what young Kaizuka has been saying."

He paused for effect and quite a few people clapped, not, I think, because of what he'd said but for the agreeably simple, no-nonsense manner in which he'd said it. After the feast of crude invective this tasted light and pleasant, like ice cream after a heavy, cloying meal. He raised one hand to restrain the applause and then went on.

"My sole experience of Kaizuka's university was a mere one year spent there some twenty years ago during which I gave a single lecture course on the history of Western art. No more than that. At the present moment I am teaching at no university. I have just recently stopped doing so, in fact. To be more specific I should explain that, although I tended to neither faction, being neither hawk nor dove, at a joint negotiation assembly I was suddenly, quite by accident as far as I could see, set upon by some excitable student who wreaked violence upon my tie. Since he was half choking me to death I was obliged to knock him down, and consequently had to resign."

This confession caused a wild explosion of laughter. There was an immediate atmosphere of goodwill created toward him, and even the

337

shout condemning his tough methods of instruction was extremely friendly.

"Oooh, that's a lie," whispered Yukari. "He never knocked anyone down."

Mr. Nonomiya continued: "I have been thinking, if this meets with everyone's approval, that I might be permitted to make the congratulatory address. Perhaps you could indicate your opinion first of all by a round of applause."

Kaizuka, apparently dumbfounded by this sudden change in the situation, did not applaud, but everybody else did with cheerful handclaps which went on for some time.

"Thank you, indeed. Now I wish to ask Mr. Kaizuka for his opinion. How do you feel in this matter?"

Kaizuka quickly nodded his acceptance, but Mr. Nonomiya was leaving nothing to chance.

"Are you quite sure there are no conditions you would like to impose?"

"Just to say a few words afterward. That's all."

Kaizuka spoke in a very different tone from the one he'd adopted up to then, and my father-in-law produced a nod-*cum*-bow in acknowledgment of his one condition.

"I think there can be no objection to that, providing nothing else unforeseen occurs. It is, indeed, in accordance with the agenda as already set down. Right, so I shall start, if you'll be so good as to return to your seat."

The prizewinner went back to his seat, placing his certificate, prize, and prize money on his lap again, while Mr. Nonomiya nonchalantly set both microphones together in the center of the dais and faced them. Out of the corner of my eye I noticed Kawashima leaving, but very few other people did, being quite taken up with my father-in-law.

So the congratulatory address began. The two *Ginga* photographers came forward again and took pictures as the address proceeded, although I must say it was less like an address than a lecture and less like a lecture than a long session of rambling, desultory chat, so fully did it break with all formal conceptions of what this sort of thing should be.

"The prize Mr. Kaizuka received a while ago was a watch, although, to be more specific, it was no ordinary watch but a very special kind, of which every part is black: the sides, the winder, the face, the strap, the hour hand, the minute hand, the second hand, even the figures on the dial; all black. Naturally this is not something any ordinary person could buy. It is for the use of a photographer ... for a man who takes news pictures. I am told such watches are only made to order in a workshop on the shores of Lake Suwa. If one wonders why a news photographer requires a watch of that kind, then I suggest you look at the clothes he is wearing today, those same clothes in which he goes out to take such pictures—without, of course, that artificial flower— and you will understand. Black is the best color for such work, since in black one does not present a target to the enemy.

"As regards the camera itself you will find that most models come in two types, black and silver. The body of the camera is either painted black or left its original metallic color. The price is normally identical in either case, and yet it is the amateur who uses the silver one, the black being chosen by the professional (or by an amateur pretending to be a professional). At most camera stores there are relatively few black cameras. If you knock or scratch a black camera the paint flakes off, making it look most unprepossessing, and the normal amateur dislikes such things. However, where news photographs are to be taken, the professional uses a black camera, not because he is concerned with people admiring the look of his camera, but for a practical reason. A black camera will not glitter in the sun and provide an object that can be aimed at, nor will it be conspicuous at night. Even with a black camera, however, only the body is black and other parts of it remain the original silver, and those photographers who go to shoot war pictures in Southeast Asia or Africa paint over, meticulously with their own hands, all those parts that remain silver, even the very smallest. I have, indeed, heard the following story. A photographer in a foxhole raised his camera above his head to take a photo with a telescopic lens, but at that moment some tiny part of his camera shone, providing a target for the enemy, and so he was shot through the wrist and crippled for life. That sort of thing can happen.

"I believe you will understand from what I have just said how appropriate has been the choice of a black watch as the *Ginga* Photography Prize, since it has been awarded to a news photographer.

This is not something that we of the selection committee proposed, but must have been the editorial staff's idea, and I think no praise could be too high when complimenting them on the excellence of their choice. Particularly in the case of a young, highly talented photographer like Kaizuka who takes violent news photos on these battlefields here at home, the front lines of metropolitan strife, it must be considered the perfect gift. It is with the greatest expectancy that I wait to see what further exploits this young man, dressed in black from tip to toe, whose teeth alone are brilliant white, will perform in days to come."

Some people assumed this was the end of the address and clapped their hands accordingly. Yukari clapped, so did Otoyo, and I must admit I did as well. However, my father-in-law merely restrained such applause by gently raising his left hand and immediately went on with his speech.

"For these reasons we may well admire the remarkable pertinence of selecting a black watch rather than an ordinary one, although I must confess that I personally have some slight doubt as to the relevance of a watch, of a timepiece itself, on such an occasion. If I were to state that I thought the gift of a watch was, in fact, strange, no doubt you would all point out a clock or watch was almost invariably given in the case of literary prizes, and insist that photography was as much an art as literature. Now, as I see it, the problem lies rather in the vicinity of the concept of art itself. Why do we feel that clocks are fitting to the arts? Or, to be more precise, why do we feel a wristwatch is right for an artist? Taking this question as my starting point I should like to consider the role of the photographer in contemporary society.

"Let me begin with something that happened to me during the last war. One day I happened to find myself, quite by accident, in the same hospital elevator as the great Kikugoro VI. He was attended by nobody and so there were just the two of us in the elevator. We traveled up to the fourth floor together, whereupon he bowed lightly but courteously to me and got out. That is all that happened; and yet what I wish to stress is just one thought that occurred to me a little later, which was that a wristwatch did not seem to suit that handsome old gentleman. I did not, in fact, realize it had been Kikugoro until after I emerged from the elevator at the fifth floor and walked quite a way. Now, of course, if he had been wearing kimono on that occasion we would have to take into account the obvious clash between his Japanese dress and the Western object, the watch. Obviously if Cézanne, for example, were to draw a wristwatch on the arm of one of Utamaro's beauties the result would be an obvious discord. However, Kikugoro, well known for his advanced, Westernized tastes at the time, was actually wearing a loud tartan check suit. The point I am making is that there was an essential incongruity between the Kabuki actor, no matter how up-to-date he may have been, the quintessential Kabuki actor, and the wristwatch he was wearing.

"Let me give one more example, this time taken from Western sources, although something from my own experience again. I made a tour of the West some time after the war and one thing—a trivial point perhaps—that I found strange, sometimes in America and often in Europe, was the fact that Roman Catholic priests should wear watches. I particularly noticed this on the package tour I made through Spain—I confess to a certain shame, as an art critic, at having 'done' Spain in this summary fashion, but the fact is I was short of money. Together with me on this tour was a Catholic priest from Norway, and despite his being dressed in the traditional black cassock he also wore a watch, and this watch and the obvious fact that it simply did not look right on him was a source of constant unrest for me. I quite honestly felt like advising him to stop wearing it, but we weren't on particularly intimate terms and so I just kept quiet. However, I found about six months to a year after I returned that French people seemed bothered by the same kind of thing, as I realized when I was reading a novel by Aragon, a French poet who also wrote fiction. In this novel a man asks his priest the following question: 'Father, is it permitted for you, a priest, to wear a watch?' and the priest replies, 'Yes, my son, it is, for these days the Church herself has been modernized.' Very similar to my own reaction, don't you think?—at least there is a genuine thread connecting the two. Here I should like to draw your attention to the concept of 'modernization' as mentioned by the character in the Aragon novel, for it will play a major role in what I have to say later on, although, for the time being, I wish simply to take it as demonstrated that the wristwatch suits neither a

Kabuki actor nor a Catholic priest, and will now take the argument a few stages further.

"What, then, would be a profession for which the wristwatch would be congruous? In order to clarify this issue the *yakuza* or gangster movie will be found to be extremely instructive. Yes, that old-fashioned stuff with its fixed ideas of right and wrong will be of help to us. The fact is that, when I was a university teacher, I did go to see a few—only two, in fact—since I felt I ought to try to understand the tastes of my students. Because it was the first time I had seen such films I noticed a lot of interesting things. In particular I made what I feel is a major discovery: generally speaking a *yakuza* never wears a watch. Of course, I am not talking about the real kind, but of those who appear in the movies. We see some handsome middle-aged fellow, informally dressed, with a Japanese umbrella in his hand, walking briskly along. All alone he barges into a place where there are huge numbers of his enemies, and begins a free-for-all that is doomed to end in poignant tragedy. He knocks down one or two with his umbrella, then gets possession of one of his opponents' swords, and kills ten or twenty of them, by which time his kimono has been torn to shreds, the tattoo on his back shows through, and the final bloody tussle has started in earnest. Naturally he gets chopped down eventually, but during that climax they give detailed shots of the movements of his hands, and you can be quite sure that he is indeed not wearing a wristwatch. At least that was certainly true of the two films I saw. Naturally I could not feel confident on the evidence of just two films, and I remember asking my students if this was also the case in other *yakuza* movies, but all they said was they didn't pay attention to odd things like that, although one of them did admit, now I had mentioned it, he had a feeling that it might be so.

"The phrase 'odd things' in this case surely has a more profound meaning than those students were aware of: meaning, I presume, that the fact of a gangster not wearing a watch in such films was a fixed convention, and for people who always watched such movies, for *yakuza* film buffs, such conventions were things one would not be conscious of, would not even notice. This is, I feel, the situation the phrase reveals to us, and I, being a pure novice in the art, did indeed notice all such 'odd things.' To give a quite different example of this

342

(and I must apologize in advance to the ladies in the audience), when we look at a nude painting, Giorgione's *Venus* for instance, since no pubic hair has been drawn we do not necessarily conclude that the lady is suffering from some form of alopecia in that area. One would have to be extremely illiterate in artistic matters to think so. This is rather wandering off the point perhaps, but I did once have the following experience. I was looking at a painting in a museum and nearby there was a nice-looking young mother with her small son, and suddenly the little boy shouted out in a high, piercing voice, 'Look, Mum, she's got no fuzzy.' No fuzzy... Well, I see no need to expand on the word. The mother turned quite red ... but no more need be said, except to point out that my reaction at the cinema was of a kind with that child's reaction in the art museum. What I am saying is, if I may be allowed to use a more difficult terminology, the *yakuza*'s not wearing a watch is *une convention fixe*, an established convention, an unshakable formulation which accompanies that genre as inevitably as do the gaudy colors of the Meiji print.

"Still, the question is why should this convention have come into being? Now, you may well reply that obviously a watch does not go with Japanese dress, but the problem then remains the same as it did with my account of Kikugoro VI just now, for the *yakuza* wearing Western clothes does not wear a watch either. That was certainly the case in the two films I saw. An odd thing, don't you think? After all, even these gangsters must have appointments to keep. Indeed they do, indeed most certainly they do as they are portrayed in these movies, for they seem to be such great favorites with the ladies that they are perpetually having secret trysts with them, be it in some graveyard as the cherry blossoms fall, or beneath the willows by the riverside. Do they ask the time of day of some member of the general public, thus ensuring they arrive on time? Or is it that these outcasts from the social world, these lone wanderers, have acquired the habit of peering into strange houses just to read the time and so have no need of watches of their own? Whatever the answer may be, I confess it was a question that just would not go away.

"Now this form of argument, whereby realistic standards are used to make nonsense of a non-realistic art form, was often used by Edo popular hacks to mock the Kabuki drama of the day, and has but little

343

validity as a critical tool, so I shall return to an assessment of the modality of the *yakuza* movie, by which I mean to argue about the form it actually takes. Here I shall put forward one exception to the general rule as already stated, and one that I consider of major significance in the unraveling of this problem. One person in the two films I saw was, in fact, wearing a watch—a Patek Philippe, it seemed to be—and he was a boss of considerable standing. I cannot speak with total confidence here owing to the paucity of my data, and yet I still feel that this one exception is extremely suggestive. I say this because, if we speak of the man in very precise terms, then he was not so much a *yakuza* as a major power *behind the scenes* of the real social world, a man who had leading conservative politicians at his beck and call. His function in the movie was as the leader of the enemy faction. Here I prefer to ignore the ideological implications of his affinity with the conservative party, since political ideas are not ones I consider my forte, and I also feel it would serve little purpose to concern ourselves with them here. What I do wish to stress is the question of whether he can properly be considered a true *yakuza*; and this is the point that must inevitably be stressed, for the conventions of the film indicated that he was not one. The old man with the expensive wristwatch was a treacherous person who did not conform to *yakuza* custom. Here we had a *yakuza* who was pretending not to be one, a nasty piece of work behaving as if he were an ordinary, respectable citizen.

"Now let's go over that again. Please, no cries or groans of complaint, I beg you. Right. Now, as is quite clear from the case of this man, in the *yakuza* movie a gangster wears a watch when he is pretending to go straight, when he is behaving *as if* he were a respectable member of ordinary society. Therefore the watch symbolizes the world of the ordinary citizen, but the *yakuza* is outside the orderly framework of that world. At least the leading spirits among them, those who represent the *yakuza* ideal in its purity, are outside it. For that reason they have been able to avoid wearing a wristwatch, that handcuff which would attach them to the society of the ordinary citizen. They need attach no watch to their body, they need carry no watch, and that is precisely the mark of their freedom.

"If we think in these terms, then the fact of those university students sitting, each with a watch strapped to his wrist, applauding *yakuza* exploits in the darkness of the cinema can be seen as a pertinent summing up of the psychological condition of contemporary youth. There they sit, our future citizens, and each has tied to his left wrist the sign of his desire to grow up into a worthy citizen himself. And yet, deep in his heart, there also exists the vain, empty dream of how wonderful it would be if it were possible to become something other than a decent citizen. He grows intoxicated with the tragic beauty of the blood-covered hero in the final decisive struggle. He claps wildly. And, at that moment, his left hand with the watch strapped to its wrist, and his right hand with *no watch* strapped to its wrist, beat violently against each other. How painful, how unbearably pathetic, is this sight, as all the ambiguity of his psychic situation, his wish to be a citizen and his rejection of that status, his desire for the citizen's life which he has not yet experienced and his fear of it, his love for it and his hate, link together in desperate contest, in a fight to the death. I certainly experience deep feelings of pathos, and I wonder if my audience does as well. A glass of water, please."

"Yes, sir," said a woman's voice just behind me, one of the editorial staff, who had presumably responded quite accidentally since my father-in-law happened to be looking in her direction. This made everyone laugh, and it didn't sound to me as if they were all restless at the thought that there was more of this to come. In fact scattered applause was mingled with the laughter, and we three joined in with it although ours was a little late. The audience had perhaps been taken by surprise at this unusual theoretical treatment of the *yakuza* film genre, but it had at least given some sort of answer to the question why the younger generation could enjoy old-fashioned movies of that kind. Even if they were still only half convinced about it, they seemed happy, even grateful for what they were hearing, and certainly interested.

Mr. Nonomiya didn't wait for his glass of water but continued.

"I shall now make a sudden break in my discourse and move away from contemporary Japan to eighteenth-century France. The royal princess of Austria, Marie Antoinette, married into the French court at the age of fifteen, which would have been in the year 1770—or was it 1771?—well, round about that time anyway—and as a wedding present she received fifty-one fob watches. Here I should point out that the wristwatch did not exist at that time, being a twentieth-century in-vention, and also that the watch was an extremely expensive luxury restricted to members of the aristocracy and the very wealthy. For the upper classes, it seems that to have carried on one's person a device that gave the correct time was considered the equivalent of having made the mental abilities of a genius one's own private property, and no doubt this was a reflection of the ideas of the Enlightenment. Marie Antoinette's watches, however, not only reflected such En-lightenment thought, but also the rococo art of the period. As befit-ted a wedding gift to celebrate a marriage between the mighty houses of Hapsburg and Bourbon, the fifty-one watches were all perfect specimens of luxury and elegance, glittering with gold, silver, dia-monds, rubies, pearls, and other precious stones, and with minia-ture portrait paintings set inside them. Thus she received fifty-one watches, any one of which would have cost hundreds, even thou-sands, of times as much as a Piaget lady's watch today. I assume the meaning of the gift is now quite clear. It was the perfect expression of wealth and power."

At this point Mr. Nonomiya took the glass of water a hotel waiter had brought him, drank a third, and then returned it.

"Thank you. Yes. Now, Marie Antoinette's husband, Louis XVI, according to his biographer, suffered from phimosis and was conse-quently impotent. I apologize for mentioning this indelicate matter, but in this case the responsibility rests not so much with Louis's biographer as with the king's, er, *organe mâle*, and certainly very little with myself. Thus for seven years after her marriage she was obliged to remain *virgo intacta* until Louis underwent a quite simple operation which at last put him in the position to possess a woman. Still, during those two to three thousand nights passed unfulfilled as a wife who was yet a maid, might it not be that she spent the time gazing at those fifty-one watches, those pure marvels of rococo art? It seems more than likely to me, I must say. Obviously for that purpose one watch alone would have sufficed, while all the other fifty watches she had received as wedding presents would merely have been ticking away quite meaninglessly; and thus one can see the essential meaning the watch must have had for Marie Antoinette. For her, whose whole life was leisure, the watch could have had no practical meaning. At court the watch was an expensive bauble, nothing more, in the same way that for a great Hollywood star a fur coat does not serve in any way the functions of preserving warmth or keeping out the cold.

"And yet, just as our Hollywood star will buy various fur coats, a mink, a leopard skin, a chinchilla, so Marie Antoinette was something of a collector of timepieces. Of these the most famous was one she ordered from the greatest clockmaker of her day, Bourget, who started work on it some years before the fall of the Bastille but did not complete it until the nineteenth century had begun. By that time his royal patroness was already dead, executed by the guillotine ten years before. This clock, the greatest masterpiece in the history of clockmaking, was named the Marie Antoinette, and yet the fact that her name should have been given to something she never actually used seems to underline the essential irrelevance of the object as such to Marie Antoinette, there being an absence of connection, a lack of true relevance in her existence, to any kind of watch, clock, or timepiece.

"Therefore, if the clock or watch is not to be an ornament or a plaything but an object of use, whose object will it be and what will it be used for? The answer is simple. Its owner will be the citizen; the laborer sells his laboring time for wages and the clock's function is to measure that time precisely. It must also be a device that determines when labor is to begin and when it shall end. In a pastoral situation where the work force is small, there is no reason why this should not be decided in an approximate way by the movements of the sun, but labor in a huge factory cannot be entrusted to such measurements and the clock becomes absolutely essential. Thus what was a plaything for Marie Antoinette becomes the basic tool of his trade for the entrepreneur, the one who manages that factory. This manager, this businessman, is our citizen, and so, to put the matter in the broadest possible terms, this is the meaning of the clock in our modern civic societies. It means work time; it also means interest time, the time during which money turns into more money. The clue to the meaning of the clock towers in the great cities of Western Europe, such as Big Ben in London, is, I presume, to be found in that direction. If, in the future, men should occupy these clock towers, disturb and derange the great clocks and the time they showed, here would be true treason against civic society, the will toward revolution.

It would also be a very splendid practical joke, a profound piece of scaremongering, creating a confusion and turmoil that would actually mean something.

"It is well known how Sohachi Kimura, in his descriptions of Tokyo in the Meiji period, loved to write about clocks and clock towers. Indeed, Ichiyo Higuchi has written in her novel *Growing Up* of the Tokyo of that time and how 'the season is now approaching when the dragonflies will scatter over the paddy fields and the quails will cry from the margin water channels. Then at morn and evening the chill autumn wind will blow over them, and in Josei's store the odor of mosquito incense will give way to the scent of charcoal burning in his body-warmer, and from Tamura's by the stone bridge will come the melancholy sound of the pestle pounding, and the clock at Kadoebi will seem to have taken on an even sadder tone.'

"Remembered that pretty well, haven't I? Not all that surprising with a book read during childhood. Kadoebi was a large establishment in the Yoshiwara red-light district with a clock on its third floor, but just one of a number of clocks in the city at that time. Rather than see this as a simple imitation of Big Ben it would, I think, be more correct to consider it an attempt to copy modern Western society in some tangible form, an indication of the passion for civilization and enlightenment that characterizes that whole period. The fact that this clock tower, this symbol of modern society, should then become a signboard for a bawdy house probably indicates the character of Meiji Japan better than anything else. Of course, all these clocks were of foreign make and there was a dreadful to-do if something went wrong with them, which happened quite often apparently. There is the tale of the clock tower at the Guards Barracks at Takebashi, the oldest one of all, that when the great clock failed to sound the hour the soldiers would be terrified and say it was the ghost. Apparently, when the barracks were first built, an English engineer used to live in a room in the clock tower, right at the bottom of it. He had someone to look after him (as they called it then), meaning a mistress, but she died of some illness and whenever the clock went wrong they said it was because of the curse her dead spirit had put on it. The fact is there is a clock tower in the university where I used to work, and that clock has been stopped for the past ten years, standing at ten to twelve all that time. I mention this not to laugh at Meiji Japan, for every time I used to look at that clock I felt it demonstrated precisely the state of our universities now, bound hand and foot by red tape, stifled by the bureaucratic machine, with education and research totally disregarded. One thing about a clock in a tower, even if it's electric, is that once it breaks down it's very hard to get it going again. The students used to joke about that clock, saying how its always being ten minutes before lunch indicated their own perpetual state of unsatisfied hunger—both for actual and for spiritual food, no doubt.

"Now, in Geneva, some fifty years before the birth of Marie Antoinette, there lived a clockmaker who had two sons. The elder son was apprenticed into a master clockmaker's house during boyhood, but toward the end of that period he ran away and was never heard of again. The younger one was apprenticed in the same way, and he also detested it and set out on his travels ... and some decades later was one of the leading thinkers in Europe. His name was Jean-Jacques Rousseau. Perhaps the easiest way to think of this is to consider that when the nuptials of Marie Antoinette were being celebrated in the Palace of Versailles, Rousseau was in a room in that street which was later to be named after him, writing his *Confessions*.

"In the *Confessions* there are two episodes concerning clocks—as has already been pointed out by the scientist Dr. Bronowski—which are of special note. One of these is the attempt he made to teach Thérèse Le Vasseur—first his servant and later his common-law wife —how to tell the time, which she found impossible no matter how hard she tried: an episode showing quite clearly how much he loved and admired her ignorance. Perhaps it might be truer to say how much he envied it. The second was some years later when he left Paris and went to live in seclusion and realized to his great delight that he would no longer need a clock, so he instantly sold it. Rousseau wrote that the moment he sold that clock was the happiest in his entire life.

"As the son of a clockmaker and the brother of a man who had failed to become a clockmaker, and also, by his own confession, a failure himself as a man, his life is illuminated by these two episodes. I shall not, in either of them, attempt to see any Freudian expression of hatred of his father, for the emotion seems directed at a much

349

larger object than a parent. The selling of the clock would seem, indeed, to be a striking example of his rejection of the citizen's orderly life and the beliefs that underlie it. The truth is that, while living in a civic society, he really loathed it; while remaining proud of being a citizen, it was a condition from which he wished to escape. For someone like Rousseau, with his passionate longing for the simple, natural life of the savage, the existence of Thérèse, who couldn't tell the time but was beautiful and gentle, must have seemed a living proof of the virtue of the noble savage. Rousseau contrasted the natural person and the civic person, the savage and the citizen, and he spent the whole of his life attempting to reconcile the two.

"Thus the ambivalence this Swiss thinker experienced in the early days of the modern civic state, the love-hate complex which being a citizen aroused, has proved prescient of the paradox of the citizen that has existed ever since. The fact is we citizens all desire—no matter how varied the intensity of this desire may be—to cast away the watch that handcuffs us to civic society, and so escape from society itself. There may be some who can maintain there is no such inclination in their hearts, but they must be very few indeed. We are bound to say, therefore, that it is our own images we see, as if we were looking in a mirror, when we observe those students applauding the struggles of those watchless *yakuza*, both hands clapping, one hand bound by a watch, the other one free, but both coming constantly together.

"And yet, even within our society there are ways of escaping the order it imposes. The best example of this is the sexual act, for by its intensity and intoxication we experience a time not measured by the clock. Or perhaps we even experience timelessness, for during that time, be it but an instant, it is as if all the clocks and watches have been confiscated and cast away. In this sense Rousseau's *Confessions* is the eighteenth-century French version of *My Secret Life*, written in the Victorian age by an anonymous English gentleman, itself a Victorian version of eighteenth-century French life. Probably Rousseau was attempting, by his dissolute behavior, to escape from the framework of modern society. It may well be that as Rousseau drew his idealized portrait of the noble savage, some sense of the unfettered sexual life of the real savage lay at the bottom of his unconscious. It would have to have been unconscious since ethnological studies had made no advances whatsoever at that time, and so much taboo surrounded the discussion of sexual practices in uncivilized lands that he could surely not have known about them.

"This admiration for the savage, for the uncivilized and the simple, which began with Rousseau, this 'primitivism' has held a great attraction for the artist. In literature there are the novels of D. H. Lawrence, of Chatterley fame, where sex is transformed into the mystical, and primitive cults and rites are given serious attention. As another example we have Dostoevsky with his respect for the child and the idiot, the boy Kolya and Prince Myshkin. Also Yeats's myth, Hemingway's blood and violence, his bullfighting. I have listed these rather crudely just as they came to mind, but there are plenty more. In the realm of the fine arts we have Picasso's discovery of Negro sculpture, the farm laborer motif in Millet and Van Gogh, the influence of spontaneous children's drawings on Miró and Klee. What deserve special mention are the cases of Gauguin, the escapee to Tahiti, and Douanier Rousseau, who delighted in painting Mexican scenes; not to be confused with Jean-Jacques, for this is Henri Rousseau. I particularly stress the two since Gauguin worked in a bank and Rousseau was a customs official, and thus both were solid, respectable citizens. Naturally, as you no doubt already know, Gauguin gave up his job in the bank, but Douanier Rousseau remained a Sunday painter, and is said to have happily harmonized the life of a customs official and that of a painter, though I myself have doubts about that, for it looks like a mere keeping up of appearances to me. After all, those paintings of lions in the jungle, gypsy girls asleep, those pastoral fairy tales, those pictures like nursery songs, can surely only represent a powerful desire to escape from the restrictions of modern bourgeois society, to run away. In fact Henri Rousseau committed two crimes in his life, which seems out of keeping with the innocence of his painting. One was the misuse of public funds, for which he was sentenced to a month's hard labor, and the other was a case of fraud for which he was given two years' imprisonment, although both were in fact suspended sentences which he did not actually serve; but I maintain these minor offenses were an attempt to realize his dream of escape from the order of society. If you look, for example, at a painting of his showing one of the more cheerful aspects of life in society, a wedding, you will notice that one extraordinary facet of the work is a black dog painted large in the foreground, and I have thought for some time that the presence of this ominous animal represents his own feelings of malice toward society. Which means that, as far as their biographies are concerned, we can see this conflict between the artist and society quite openly in the case of Gauguin, although with Rousseau it lies more deeply concealed; but if we look at the works they created, then both show quite clearly the same lack of rapport, indeed the confrontation that must occur, between the two.

"Jean-Jacques Rousseau, by his brilliant analyses, was not only responsible for making primitivism a popular idea, but foresaw this confrontation between the artist and society which has continued for over two hundred years and will, as I see it, go on for some time to come. Obviously the confrontation will take different forms, in the same way that the same profession will appear differently to different kinds of men. But since the artist is a person who aims at a world of autonomous artifacts, this in itself will mean he is in rebellion against bourgeois society as such. That, I believe, is the proper way to consider this question. The artist is not in opposition to society because he transgresses good manners and respectability, or because the content of his works is immoral; or at least not solely for that reason. After all, there is more immorality among the citizens themselves, and always has been—society being full of immoral aspects. No, the question is a much more basic one than that, for I cannot help feeling the conflict between the artist and society arises from the fact that the artist is concerned with a quite different time to the one recorded on the clock towers in the public squares of the great cities. I am aware that the exaggeration I am about to make may well lead to misunderstanding, but I shall state that art is a criminal act aimed at destroying the clock towers in our public squares.

"In the Museum of Modern Art in New York there is a painting by Salvador Dali, *Persistence of Memory*, which I believe many of you will already know. That surrealist masterpiece, where the pocket watch has become soft and folded, deprived of its essential form, represents, I believe, more than any other work, the shadowy dream of the artist, of the man who lives in society and yet bears malice toward it, who constantly plans his quite solitary, singular rebellion which he calls his art, and just as constantly practices it.

"If one considers the matter in this way, then it is surely a weird custom that clocks or watches should be given as literary prizes. One might well say, indeed, that the whole thing is a kind of plot to domesticate men of letters in a way appropriate to civic society, a chain by which animals yearning to be wild can be retained as livestock, a plan to turn them, not into aristocrats or *yakuza* outlaws, but factory managers. It may even arise from the malicious idea that their trade is to create disposable products whose function is to help the citizens pass their leisure time, a trade for which a watch would indeed be a fitting symbol. Again, one might argue that when the man of letters writes, besides removing the watch from his left wrist, he also performs his work with the right hand, on which there is no trace or scar left by this bond that handcuffs him to society, and so it does not matter. However, there is another possible approach to this question, if one takes into account the fact that poets do not seem to be given watches when they win prizes. One could see this custom as something related to the basic character of the novel as an art form, one remarkable for its impurity, its vulgarity indeed, having a structure that is truly no structure, devoted as it is to the relating of ordinary events in the everyday world of the present; and so one could say that the watch, that symbol of modern civic society, is a totally appropriate award.

"I shall now enter upon my main argument. Let us leave the question of the watch as a literary prize, and think of it as an award for photography. Is it the right kind of thing? In particular, what kind of thing is it when the prizewinner is a news photographer, and one of anti-establishment inclinations? Naturally those who selected this prize did so in the benevolent, pious hope it would be useful, and that was their sole consideration. But if we view the matter in a purely speculative light, how should we consider their choice? Here, naturally, the important issues are the basic ones: namely, what is a photograph and what is a man who takes photographs?

"Normally people think of photography in relation to painting very much in the same way that they consider fiction vis-à-vis poetry. They think of it as short on purity but long on usefulness, a popular art form, one lacking in formal status. As a person engaged in celebrating the award of a photographic prize I am aware of the perhaps indiscreet nature of what I have just said, but that is what we can call the normal, accepted, commonsense view of the matter. However, merely reverse the terms of the argument and all these characteristics become the strengths of the photographic art. It is often said that the novel occupies a position right next to actual human life; but photography faces life and society head-on, from that close-up position unhesitantly obtaining images with the swift click of the shutter. Here, indeed, are immediate riches; or here, indeed, is a rich immediacy. By which I mean that just one slight error, just one foot wrong, and we have what is a mere record or mere propaganda, and the danger of that happening is, I feel, much greater than in the case of the novel. Also, of all photographers, the one who is most directly confronted with that danger is the newsman.

"Now, in the case of a news photographer who has no talent, everything is simple. He takes pictures that merely record or advertise, and whether he claims they are art or admits they are not is beside the point, for they are not; and they are not because in no way do they run contrary to the decrees of bourgeois society. There is no reason why such a person should not wear a wristwatch; indeed it suits him very well. However, with a photographer of true talent, even of genius, what do we find? We find him creating art even when he had no intention of doing so. He means only to create a mere record or to provide propaganda and yet he brings forth beauty. He means to provide an imitation of the real world, but as he imitates we find he confronts us with a totally imagined world. He is an artist despite himself, *un artiste malgré lui,* and yet one of those artists who belong firmly to the romantic tradition. I need hardly add that the doctrines of romantic art all lie firmly under the aegis of Jean-Jacques Rousseau.

"For our unwilling artist, for our artist in spite of himself, what will this black watch on his left wrist signify? And will those images he takes in order to propagandize, in order to proclaim those political beliefs he cherishes, those records of commotion, riot, and rebellion— will they truly serve, as he believes, as propaganda for the society that will succeed this one, a society created by escaping from our present civic state? Or is it not, instead, something he dreams in the hidden depths of his mind, a dream of a country beyond the one we know, as the banker Gauguin dreamed of far Tahiti, a marvelous model made only of light and shade? Thus the wristwatch that Gen Kaizuka will wear has been made completely black: black hands, black dial, black everything, to indicate that this, although a watch, is not indeed a watch that represents bourgeois society. Here, surely, is a truly romantic device, an instrument of darkness measuring darkness. This being my view of the matter, it is with deep interest and concern that I shall follow the career of young Kaizuka, freely wearing or obliged to wear his black watch on his wrist; and I look forward to the works he will produce. Ladies and gentlemen, thank you very much."

Before he'd even started to bow the applause broke out, and as he lowered his head everybody was clapping their hands. Part of that response was obviously relief that at last this long address was over, and no doubt part of it was an expectation that one would soon be able to get a drink; but for the most part the applause did seem to indicate admiration and approval. The argument in the second half had been perhaps a little too involved, probably because the speaker himself had been exhausted, so a number of logical jumps had occurred and the thread of the whole thing seemed to have been lost in some places as abbreviations had been made and shortcuts taken. Still, the first half had been easy to follow and also interesting, with just the right touch of the erotic, too; and it was only proper that people should have thought highly of it. He had treated the young prizewinner very kindly despite the way he'd been carrying on, and yet there'd been a hint of mild reproof in some of what he said, which was all to the good. Of course, the main thing was that he'd been able to keep going for so long with a speech completely off the cuff, and the tumultuous nature of the applause was very much like the kind directed at a man who'd been able to walk on his hands for five or ten minutes. I must admit that during the speech, at that point where he was talking about Louis XVI's problem with his male organ, I began to think it would be a good idea to have him give a lecture at my company; and then, the next moment, I realized my father-in-law was putting on this performance for that very reason, having brilliantly seized the opportunity provided by the extraordinary events of the day to ensure that requests for lectures would come in from various quarters. Now there, I thought, was an initiative one could really admire, and it added to my satisfaction with the way the audience was responding.

Still, the earsplitting clapping didn't continue for long. Kaizuka stepped forward as soon as Mr. Nonomiya had completed his bow, almost as if he were brushing him out of the way, and began speaking into the microphones.

He was in an extremely unfortunate position. First of all, people were sick to death of talk and wanted no more of it. Secondly, in comparison with Mr. Nonomiya who had years of lecturing experience, Kaizuka's use of the microphone was incompetent, an incompetence made worse by the fact that he was in a very excitable state. His voice was much too loud, and quite a lot of what he said became an unintelligible screech which echoed about the hall. People winced at the noise, and as they winced they also felt contempt for his lecturing skills, quite different from his predecessor's, lacking those illustrative stories and fine rhetorical flourishes that aroused one's interest. Much as they'd enjoyed observing Takezo Kawashima having the daylights beaten out of him by Kaizuka, now they were rejoicing in the spectacle of Kaizuka suffering a defeat at the hands of my father-in-law.

The youth in the black jacket and black trousers began breathlessly:

"That's all wrong, all that about the clock being at ten to twelve. He's got it wrong. Got it wrong because. . ."

This method of speaking, or rather shouting, caused immediate laughter, although it didn't give him pause, for he went on:

". . . it's not ten minutes to noon. Not ten minutes to lunchtime, so no one's going to feel hungry. So it's stopped. Right. Still, ten minutes later . . . of course, the clock's got to be mended, got to be put right first. Then, if it's. . ."

A lot of people were laughing quite openly by the time he'd reached this point, and their laughter was obviously unfriendly, some of it even contemptuous. But Kaizuka went on:

"The great bell would strike twelve times. Okay. But that would mean it was tomorrow. The day would have changed. A new day. Are you with me? Okay, then. It's not 11:50 A.M. now; it's 11:50 P.M. Ten minutes to midnight. It's pitch black. That's how it is."

This imposing image certainly impressed people, or at least it took them by surprise. They all became quiet again, and one person at the back clapped loudly. I saw that Kaizuka had been visibly encouraged, but, at the same time, someone to my left a little way behind me bawled out in a crude voice:

"Put that clock right and you'll find it's five o'clock."

At this the audience collapsed laughing, although I imagine there was more than one reason for this. Naturally, if one were to repair a clock that had stopped at ten to twelve it would mean adjusting it to the right time, and obviously the odds against it striking midnight ten minutes after being repaired must be enormous, so presumably people were laughing at their not having noticed that. Again, some people were probably jeering at Kaizuka for not having noticed it himself and for persisting in lecturing away at the top of his voice. Perhaps some people had burst out laughing at this quick-witted way of reminding everybody that valuable drinking time was already being lost. I also felt quite a lot of them were laughing at the crude voice itself. I know I also laughed, but even in my own case I can't work out exactly why.

This storm of hilarity obviously shook Kaizuka. He was made sufficiently angry, however, to grab hold of both microphones, one in each hand, and before the audience had quietened down he started off again.

"All right, then. This is the point. Revolution. . . . . . Photography as an art, that's a lot of old hat. I'm not interested. If someone's got talent or not doesn't. . . . . . The problem is. . . . . . First of all, the word 'citizen' just mixes up the capitalists and the workers, doesn't it? What's just been said . . . . . . funny. . . . . . ."

From this point on the speech became really ragged, and one could only make out bits of it.

"Present system . . . . . . adhesion . . . . . . this present point in time . . . . . . lay explosives under . . . . . . repudiation as the ideological starting point. . . . . . ."

These fragmented cries sounded like a ritual form of curse. I could no longer bear to look at his contorted face as he went on raving, it was much too painful. Rather than produce these ready-made, hand-me-down phrases he'd have been much better off lecturing them on "city death," I thought regretfully and turned my eyes away. I noticed the president and the managing director were whispering to each other, obviously discussing how they could bring it to an end.

They were relieved of their worries, however, by another strange event. Somewhere near the door at the back of the hall a thick, guttural voice shouted out something unintelligible. This was followed by a woman's voice telling him to stop it. The drunken voice then called out words that could be clearly heard this time.

"Students. All hopeless. Ought to pack it up. . ."

An old man made his way down the center aisle toward the dais, followed by an old lady in kimono who looked peculiarly calm considering she was trying to restrain him.

"Please, Yama," she said, "I'm asking you, so please. . ."

It was Granny Utako and her lover. On making this discovery Yukari, Otoyo, and I all gasped out in surprise together, and also half stood up on the same impulse as the two of them passed by and stopped before the dais. Granny's face was red in patches, but she seemed to be more exhilarated than embarrassed by his drunken state, smiling happily as she told him to stop all his nonsense. It seemed to me like the happiness one can hear in the extravagant tones a mother's voice takes on when she's reproving her child for some naughtiness, the reproof being a mere gesture, since she's actually enchanted by what the wicked little rascal has been up to.

The man in the cap, fresh out of detention, raised his right arm slowly as the buzzing and snickering of the crowded hall continued, and pointed at Kaizuka.

"You students. You're all words. Just words. . . Students shouldn't try to talk . . . clever. . ." he shouted.

The young man in black was so amazed he couldn't say a word in reply, while Hirayama, wearing an ancient-looking three-piece suit and a shirt with no tie, suddenly turned around with surprising speed to face the audience, staggering only slightly as he did so, and began to address them with great good humor.

"Talk about revolution. Huh! Nothing as sinister as that, I can tell you. Playing about, that's all it is. Look at me. Just throwing stones for a bit of a laugh, I was. Then I got picked up, and I'm glad to be able to report that this day, this very day, they let me out after two weeks in

358

the nick. Had a few beers to celebrate. Not all that much, mind...
Revolution. Who do they think they are? Why can't them students
give their names like everybody else? Say it out straight like a man
without all that carrying on? Then maybe we could all stop wasting
each other's time. The police are workers too, you know. It's a crying
shame the way you lot won't try to help them."

Granny's lover had rather delicate, somewhat oily features, but also
a tough-looking physique considering his age. While he talked, Granny Utako stood at his side keeping up a series of interjectory complaints, such as "Oh dear, what a thing to say," or "It was all thanks
to Mr. Kaizuka," or "Come on, let's go now," but these tended to
sound more like supplementary comments supporting what he had to
say, or even like those high-pitched ejaculations the accompanying
musician lets forth at times during the recital of an old-fashioned
ballad. Everybody laughed boisterously, not only because the dicker-
ing between these two was so funny but because Kaizuka, who had
relinquished his hold on the microphones and now stood in a daze immediately above the two, looked so ludicrous. In particular Granny's
remark that "it was all thanks to Mr. Kaizuka" was found especially
hilarious because, of course, nobody had any idea what she was talking about.

Hirayama misunderstood this irresponsible laughter as encouragement, so he continued happily:

"Look, what I say is, how about some consideration for each other,
a little kindness for a change. Now, when that policeman nabbed me,
well, he was a bit rough, I say he was, but that couldn't be helped. I
mean, the reason I got out today is because of the kindness of a very
decent gentleman. He got in touch with one of the bigwigs in the
Metropolitan Police, and they settled everything in a friendly way.
That gentleman's name is..."

"Oi, stop that!" cried Kaizuka from the dais, his face having suddenly changed color. The voice boomed out via the microphone but had
no lasting effect on Hirayama, for now he appeared to be striking a
deliberate pose, raising both arms into the air.

"That gentleman's name..." he repeated, whereupon Yukari jabbed
her elbow violently into my stomach, and Kaizuka shouted out to
him again to stop. This time it was only the sound of his actual, non-

amplified voice, for he had tried to jump down in order to restrain Hirayama, but got his foot caught in the microphone cord and crashed full length upon the dais. As people stood up to get a better look Hirayama finally announced the gentleman's name.

"The chancellor of the exchequer."

As I saw it he'd mistaken MITI for the Ministry of Finance, but for the audience, of course, it was plain gibberish, and since they all felt they'd stood up just to be told this obvious nonsense they laughed again, and it was during the laughter that Kaizuka rose once more to his feet. Granny, as was her habit when she was amazed by anything, had raised her clenched right hand and flashed the fingers open, and she went on standing there in that pose. Hirayama, feeling even more encouraged by the additional laughter, which he insisted on misinterpreting as more approval, had opened his mouth, obviously prepared to go on with his address.

However, it was now Hirayama's turn to be taken aback. The plump, fair-faced editor, face wreathed in smiles, had ascended to the dais, taken one of the microphones in his hand, and was now saying the following words:

"Well, certainly an afternoon full of surprises... At this point, however, I am obliged to announce ... I am quite desperate for a drink. We will now adjourn to another room, where the party's to be held."

Cries of assent greeted this announcement, accompanied by a burst of clapping of an intensity that had certainly not been heard so far. People left their seats with shouts and whoops of delight, and this remarkable prizegiving ceremony had ended in appropriate absurdity.

18

"If all prizegivings were like that they'd be worth going to," said Kentaro Horikawa. "I'm glad I came."

He had a glass of whisky in one hand. With his other he put a cigarette to his lips, and a bar hostess, employed to help out at the party, lit it for him. One of the journalists who'd come forward at the time of the Kaizuka disturbances to lean against the wall and make notes was also holding a glass of whisky, and asked Horikawa with a quizzical look what had happened to his own wristwatch.

"I was really very fortunate today. I forgot to wear it."

"That means you're outside the framework of modern civic society, does it?"

"That's right."

The hostess butted in, trying to wheedle the novelist into going to the bar where she worked after this, but he was unenthusiastic about it, saying the drinks cost too much there.

"Still, surprises me the way people like lecturing. I can't stand it myself."

"Oh, they're not expensive, really. Oh, please do."

"Exhibitionism, I suppose."

"Must be. Used to be called presumption in the past. Its stock seems to have gone up lately."

"The influence of television. . ."

"Goes back further than that. Remember during the war the way the local barbers and grocers became leaders of neighborhood associations and gave lectures on air-raid precautions and suchlike? I suspect it all started round about then."

I moved away from the vicinity of these two amusing people toward the center table. I was due to go on to another party but was feeling pretty hungry. On the nearest silver platter there were pink slices of smoked salmon. I put my whisky glass down on the white tablecloth and helped myself to two slices on a plate. Then Carrot Otoyo approached.

"So this is where you were."

"Would you like some? It looks good."

"Maybe I will."

I added a fork to my plate and passed it to her, and took some more for myself.

"How's Granny getting on? It's so crowded here I've no idea..."

"In the corner over there." She indicated where with a jerk of her head. "She's sitting down all nice and friendly with that drunken old man, the one she calls Yama. You're not supposed to sit down at a party like this, are you?"

"Well, if you're old. Anyway, considering what's been going on today, bad manners have ceased to mean anything."

"Really," she said, as if sighing with relief, smiling slowly.

"What about Kaizuka?"

"Oh, he's in an awful state. He's sitting on the dais and just won't move."

"Has he injured himself?"

"Doesn't seem to have. He's insisting that everyone has to come back and listen to what he has to say. He says that was the understanding he'd been given, only he puts it all in a much more difficult way. Of course it's hopeless. At first the editor and Mrs. Mabuchi and I tried to talk him out of it, saying all sorts of things to persuade him, but the editor soon went away, and then so did I..."

"So Yukari's doing all the persuading by herself?"

"Still, she'll soon be here, I expect," she said, drinking up her whisky before asking me in a whisper if they had any saké.

"I should think so," I said and asked a passing hostess for some.

I was then spotted by my jovial father-in-law, who called out to me and started to approach, but he was stopped on the way by a fat little man of about fifty with a moustache. The man said in respectful tones that he was employed in some advertising capacity somewhere, bowing low and producing his card, and praised my father-in-law's address in exaggerated terms.

"Oh, just off the cuff, you know," he replied happily. "Put together from things I'd read in various books."

"The fact is, sir, my dead grandfather used to be something of a playboy, you know, and he actually saw the great fire in Yoshiwara from the top of the Yoshiwara dike."

"Oh, really ... your grandfather... Dead, is he?... I see."

"He often talked about it. I can remember the exact date of the fire, he said it so often. The ninth of April, nineteen hundred and eleven. Anyway, that clock at Kadoebi made a terrific noise, he said, when it all burned up and the works came crashing down. Tremendous clattering sound..."

"Ah."

"Tremendous clattering sound..."

"That is a most interesting recollection—most valuable in terms of cultural history," my father-in-law replied, making a friendly acknowledgment and setting forth again, when this time a fat man around thirty approached and produced his card.

"I go to *yakuza* movies every week, and I found your talk extremely interesting. The kind I like are the ones about women gamblers, you know, when they hold the dice like that and raise their arms..."

The man had mistaken him for a passionate fan like himself, and launched into an account of his own ideas and recollections, which Mr. Nonomiya handled with the occasional "I see" and "I quite agree," as if he were genuinely following what the man was talking about, bringing it to an end with a polite bow and finally arriving where I was.

"You seem very popular," I said.

"No, no," he said, blushing with pleasure. "I only did it because it suddenly occurred to me as the one way to bring things to a satisfactory conclusion, but I'm afraid I went on for much too long and made rather a nuisance of myself. Still, it seems to have gone down quite well. I've been asked to give two lectures on the strength of it."

He was obviously satisfied with things, but added:

"Is Kaizuka really performing some sit-down strike?"

"Yes, apparently," I said, and Otoyo explained that at first he'd been thinking of using the microphone and addressing the empty hall, but had at least realized how stupid that would be so he'd given up the idea. She now held a glass of saké in her right hand, and my father-in-law turned to her and gave a large nod.

"Well, he's young, so he soon loses his temper. Not all that surprising, I suppose. . ." he said, although there could be little doubt he was making a veiled hint of dissatisfaction with the aspersion cast on the mediatory effects of his own lecture. "He complained I'd mixed up capitalists and workers, but the citizen is, originally, a gentleman, a member of the master class, a bourgeois. The fact that working-class people these days are pretending to be citizens is just a vulgar piece of inverted snobbery."

Since he had now started a reactionary counterargument to Kaizuka's remarks, I thought I'd better put in a few words that could be seen as friendly to either party.

"Well, he's a young man with a mind of his own. Even so, things like that will happen. But that's the way it goes, surely?" I said, and then attempted to stress the legal aspects of the case. "After all, it was agreed that he'd be allowed to speak providing *nothing else unforeseen* occurred. He was promised he could say *a few words*. Then, when he'd just started on his few words, something unforeseen did occur. . ."

My father-in-law seemed unimpressed by this legalistic quibble and took a large sip of whisky.

"I don't know, but young people nowadays seem to talk quite differently when they're speaking to an individual and when addressing a large audience. I don't think one can go as far as to talk about a split personality, but I must say the old distinction between the public and the private seems to require a new interpretation these days."

This was an obvious criticism so I followed suit with a few critical remarks about contemporary youth, and then tried to put in a good word.

"Still, as Granny said, he really did help her during the riot two weeks ago. I don't know what might have happened if he hadn't been there. He's a very considerate young man, at least in private. That was quite clear by the way he behaved when there was a danger of my name being mentioned."

"Your name?" my father-in-law repeated suspiciously, and so I explained (lowering my voice, of course) what had been going on between Granny and her lover, and what conclusion we'd expected to his speech. Right from the beginning, despite being awkwardly conscious of Otoyo's presence, he showed a striking interest, and once he realized she knew all about it, his interest was transformed into a veritable passion for this piece of gossip, and he asked a number of questions about Hirayama.

"I wonder why he thought Mr. Mabuchi was the chancellor of the exchequer?" Otoyo asked.

"Could have misheard, or might have been a failure of memory," my father-in-law replied immediately. "Then it might have been out of vanity, trying to show himself as a person of importance with connections in high places. A criminal could well behave that way, you know."

In this case he was only using the word "criminal" to indicate someone arrested for throwing stones at the riot police, and Otoyo expressed a ladylike surprise and interest in the phenomenon.

"So that's how it was. The young man was bravely sacrificing his own interests in order to protect your honor," he said in an old-fashioned way. "Still, it was very rash of me to invite Mother to a place like this. I can't imagine why I ever thought of such a thing."

He gave a sigh, and this prompted Otoyo to take up the case for the defense.

"But if Utako hadn't come in at that moment . . . well, really. She came just at the right time, I thought. Otherwise it would have been even worse for poor Mr. Kaizuka."

"As it turned out, of course, you're right. The trouble is she is so completely undiscriminating. You won't know about this, naturally, but I've had nothing but trouble from her for years."

This querulous remark presumably aroused loyal feelings of outrage in Otoyo, for she knocked back two fingers of saké and said:

"Still, she's a good person, a real good sort."

Mr. Nonomiya made only a halfhearted attempt to respond in the same terms:

"She's a good person, all right. The trouble is she does tend to get rather carried away."

That was an unfortunate remark, since Otoyo herself was sufficiently carried away by it to make an uncalled-for confession.

"Impetuous, yes. But isn't that just because she's so good-hearted? Yes, she does get carried away. Perhaps goes a bit too far. Like that time when I broke out of jail, she didn't have to go as far as that. I only wanted her to cover up for me a bit, but instead she did just about everything she could think of."

The glass fell from my father-in-law's hand and shattered on the floor, although he went on staring at Otoyo's face for some time. Not surprisingly it had come as a real shock to discover that this ordinary (he'd assumed) if attractive middle-aged lady standing before him was actually a convicted criminal who'd also broken out of prison. The burglar Carrot Otoyo herself finally realized what she'd said and gave a little cry, placing her hand swiftly over her mouth. Luckily, just as the waiter was bending down to sweep up the bits of glass, the company president came up with another man, expressing in a loud voice his thanks for the way he'd praised their choice of prize, and a hostess also approached and offered him another drink; so Otoyo chose this opportune moment to glance quickly at me and move off in the direction of Granny and Hirayama.

The president introduced this man and another to my father-in-law. One of them was a drama critic and the other was a director of a different publishing house. My father-in-law then introduced them to me. The drama critic praised him for his delivery, and the director asked him when the wristwatch had been invented, in an attempt to find something to talk about.

"I believe, sir, you said it wasn't until the twentieth century..."

"Yes, quite right. I am not, in fact, any sort of specialist on the subject and so I can't claim to be absolutely sure, but I believe it was at the time of the Boer War in South Africa when an English officer, tired of perpetually having to take his watch from his pocket, thought up the idea out of pure frustration. That would put it at 1899, or thereabouts. A man in military uniform is, of course, fairly wound about with various kinds of strings and straps, for his canteen, his telescope, and so on, and it must have been a real nuisance getting the watch out. Being a pocket watch, naturally it would have been pretty large, sticking out on both sides of his wrist, I imagine."

While this conversation was going on I also moved off, but in the opposite direction to Otoyo, intending to go back to the hall and persuade Kaizuka to give up his protest and come back with me to the party. I was worried about Yukari, but most of all I felt sorry for Kaizuka (though I suppose one could say he only had himself to blame) and felt I owed him a debt of thanks anyway. I found Yukari, however, near the entrance to the hall, happily talking to Oguri.

"Hello, is Kaizuka carrying on his sit-down all by himself?" I said to Yukari, who had a dark glass of Coca-Cola in her hand.

"No. He's given up. On reflection, he said, he'd decided it was a stupid thing to do. He told me to keep these for him."

She was holding the prize and the prize money, plus the certificate which had been folded in two, under her arm.

"She won't let me have them no matter how much I offer to hold them for her," said Oguri with a smile. "Perhaps she's worried a stranger like me might run off with them."

"A reasonable anxiety," I said. "Still, where has he got to?"

"I imagine at this very moment he's engaged in a quarrel with that drunkard, about the students and the revolution. . ." Oguri said.

"That's more than likely," I replied glibly, although I found the idea extremely improbable. "Whole thing was an awful mess anyway," I muttered, helping myself to a whisky from the tray a waiter had proffered. Oguri smiled.

"I always thought there was supposed to be a rule that politics and religion shouldn't be mentioned on social occasions such as parties. It must have come from abroad, that one, because it's pretty meaningless here. The Japanese have never thought seriously about God, and being even less serious about politics is a form of common sense in this country."

"And yet, quite recently, suddenly. . ."

"That's it," he said. "The old Japanese traditions really ought to be kept up. The times have certainly changed and I don't even seem to have noticed it happening. It's like that clock he was going on about— I don't mean his interpretation of it—which struck midnight ages ago while I was just standing about in a trance not noticing the new day had begun. And now see how busy and excitable the world has become."

"Sounds like a sequel to what you were saying about being tall," Yukari put in.

"What's that?" I asked.

Oguri explained what he and Yukari had just been laughing about. He'd been excessively tall right from primary school days, something he'd thought was a major handicap, so he'd forced himself to stoop in order to be as much like the others as possible. This had turned into a habit, hence his permanently rounded shoulders. Still, a lot of young people were tall nowadays, and nobody of his size would be considered a freak the way he had been, and he regretted now he hadn't kept his back good and straight and acquired a decent posture. He felt he'd been a complete fool trying to conceal the way he was.

"I see. Not merely a change in average height but in social attitudes as well," I said.

"Still, it was your own fault for trying to be like everyone else," said Yukari.

"That's a very contemporary way of thinking," Oguri persisted. "Up until recently, not being different was always considered a virtue." He had another sip of his drink and then made a very strange proposal. He suggested that since I was all right in that respect, being neither tall nor round-shouldered, I should stand for prefectural governor back home on the progressive party ticket, for I was bound to be elected. I dismissed the idea with a wave of the hand.

"Come off it. I've already rejected a similar proposal, anyway. Well, not all that similar, as it was for mayor, and for the conservatives as well."

"No, I think the progressive ticket is right for you."

"Why?"

"Look at your record. Refusing to go to the Ministry of Defense would go down big. Make that your sales point, because that really is something. Stand there proudly before them as the man who chose to preserve peace, and the women's vote is all yours. After all, you're not round-shouldered. That youthful graying hair is quite distinguished. Make sure all your photographs are taken *en profil...*"

What I should have done was just laugh at an obvious joke and take no more notice, but I was unwise enough to reply:

"Still, if I did go for something like that it would be under the conservative banner. Of course, I'm not going to stand anyway."

This gratuitous remark brought the conversation to a brief standstill, and for a moment Oguri's face was quite serious as he looked intently at me. Yukari was staring silently at me, too.

368

"Would you?" said Oguri, and then, very slowly, "Yes, I suppose you would."

"Certainly I would. I mean, just look at the political situation in this country today. The place is swarming with fanatical conservatives. That's especially true of my home town which, as you well know, is an absolute conservative stronghold. Naturally, my great-grandfather played his part and more in making that come about. If you want to do anything in that part of the world you're bound to go that way. If you don't want to get anything done, of course, then that's a different matter. It's hard enough getting elected on a progressive ticket in the first place but, just for the sake of argument, let's assume an election could be won by youthful enthusiasm and all the rest of it. Then what would happen? I'll tell you. Nothing, because a progressive governor would be able to do nothing. Anyway," I added, laughing, "we shouldn't be talking about politics at a party, should we?"

"You're quite right," said Oguri, "but perhaps this only shows that, surprisingly, we aren't lagging behind the times after all."

This was no attempt to change the subject, however, and although his tone of voice remained as frivolous as ever the expression on his face was perfectly serious.

"If I may be allowed a comment as an idle spectator, I must say I feel it would be a great pity to abandon this project. 'Progressive Governor in Conservative Stronghold'—now that's my idea of a headline," he said, apparently pleased with the irresponsibility of his own remark, and continuing: "After all, would it matter all that much if, as governor, you weren't able to accomplish anything? Surely there'd be sufficient significance in the fact that you'd managed to win an election on the progressive ticket. Or is that an odd way of thinking?"

I found myself being led astray by Oguri and entirely forgetting that what we were arguing about was the purest of fictions.

"I can't go along with you there. After all, this isn't a question of ideas or ideologies, is it? The issues are much more practical. If you look at the people in that region who support the progressives, there's hardly a single person of any ability among them. You can probably work out why. Anybody who's a bit clever or talented goes to the conservative side. There's nothing that can be done about that. Besides, as people, I wouldn't trust any of them on either side. As far as that goes the conservative lot might be slightly better. It's very much like central politics in that respect."

"Maybe you're right," said Oguri, nodding; and then he turned to Yukari and asked her gently if there was something the matter. I looked and saw that my young wife, standing by the wall with its pink, white, and gold patterned paper, was looking strangely depressed as she gazed at the two of us, principally at me. She was, in fact, observing, perhaps reappraising me, with eyes quite different from the way they normally looked, and she didn't reply to his question. She was like a child lost in a town suddenly grown unfamiliar, who could only gaze in confusion on something she thought she knew, in near panic, not knowing which way to go.

"What's wrong?" I also asked her.

"Somehow," she finally said, "the image has suddenly changed."

"My image?"

"Yes. I feel a bit confused. That's all."

"Ah, you were imagining your husband as governor cutting tapes and so on," said Oguri, trying to make a joke of it.

"No. Not that," she said, and then added something I'd never even imagined as a possibility: "He said it was your example that encouraged him to do it."

"My example?..."

"That's what he said. That rebel act just now. He told me so."

"But what had I done?"

"Don't you know?"

"No."

"The Ministry of Defense business."

"But that was only..." I cried in an unintentionally loud voice, but it was swallowed up in the hubbub of the party, the laughter of the guests and the sexy chatter of the hostesses. For a moment I felt as if I were suddenly enclosed in a transparent cocoon amid it all. As I stared at her with wide-open eyes I must have had the most vacuous expression on my face.

"Ah, I see," said Oguri in a kind of groan, and then he explained the matter at high speed for my benefit, since I was still looking baffled.

"What it means is that the young man saw your refusal of that transfer as a very honest, indeed heroic, act of rebellion. Most people would look at it like that, in fact, but the difference in his case was that he wanted to emulate you. Then by chance he found that the boss of the selection committee for this photography prize he'd applied for was a very dodgy kind of professor at his old university who'd been up to no good at the time of the student troubles there. It hadn't meant much when he first submitted his pictures, but once he'd won the prize it began to worry him. When you're young there's a tendency to blame yourself for all sorts of things, as if you'd taken the responsibility for everything in the world upon your own shoulders. That's where the desire for ideological consistency, a kind of intellectual purity, comes from—something that I think, by the way, should be respected. At least I personally feel more sympathetic toward it than otherwise. So he wanted his own behavior to make sense, even if only to himself. He wanted his actions to be consistent with his beliefs, and thought the way to do so was to behave in that spectacular fashion. Still, he couldn't quite make up his mind. But there was one thing that encouraged him to do what he felt he had to do, and that was your example, because Eisuke Mabuchi had stuck to his principles, a bureaucrat at MITI had made that anti-war, anti-militaristic gesture... Something along those lines, wasn't it?"

"He didn't spell it out quite like that," said Yukari, but she was admitting it was pretty near the truth even if the words weren't the same.

I looked down at the floor and gave a deep sigh. Oguri laughed and asked what I was sighing about, because he couldn't see why I should; but Yukari ignored my sigh.

"And now you talk like that, all reactionary and facing up to reality. I don't know what I'm supposed to think. The image is all wobbly and blurred now. Which is the real you?"

She sounded halfway between laughter and tears, as if she were struggling to find words to explain what she meant. I could reply to neither of them, being so amazed that an incident in my past which

I'd thought all over and done with years ago should have this power to work upon the present and spark off an incident that had excited and confused so many people. I thought it was probably like what a mountain climber must feel when he learns that a magnifying glass he lost in the mountains has caused a forest fire.

"Well, no matter," said Oguri, trying to cheer me up. "It's an ill wind, as they say, and at least Mr. Nonomiya's trade is flourishing, thanks to you. An act of filial piety, indeed. Young Kaizuka will be left out in the cold, of course, and the editors will try to kill him off; but you can't be sure how it'll work out because the young subeditors will probably still want to use him. The times have changed after all."

"Left out in the cold?" asked Yukari, but she received no answer, for Oguri had addressed a middle-aged man in a purple suit with hair like a shaggy poodle, and gone off to speak to him. I was thinking I'd have to be leaving shortly when someone tapped me on the shoulder, and I turned around to be confronted by the pale, shiny, smiling face of Otoyo, who said to my wife:

"What's this? Coca-Cola? Try some saké, young lady. You can take it, I'm sure."

I asked her how Granny was getting on, and she replied:

"Sleeping peacefully, whistling away, the two of them. And young Kaizuka's sitting beside them, drinking hard, with a dreadful look in his eye..."

19

I arrived at the next party a little late, and there were people I had to spend time with afterward so I didn't get home until 11:30. The house was completely dark. Neither Yukari nor Granny had returned.

I telephoned Yukari's parents, but they knew nothing. It took me some time to get this negative information since Mrs. Nonomiya started off with her own complaints about her husband's not being home yet, and she went on about that. When she'd finally admitted she knew nothing about either of them, the ex-professor seemed to turn up, and she started on about him again, until a horribly drunk father-in-law came to the phone and began singing an old dorm song from high school. This gave her another reason to tell him off and he put down the receiver.

I slept very badly that night, waking up every hour or so and each time looking at my wife's bed, but the bedside lamp, which had been left on, only shone in vain on the fact that she wasn't there. I didn't worry about Granny at all.

20

The dazzling sunlight of a beautiful day woke me up the next morning, not surprisingly since, besides failing to undress last night and so sleeping in my shirt and trousers, I'd forgotten to close the curtains. There was still no Yukari in the neighboring bed, and the bedcover was neatly in place, the only sign of any disturbance being my jacket and tie thrown diagonally across it.

The bedside clock said it was seven o'clock, and my wristwatch, which I'd taken off and laid beside it when I went to sleep last night, registered exactly the same time to the minute. The company car would be here for me at eight. I got up and went downstairs, looking in Granny's room just to make sure, and then took a shower, sensing the deep silence of the house as I did so.

Once I'd changed I telephoned Yukari's parents, but neither she nor Granny were there. My mother-in-law made a great to-do about it and went to wake up her husband, although all he could do was apologize for the anxiety I was suffering, and then give me an account of the various bars he'd been taken to by the editor of *Ginga*, which was all to no purpose. The one thing he said that could be considered information was that when he'd got around to noticing such things he'd realized neither Yukari, nor Granny, nor Hirayama, nor Carrot Otoyo, nor Oguri, were present any more at the party. I sighed, and my father-in-law apologized for the umpteenth time, and then added in a ponderous, unhappy tone of voice:

"It does look as if they might have had, well, something like a head-on collision in a taxi. Better get in touch with the police right away."

"Yes, well, I had thought of that. Still. . ."

"Um, yes. Yet if they had met with an accident on their way home from the party, given the considerable length of time that has elapsed since then, it seems only reasonable to assume that something . . . particularly when there has been no contact from anyone as yet."

"Yes, but. . ."

"If one of them were conscious, then contact would be made. Since it has not, one is forced to the regrettable conclusion ... although nothing conclusive can yet be said, of course."

I said nothing.

"However," added my father-in-law, now completely reversing his argument, "perhaps the wiser plan would be to wait a little longer. Probably best not to be too eager to contact the police, the reason being. . ."

"Yes."

"Mother has acquired that kind of record, and it may be she has caused some form of trouble again. I'm not necessarily speaking of any *affaire criminelle* but just some sort of trouble. If we were now casually to telephone the police announcing her absence, it could well serve as a means of informing against her, don't you agree?"

"Um."

"Therefore it behooves us for the time being to consider whether it might not be wiser to continue a calm appraisal of the situation."

There was little point in trying to argue the matter with an old man with a hangover, so I brought the conversation to a close in some suitable way. But, on consideration, I suppose I must have been affected by his opinion to some extent, since I had intended to ring the police if there'd been no communication received at his house, and yet I didn't. I began to think there well might be some possible link between the disappearance of the two and Granny's "record." It was also a fact that both Hirayama and Otoyo had records as well, so it made the suspicion all the stronger. Still, this notion was destroyed by Oguri's reply when I phoned him immediately afterward. By the tired voice in which he responded I was aware I'd woken him up, but after he'd muttered how strange it all was he gave me a piece of information that was doubly disturbing, being so imprecise and open to varying interpretations. He said he'd talked briefly to a number of people at the party, then returned to Yukari, with whom he was engaged in jocular small talk about Mayo and other subjects when he happened to notice Kaizuka walking briskly out of the room. He was obviously leaving for good, so Oguri told Yukari she'd better hand over the prize money and other things to him now. Yukari ran after him, and that was the last he'd seen of her.

I gave something like a groan in response, so Oguri went on:

"Of course, she might well have come back. I was talking to a variety of other people, and wasn't particularly paying attention. I think Otoyo had already left. Wonder if she managed to sell all her carrot wine?"

This seemed something pretty irrelevant to be worrying about at this particular moment, but he continued:

"Granny went off with that old man of hers. That was before Kaizuka left."

"Um."

"Well, that's about it."

"Is it?"

"Wouldn't be a traffic accident by any chance? Perhaps you should try her parents' home."

"Already have. Anyway, since the two of them weren't together. . ." I said, not quite sure what to say next when I suddenly felt I couldn't bear the whole thing any longer, and let some of my frustration pour out. "Ever since we've had Yukari's grandmother in the house things have all been going wrong. I suppose I've told you this before anyway. Still, she's caused nothing but problems throughout her life. Look at the way she behaved yesterday. I mean, she's just a mess; there's no sense to what she does. Sometimes goes days without cleaning the passageway, so it gets thick with dust. And we still haven't been able to find a replacement for Tsuru."

How much sense this kind of grumbling could make to Oguri I'm not sure, although he replied that he'd heard something about it yesterday from Yukari; and then he asked if I was going to work today, speaking in a tone of such courteous, distant concern that it conveyed to me all too clearly how wretched I must appear to a third party.

"Yes, I'll have to be leaving shortly. Got three meetings today. Always busy with something or other. Sorry to have woken you up about this."

"That's all right; it was time for me to get up, anyway. I'm sorry I couldn't be of any help."

I made a similarly wooden statement of thanks and rang off.

I tried shaving with my electric razor while heating up a saucepan of milk, but didn't manage it very well, particularly around the Adam's apple. While I was struggling away with the razor the milk boiled over, which meant getting another bottle out of the fridge to mix with it, so I drank twice as much as I'd intended to. I scribbled a message, which I left in the hallway, had a quick look around to make sure everything was locked and all the proper things switched off, and when I got outside I saw the company car had already arrived, the driver solemnly dusting it with a long-handled feather brush as though performing some religious incantation over it. We greeted each other, with me managing to achieve a certain bright cheerfulness in my voice, and the driver sounding much more jovial and happy. However, at that moment a taxi, driven in merciless style, screeched to a halt in front of the house, and Granny Utako got out.

Granny smiled at me in what seemed an embarrassed attempt to conceal the awkwardness of her returning home at this hour in the morning, or it may have been the sun in her eyes that made her screw them up like that, or both. I told my driver to wait a moment and called out to Granny to hurry on into the house for, after her taxi had driven off, she'd just stood there dithering and looking at me in a bemused way. But she responded to my command all right, and with a hoarse cry set off toward the house at almost a run.

I opened the door and stood with her in the entrance hall, giving her a brief account of the situation, while Granny explained at some length that Hirayama had said he didn't feel too good so they'd gone outside to get some fresh air, and from then on she knew nothing about what might have happened at the party, though she'd rung up three times yesterday evening but nobody had answered.

"Well, that's as it may be. The point is you must get Yukari to ring me at the office as soon as she comes home. And you must stay in all day. You mustn't put a foot outside. You're in charge of the telephone, all right? And phone the Nonomiya house to tell them you've got back safely."

Granny nodded to all this and then mumbled:

"I wonder what's happened to her? Really that child..."

"I don't know and I can't even start to guess," I replied, and just then the telephone rang. It made a noise twice as loud as usual and seemed so very urgent I leaped up into the house with my shoes still on and scampered down the passageway, convinced it must be Yukari. However, it wasn't her voice at the other end but a man complaining what a dreadful time he'd had in Fukuoka. I had to give him my name twice before he cottoned on, whereupon he made a very curt apology and rang off just as sharply.

In the car I opened some papers on my lap and passed my eye over them each time we were held up in the traffic, hammering the relevant figures into my head. I had to give a report at one of today's meetings, but I'd always found it pretty easy to mug up things in this way, and even on a very special morning like this the ability remained practically unchanged.

When the car had stopped for the umpteenth time the driver said:

"Seems like there's going to be a new manager at the Tochigi factory, doesn't it, sir?"

"At Tochigi?"

"Yes, sir."

"That's news to me," I said, which seemed to take the edge off his confidence.

"Must be a mistake, then, I suppose," he mumbled, and I replied that he wasn't a very reliable source of information, pointing out two other instances where he'd got hold of the wrong end of the stick; and yet I noticed what had begun as a jest on my part was starting to sound spiteful so I quickly shut my mouth. The driver seemed unconcerned, however, and asked me, with a brief laugh, to stop bullying him, while I apologized for taking his mind off his work. The line of cars slowly began moving again.

I had one meeting that morning and two in the afternoon. The first one dragged on into the lunch hour, and although I was expecting a visitor at exactly one o'clock I still insisted on going out for lunch because it gave me a chance to telephone home. So the first thing I did was find a phone booth, call up a nearby restaurant and order a simple meal, and then ring home. On the second ring Granny picked up the receiver, which showed she was doing as she'd been told. Yukari had not come back yet.

I then dialed the number of Oguri's company to discuss with him what I ought to do, but he wasn't there. The switchboard operator asked me my name but I didn't bother to give it. As I was about to leave the booth I noticed two fat volumes of the telephone directory, and I found myself looking up Murata's number, putting in the coin, and even dialing the third of the seven figures before finally replacing the receiver and listening to the rattle of the returning coin.

"Stupid. Stupid. You're like a complete lunatic," I reproached myself out loud, and my voice echoed in that confined space.

The restaurant was crowded and the food I'd ordered wasn't ready. I was obliged eventually to leave without eating because of the time, but in fact I had no appetite. I walked slowly back to work although I ought to have hurried.

During the third meeting, which wasn't of any particular importance, there was a phone call for me. It was from Oguri.

"You're in conference?" he said, and then, in a whisper, "Back yet?"

"No. At least, only one of them."

"Your wife?"

"Not yet."

"All right, then. Take this down. You ready?"

Oguri had me write down an address, and I asked him the obvious yet unnecessary question.

"Whose is it?"

"It's his apartment. I've tried all the magazines I know of. Probably worked out what I was after, but I don't know. Anyway, he's not at any of them. One said he'd promised to show up this afternoon but he hadn't done so. Everyone's looking for him because of the morning papers. You haven't seen them? Anyway, go to this address and see what's up. If you can't find out anything there you'll just have to report it. Okay then."

He rang off without any of the usual formalities. I handed the telephone to the man next to me and indicated to another that he should go on with what he'd been saying.

I had dinner at the counter of a small eating place I happened to come across. I ordered food and drink and then rang home, but Granny said Yukari hadn't returned yet and burst into tears. She was still crying as I put down the receiver. I asked the man behind the counter to let me have all the morning newspapers he had, which amounted to two ordinary dailies, one specialist economic journal, and also a

379

sports paper which seemed to have been left behind by one of the customers. The two dailies had reports on yesterday's "rebellious act" by Kaizuka. One of them was mainly a sort of encomium of Kaizuka's behavior, and the other gave over most of its space to a strong denunciation of the distinguished photography critic (neither of them mentioned Hirayama); but the main impression I received in both cases was that they were less concerned with reporting the event than turning it into a joke. It felt like reading an account of something totally different to the actual incidents I'd witnessed.

I had just one small flask of saké and forced myself to swallow a bowl of rice, tea, and pickles to finish off the brisk meal, then took a taxi. Kaizuka's apartment was extremely difficult to find, and for a while I was completely lost. I asked passersby and also at a tiny tobacconist's, but received only the vaguest of answers, although since it turned out that it could only be reached by going through a large temple gate, turning right, and going on well into the grounds before finally coming upon a two-story building in the darkness, perhaps it was unreasonable to expect anything but imprecise knowledge of its whereabouts. Anyway, I did eventually find the wooden apartment building, and took my shoes off in the entrance hall. There was a smell of fish being grilled and the sound of two television sets. I soon found Kaizuka's room. It had his visiting card fixed by the door, although the glue had come unstuck at the bottom right-hand corner. I stared at it for a while and then knocked on the wooden door, but there was no reply. At my feet I noticed three editions of the same newspaper (two evening and one morning) and a bottle of milk, while two visiting cards had been inserted in the gap between the door and the doorpost. I took them out and looked at them. They were both from journalists working for the weeklies, and they'd written on them that they wanted to interview him about the prizegiving and would come back later. Even so, I knocked again just to make sure.

"Mr. Kaizuka," I called out. After a while I heard one of the doors behind me open, and I turned around.

"Oh," a woman's voice cried. "What are you doing here, Mr. Mabuchi?"

I think I must have looked at the woman's face for a long time. She was wearing a red sweater over a white blouse and gray slacks, but it was the reddish brown hair that made her unrecognizable. One minute, then two minutes, perhaps even a longer period of time passed, till finally I said her name in a low voice:

"Otoyo?"

Carrot Otoyo smiled. I had completely forgotten she lived in the same apartment house as Kaizuka. I'd seen the name Hagiwara scrawled on a piece of paper on one of the row of shoe lockers in the entrance hall and also on the door across the corridor, but had thought nothing of it.

She told me Kaizuka didn't seem to have come back last night, nor had he been there today. Seeing how preoccupied I looked she went on:

"Was there something you suddenly had to see him about? Anyway, please come in, though I'm afraid it's all rather a mess. At least I'm glad it's you and not a reporter."

She spoke in a friendly way, saying how awful it had been with those journalists coming and going all afternoon. I accepted her invitation.

The robber's den was six mats in size (the same as Granny's room back home), impeccably clean and tidy, nothing like what I'd expected. Still, I felt some incongruity between her red sweater and slacks and the large traditional doll in a glass case. The quilt over the *kotatsu* was in a traditional pattern too, and the cushion she offered me had a folk-craft design. I put my legs inside the warm *kotatsu* and looked at the calendar on the wall with its views of Paris, while Otoyo switched off the television, knelt down in front of the mirror, and quickly put on a wig.

"There you are," she said, turning to face me. "It's me now, isn't it?"

"So that's what it was," I said.

"That's what it was."

The black hair brought out the whiteness of her face, which smiled just a little smugly at me, and she explained that a surprising number of women with white skin had reddish hair, although my wife was one of the exceptions. I looked at the black hair with interest, but this seemed to embarrass her and she produced a bottle of whisky, which I declined. Then she asked:

"Still, what did you want to see Mr. Kaizuka about? I mean, I could always pass on a message."

I puffed away at my cigarette for a while, hesitating as to what I should do, but at last began to explain the situation, although my voice sounded very dejected as I did so. Otoyo listened to me in silence, and finally commented:

"Still, you can't be sure anything like that has happened, can you?"

This certainly cheered me up a bit, but she went on to say:

"I suppose you haven't been paying her any attention lately, have you?"

"No. Not for ten days. Might even be a fortnight."

I replied quite frankly to her much franker question and then, once again (and how many times I'd thought about this since last night I do not know), remembered gloomily how Yukari had told me he was equipped with a really enormous one.

"Well, that's no good, is it?" she said, reproving me with a very serious look. "Doesn't matter how busy you may be. If a woman doesn't have it, why, she can get a nosebleed."

I was impressed by the unhesitating way in which she delivered this information, even if I was skeptical of its truth; and she herself seemed not all that sure when I expressed my doubts.

"That's what I heard at Tochigi. I've never suffered from it myself. Perhaps it's just an old wives' tale?"

She began talking about the inmates at Tochigi and their various lesbian affairs, their quarrels, their concern with their appearance. She said the desire to look nice was even stronger than the desire for a man, and since the use of razors was forbidden the women prisoners broke pieces of glass and used the fragments to shave themselves. She explained in detail the various knacks required in breaking the glass and honing it, the proper way of holding it and so on; although she proudly maintained at the end of this account that she'd never once tried anything so risky herself, so I assumed this was probably as reliable as the talk about nosebleeds. As she saw it, there was no point in making yourself look nice with only the prison staff to look at you, and I laughed in agreement with her sentiments; but as the peal of laughter came to an end it was suddenly replaced by a sigh of quite accidental intensity. Otoyo looked straight at me.

382

"Now, you mustn't upset yourself like that. After all, you may just have somehow missed each other for some reason. Try to look on the bright side. Just wait a bit longer."

She produced two glasses and poured whisky into them, and as we sipped away we began talking again, although my own role was simply to sit there and listen.

In order, perhaps, to cheer me up in some way, Otoyo had chosen a different topic for our conversation. She said how very interesting yesterday's speech by Dr. Nonomiya had been, giving a little shake of the head to indicate how much the whole thing had impressed her.

"You mean about the *yakuza* movies? Or the story about the ghost of the dead mistress haunting the army clock tower?"

"Well, yes, that was very interesting too," she said, hesitating a little and then: "Shall I tell you how I first went wrong? It was to do with a clock, in fact."

"Oh," I said, although as I listened I found it wasn't really about a clock at all so much as a kind of love story, a simple tale of unrequited love. When she was eighteen she'd been employed in the office of a certain large business enterprise. Working in a different section was an unmarried university graduate who commuted from a long distance away and was constantly late. So, when she heard about this at lunch one day, she felt sorry for him and offered to clock in for him each morning when she punched her own card. He was delighted with the idea, but after a year or so his misdemeanor came to light, and he was called before the personnel section to explain his behavior. She herself didn't get into any particular trouble about it, only he told her not to do that with his card any more; and he wasn't particularly nice to her afterward, getting married within a few months.

"Was there anything really going on between the two of you?"

"Of course not. Hardly likely to be. I just thought he was rather super, that's all. Perhaps he took me to the movies once or twice. Still, it does show, I suppose, that I tend to prefer the intellectual type. Someone like you, for example."

"Thank you."

"I came to hate that time clock. I couldn't bear to look at it even. I think that was probably the reason I gave up my job there. At least that's what I was thinking yesterday as I listened to that talk."

"I see. Civic society as a time clock," I said, and then smiled. "Labor supervision must have been lousy if you could get away with a game like that for a whole year."

"I suppose he's probably in charge of his own department by now," she said, with a sad, romantic little smile. "Perhaps even a director."

It was an ordinary enough tale of adolescent infatuation, yet I felt a certain admiration for her intelligence since it required some wit to select from one's past experience a story that illustrated pretty neatly the main theme of what my father-in-law had been saying. At least it showed she'd more or less understood him. She poured some more whisky into both our glasses.

"Still, Mr. Kaizuka is, well, a very nice person, but not the kind I'd go for."

This remark pleased me, presumably because I saw it as relevant in some way to the possibility of a relationship between him and Yukari; for if this intelligent woman said Kaizuka was unattractive then it must be an objective fact and, consequently, he could have no attraction for Yukari either. How much I was persuaded by my own specious argument I don't know, but I said:

"Oh, no good, is he?"

"Not for me. I prefer either a more *yakuza*-type man or someone more intellectual-looking. Kaizuka's neither one nor the other. Then I've never liked younger men..."

"Never? Never at all?"

"Not once. I'll still be the same when I'm an old granny," she said, gazing at me and whispering: "Now, you're just right in those respects. You're an older man, an intellectual..."

"Hold on. This could turn into something serious."

"Well, I could hardly make a play for a man who's come here looking for his wife, could I?"

"I suppose not."

"So we'll have to make it some other time. Still, the very first time we met—which was only yesterday, of course—I thought you weren't at all bad, I can tell you. Just my type, I thought."

She smiled as she said this but, despite the provocative nature of the sentiments expressed, she made no attempt to snuggle up close or anything like that, and remained sitting very properly on the other side of the *kotatsu.*

"Well, I'm very glad, I must say," I said. "I'm very grateful. Thank you. As the saying goes, if one god rejects there's another who saves. Let's hope we can meet in better circumstances next time. Things are a bit too grim at the moment."

"Well, then, perhaps I might have a visiting card now. I could ring you sometime," she said with a mischievous look. "It's all right; I won't use it for anything devious."

"I'm sorry, I forgot."

"Forgetfulness, was it? Why, yesterday you were going to give me one and then decided not to."

"Unmasked, am I?" I smiled as if I'd indeed been caught in the act, and handed her my card. "Please do phone me. At work, that is. They're pretty well bound to know where I am if I'm not in. I rather like the idea of an affair with someone as attractive as you, I must admit. I'll have to go into strict training a week beforehand, of course, drinking lots of carrot wine. . ." I drank my whisky down and continued: "Now that's decided I think I should be on my way. It looks as if I'll simply have to report the whole business."

I stood up, but Otoyo remained sitting and asked me, with a slightly dubious note in her voice, if that meant I was going to tell the police.

"It's all right. I'm not exactly informing on anybody . . . or maybe that's what it boils down to? Still, it could be a traffic accident. It could even be abduction or something like that."

"I suppose so. There's really no saying what it might be," she said with feeling and stood up, too; but then her face became suddenly very stern. She placed her finger to her lips and shushed me to be quiet. I could hear a man's voice coming down the corridor. It was followed by a woman's. They passed by whispering something to each other, and opened the door of the room opposite. The man's voice seemed to be Kaizuka's, but I couldn't be sure, and I had no idea if the woman's voice was Yukari's or not. Otoyo certainly looked very intense as she exchanged speaking glances with me, and she whispered encouragement into my ear, though what I was being encouraged to do I couldn't quite work out. Anyway, I nodded to indicate I would do as she said, although I supposed she had as little idea of what I should do as I had.

The fact is that, up to that moment, I'd assumed Otoyo had simply been pretending to be interested in me as a way of cheering up a man who'd recently been cuckolded; thus it was little more than a joke or, to put it more bluntly, a lie. It was on that assumption I'd given those various cheerful, careless answers to her provocative remarks; and I don't think this involved any prejudice on my part but was merely my habit of always classifying things in a methodical way. After all, there was something a bit too eccentric about the idea of a love affair between a government official turned director of an electrical goods company and a habitual criminal. Even so, I now found her body pressing suddenly against me, and I responded by holding this plump yet somehow slender-feeling frame; and as her white face with a rather desperate expression on it approached me and stopped immediately below mine, my lips touched hers and her eyes closed promptly like the shutter of a camera; then her tongue probed naturally inside my mouth, did one short circuit and quickly withdrew, as she also drew her body artfully away. Carrot Otoyo the burglar's tongue tasted extremely sweet, like the fig syrup that a maid (not Tsuru) in the huge kitchen of my home in the country had let me have a taste of sometime during my childhood.

As I just stood there, Otoyo wiped my mouth with a face towel on which there was some cream, leaning her head to one side in a slightly embarrassed way and smiling. I said, much as if I were whispering to myself, that this was only part payment of the bill, after which I raised my right hand in farewell. Otoyo went on standing there with her head tilted to one side, as though still somewhat embarrassed, saying nothing but looking unquestionably erotic. Once in the corridor outside I had a few deep breaths, then took out my handkerchief and wiped my lips with great care, but obviously Otoyo had already done this very efficiently since the handkerchief remained completely white. As I looked at it, standing before the communal kitchen area, I let out another sigh, a large sigh which was somewhat different, in its degree of complexity, from the way I'd sighed before. There was, after all, the awareness that Carrot Otoyo seemed somehow or other attracted to me, and that was a pleasant, happy feeling; but my mind was equally occupied by a reawareness of the unhappy fact that I was, apparently, a cuckolded husband. The situation was so complex I felt like sighing again, but I contented myself with simply stroking my face slowly with the palm of my hand. For a moment I considered the idea that the woman in Kaizuka's room was actually Mayo, a fiction of enormous attraction for one short moment; but I then shook my head severely as if dismissing this piece of soft, wishful thinking and knocked on Kaizuka's door.

The voice that replied was obviously his. The door slid open a foot or so and Kaizuka saw who it was; or, rather, the door suddenly stopped opening after a distance of ten inches, and his face remained held in the unusually long, narrow frame provided by the edge of the door and the doorpost, hanging there like a portrait, his mouth quivering with astonishment. His expression told me quite clearly it wasn't Mayo in his room. I said nothing, and neither did he at first, but finally, in a voice of such gloom it seemed to be offering his condolences, he said:

"She's here. Would you mind waiting a moment?"

I nodded in reply, and the door closed. I could hear them talking but was quite unable to make out what they were saying. I had to wait quite a while, but when at last Kaizuka opened the door this time he opened it wide.

"Come in," he said, and bowed his head.

The room was exactly the same as Otoyo's in shape, but gave a totally different impression. There were huge blowups of his own work stuck all over the walls, but the main difference was the way the built-in cupboard, normally used for storing bedding, had an extension made of plywood built onto it; obviously he used the enlarged cupboard as a darkroom. As proof of that assumption the electric light on the ceiling had a forked socket in it, one socket holding a white light bulb and the other a black cord that ran down inside the plywood construction. Since the room now had no cupboard it was naturally in a chaotic state, with clothes hanging on the walls, the bedding piled in one corner (looking as if it had only just been tidied away), and heaps of magazines and books and boxes and odd bundles and bottles of whisky all stacked together. The three newspapers he'd just taken in had been placed on top of the bedclothes. The one thing that did seem clear was that this wasn't the bedding he and Yukari had slept on, since he hadn't returned here last night; and what also came immediately to mind was the thought that it was very unlikely Yukari would think of living with Kaizuka in squalor of this kind.

While I was just standing there beneath the light Yukari said:

"I knew you were here. Your shoes were in the hallway."

She had a very tense expression on her face and appeared to be looking through me at some point on the wall at my back. Her face was not so much white as gray, making a funny contrast with the exotic colors of her lamé jacket and the mauve pantalons.

"Yes," I said in a weary, irked tone of voice. "Otoyo let me wait in her room." I was trying to speak in as toneless a manner as I could manage, with an equally expressionless face. "I've got things to say to you, but they can wait. I want to speak to Kaizuka first."

Kaizuka offered me a cushion with green horizontal and vertical stripes on it. It was perfectly clean. I thanked him and sat down cross-legged. So the three of us sat in this very confined space—some four square yards, about a third of the room—and although Kaizuka was also sitting in informal style I was the only one with a cushion, so I felt myself to be in the position of a guest and thus obliged to make some kind of small talk. Consequently I inquired whether that plywood extension was indeed a darkroom, and if it had running water laid on; and Kaizuka replied that he had to carry it here in a bucket and other containers, also giving an account of a minor disaster he'd had recently which made me smile. Yukari also smiled, but in a modest, retiring way. While we were still smiling he shifted into a more formal, kneeling position, and began to speak of "the events of last night" in a very different tone of voice; but I immediately interrupted him, saying there was something else I wanted to talk about first.

"There's this one thing I need to explain, you know: my refusal to go to the Ministry of Defense. There seems to be some misunderstanding on this point, and I also gather it appears to have had something to do with your conduct yesterday. One problem is that I may have misunderstood my own motives to some extent, perhaps even to a fairly large extent. That's how it feels to me now, anyway. I've been thinking about a number of things since yesterday, and one of them has been this."

I gestured to him to sit more comfortably again, and he reluctantly complied. So I began an explanation of my behavior, starting off with my reasons for taking up employment at MITI in the first place.

"It's all a very long time ago, when I would have been the same age as you are now. I have to start with that or otherwise I don't think I can make the reasons for my later behavior clear."

I explained it was not very long after the war had ended, when everybody was still poor and the Japanese economy was in so confused a state no one knew what was going to happen to it. Although I'd graduated from the economics faculty at university I didn't feel like going to work in a business company. In fact I didn't know what I wanted to do. I was on friendly terms with a painter in the neighborhood and often used to visit him, and so, according to the terms of the argument my father-in-law had put forward the day before, this should have indicated some rejection of civic society on my part. But I'd no literary or artistic inclinations, and I don't feel I had any particular dislike of society as such either. In fact I still think I'd entered the economics faculty because I believed the most important things in life were the business and industrial aspects of everyday social existence, ideas that had predominated in my family since the time of my great-grandfather. Perhaps, indeed, the reasons why I hesitated to join an ordinary business company lay in the state of Japanese society at that time. It seems very odd now when one thinks about it, but the prewar ethos still persisted even in large business corporations, and personnel questions weren't related to individual ability but to a form of clannishness whereby promotion was mostly determined by who was related to whom. So I had serious misgivings about the sort of position I'd be able to achieve if I went into business, and the kind of work I'd be allowed to do, quite apart from the question of whether I'd be a success or not. I wasn't exactly thrilled by my prospects, and when it was suggested I should enter a company in the Kansai area whose president was one of my great-uncles, where I was bound to get on for family reasons, I wasn't interested either. After giving the question a good deal of thought I came to the conclusion that the work offering me the most freedom and scope to prove my abilities was in government service and so, despite the fact I was an economics graduate, I began to prepare for the higher civil service exams. Thus I became a civil servant for the perhaps surprising reason that I was seeking personal freedom.

This was a period of major change in the Japanese economy, the time of the great switchover, the start of the new prosperity, call it what you will, and that was probably the reason why I found my work at MITI much more fruitful and worthwhile than I'd expected. I found the opportunity to give guidance to a variety of business enterprises fascinating, though perhaps one could say I was merely indulging a common desire to wield power. However that may be, the fact is I felt that, of my age group, we at MITI had been given the widest scope to do work of genuine importance and on the largest scale, and I was satisfied with what I was doing and glad I'd joined this branch of government service. I was also confident the standard of my work was certainly the equal of that of any other career civil servant.

This being the case, then, why did I become a candidate for transfer to the Ministry of Defense? Well, those who were moved from MITI to the M. of D. were not in fact of inferior rank, since the sums of money being handled for the Self-Defense Forces were considerable, and if the people in charge were a motley crowd of incompetents then it would reflect on the credibility of the ministry itself. However, although those who went there were certainly not from the bottom of the pile, neither were they from the top. If one grades the top-class civil servants as A, A minus, and A double minus, then the ones who went to the M. of D. were A double minus. In my case, though it may sound a bit funny coming from me, I think I saw myself as being more of an A-minus than an A-double-minus man. Later on I understood, in fact, there'd been a deliberate change of policy here, since the money to be spent on defense was due for a major increase, and an A-minus person like myself being transferred there reflected this change of thinking on the part of the higher powers. That, however, was something I would only work out later and of which I knew nothing at the time, so this distinction between an A minus who wouldn't go and an A double minus who would meant a great deal to me, as it would to any civil servant. It may look trivial to an outsider, but it's a matter of supreme importance for a bureaucrat, and it's in such things you can see how the bureaucratic mind really works.

There was one more factor involved in my refusal, and this was a genuinely trivial one although it mattered enough at the time. Immediately before the personnel director called me in to see him, I happened to meet the chief of one of our departments (a person with whom I'd never been able to see eye to eye) in the men's room. As we both stood there relieving ourselves he said to me:

"Gather you're up for it this time. Well, it'll do you good to rough it for a bit, and then you can come back to us."

Since I showed by my expression I didn't know what he was talking about, he showed by his own that he knew he'd put his foot in it completely, but he tried to bluff his way out with a large, cheerful laugh.

"Oh. You haven't heard yet?" he said, and I acknowledged by my awkward, puzzled smile that I hadn't. Then, almost as soon as I got back to my desk, there was a call from the personnel director saying he wished to see me.

When I was alone with this ever cheerful and pleasant gentleman in the long, narrow room that was his inner office, there's not much doubt these two factors did influence the way I felt. The personnel director himself seemed to be aware to some extent of what was going on inside me, for he made a positive effort at flattery, insisting there'd been a policy change and I was the wedge or linchpin to be driven into the Ministry of Defense in order to bring all this about. Surprisingly this wasn't, in fact, a lie, as I realized later from the kind of people (with one or two exceptions) who were actually sent there, but at the time I wasn't to know this and was pretty suspicious of the whole thing. I think I still remained unconvinced at the end of the session, or at least only half convinced. It was also true that the remark about "roughing it for a bit" obviously had some effect on my attitude, though I don't think it bothered me all that much. I still wonder, however, why I felt, as the "offer" was being made to me, that I would probably be allowed to reject it and suffer no serious consequences. Was that assumption based on the idea that freedom of choice in one's work really existed? I don't really know, and I can explain in no better way than that; no doubt it was also only a vague, unconscious belief, if belief it was, although it must have been deep-rooted enough. I must have really trusted in the rightness of my objections, for I said quite bluntly that I didn't much like the idea.

"Couldn't my case be reconsidered, perhaps? I really do want to be allowed to continue with MITI work, even if that means being sent away from Head Office."

I made this request in a very quiet, relaxed tone, and it certainly wasn't a demand. Yet just as certainly it could only have been interpreted as a refusal, and it was. That's how I see it now, anyway.

Obviously a more detailed explanation of what I mean by freedom of choice in one's work is needed if I'm to be properly understood, but I think first I should give some indication of my attitude to war and the military. I was just too young to have gone into the army, or even to take the medical, and so I didn't grow up with any powerful feelings about the horrors of war or of hatred toward the military. In the same way that I had no anti-militaristic or anti-war feelings as a young man, I also lacked any tendency toward emperor worship or similar right-wing modes of thought, but was a very normal youth. While I was being a normal youth Japan lost the war and became a country without armed forces. But before that happened I never once thought of applying to a naval or army academy or a military flying school, nor did anyone suggest I should. The reason for this, I should add, was the snobbish feeling that such places were for the children of poor households who couldn't afford higher education by other means. Another awkward admission I have to make is that, other than thinking it was a good thing the military should have disappeared with the end of the war, I don't imagine I ever thought deeply about the matter. The same applies to the whole debate about the Self-Defense Forces as well. I sometimes wonder now, not very seriously of course, whether that order to proceed to the Ministry of Defense wasn't some kind of punishment for being so lazy about these things.

What really mattered to me, as it still matters, was freedom of choice in the work one did. I don't think I felt any objection to the Self-Defense Forces as such, providing I wasn't myself involved. It's true that I personally wanted nothing to do with a military establishment of that kind, but the strong sense of rejection, even repulsion, I felt was a purely intuitive judgment, not something I'd worked out. You see, what I mean by the freedom to choose one's work is something very simple and basic, the freedom of choice the son of a shipyard worker has when he chooses to be a gardener because he likes to see flowers in bloom, or a farmer's boy has when he chooses to do research in physics. Naturally this freedom is limited by the kind of ability someone has, but the principle I believed then, and still believe in, is that such choices are possible. I felt I'd joined MITI because I'd chosen to do that kind of work, and *not* in order to get mixed up with purchasing goods for the military. I just felt that I personally didn't want to touch that kind of thing. When I refused to do so, what I was really saying was, although I accepted that the state required objectionable things like an army for external defense and law courts and prisons for maintaining internal order, that didn't mean I had to like such things. In fact I knew quite well I would absolutely refuse to become a prison warder, or even a chief warden, myself. I suppose I can be accused of pure egotism here, but it just is a fact that there are things people don't want to do, things they find genuinely objectionable, and one must recognize the right of others to think and behave in the way that they do. Those are, at least, the words I'd use now to express my feelings of that time, although they weren't properly thought out then, being just an unconscious principle underlying the way I behaved. I admit I've only become really conscious of this principle recently, and at the time I just felt I wanted to go on doing my work at MITI. I had no critical attitude toward the Self-Defense Forces, as I can clearly remember saying to the personnel director; he accepted what I said without any question, and the matter was never raised again.

Another thing that people outside the service may find a little difficult to credit is that there'd been more than two or three cases of people refusing such transfers, and these refusals didn't seem to have damaged their careers in any particular way. The right to choose one's work was, to a real extent, acknowledged; and if they hurt themselves at all, then, as such wounds go, it was only a minor graze. For example, there was one man who refused to go and work in a technological institute because it was an extra-ministerial post, and another who objected to a transfer to the Fair Trade Commission. It's true that the man who'd objected to going to the F.T.C. gave up his job after a year, but during that year he wasn't punished or badly treated in any way, and in fact his decision to resign was dictated by his wife's family (he became a director of the company of which his father-in-law was president). I assumed, or half assumed, I could expect my own case to be dealt with in a fairly similar way, and the truth is my refusal didn't seem to have been taken badly. Anyway, after ten minutes or so (it might have been nearer five), the personnel director smiled wryly and said:

"Well, think it over a little more. There's no need to decide the matter here and now."

That brought the discussion to an end; in fact it brought an end to the matter itself, for quite openly a few days later somebody else was transferred to that post, and after six months I was promoted to the rank of section chief in the same head office. Thus the whole business was sewn up with nothing at all dramatic taking place, an example of the way civil servants will try to control any situation by covering up for each other, and by the principle of peace at any price which can be seen running right through the whole affair. I've no doubt various things were said about me behind my back, but the only judgments I actually heard referred to my "eccentricity" and "bravado," words that (when applied to a career bureaucrat) don't necessarily have critical implications.

However, judging from the way my career went after that, some sort of sanction seems to have been placed on me in the sense that I appeared to have been demoted in status, not merely to A double minus but to plain B. One reason for this would have been a kind of settling up for the trouble taken covering up for me, but there was also perhaps the feeling that the affair had demonstrated I'd only been a B-caliber person all along. Whatever it might have been, as I— the interested party—saw it, this wound was a bit more than a graze, and worse (though the difference is a subtle one) than what I'd prepared myself for during that five- or ten-minute interview. Even so, I must stress it was only a very little worse. Therefore, taking a strictly objective view, all it really demonstrates is how a man well versed in the conventions of government service did manage, in fact, to get his own way. If there was something of the spoiled child in the way I behaved, it arose from a minor miscalculation as to how much I would have to pay. I may not have liked having to pay anything, but that's all it was. If I can still be considered as having resisted the system, then it was only to that small degree. One could also say (and I am prepared finally to admit this much) that right at the very bottom of my attitude there may have been some of that anti-military prejudice one can expect in someone who grew up during the war, but it would only have been a minor motive among others of which I was also unaware. What I did was, in effect, to whisper a word in defense of my belief in the right to choose one's work, and it was a completely private action. The curious admiration it has caused can only be put down to various generous misinterpretations.

That is a general outline of the account of my behavior I gave to Kaizuka, and my final words were:

"At the party yesterday Oguri joked that I ought to stand for governor under the progressive banner, selling myself as the anti-war candidate and getting the women's vote. I was bound to win, he said. He was talking about the prefectural election back home, of course. You know him, I think—he's the editor of a publicity magazine for a beer company and is very tall. Still, the whole thing was completely beside the point because I'm just not like that. It could only be an impractical joke because I'm no progressive and I'm not opposed to the system. Nor, on the other hand, have I any intention of becoming a conservative politician either. The one thing I really care about is protecting what I consider the major premise or precondition of any society, namely freedom. To protect that freedom in my own case is something I'm determined to do whatever happens; and where other people's freedom is concerned, I want to defend it as far as that's feasible."

Yukari had been gazing downward, but now she looked straight up at me. Since I found her stare oppressive I broke off for a moment, whereupon Kaizuka said in all apparent seriousness:

"No. I still don't believe that was a misunderstanding. You did something that needed courage, and you did it all on your own... Still, it was an odd kind of defiance. After all, if you accept the existence of an army for external defense of the state, and law courts and prisons within that same state, then it must mean you accept the existence of the Self-Defense Forces? Or perhaps bringing in the factor of the state confuses the issue?"

"No," I replied. "It probably helps clarify it, if anything. After all, society as we know it depended for its birth, and has depended for its existence since then, on the fact of the modern state, as you can see quite clearly in Britain, France, the United States. It would be a mistake to think about society in isolation from the one thing that provides the base on which it stands. If you want to be brutally frank about it, then there's no reason you can't say that modern society was brought to perfection through the existence of imperialism."

"So although you accept imperialist aggression you objected to working in the Ministry of Defense? Doesn't that mean you're prepared to stand by and watch the state do evil just so long as you don't have to dirty your own hands?"

"Dirty my hands?..."

"I wasn't implying anything personal..."

"I don't, in fact, approve of aggression. I have a proper hatred of war. However, if you probe beneath the society of which I approve, then you discover the modern state; you don't really need to probe, either, since it just happens to be obviously there. The history of the modern state has involved imperialism, and no doubt still does in some form or other. That's simply a fact, and I don't wish to pretend I'm ignorant of what the lineage of civic society as we know it actually is. I treat it seriously on the basis of that knowledge, not in spite of it. I value our society, not in a cheerful, yea-saying kind of way, but rather the opposite: with feelings of sorrow, even gloom. More than that I'm ashamed to say I neither know nor understand. It's rather like, for instance, the care you might feel and show for a woman even though you're perfectly well aware of her dubious past. After all, she has other virtues and they can be loved. There's nothing that can be done about the past, anyway. If you consider the wealth of the house in which I grew up, for example, nearly all of it was created essentially out of the confusion surrounding the political conflicts at the beginning of the Meiji period, although we weren't exactly traders in death or anything like that. But I'm not prepared to grovel and apologize for my birth and upbringing because of that—nor do I feel like boasting about it either."

I don't think this was all that adequate an answer, and Kaizuka looked a little disconcerted by it; but after hesitating a while he replied:

"You're very frank about it, I must say. Still, there's some sort of deceit, surely, in exposing what's wrong with society in that very honest way and still appearing to support it as well. Perhaps I'm not choosing my words right, but it looks to me like some sleight of hand on your part. I also get the impression that your argument tends to stress some cheerful, unreal image of society by shifting all its dark, negative aspects onto the idea of the state."

Kaizuka smiled kindly at me, and in his expression I could see an obvious happiness at being able to put the real problem of the moment (how to handle the question of adultery) to one side for a while and focus on the gayer topics of politics and society. Yukari swallowed back a yawn, and I had no answer to make except to say I saw his point, smile wryly, and light another cigarette. Kaizuka looked quite satisfied now and he continued fluently:

"You remember we talked one evening, in that coffee shop, and I said I'd prefer village life to living in a town? You told me off about that..."

"I didn't tell you off..."

"... So it stuck in my mind, and probably it's true it's not so much any actual village I'm thinking of but some highly idealized fantasy of village life, and I have romantic feelings about an abstraction called anarchism. Which means, I suppose, I'm dreaming of the society that will emerge after what you and Mr. Nonomiya refer to as civic society has come to an end..."

"I think you're right and, if that is the case, I understand that feeling. But what that society will actually be like..."

"Wait a moment," said Kaizuka hastily. "What I found strange about his account of society was the only people who seemed of any real value were artists. If members of the working class aren't considered citizens, then 'citizen' becomes a class concept and means a capitalist, just that. If he's not a capitalist the citizen can still only be a factory manager or someone like that who measures work time with his clock. I hope this doesn't sound too critical of your father?"

His last remark was aimed at Yukari. He turned toward her, then looked back at me:

"Still, it's surely only a picture of a comparatively early stage in the history of modern society? That's how the classification of citizen and artist looks to me, anyway. To put it crudely, at that period there was no reason to suppose the system might be overthrown, and those who wanted to express some slight form of opposition could only do so under the guise of art. The fact that Mr. Nonomiya insists on still using that picture of society even now merely indicates how much his ideas are those of a man firmly entrenched in the society he thinks he's criticizing. . ."

"Um," I nodded, then thought a while and said: "You're quite right, of course, but it's inevitable, surely? Her father is, unlike yourself, right up to his neck in civic society, and at the same time he considers himself some sort of artist. I'm right up to my neck, too, up to my nostrils in fact, although I'm no artist and don't see myself as one. Even so, perhaps even because I'm right in it, I'm well aware that our society is old, tired, doddering, sick. That's certainly the way I experience it: my basic feeling is that our society is sick. Still, unlike yourself, I want to revive this sick society, nurse it back to health, do something for it. . ."

"Why should you?"

"First of all because I get no picture whatsoever in my head of the society that you say is going to replace this one. Then I appreciate, I value highly, the things that are good in this kind of society. It's like an old cup, cracked and chipped and broken. I don't have another cup, and I rather like this one, so I glue the bits together and mend it somehow, and now I want to use it with great care, gently, tenderly. . ."

"Yes."

"It's like the one wife–one husband system in marriage," I added, and Kaizuka nodded in agreement, probably because he was feeling in a good mood. Obviously what ought to have made me think about marriage in this situation was Yukari's adultery and that alone, but I didn't seem to find it at all ridiculous to launch into a theoretical discussion of monogamy at this time and before this particular man.

"Ah," he said.

"Exactly like the marriage system," I repeated rather stupidly.

"Could you explain in a bit more detail," he said quietly.

"Well, the marriage system isn't just a question of any individual marriage or any particular couple," I started to say, but for the first time I realized the absurdity of what I was doing, and hesitated.

398

Kaizuka, however, seemed quite indifferent to it all, and now I'd got this far I saw nothing for it but to go on.

"No, it's a question of the system itself. There are a great many things wrong with the system, of which the majority of people are probably aware. Still, there's no obvious alternative, so we've no choice but to persevere with it. So we care for it, the way we look after our broken cup. Her father might maintain, of course, that the monogamous system was simply something we imported from the West during the Meiji era."

"Like the clock tower?"

"That's right."

This reply of mine produced a strange silence from Kaizuka, and I was just beginning to wonder what was wrong with him when he suddenly flushed a bright red.

"Are you trying to be sarcastic?" he said, starting to get angry. "Because if you are then that's all right by me, although I find it a bit peculiar on your part. After all, you were the one who deliberately avoided the issue when I was ready to make a clean breast of it, and I can't think why you should decide now that you want to start being objectionable."

"I'm not trying to be sarcastic or objectionable," I protested, but he wasn't prepared to be put out of his stride.

"In that case I'll say it out straight. I spent last night with Yukari," he said defiantly, but then he suddenly became quiet again and gave his account in a small, nervous voice. Yukari had become very tense, and looked equally at me and Kaizuka. In fact she seemed to be looking equally *through* both of us, although not so much at the wall but as if she were seeing, as she probably was, the events of the past twenty-four hours as he related them.

As Kaizuka was leaving the party, Yukari had run after him and handed over the prize money and his other things. He then invited her to have dinner with him somewhere as a way of thanking her, and Yukari was only too glad to accept since she'd had almost nothing to eat; but first they did some bowling, then some drinking, then some dancing, becoming intoxicated with the drink and the dance, and so spent the night together in a hotel. They didn't eventually eat until lunchtime today, and though neither of them had any idea what was going to happen next, they both had a very solid meal (made possible, of course, by his prize money) in an expensive restaurant that Kaizuka had only known before by name. In fact it wasn't until they'd eaten their thick steaks in the bright light of day that they became fully aware of what an impossible situation they'd got themselves into. The conclusion they came to was that they'd have to discuss it with someone else, but the image of that suitable someone just wouldn't arise in their minds. Finally Kaizuka suggested perhaps they should discuss it with me, but Yukari was furious with him for considering such a thing, so they went off to the bowling alley again and then had dinner in a spaghetti restaurant...

Having got this far Kaizuka again changed his tone to one of commiseration, much as he'd done when first inviting me into the room.

"I feel sorry about what I've done to you but ... I don't think I've personally done anything wrong."

There was a slight pause.

"I don't like telling lies, so it's best for me to say what I can't help feeling."

"Yes, I suppose so," I said. "I think I know what you mean. By which I mean that I'm not myself in all that much of a rage about it. In fact I've been wondering since last night why I'm not angry, and I suppose it's because if I were to work myself up into a rage it would have to be on account of the system itself, and that, quite honestly, I'm not prepared to do. I don't particularly believe in it, and certainly not in ethical terms so much as in ones of pure convenience; it's something I use, like that cup. I became aware of what I really thought on the subject quite suddenly last night when I was sitting at the counter of a small cafe, eating dinner. It was then I finally realized I accepted the relationship that exists between me and this society. That's how it seems to me, anyway, although I don't want you to get the wrong idea and think I'm pleased at the way things have worked out, because I'm not. It's a damned unpleasant situation for me. I loathe it, and not because it's inconvenient for me either..."

After that I thought a little, and then proceeded:

"I'm not annoyed because of some moral affront to the marriage system—I just don't think that way. It's something much simpler, something gone wrong between one man and a woman, and I don't know what to do about it. I'm confused, I'm sad, I'm bewildered ... that's how it is."

Kaizuka had been sitting with drooping head for quite a long while, but now he cried out excitedly in what seemed like contempt for what I'd said, and then put his feelings into words.

"How can you talk like that? So calm, so collected, so objective? You're just trying to pass the whole damn thing off."

"Pass it off?"

"Yes. You want to think everything's all right really. There's nothing to worry about. Yukari's young and there are no children. If the worst comes to the worst you can always get a divorce. You're just avoiding the whole issue."

"I see," I said, thinking that when he talked about the worst it was only as far as he himself was concerned.

"I've already told Yukari and now I'll tell you: I've no intention of marrying her. First of all I just couldn't afford it. That would've been the case even if that hadn't happened yesterday, but now it's even more true."

"I don't see why. There's been plenty of support for you. In today's papers it..."

"I read them at the restaurant. Still, I'm bound to catch it from now on. I know I am."

"It was a question of love, you see," said Yukari, speaking quite suddenly into the silence that had fallen between the two men, and continuing as though talking to herself: "There wasn't enough love shown to me, so this happened..." and I understood then that she wasn't referring to Kaizuka.

"Oi," I shouted. "What do you mean by that? Give me an example." I thrust out my jaw aggressively.

"Well, for example ... the bed problem."

"The bed problem?" muttered Kaizuka—not me, because I couldn't reply, or even nod, but just held my breath. The thought of all the intimacies of the bedchamber being now laid bare (confronted by the fact, for example, that however busy I might be that didn't excuse my paying her no attention for a fortnight) was horrifying, and I was particularly aghast at the prospect of being judged liked this in front of a third party, the ultimate humiliation for a man. However, Yukari was talking quite literally about the bed problem, and wasn't being euphemistic about something else.

"It was awful of you to make me use the same bed as your first wife. I really hated it... I hated it... Anyway, that sort of thing."

When she'd finished speaking she closed her eyes in a grave manner as if to endorse what she'd said, and only the false eyelashes that decorated her tired face, and now seemed remarkably long, flickered occasionally.

"But look here, Yukari," I said, addressing that face. "You've never said a word about this before. After all, it would cost a fortune to have another pair like that made."

"I couldn't say anything because it would have looked strange. I knew I'd be told off if I did, too."

"Still," said Kaizuka, looking as if he sincerely wished to mediate between us. "It's not all that easy nowadays to get rid of an old bed."

What really calmed me down, returned me to a normal state of mind in fact, was the sheer absurdity, the ludicrous nature, of that remark. I was suddenly able to understand and accept my present situation for what it was, and knew exactly what I had to do.

"Look, I think I've just about finished what I have to say to you. Now I want to talk to Yukari, so would you mind not interrupting at all for a while and just leave the two of us to get on with it?"

Having requested his cooperation I turned to my wife.

"Well, what are you going to do? Are you going to go to Tochigi, or are you going to stay with Kaizuka? In either case..."

She had opened her eyes, straightened herself up, and was listening to me, but on hearing this she could only cry out the word "Tochigi" and gape at me in horror. She repeated the word and I replied that it wouldn't be forever although I wasn't sure how long. This brought a cry of protest from Kaizuka despite his promise not to interfere.

"You must be crazy. You're not seriously threatening to put her in... prison?" he said, his voice tailing away as the confidence drained out of it. "You do mean the prison, don't you? Perhaps you..."

"No, I do not mean the prison. At today's board meeting they decided to make me manager of the factory in Tochigi. Of course I still remain an ordinary director. I'm also expected to take up the new post as soon as possible."

I explained the situation to them. The whole thing had been decided by the president and the managing director alone, and had come as a total surprise to me (although my chauffeur seemed to have known something about it). It wasn't, in fact, a form of demotion, but had come about because production at the factory seemed to have suddenly gone haywire; so I'd been asked to go and straighten things out, and naturally there'd been no way of refusing. In the past the appointment as factory manager had always been taken up in leisurely fashion, even urgent cases being allowed at least a month, but I wanted to get out there as soon as possible. I would rent out our present house to someone and live in company housing while in Tochigi.

"So you'll be managing a factory," Kaizuka murmured.

"That's right," I said. "Just the trade you were talking about: measuring work hours with a clock."

I stood up and turned to Yukari.

"Anyway, I'm going home now. I didn't come here with the aim of making you come back with me. You'll have to work out for yourself what you want to do. You can come back if you like, and if you choose not to then that's all right with me. Decide yourself how you feel."

Yukari gave a little nod but said nothing. Her face reminded me of a delicately worked piece of ivory, soiled ivory. I decided there was no need to say anything more to Kaizuka, and left.

I walked quickly through the dark, driven on by the night wind disturbing the branches of the temple trees, as though pursued by something in that sound. I felt Yukari would probably come back to me, although I couldn't depend on it, feeling there was a seventy percent chance, or sixty, perhaps only fifty, and as that possibility seemed to decrease I was haunted by memories of things we'd done together, clear images of good, happy things of morning, afternoon, and night, and these added to my torment, although I couldn't work out if this was the suffering of a man who was going to lose his wife, or his sadness at the prospect of his mistress leaving him. I came to the main road and waited there, soon managing to pick up a taxi.

After the cab had set off I began to think about Yukari's unhappiness over that bed, wondering if she'd felt like that right from the start. But even if she'd just thought it up after struggling and failing to find anything else to complain about, it must still have meant enough to her to make her say it straight out like that. In the dim light of the taxi I thought how women got upset by such peculiar things and then kept quiet about them, and I suddenly remembered my first wife and wondered if she too had been dissatisfied in various ways like Yukari, and whether she'd died without ever mentioning them. And if she had, then what things had she hated in me, I wondered, feeling again close to her and yet sensing what a mystery she'd been essentially, something unfathomed, eventually unknown. I had much to recall and question, although it was strange I should have wondered in her case too whether she'd been my wife or my mistress. It was strange because quite obviously there was no room in which to consider the daughter of an M.C.I. official as anything but a wife, and certainly no mistress. What was even stranger, however, was that the certainty, the obviousness, of the fact became less and less obvious as I thought about it, its clarity becoming vague, troubled, and confused. I even began to think the reason I'd had such a strong sense of her being my wife and nothing else was because the house had always been so tidy while she'd been alive; a fact, however, that really reflected nothing but the existence of Tsuru, our maid.

Yet as that possibility crossed my mind the driver asked me which road he should take.

21

Six months passed. I was now accustomed to the work as factory manager, and life in Tochigi was going smoothly.

The thing that had been most welcome on coming to this town was finding an old lady living nearby who was prepared to do the housework for us, and who did it well. So the servant problem was solved quite casually. This cheered Yukari up considerably, and she said that when we were back living in Tokyo again she was going to be very busy working for fashion magazines that catered for the "married lady," and was determined to take a maid back with us. I had my doubts that things would work out so easily, but I made a point of only saying, whenever she raised the subject, that we'd see when the time came. I had these doubts because our present maid was old and lived locally, and I'd no idea what would happen if she became ill and had to take to her bed. In fact it wasn't something I much liked to think about, and I felt a similar uncertainty about the demand for Yukari's services when we returned to Tokyo in two or three years' time, since I really couldn't see her being slim enough. During these six months I thought she'd put on a lot of weight, and although she claimed that married women's magazines liked their models on the plump side (which meant a little fatter than she was now), the subject was a bit beyond me, and so finally I had no ideas about the matter at all.

Recently Yukari had begun to put much more effort into the housework. One reason was there was much more pressure from the neighbors in this part of the world, but the main factor must have been that the Kaizuka affair had made her realize there was no choice for her but to live as my wife, and so she became more wifely in her habits. It seemed to me she'd understood what it meant when a marriage started to fall apart merely because the maid had left, and that a lot of the responsibility lay with herself.

What had happened was that, an hour or so after I'd returned home from Kaizuka's apartment, Yukari came drifting back as well. The outcome was simple enough. I'd been upstairs in my study looking through some papers, and when I went downstairs there was Granny sitting in the passage blocking my way. Yukari was standing in the entrance hall beyond her. Granny pleaded with me desperately on Yukari's behalf, bowing her head on the wooden floorboards (even onto a slipper that happened to be in the vicinity) in abject supplication. Yukari also muttered something in the background, although I couldn't hear what it was. So, before anything practical or pertinent had been said, I told Yukari to come inside at least, and that was that.

Two days later I went to Tochigi to take over my duties there, stayed overnight, and caught the train back round about noon. I had to go off to the office right away and so didn't get home till late, but both Granny and Yukari had waited up for me, saying there was something very important to discuss. This important thing was the very unexpected, indeed remarkable, suggestion that Granny should leave us and go and live with Hirayama. Hirayama had apparently been working some swindle with the expenses in his post as caretaker of an apartment building, and this had now come to light. He'd "retired" from the job, on the understanding he would return the sum he'd appropriated in a series of monthly payments, and was now looking for work. His divorced daughter was going to move out and find a job as a live-in maid somewhere. Granny herself meant to put to use the craft she'd learned in prison, for she was going to work in a hairdresser's and live with Hirayama while both of them went out to work.

I was secretly delighted to hear this, since it was an answer to my prayers and we wouldn't have to take her to Tochigi with us; but Yukari felt we didn't know how far Hirayama could be trusted, and no matter how much Granny might love him she ought to think longer and far more seriously before allowing him to come and live in her apartment. Granny announced that she'd thought about it a lot already, but it all came down to the fact that it would be strange if she just stood by while the man she was fond of was in trouble and not try to do something about it. Also Hirayama knew she had a place to live since he'd spent the night there after Kaizuka's prizegiving party, and so it would be very peculiar if she didn't offer him a room. She was obviously very serious about the matter, and showed no inclination to sleep despite the lateness of the hour.

Since the discussion didn't seem to be getting anywhere we decided to ring up my father-in-law and talk the matter over with him, for Yukari said he was still bound to be up. His response to the suggestion was certainly surprising. After listening to my account he said:

"So Mother has finally grown up at last. Eisuke, we've much to learn from her attitude toward life. She has discovered, by her own unaided research, that solitude is the condition of life for man in the city, and that the sole solution is to live that solitude to the full, to give it total realization. And nobody has told her that—she found it out quite by herself."

He was so impressed that I felt called upon to put in a minor objection:

"But she's going to live with that caretaker Hirayama, so she can't really be said to be living in solitude..."

"No, no. It's still solitude. Think more carefully about it and you'll see that, even where there's love, there is still solitude. The city and existence—the urban as the existential, the existential as the urban—I mean, that's something we intellectuals know with our heads but find extremely difficult to put into practice. Whereas a person like her ... well!"

He groaned again in admiration, whether because he was as pleased as I was at having got rid of this nuisance (only he'd chosen a high-falutin and long-winded way of saying so) or because he really did admire her, I found it difficult to tell. Anyway, while I was wondering which it was I suddenly found myself seeing this decision of Granny's in a heroic light too. In particular I was struck by the feeling that there must be something that sustains and nourishes solitude, although I couldn't think what it might be; and when I came to the desolate conclusion that solitude sustains itself, alone, I found myself genuinely moved by that bleak, desperate idea. Perhaps the reason I made love to Yukari the same night was some kind of sentimental hangover from that emotion. She responded passionately, which left me feeling jealous.

The following week was occupied by the chaos of getting ready to go to Tochigi, and Granny moved out during the confusion. We let the house to a young couple just back from America who were distant relations of a director of the bank that did the company's business. The first thing I realized after I got there was that it hadn't been at all clever of me to be in a hurry to take up this appointment. In fact I'd been a complete fool to let the whole business be signed over to me at such speed. Each invoiced item of stock the factory had on its books should have been carefully checked to make sure it was really there, and I now understood why former managers had spent so much time taking up the post in the past. I'd hardly bothered about such things at all, merely glancing quickly through the documentation, so no wonder the productivity recorded on the last day of March for the half period looked really awful. Clearly I was the victim of some kind of racket that had been going on there, and since nobody (not even the managing director, Mayama) had give me the least inkling that such a situation existed, let alone advice on what I should do about it, I gained some idea of the ill will my colleagues bore toward me— although this is no doubt something all ex–government officials are bound to experience at some time in their new careers.

However, productivity went up in the new term for which I was responsible, and one thing I particularly prided myself on was providing a radical solution to a problem that had always vexed previous managers, that of the scarcity of labor. Toward the end of January a number of women employees left one after the other, and everything was tried to solve the shortage until finally I decided to replace the usual management meeting with a brainstorming session. This proved to be a good idea, and was based on methods I'd employed when head of the planning department in Tokyo to work out sales promotion of new products, combined with various hints I'd picked up from Oguri about a publicity conference at his beer company. What I did was make everybody sit just anywhere at the conference table and say the first thing that came into their heads; but for the first thirty minutes all we heard were the most dreary suggestions, which bored everyone to tears, until finally a middle-aged man who'd said nothing so far suggested halfheartedly that the only place in Tochigi where there were plenty of women was the prison. This had everybody ready to burst into hoots of laughter, but just before they did so I got in with a cry of "That's it!"

That was indeed it and, once I had the idea, it was simple enough to put it into practice. All I had to do was get working on the prison warden (by good fortune the chief of the prefectural police happened to have been a senior of mine at high school), and make a real nuisance of myself with the Ministry of Justice in Tokyo. So from April onward a few dozen women prisoners began arriving by bus at eight o'clock each morning and leaving at five. They were set to work in a separate part of the factory, away from the other staff, but they shared the same canteen at lunchtime except that they sat at their own tables. During the lunch break they were allowed to play volleyball and dodgeball, which I joined in, and still do. Up to this moment nothing at all has gone wrong and I feel the system should continue to work all right. My quite unprejudiced treatment of these women has amazed everyone at the prison, from the warden downward, and earned the admiration of people in my company, too, although each time I hear what a marvel I am I simply want to laugh, since I haven't taken a single risk. I signed a contract whereby, first of all, if any of the prisoners should escape while they're in the factory it wouldn't be my responsibility, and also (a point concerning which the warden doesn't seem properly aware), if there should be any kind of recession, I'm always free to bring our joint venture to an end. I must say I really have to thank Granny Utako for providing me with the first inkling of how to solve our labor problem. Of course, looking at it in strictly logical terms, it does seem odd that a man who refused to work for one of the two most unpleasant aspects of the state, namely the military, should have achieved so close a relationship with the other, the penal system; although I personally feel that prisons have always been rather more in my line than the military. In fact this connection I'd established with the penal system perhaps indicated something basic in my character. I don't suppose there can be all that many people in whom the solid virtues of the citizen seem to coexist in exactly equal proportions with their opposites. My wish to rebel balanced my desire to conform, yet I permitted conformity to control my life, and so the role I'd been given as a factory manager who set female prisoners to work was, in fact, right up my street. I'm perhaps exaggerating here, but it is at least conceivable that the reason Granny got so drunk, on that fateful evening of the Dolls Festival when she first visited our home, was because she'd soon worked out the kind of person I was. She'd seen the rebel in hiding there just beneath the skin.

One thing that was really very funny was what the warden said about ten days ago when he was in my office at the factory.

"It's a pity we aren't allowed to bring the girls who're in for murder, Mr. Mabuchi. They're extremely good at hairdressing; run a beauty parlor in the prison. The cleverest of our girls are always the killers, though you'd probably never have thought so, I suppose."

I dearly wanted to say that my wife's grandmother had in fact been one of them and was now putting the skills she'd learned in his prison to good use, for we'd had a letter only the other day saying she'd been offered a job as the matron of a boardinghouse for young women working in a large hairdressing establishment. Naturally I said nothing of the sort, assuming an innocent expression while voicing amazement at what he'd just told me. It seems very likely, in fact, that Granny will take the job. Hirayama is working as a company guard, but he has those monthly payments to keep up so life isn't easy, and she feels she can't refuse an opportunity to make money when it's there for the asking. Although she'll be a dormitory matron she can return home once a week, so the work won't hinder their living together all that much. Her letter also said Hirayama's daughter had gone to work as a live-in maid for a man in his sixties who owned one of the apartments where Hirayama had been caretaker, and it seems likely she'd established a relationship with him some while ago.

Ever since that prizegiving day, my father-in-law has achieved more and more recognition, and is now leading an extremely busy life of lectures and articles. He has even appeared on television recently, on a late-night show, in charge of the art spot entitled "Nudes of the World," so he can be said to have really made it. Yukari and I did watch the program once and found it a bizarre mixture of marginal scholarship and obscene anecdotes. The only problem he's facing at the moment is that Yukari's younger brother has decided to drop out of college and become an actor in some very minor theatrical group.

Like father like son, is my own feeling, and he has little right to reprove his son for his casual attitude toward the benefits university status confers.

I heard something about Tsuru a few days ago from Oguri when I was paying a visit to Tokyo. Apparently the snack bar where she worked had attracted no new customers but merely lost those it had already, and was on the verge of closing down when Murata decided to turn it into a noodle shop. This was a tremendous success, with customers almost fighting to get in. Oguri had plugged the shop once in his magazine at Tsuru's request, but he smiled at the idea now, saying it would be almost indecent to make more money than the shop must be doing at the moment. I was very pleased to hear this and thanked him for his attentions to Tsuru. He gave me an old-fashioned look and asked if I really hadn't known about it, hinting that while he was still a student he'd slept with Tsuru on two or three occasions, something that genuinely surprised me. Still, what was even more surprising was the suggestion (a quite unproven assumption on Oguri's part) that Murata had got Tsuru out of my house by making her think he was in love with her, or by at least some kind of sexual ploy. Oguri spoke with a good deal of assurance, but I remained only half convinced.

He asked how we were getting on in Tochigi and was most impressed by the way I'd handled the labor shortage, praising me extravagantly for the uniqueness of the solution, which must soon be given the recognition it richly deserved. He then hesitated slightly before finally saying he'd bumped into Kaizuka the day before. Kaizuka didn't seem to recognize him and just walked past, but Oguri called out his name and asked him how things were going. As might be expected, he'd received no commissions whatsoever for four months after that fatal day, but managed to make a living as a construction worker. Then, during the fourth month, he'd been given a large commission by a publicity company, with whom he'd had no connection at all before. It was a full-page newspaper advertisement, so his luck had finally turned and now he was getting orders from a number of different quarters. I remembered seeing that particular advertisement myself.

"All that manual labor has filled him out. He's about twice his previous size, really powerfully built. Looks well, too, except his teeth have become pretty dirty. Still"—Oguri smiled a little—"I suppose his real struggle with the system is yet to come."

"Yes, I suppose so. It's still all to come for him," I agreed, and then asked him, "How about your own struggle?"

I wasn't, in fact, referring to anything in particular, but Oguri seemed to misunderstand me, for he told me how Mayo had given up being a model and become a bar hostess instead, and how he'd been to the place where she worked and on the way home had finally managed to persuade her to sleep with him.

"Ah, so it was all right now that she wasn't a model?"

"Well, I don't think that had much to do with it," said Oguri, looking a little shamefaced, and adding, "It wasn't up to much, anyway. The wild rose smells sweetest when unplucked."

He was obviously being very serious, and although the handling of the wise saw was as comically wrong as always, I didn't laugh or even smile.

The one person of whom I know almost nothing is Carrot Otoyo. According to what Oguri learned from Kaizuka, a few days after my visit to that wooden apartment house she suddenly had the movers in and departed. Apparently she said she was going to Yokohama, but nobody knew if that was true or not. So our promised love affair remains, as it were, in a state of suspended animation, although this doesn't mean I shall ask the police to make inquiries into her whereabouts. All I can do is hope and pray she'll have the good fortune to avoid the fate that could, perhaps even in the near future, condemn her to working in my factory.

定価3,400円
in Japan